y George Kimball

gs
Hagler, Hearns, Duran and the Last Great Era of Boxing

in Deep

's Fools
, Tromped, Kicked and Chewed in the NFL (with Tom Beer)

nan of the Boards (with Eamonn Coghlan)

can at Large

ighter Still Remains
bration of Boxing in Poetry and Song from Ali to Zevon
with John Schulian)

e Fights: American Writers on Boxing (editor, with John Schulian)

Manly

george kimball

Manly Art

(They can run — but they can't hide)

McBooks Press, Inc.
www.mcbooks.com
Ithaca, NY

Published by McBooks Press, Inc. 2011
This Compilation Copyright © 2011 George Kimball

Cover paintings © 2011 Tom Russell
Author photo © 2011 Anne Tangeman—Taken inside William Burroughs' Lawrence, Kansas, home.
Cover and interior design by Panda Musgrove.

Library of Congress Cataloging-in-Publication Data

Kimball, George, 1943-
  Manly art : (they can run but they can't hide) / by George Kimball.
     p. cm.
  ISBN 978-1-59013-571-6 (hardcover : alk. paper)
  1. Boxing--Anecdotes. 2. Boxers (Sports) I. Title.
  GV1135.K56 2011
  796.83--dc22

                         2010044552

Visit the McBooks Press website at www.mcbooks.com.

Printed in the United States of America

9 8 7 6 5 4 3 2 1

This book is for Pete Hamill and Tom Paxton and for our pals running bar tabs at the Great Saloon in the Sky:

Val Avery, Tommy Butler, Liam, Tom, and Paddy Clancy, Dennis Duggan, Fred Exley, Joe Flaherty, Wes Joice, David Markson, Frank McCourt, Archie Mulligan, Jack Newfield, Joel Oppenheimer, Mike Reardon, Paul Schiffman, José Torres, Dave Van Ronk and Vic Ziegel

Table of Contents

Chapter III—At Ringside

Chapter IV—The Good, the Bad, and the Ugly

Chapter V—The Final Ten-Count

Chapter VI—The Last Great Heavyweight Rivalry

Foreword *by Carlo Rotella*

You have in your hands a rare and precious thing in the 21st century—the work of a professional boxing writer. There are few such pros left, and none on the way, as far as I can tell. George Kimball is one of the very last of the breed.

Professional boxing writers, as a class of journalists, can exist when writers who care about the quality of their reporting and their prose can make a decent living writing about boxing. Something similar holds true for boxers. For both sets of practitioners, there has to be some kind of balance between doing it for love (so to speak) and doing it for money—not a lot of money, necessarily, but enough to temper enthusiasm and cynicism with the rigor that comes of delivering the goods to earn a worthwhile wage.

Once upon a time, when boxing's only peer as a popular sport was baseball, a lot more men could make a living at the trade, which made for more bouts, a thicker network of gyms, and more and better boxers. Similarly, newspapers were obliged to employ reporters who specialized in boxing, and boxing magazines had stables of writers who addressed large readerships. Some of these golden-age fight scribes were better than others, of course, but together they played an important collective role. Their grasp of the complicated fit between two very different kinds of sophistication—the boxer's difficult craft and the dark arts of the fight business—supplied a crucial third force to offset the often uncritical passion of fans and the promotional fairy tales peddled by the backstage powers who profited from boxing.

These days, with boxing consigned to a remote niche in newspapers and magazines, and with most writers who regularly cover fights working for websites that pay starvation rates, the "decent living" part of the professional equation is hard to come by. Too many writers filing copy from ringside have to do it as a hobby, or because it feels good to sit up close and wear press credentials around your neck and act like an insider. The result is that too often they write like fans or volunteer publicists. That's one big reason why the body of informed, substantive, well-reported, well-crafted, timely, time-less, independent-minded, entirely professional fight pieces that make up this book are, as I said, a rare and precious thing in the world today.

That George Kimball wrote them mostly after he'd "retired" is an indicator of the current state of affairs in the fight-writing world. Print and online editors won't let him retire in peace. He learned his craft as a newspaper beat reporter in Boston, for a decade at the *Phoenix* and then for 25 years at the *Herald,* which means that he's far better at the job and more experienced than anybody else those editors could find. His career spans the end of the era of the boxing beat writer at a newspaper—an era he helped prolong by exploiting the rise of the local middleweight hero Marvin Hagler to force the *Herald* to let him cover boxing regularly—and the beginning of the online era. He's one of the very few boxing writers worth reading when he goes long online, and that's precisely because he internalized the virtues of the news-paper beat reporter's often highly constrained trade.

As you read these pieces, consider how much went into even their most effortless-seeming paragraphs. Kimball's long-range perspective, both his knowledge of boxing history and his extended personal familiarity with the fighters and other characters he writes about, enriches every observation. A just-right blend of connoisseur's joy and seen-it-all worldiness enables shrewd judgments of talent and also a penchant for penetrating the fight world's pandemic bluster and lies to arrive at nuggets of truth. He strikes a crucial balance between by-the-book reportorial legwork and disciplined personal judgment, and he mates the theater critic's eye for ring drama to the investigative reporter's nose for murky dealings. Again and again, his lit-erary sensibility and cask-aged sense of humor strike resonant notes from double-checked facts.

Kimball makes it all look easy—or, if not easy, then smooth and natural. And by now it does come to him naturally. But you're looking at the accrued benefits of decades of writing about boxing for a living. In other words, you're looking at the work of a professional boxing writer. Enjoy it, and treasure it. Unless and until he puts out another such collection, we probably won't see its like again.

Chapter I—The Way It Was

Survival of the Greatest

More than two dozen men have claimed the heavyweight championship in the three decades since Muhammad Ali last owned that title, and they could, almost without exception, walk unrecognized down the main street of any major city. But, as the late publicist Irving Rudd once noted, "If Ali went into a hut in Africa, a village in Asia, the outback in Australia, or a marketplace in South America, the people would look at him, smile, and say 'Muhammad Ali!'" We're just guessing here, but you could probably add to that list a *boreen* in County Clare.

My children have often noted, more out of amusement than actual annoyance, that they grew up in a house in which there were more photographs of Muhammad Ali on the walls than there were of themselves. Of course, some of these included Ali *and* the kids: there is one, for instance, of Ali, a beatific smile on his face, holding my now-twenty-five-year-old daughter beside the swimming pool at Caesars Palace. I can date that one to the week of the 1986 Barry McGuigan-Steve Cruz fight, because Brian Eastwood's face is in the background.

Last Friday in the Bronx, Ali was honored prior to that evening's New York Yankees-Boston Red Sox game. Not only did the predictable chants of "Ali! Ali!" resound during a standing ovation 50,000 strong, but millionaire ballplayers from both teams also halted their pre-game preparations, dropped their gloves and bats, and raced over to meet, and perhaps touch, a man who had stopped boxing before most of them were even born.

He was arguably the best heavyweight who ever lived, but the boxing accomplishments of the three-time world champion don't begin to explain the almost universal reverence in which the mythic figure is held in his dotage. Great boxers such as Joe Louis, Jack Dempsey, and Sugar Ray Robinson retained a certain popularity after their careers ended, but you didn't see any of them flying around the world to light Olympic torches or negotiate the release of hostages.

Dempsey operated a midtown saloon in his post-combat years. Robinson scuffled to make a buck as a song-and-dance man, while Louis became first a cartoonish wrestler and then a "greeter" at Caesars Palace. The financial motivation of Ali, who can still cause a traffic jam just by stepping out of a limousine, is somewhat different. He is constantly on the road these days, raising funds for children's hospices and for his nonprofit Muhammad Ali Foundation.

Proximity to famous athletes generally leads to a rather jaded view for those in this profession, if only because exposure to the human frailties of widely admired figures almost inevitably causes disappointment. From the time he first came to our attention as a sleek teenager at the 1960 Rome Olympics, it was apparent that this was a boxer unlike any other who had come before, but admiration for Ali the fighter doesn't begin to explain why he remains such a beloved figure today.

Dr. Wilbert McClure, the Boston psychologist who was his roommate at the 1960 Olympics (and who, along with Ali and Sergeant Eddie Crook, was one of three American boxers to win gold medals at those Games), noted of Ali: "He always carried himself with his head high, and with grace and composure. We can't say that about all of his detractors."

His stature was enhanced, of course, by the brave stance with which he risked everything in his opposition to the Vietnam War. ("When Ali said 'No, I will not go,'" the noted journalist David Marash wrote in a profile for Al Jazeera that never saw the light of day, "it turned a *boxing* champion into a *moral* champion.") And that reverence in which he was held has continued to grow as he has matured gracefully into a universally beloved figure.

The irony is that a man once known for his quick wit and boastful jibes has been rendered as silent as a statue of Buddha. The Ali of today would probably have more to tell us than at any previous stage of his life, but between Parkinson's syndrome and the medication he must take to control it, he is able to speak only with great difficulty—and that's on a good day. "He always spoke to the people," says Howard Bingham, the renowned photographer who has been Ali's best friend for more than 40 years. "Now *they* speak to *him.*"

Many who have watched the specter of his trembling hands and his tortured attempts to speak leap to the conclusion that there has been a concomitant loss of cognitive function, sort of the way deaf people are sometimes assumed to be retarded by those who are themselves just too stupid to know better.

But Ali is not punch-drunk, or even close to it. His motor functions have been diminished, but his mind has not. "It's like he's trapped inside his body," said his daughter Laila. "He can think, he has things he wants to say, but his lips sometimes don't move to get it out."

The Ali who returned from a three-and-a-half-year exile to twice regain the heavyweight championship was a very different boxer from the one who had defeated the fearsome Sonny Liston to win his first, and the fact is that the world never saw him at his peak. Before they took his boxing license away and stripped him of the title in 1967, he was not only faster than any heavyweight who had ever lived but had continued to improve with every fight.

His second incarnation brought some of the more thrilling contests in the annals of the sport, but he could no longer rely on quickness and uncanny reflexes.

"I was better when I was young," Ali acknowledged to his biographer, but "I was more experienced when I was older. I was stronger; I had more belief in myself. Except for Sonny Liston, the men I fought when I was young weren't near the fighters that Joe Frazier and George Foreman were, but I had my speed when I was young."

Particularly in the 1974 Rumble in the Jungle against Foreman and the 1975 Thrilla in Manila against Frazier, this second incarnation of Ali demonstrated something the first had never had to prove: that he could take a punch.

In the former fight he sacrificed his body in order to exhaust Foreman with a scheme he later described as "rope-a-dope" ("And," recalled Foreman, "I was the dope!"), while the latter contest was a near-death experience that put both men in hospital.

In a private moment years later, when the Parkinson's had begun to work its ravages, I asked Ali when he might have hung up the gloves if he had it to do all over again. He thought about it a bit before replying in what was barely a whisper: "George Foreman." Of course, if his career had ended on that high note in Zaire, the world would never have seen his third fights against Frazier and Ken Norton, but neither would it have had to endure its sad conclusion against Larry Holmes and Trevor Berbick in the 1980s.

Bill Nack, who chronicled many Ali fights for *Sports Illustrated,* recalled that when Ali's Parkinson's syndrome first began to present itself, "he was mumbling and starting to slur, just a little bit. I remember thinking: 'Is he just tired?' Then I thought about all the times Joe Frazier had hit him and I realized he *wasn't* 'just tired.'"

There are Parkinson's sufferers who never took a single punch, but even Ali concedes that his present affliction is almost certainly the product of damage accumulated during those later fights.

A lion in winter, he may now be paying the price for all the joy he provided us then, but pity would be misplaced. Ali remains, as his longtime physician, Dr. Ferdie Pacheco, once put it, "in a complicated society, a simple, happy man."

"He always thought that once he stopped boxing, people would forget him," says his biographer, Tom Hauser. "He really didn't understand how important he was."

The Irish Times Weekend Magazine
August 2009

Those Grady forebears had been rattling around in the Clay family closet for years, but when Ali came to Dublin to fight Al (Blue) Lewis, he didn't want to hear about them. At the time Ali was still a couple of years away from his conversion to traditional Islam, and in the theology of Elijah Muhammad it was assumed that if a man had white ancestors it must have been the result of a master raping his slave. By 2009 Ali had come full circle, and when he visited Ireland this time it was for the same reason thousands of other Americans do each year: to trace his Irish roots.

The Great St. Patrick's Day Hooley

McTigue and Siki

There is some irony, as well a bit of symmetry, to the fact that the Irish Arts Center is located in the Hell's Kitchen section of mid-Manhattan, just a few blocks removed from the spot where Battling Siki, with two bullets in his body, had crawled to his death in 1925.

Curated by Jim Houlihan, the Fighting Irishmen exhibit opened at the Irish Arts Center three years ago for what was intended to be a limited run. The fascinating collection of boxing ephemera that included everything from Barry McGuigan's shorts to Dan Donnelly's arm proved to be so popular that it has been on display ever since. At the conclusion of its stay at the Arts Center, it moved on to the South Street Seaport Museum, and from there to the Burns Library at Boston College. Next week it opens a six-month engagement at the Ulster Folk Park in County Tyrone, and there are plans to bring it to Dublin after that.

Subtitled A Celebration of the Celtic Warrior, Houlihan's Fighting Irishmen collection has also been the subject of a BBC documentary, which was screened at the Arts Center Tuesday night, along with Andrew Gallimore's 2007 film *An Troid Fhuilteach* (A Bloody Canvas), which explores the light-heavyweight title fight between Mike McTigue and Battling Siki that took place in Dublin on St. Patrick's Day of 1923.

For 86 years—until Bernard Dunne knocked out Ricardo Cordoba to win the WBA 122-pound title two months ago—McTigue's win over Siki remained the most significant upset in Irish boxing history, and its outcome has been the subject of some controversy ever since. There have been several attempts to recount its details in recent years, and Gallimore, a renowned Welsh filmmaker, has retold the story, assisted in that endeavor by still photographs and grainy newsreel footage shot on the night of the fight.

Although the invitation to the Irish Arts Center viewing described the McTigue-Siki fight as "a sensation attracting the attention of the world's sporting press," and as "an unknown chapter in Irish history," it would seem pretty hard for it to have been both.

Since Gallimore's documentary was produced for Telefis Éirann, an Irish-language channel, and much of the dialogue is spoken in Irish with English subtitles, it would be easy to assume a pro-McTigue bias, but in fact the strongest opinion is offered by Siki's American biographer Peter Benson, who says that McTigue's win represented a likely larceny.

The 1923 newsreel footage Gallimore used had actually surfaced 30 years ago after being discovered in the British Archive, and it served as the basis for a lengthy *Sports Illustrated* retrospective by the late Robert Cantwell. Cantwell's reconstruction of McTigue-Siki was entitled "The Great Dublin Robbery" and also concluded that Siki deserved the decision.

On the other hand, John Lardner, in his classic 1949 *New Yorker* profile of the Senegalese warrior, wrote that "the operation for the removal of [Siki's] crown was painless. The decision went to McTigue on points. There was nothing particularly wrong with this verdict, I am told by a neutral eyewitness, except that McTigue did not make the efforts or take the risks that are commonly expected of a challenger for a world's championship. There was no need to. In the circumstances, nothing less than a knockout could have beaten him, and he avoided that possibility by boxing at long range throughout."

The suggestion that McTigue was the beneficiary of a hometown decision was also addressed by the eminent African American boxing historian and essayist Gerald Early, who concluded that "Siki probably would not have beaten McTigue if he fought him in New York, Osaka, or Tangiers. He simply did not fight well."

Still, the background of the fight and its historical context make for a fascinating study, and with some significant input from Irish boxing experts Patrick and Thomas Myler (who if nothing else serve as a counterpoint to Benson's sometimes runaway enthusiasms), Gallimore's film explores it well.

Although he did manage wins over some of the best fighters of his day, by almost any standard McTigue was a career journeyman with a record of 82-25-7 when he, accompanied by his family, returned to his homeland in June of 1922.

McTigue was born in Kilnamona, near Ennis in County Clare, but when he arrived at Ellis Island ten years earlier he had listed his citizenship as "British–of Irish ancestry."

Despairing of what he was earning on mostly small-time New York club shows where he lost nearly as often as he won, McTigue hoped to fatten up both his purses and his record on the other side of the Atlantic–and he was prescient on both counts. Before the year was out he had dispatched three opponents in fights in England designed to advance his candidacy for a possible challenge to the world title. In that quest, his quarry was not Siki, but the incumbent champion, Georges Carpentier.

Still considered among the all-time great 175-pounders, the "Orchid Man" had won the European heavyweight and light-heavyweight titles in separate fights in 1913, and retained both through what was by all accounts heroic service as an aviator during the first World War. (During Jack Johnson's Mann Act exile he had also won a 1914 fight in London for something called the "White Heavyweight Championship of the World.") In 1920 he had traveled to the U.S., where he knocked out Battling Levinsky in Jersey City to win the world light-heavy title, setting the stage for his 1921 challenge to Jack Dempsey.

That bout matched a French war hero who had been awarded both the Croix de Guerre and the Médaille Militaire against a man whose non-service had labeled him a "slacker" in some quarters. Carpentier's gallantry didn't help him in the ring against Dempsey. When the two met at Boyle's Thirty Acres in Jersey City, the Manassa Mauler knocked him out in four. Carpentier made one subsequent light-heavyweight defense in 1922, defeating Ted "Kid" Lewis in London, before agreeing, on short notice, to fight Siki in Paris on September 24th.

Siki had turned professional before the war but was a modest 8-6-2 before abandoning the ring to serve in the 8th Colonial Infantry. Born Amadou M'Barick Phal in what was then French West Africa, Siki had reportedly been the bravest soldier in his unit. His legs bore scars from his shrapnel wounds, and he had been awarded the same honors as Carpentier (the Croix de Guerre and the Médaille Militaire), lending a certain cachet to a bout between the two, even though, as Benson notes in *A Bloody Canvas,* many Frenchmen regarded Siki as a savage, "one step removed from a baboon."

(Though an uneducated product of the colonial system, Siki was reportedly fluent in as many as ten languages, but, the *New York World* once unkindly noted, "He speaks seven languages, but his total vocabulary is limited to 157 words—counting profane expletives.")

Since resuming his boxing career in 1919, Siki had gone 45-1-2 against largely undistinguished European opposition. Carpentier apparently did not consider him a serious threat, particularly in a bout whose outcome was by most accounts pre-determined. (Benson says that the script called for Siki to go down in the first and second and then be counted out in the fourth. For his cooperation Siki was to receive not only his own but Carpentier's 200,000-franc purse. Carpentier, who was both a co-promoter of the fight and a part-owner of the 55,000-seat Buffalo Velodrome, could afford to be generous.)

Siki was knocked down in the first, and none too convincingly at that, and again from a harder blow in the third. By then Carpentier had begun to berate him with racial slurs.

Whether Siki became enraged at this point or whether he had never intended to go along with the fix remains open to dispute, but in either case from the third on he began to fight with a fury, battering Carpentier around the ring and finally knocking him out with a left hook in the sixth.

Carpentier, claiming he had been fouled, rolled around on the canvas holding his leg. Referee Arthur Bernstein, who was reportedly a party to the set-up, thereupon disqualified Siki and declared Carpentier the winner. This in turn produced a near-riot among the outraged spectators. Twenty minutes after the conclusion of the bout, Victor Bryer, the president of the French boxing federation, entered the ring and overruled the referee.

Thus it was that by the time McTigue and promoter Tom Singleton arrived in France to open negotiations, the world's light-heavyweight title no longer belonged to Carpentier, but to boxing's "Natural Man."

Although Siki had also won the European heavyweight and light-heavyweight titles (Carpentier's white heavyweight title was for obvious reasons not on the line), as Lardner noted, those trinkets weren't much more valuable then than they are now. Singleton was, however, able to persuade Siki's French manager Charles Hellers to sign for a light-heavyweight defense the following March 17 in the Irish capital.

Agreeing to a fight against an Irishman in Dublin on St. Patrick's Day, it was later remarked, made Hellers "either the bravest man in the world—or the dumbest."

Whether Siki even realized that the date coincided with Ireland's National Holiday remains a question, but McTigue's spotty record and the fact that both men would be fighting before an unfamiliar audience (this was the first and only fight of McTigue's 173-bout career to take place in Ireland) apparently persuaded M. Hellers that it was a low-risk exercise.

Moreover, Gallimore's film makes clear, Siki had few options. His boxing license had been revoked in France for an in-ring fracas in which he had been acting as a second. He had hoped to defend his title in London, but the British Home Office, fearing that a win by a person of color might encourage the Empire's already-restless colonial subjects, had issued a ruling specifically prohibiting interracial sporting contests.

There was one country, on the other hand, not only willing but eager to host such a fight. In January of 1922 the British had handed over Dublin Castle to Michael Collins, and the newly established Irish Free State was anxious to demonstrate that it belonged among the nations of the world by staging a significant international event.

Siki was nearly as profligate a spender in his day as Roberto Duran would be in his. As a result of the controversy in the Carpentier bout, he had never been paid for that fight. He might not have been anxious to travel to Dublin to fight an unworthy opponent before an audience of 3,000, but he needed money and that was the offer on the table. Professional boxing was so rare in Ireland that there was only one credible challenger in the entire country, and that was the man who had come back from America the previous summer.

Gallimore's account of the fight will correct some lingering misunderstandings promulgated by the lengthy 1979 *Sports Illustrated* treatment. In constructing his revisionist argument that McTigue-Siki was a "robbery," Cantwell was also guilty of some very bad history.

He described Eamon de Valera as "the president of Ireland," and noted that "de Valera's government ordered the fight stopped . . . but when [Dublin impresario] Lad Ray opened the doors of the [sic] La Scala Theatre at six o'clock, on schedule, the government backed down."

A year earlier Irish voters had overwhelmingly approved the establishment of the Free State, precipitating a Civil War that still raged. Collins had been killed the previous August, and the first president, Arthur Griffith, had also died. In March of 1923, W.T. Cosgrave headed up the Irish government. De Valera was on the run *from* the government, a wanted man with a price on his head, and hardly in a position to be giving orders to a boxing promoter.

Another boxing writer, Don Stradley, appears to have relied on Cantwell's flawed version of history in a story for ESPN that appeared on St. Patrick's

Day last year: "Eamon de Valera, *Ireland's president at the time,* had deemed the bout inappropriate," wrote Stradley. "When thugs threatened to bomb the La Scala Opera House where the fight would take place, Siki and McTigue began traveling with guards."

Uh, Don, once again: de Valera wasn't the president "at the time" (though he would hold that office from 1959 to 1973), but in March of '23 was engaged in a guerrilla war *against* the government. And those "thugs" you're talking about? They were *de Valera's* thugs. And the guards belonged to the government, which provided a squadron of armored cars to escort McTigue from his training camp in Lucan to the city center for the fight.

Henry Luce's *Time* had published its first issue on March 4, and while the view of the proceedings by the magazine's European correspondent was somewhat jaundiced, at least he knew one side from the other in the Irish Civil War. The March 24, 1923, edition of *Time* said "the normal interest of the Irish populace in fighting was augmented by the 'decree' of the outlaw Republicans forbidding the bout. Free State bayonets spiked the decree and a bomb explosion a stone's throw from the ring was the only interruption. Two children were wounded."

(With part of the crowd already in the house at La Scala, the IRA tried to disrupt the fight by blowing up the cable providing the electricity. They attached a land mine to the wrong cable, and blew out the doors of another movie house up the street.)

On the other hand, the *Time* correspondent seems to have been only vaguely aware, if he was aware at all, that McTigue was a native Irishman. The magazine described him as a "third-rate American fighter," and in providing the bout's result noted that "the American received the decision on points."

Put it this way: It has taken its place in boxing lore, but Maurice Walsh's *The News From Ireland,* a recently published book detailing the activities of a veritable army of worldwide press correspondents operating from Dublin in the early 1920s, doesn't include so much as a mention of McTigue or Siki. Nor is there a word about the fight in Tim Pat Coogan's exhaustively researched, 772-page biography of de Valera.

The fight footage itself is interesting but inconclusive. This was the last championship fight ever scheduled for 20 rounds, and Siki obviously had no intention of going that distance. He so overpowered McTigue from the opening bell that spectators initially feared that it might be over in the first minute. Siki's incautious display of abandon tends to support Benson's assertion that he had been assured that the fight was in the bag and that McTigue had agreed to bow out with an early exit.

No evidence supporting this theory has ever been advanced, but what does seem likely is that Hellers, who believed McTigue had no chance of beating his man, may have *told* his man the fix was in order to get him to agree to the Dublin fight.

If the plan called for the Irishman to go into the tank that night, nobody apparently told McTigue about it. He eventually got himself away from the ropes and began to box behind an annoying jab that served mainly to keep some distance between himself and the champion.

After dominating the first ten rounds, Siki ripped open a cut above McTigue's left eye in the 11th. Later in the same round McTigue, perhaps concerned that the cut might lead to an early stoppage, cut loose with the hardest punch he had thrown all night. When Siki tried to duck under the right, it caught him on the top of the head and dislocated McTigue's thumb.

Neither man was exactly guilty of untoward aggression over the last half of the fight, but McTigue increasingly pressured Siki, whose stamina was on the wane. (When his handlers poured water over the champion's back going into the 16th, Benson relates, the resultant hiss of steam "sizzled like a farrier's bucket.")

McTigue's resurgence may also have been spurred on by a rifle-toting Free State soldier stationed in his corner who reportedly jabbed him with the point of a bayonet just before one late round and, warning the challenger that he had bet him to win, whispered, *"God help youse if you lose!"*

Cantwell's view that Siki should have won the decision evidently came at least in part because either he couldn't believe his own eyes or distrusted the bowdlerized newsreel he had viewed.

"Though it is tricky to judge from the edited film, three of the last five rounds appear to be McTigue's," wrote Cantwell in what would seem a startling admission from a man describing a "robbery."

At the end of the 20th round, English referee Jack Smith so quickly pointed to McTigue's corner that the result seemed to some foreordained.

Under today's scoring system, Siki might indeed have won more rounds than McTigue, but remember, Smith wasn't handing in round-by-round totals, and his overall view was apt to be more shaped by the concluding rounds than those that had taken place more than an hour earlier.

The *Time* correspondent seemed to agree with Lardner when he wrote that "neither Siki nor McTigue showed sufficient skill or savagery to warrant the championship," but he also noted in what reads like a description of a John Ruiz fight that "in the 17th round of the scheduled 20, the Senegalese faltered about in the ring, groggy before McTigue's punches, finally falling into a clinch to hug himself safe from a knockout."

The next morning's *Irish Times* headline read McTigue Beats Siki on Points. A Disappointing Fight.

The celebration, in any case, lasted throughout the night in Dublin, and when word of the outcome reached the west of Ireland after midnight, bonfires spontaneously erupted up and down the Clare countryside.

If Carpentier had been double-crossed by Siki, and possibly Siki by McTigue, the Irishman took precautions against the same thing happening to him in his first defense. After swapping wins with Tommy Loughran in non-title fights that summer, when McTigue traveled to Columbus, Ga., to face Young Stribling in October he brought along his own referee. At the end of ten rounds Harry Ertle obligingly ruled the fight a draw, but overruled himself to declare the challenger the winner after a Stribling backer produced a gun.

Siki's title reign had lasted just six months, and McTigue's appeared to have as well, but Stribling's claim to the light-heavyweight title was over in an hour. Once he returned to his hotel Ertle signed an affidavit affirming his initial ruling, and confirmed that he had changed it only in the face of threats that he would "never leave the arena alive."

McTigue kept the title until 1925, when he lost a unanimous decision to Paul Berlenbach at Yankee Stadium. Even after losing the title he had prominent fights against Loughran, Jack Sharkey, and Jack Delaney, and two with Mickey Walker, all of which he lost. For a time, anyway, his purses reflected his status as a former champion, but the contention of *A Bloody Canvas* that he earned the equivalent of $10 million in today's dollars is downright absurd. The film also rather preposterously claims that McTigue had comfortably retired but was forced back into the ring when his investments were wiped out by the stock market crash of 1929.

If so it must have been the shortest retirement and un-retirement in boxing history. On October 18 of that year McTigue was knocked out by Jack Gagnon at the Boston Garden. The market began its descent into freefall on October 24 and had collapsed by October 29, a/k/a Black Tuesday. Two weeks later, on November 12, McTigue fought Emmett Curtice in Grand Rapids.

His overall record after the Siki fight was 23-21-6. Later afflicted by what today would be recognized as either Alzheimer's disease or *pugilistica de-mentia,* McTigue was committed to Creedmore State Hospital in Queens. (Woody Guthrie was a fellow patient.) He died there in 1966.

After losing to McTigue, Battling Siki had three more fights in France be-fore making his U.S. debut against King Norfolk at Madison Square Garden in November of 1923. Over the next two years he went 10-16-1 in fights in ten different states, the last of them a 12-round loss to Lee Anderson in Baltimore on November 13, 1925. Thirty-two days later he was shot in what was apparently a botched robbery attempt and had bled to death by the time a foot patrolman came upon his body just after four in the morning, not ter-ribly far from Irish Arts Center where his most celebrated fight was reprised on film Tuesday night.

At his wife's request, Siki was given a Christian funeral service, presided over by the Reverend Adam Clayton Powell, who in his eulogy asked the people of the world "for better treatment of the next mischievous boy of the jungles who comes to live among us."

Then, wrote Lardner, "seven Mohammedan pallbearers in turbans car-ried his body to the hearse, chanting prayers as they did so, while a crowd of three thousand people looked on."

TheSweetScience.com
July 2009

Separate But Unequalled

Sam Lacy

When he arrived at Griffith Stadium that night in 1941, Sam Lacy had anticipated, correctly, that he would have been assigned a position alongside the
other "colored" reporters, but before he could locate his seat in the separate
but decidedly unequal working press facilities he ran into Shirley Povich.

The *Washington Post* columnist seized Lacy by the arm and led him to
a seat adjacent to his own in the ringside press row. "Nobody's going to tell
you to move," Povich assured him, and nobody did.

While none of the other white sportswriters voiced their objection to the
presence of the Baltimore *Afro-American* columnist in their midst, it was evident that many of them regarded him as an interloper—although, once the
bizarre events of the evening unfolded, it became clear that the reverse may
have been the case. *They* were the interlopers, and their coverage, alongside
Lacy's, of what would rank as the most controversial ending to a heavyweight
title fight until Mike Tyson took a bite out of Evander Holyfield's ear more
than half a century later suggests that Sam may have been the only man at
ringside who fully understood what he was watching when Buddy Baer was
disqualified in his challenge to champion Joe Louis.

To say that Samuel H. Lacy saw them all understates the case. A pioneering
black journalist, Lacy was born late in the reign of James J. Jeffries and five
years before Jack Johnson bested Tommy Burns at Rushcutters Bay to win
the heavyweight championship of the world. He covered Joe Louis' championship run from start to finish, and when Sam died in 2003 Lennox Lewis
was a month shy of his final fight.

The son of an African American father and a mother who was a Shinnecock
Indian, Samuel H. Lacy was born in Mystic, Conn., but moved with his family

to Washington, D.C., as a small boy and made the nation's capital his home for most of his life.

After graduation from Howard University, Lacy's first job was with the *Washington Tribune,* a now-defunct paper, serving the minority community in the District of Columbia. He briefly moved to Chicago to write for the *Chicago Defender* in 1940 but was shortly after offered a position as a sports columnist for the Baltimore *Afro-American.*

The feisty *Afro-American* was at the time the country's pre-eminent minority newspaper, and Lacy would remain there for the next six decades. An early crusader for the integration of baseball, he (along with colleague Wendell Smith of the *Pittsburgh Courier*) helped arrange the infamous 1945 Fenway Park "tryout" of Negro League stars Jackie Robinson, Sam Jethroe, and Marvin Williams, an audition which was abruptly curtailed when someone (reputedly Red Sox owner Tom Yawkey) barked out an order to "get those niggers off the field!"

When Robinson signed with the Dodgers a year later, Lacy was assigned the Jackie Robinson beat and chronicled the exploits of the baseball pioneer through his one minor league season (with Montreal of the International League in 1946) and as a National League rookie in 1947. In their travels Lacy was subjected to many of the same indignities his subject was. In spring training in Florida and in many major league cities the two had to share quarters in segregated hotels. When the Dodgers barnstormed their way through New Orleans, Lacy, barred from the press box, had to cover the game from the stadium roof—where, to his surprise, he was joined by a sympathetic gaggle of baseball writers from the major New York papers. In Robinson's first major league season, 1947, Lacy was denied admission to the press box at Cincinnati's Crosley Field.

You won't read about these unseemly episodes in combing through the archives of Lacy's columns. Sam regarded himself not as a "black journalist" but as a journalist who happened to be black, and while he battled injustice on behalf of others throughout his career, he never wanted to make the story about himself.

While other sports dragged their feet when it came to integration, Sam's early newspaper career paralleled the rise of several black boxing champions. He chronicled the career of Henry Armstrong and was among the first to notice a rising young welterweight from Detroit who fought under the name Sugar Ray Robinson. But no boxer was more closely identified with Lacy than Joe Louis. The Brown Bomber (usually abbreviated to "Bomber" in the pages of the *Afro-American*) was the first black heavyweight champion since Johnson, a figure of such enormous pride to the community forming his readership that Lacy essentially became his personal Boswell, much as he later would be Jackie Robinson's.

And when it was announced that Louis would be defending his championship against Buddy Baer in Lacy's hometown of Washington in May of 1941, no one was happier than Sam and his colleagues at the *Afro*.

Louis was a busy champion, and the Baer fight that May would represent his fifth defense of 1941. Although the appellation that would define this interlude as Louis' "bum-of-the-month-club" had yet to gain widespread currency, *Afro-American* sports editor Art Carter did make reference to "this foolish, victim-a-month campaign that is definitely lowering his prestige."

The District of Columbia had originally been carved out of territory ceded by two slave states, and in the early 1940s Washington was both geographically and philosophically considered a "southern" city. In the run-up to the bout, the *Afro-American* pondered the question of whether Louis could expect a fair shake "here in the South," but with its large minority population, the nation's capital also represented the champion's natural constituency.

A Louis training session at Riverside Stadium five days before the bout drew 6,412 paying spectators, most of them black. Baer worked out in Olney, Md., the same day before an audience estimated at 800.

Ray Alvis, the Washingtonian who was co-promoting the event with Mike Jacobs, predicted a gate of $150,000. A week before the fight the *Afro* reported that Alvis estimated the advance sale at $55,000, adding that "$40,000 of that had been spent by colored fans of Louis, this indicating that more people of the title king's race will see him in action than ever before."

Samuel Lacy had virtually grown up at Griffith Stadium. As a boy he had sat with his father (recalled by Sam as "a dyed-in-the-wool fan") in the Jim Crow–era "colored" section in right field. As a teenager he worked as a ballpark vendor, and often arrived hours early for work so he could take the field and shag flies for the major leaguers who took early batting practice. He even had more than a nodding acquaintance with Clark Griffith, and shortly after returning from Chicago to work for the *Afro-American* had met with the owner of the hometown franchise.

Sam suggested to Griffith that the surest way to address the Senators' attendance woes in a city with a large minority population lay in signing a few black stars. Griffith argued that such a revolutionary step would lead to the collapse of the Negro Leagues, putting hundreds of colored ballplayers out of work and, not coincidentally, depriving Griffith Stadium of its most profitable tenant—the Homestead Grays, who in their Washington dates regularly outdrew the Senators.

Lacy found the owner's position unpersuasive. "The Negro Leagues were a symbol of segregation," he told *Sports Illustrated* many years later. "They were separate but unequal."

As an adult Sam had covered Senators' games for both the *Tribune* and the *Afro,* but not from the press box, which was off-limits to nonwhite reporters. Despite the presence of a black world champion in the main event, the 23,912 paying customers at Griffith Stadium were segregated by race on the night of the fight.

Sam's one-man integration of press row wasn't the only milestone accomplished that night. For the first time in boxing history an African American judge was assigned to a heavyweight title fight. Dr. John E. Trigg, described by the *Afro-American* as "a colored physician," kept one scorecard. Jimmy Sullivan was the other judge; the third tally was maintained by referee Arthur Donovan. (Sixty-eight years later the record book still listed Trigg as "Dr. Treeg," which was apparently the way *The Ring's* Nat Fleischer decided to spell it at the time. Informed of our findings last year, BoxRec.com historian John Sheppard updated the information and created a listing for Dr. Trigg.)

Washington would hardly have been considered a big-time boxing town, but it represented the sixth new venue in as many fights for Louis, and the Baer fight would be the only one of the bum-of-the-month series to take place in an outdoor arena. The International Boxing Club had ceded supervisory jurisdiction to the District of Columbia Boxing Commission, which was apparently nearly as much of a joke then as it is now. In the pages of the *Afro,* sports editor Carter noted that the local commission, "unaccustomed to big fights, wasn't prepared for such a happening," and that workmen had installed the timekeeper's bell under a ringside table, which muffled its sound and contributed significantly to the confusion surrounding the denouement of the main event.

The younger brother of former heavyweight champion Max Baer, Jacob Henry (Buddy) Baer might have lacked the notoriety of his older sibling (who had killed one opponent in the ring and was widely held responsible for the death of another), but at an imposing 6' 6 ½" and 240 pounds he was even larger and stronger than Max. Just a few weeks shy of his twenty-sixth birthday, he had won 50 of his 57 career bouts, and only four of his victims had survived to hear the final bell.

"The man's bigger than I am, a year younger than I am, and can hit," admitted Louis.

Just a month earlier Baer had successfully auditioned for his role in the title bout by knocking out Two-Ton Tony Galento in three at Washington's Uline Arena. Less than two years earlier, Galento had given the champion all he could handle, knocking Louis down twice before succumbing in four, and on the strength of their respective performances against a common opponent, Baer seemed confident of his chances.

"I took all of Galento's best punches without going down," he pointed out. "I'm told that four of the left hooks he hit me with in a row were as tough as the one that floored Joe. If Tony Galento could knock Louis *down,* I can knock him *out.*"

Few experts seemed to put much stock in Baer's boasts, but in the first round he sent a gasp through the crowd when he knocked Louis down and right through the ring ropes with what was described as "a corking good left hook." The punch knocked Louis through the ropes, and only an acrobatic landing prevented his head from thudding off the canvas.

Dazed, Louis came to rest perched "no more than two inches" from the edge of the ring apron, and very nearly tumbled over the edge and into the first row of sportswriters.

In a 1923 title fight at the Polo Grounds, Luis Ángel Firpo had knocked Jack Dempsey into the press section. On that occasion, several newspapermen, including Walter Winchell, Hype Igoe, and Paul Gallico, had assisted the Manassa Mauler by helping him climb back into the ring in time to beat the count, but Art Carter seemed to doubt that the Washington scribes would have done the same for Louis.

"If he had fallen into the press row, I hesitate to think what may have happened with a very hostile press in position to delay his return to the ring," wrote Carter.

It was the first time in his career Louis had ever been knocked out of the ring, and the episode apparently startled both combatants. Once Joe got back in the ring, he and Baer had both headed toward their respective corners, only to have Donovan order them to resume hostilities. There were still almost 20 seconds left in the first.

None the worse for wear, Louis resumed his two-fisted attack and handily won each of the next three rounds. He was similarly dominating the action in the fifth until, at close quarters, Baer unloaded an uppercut that ripped open a cut above Louis' eye.

Louis had been cut just once before, and that had been the result of a head-butt from Red Burman. This was the first time in 48 fights he had been cut by a punch.

Arthur Donovan was the pre-eminent referee of his day and almost as familiar to Louis as the champion's own cornermen. He was the third man in the ring for nine of the Brown Bomber's title fights, as well as four others in which Louis, on his way up the ladder, had faced former world champions. (Included among these latter had been Joe's fourth-round KO of Max Baer in 1935.)

Donovan's performance in the Washington fight was an aberration—a case of a good referee having a bad night—unlikely to appear on any highlight films of his officiating career.

After his early display of bravado, Baer was on the wane. Inspired by the sight of his own blood, Louis picked up the pace, and Baer was visibly staggered by the champion's onslaught late in the fifth.

Louis floored the giant challenger with a hard right in the sixth. Baer made it to his feet by the count of five after the first knockdown but probably should have been counted out the second time Louis put him down. Timekeeper Charley Reynolds actually did get to "ten" with Baer still on the canvas, but Donovan had misheard Reynolds' count and only reached "nine" before Buddy struggled to his feet.

Under similar circumstances in Lewiston, Maine, 24 years later, Sonny Liston was ruled to have been knocked out by Muhammad Ali even though referee Joe Walcott had missed the timekeeper's count; but on this occasion the fight continued, with just seconds remaining in the round.

Intent on finishing his foe and with the crowd now at fever pitch, Louis raced at Baer, fists flying. Louis feinted with a left and then landed a right squarely to the jaw. Neither fighter had heard the bell end the round, and neither did Donovan realize it had sounded until Baer was already writhing on the canvas.

Baer did eventually make it to his feet and fairly stumbled to his corner. Manager Ancil Hoffman devoted most of the intervening one-minute rest period berating Donovan, demanding that the referee disqualify Louis for the late punch.

The extent of Baer's recovery during the one-minute rest period we will never know because when the bell rang Hoffman all but sat on his fighter to ensure that he didn't leave his stool. Ray Arcel and Izzy Klein, the seconds in Baer's corner, also remained on the ring apron, refusing to descend the stairs.

When the Baer entourage ignored several entreaties and refused to vacate the ring, Donovan disqualified the challenger.

The pro-Louis segment of the crowd was pleased by the result, if not by the precipitate conclusion, of the bout, but Hoffman's histrionics apparently struck a chord among a preponderance of ringside reporters, many of whom wrote the next day that Louis, and not Baer, should have been disqualified. Of course, most of these sportswriters were covering their first championship fight. Sam Lacy, on the other hand, had covered plenty of them, and he understood exactly what he had seen.

Yes, the final blow had been struck after the round was over, but Donovan hadn't heard the bell and neither had either fighter. Even once this had been established, the referee maintained that Louis' punch had been delivered "at the bell," though most onlookers thought it came a few seconds later.

Once rendered, the referee's ruling was, like a called third strike, irreversible.

"I made my decision and I am standing by it," said Donovan. "There is no appeal from my decisions."

Hoffman knew this as well as anyone. Even had the referee acknowledged the champion's transgression, it was so obviously unintentional that he might have taken the round from Louis, but he certainly wouldn't have disqualified him.

Hoffman also knew that his fighter had been down three times in the past three minutes and was unlikely to survive another minute of fighting, let alone another round. In appearing to stand on principle, what he was actually doing was laying the groundwork for a rematch and another payday for himself and Buddy Baer.

In this respect Hoffman's actions are comparable to, say, the attorney William Kunstler intentionally getting himself physically carried out of the courtroom of Judge Julius Hoffman (no relation to Ancil, as far as we know) at the Trial of the Chicago Seven. Kunstler knew he couldn't win in court that day, and he knew perfectly well he would be locked up and jailed for contempt. But he also knew that by portraying himself as the aggrieved party he would build a groundswell of public support, and hoped to establish a case for a new trial before a more hospitable judge.

So while the other sportswriters were falling for Ancil Hoffman's con job,

Sam Lacy immediately recognized it for what it was. But, far from angered, Lacy actually applauded Hoffman for what he recognized as a brilliant tactic on behalf of his client.

Wrote an admiring Lacy in his "Looking 'Em Over" column, "Hoffman, hardly known to this corner prior to that time, immediately captured its profound respect . . . That is the kind of manipulation that marks a real strategist and lifts a fight manager far above the rank and file of his contemporaries."

While many white sportswriters viewed Louis' late punch as an act of moral turpitude, Sam recognized it for what it was—an unintentional transgression that "nevertheless, should have been punished.

"Loss of the round was probably the most severe penalty that could be administered under the conditions, however," wrote Lacy, "and there shouldn't be a moment's entertainment of the claims that [Louis] should be shorn of his crown."

Lacy's opinion was seconded by Dr. Trigg, who told the *Afro-American,* "Though I don't think he did it deliberately, Louis' final right-hand smash to Buddy Baer's jaw was in my opinion a foul. Louis threw that blow about three seconds after I had heard the bell ring. Because of the terrific din set up by the crowd and the fact that the bell was placed in such a position that it might not be heard over the roar of the crowd, it can be safely said that Joe probably didn't hear it.

"In keeping with the rules, that sixth round should have been taken from Louis and awarded to Baer and the fight should have continued, if—which I doubt—Baer had been able to come out for the seventh."

Disqualification in a heavyweight championship fight is rare. The most obvious example came when referee Mills Lane disqualified Tyson after he deliberately bit Holyfield in the ear—twice—in their second fight in 1997. (Lane, a no-nonsense former prosecutor and judge, also DQ'd Henry Akinwande, after repeated warnings, for "excessive holding" in a fight against Lennox Lewis.) Some of the white ringside press apparently considered Louis' late punch the 1941 equivalent of the "Bite Fight," but Sam Lacy knew better.

But, wrote Lacy in his whimsical analysis of Ancil Hoffman's actions provoking the DQ, "by straddling Buddy and creating a general disturbance, Hoffman accomplished more in the way of winning public sentiment for a return go and rousing a press which up until this time had been earmarked 'recalcitrant' by the promoters than he and his whole stable of fighters could have done in a year."

In this analysis Lacy was not only accurate but downright prescient.

Thanks to his manager, Buddy Baer did indeed get a return bout. He and Louis met at Madison Square Garden the following January. The champion's seventy-five-year-old trainer Jack Blackburn, by then badly ailing and crippled by arthritis, nearly withdrew from the Louis corner for Baer II, voicing concern whether he could negotiate the steps for fifteen rounds. Louis told him if he could make it up to the ring once, he wouldn't have to do it again.

"That's a promise," Chappie reminded him, and Joe made good on it.

After Louis knocked him down three times in the first round to score a quick TKO, Baer famously said, "The only way I could have beaten Louis that night was with a baseball bat."

Blackburn passed away that April, and Louis shortly found himself in the Army.

The payday from the rematch was Buddy's last as a boxer. The attack on Pearl Harbor had occurred a month before the rematch. Buddy and Max both joined the Armed Forces, and neither ever fought again. After World War II Buddy Baer returned to California and embarked on an acting career that saw him appear in numerous movie and television roles.

Lacy continued to write his column for the *Afro-American* well into this century. After he suffered a stroke, his son drove him to the newspaper's offices, and once his hands became too crippled by arthritis to type, he wrote his column in longhand. Sam's column appeared three times a week until his death, at ninety-nine, in May of 2003. He was inducted into the writers' wing of the Baseball Hall of Fame in 1997. And when the Boxing Writers Association of America established the A.J. Liebling Award in 1995, Samuel H. Lacy and Shirley Povich were included in the first group of recipients.

Somehow, though, Lacy's name has not come up for inclusion in the "observers" section of the International Boxing Hall of Fame at Canastota—an oversight that should, in our opinion, be addressed, and at the earliest possible moment.

TheSweetScience.com
2010

A Man You Don't Meet Every Day

Pat O'Grady's unfortunate legacy is that he is destined to be remembered as the founder of the short-lived World Athletic Association, a one-man sanctioning body whose death knell was sounded by a single punch in its very first "world championship" fight—a bout that simultaneously turned Sean O'Grady into a broadcaster.

The mention of his name today conjures up images of yet another over-involved boxing father. To be sure, Pat was that, but he was *sui generis,* one of a kind.

Even old-time boxing scribes tend to recall O'Grady as the colorful buffoon who bungled away his son's championship, but in the 1960s and '70s Pat singlehandedly kept the fight game alive in the American Midwest, where he employed a Barnumesque approach to the staging of literally hundreds of club-fight cards in an era when live boxing otherwise seemed to be on the wane.

For the better part of two decades O'Grady staged cards on the first and third Tuesday of each month.

On paper, his wife, Jean, was the promoter-of-record, but the O'Gradys were keeping it all in the family long before the idea occurred to Don and Carl King. It wasn't unusual to see an Oklahoma main event in which O'Grady was not only the promoter but also the matchmaker and the manager—of *both* fighters.

"We moved to Oklahoma when I was six years old, but even before that I can remember my father running shows at the old Pan-Am Center in Austin, Texas," recalled Sean O'Grady. "My father would attend to the fighters and the logistics and my mother would show up with a briefcase filled with tickets. She'd sell the tickets and pay the fighters, all out of that briefcase.

"Then by the time I was twelve or so I was working, too," said Sean. "I'd help set up the ring, get the gloves ready, and be in the dressing room to get the fighters to and from the ring.

"I guess you could say I saw 'the good, the bad, and the ugly' side of boxing at a tender age. And the ugly side could be truly ugly. I can remember being in the dressing room with this heavyweight named Jimmy Cross who'd just gotten his ass kicked by Duane Bobick. I mean he'd been pulverized in this fight, but he's saying 'Man, I get *high* off this!' and I'm thinking '*What?*'"

Pat O'Grady had gravitated toward the fight game at least in part because he had returned from World War II with two Purple Hearts. The wounds left him unsuited for more conventional work.

"The second time he was wounded was by shrapnel from a mortar shell at Guadalcanal," said Sean. "My understanding is that he was one of only four marines in his unit who survived the explosion, but my Dad never wanted to talk about the war. The only time I ever heard him talk about it was one time when somebody got him to drink a martini. He hardly ever drank, so that one drink was enough to get him going."

Pat knew the fight game inside out, and some of it may even have rubbed off on the ever-changing stable of cowboys and shitkickers he kept trotting into the ring, masquerading as boxers.

He so successfully groomed an Oklahoma light-heavyweight named Brian Kelly that he managed to attract the great Bob Foster to Oklahoma City for a 1971 WBC title fight. Kelly was down twice in the second round and again a round later before the referee stopped it in the third.

O'Grady also developed a lightweight from Lawton, Frank "Rootin'Tootin'" Newton. Newton was an undefeated 32-0-3 fighting in the Oklahoma-Nebraska-Arkansas nexus, 1-4-1 outside it. Pat never did get Rootin' Tootin' a title shot, but he did move him far enough along to lose a fight—to Charlie "White Lightning" Brown—on the Hagler-Duran undercard at Caesars in 1983.

But long before there were Sean O'Grady and Rootin' Tootin' Newton, Monte Masters and Wimpy Halstead, there was Humphrey Pennyworth McBride.

He had been christened Claude McBride, but at Pat's behest called himself Humphrey, after the bumbling, kind-hearted giant in the old *Joe Palooka* comic strip. (When *Joe Palooka* had a run as a syndicated television program in the mid-1950s, a real-life boxer—Slapsie Maxie Rosenbloom—had portrayed Humphrey Pennyworth.)

"My father hung a nickname on every boxer who ever walked into the gym," said Sean O'Grady. "And usually they'd stick. He named Jerry Halstead 'Wimpy' because he whined all the time. Another guy was called 'Hamburger.'

The first time he saw McBride, my dad said 'You look just like Humphrey!' and from that day on he was Humphrey.

"But then a few years later Oscar Bonavena came to town and sparred with Humphrey. He couldn't quite pronounce the name because of his accent, so it came out 'Humpity,' so from then on he was Humphrey in the ring but Humpity in the gym."

Humphrey McBride stood 6' 4", his weight fluctuated between 280 and 300 pounds, and while he couldn't fight a lick he won his first 27 bouts as a professional. Never mind that 12 of his opponents had never won a fight when they met Humphrey (and several of them never *would*). The rubes, inspired by McBride's success, kept pouring through the turnstiles on weekend nights in Oklahoma and Texas.

Capitalizing on the physical resemblance to the comic-book character, Pat persuaded Humphrey to wear baggy pants with large polka dots, a newsboy cap, and a pre-shrunken sport coat. He even had a bicycle constructed with a tiny house attached to the back, just like the fictional blacksmith Pennyworth, and urged Humphrey to pedal it around the streets of Oklahoma City.

You wouldn't find very many familiar names on the roster of Humphrey's victims, but in 1972 he did win a decision over Henry Hank in Ardmore, and later that year, in Oklahoma City, he beat Terry Daniels, who only seven months earlier had lasted almost four rounds with Joe Frazier.

At thirty-seven, Hank didn't have much tread remaining on his well-worn tires, and Daniels would lose 17 of his last 19 fights, but even so, one must surmise that had those bouts been on the up-and-up they'd probably have had enough left to beat Humphrey.

But in 1972 Muhammad Ali, following his loss to Frazier a year earlier, was easing his way back up the heavyweight ladder with his own personal bum-of-the-month club. He'd beaten Al "Blue" Lewis in Dublin that summer and was looking for another soft touch with a decent record.

Humphrey fit both descriptions, and Pat O'Grady made a deal. The Ali fight was agreed upon in principle, provided Humphrey won his next fight, against another 300-pound behemoth, Buster Mathis.

Although Mathis had gone 12 with Ali just a year earlier, he was widely (and correctly) considered to be at the end of the line. O'Grady nonetheless advertised the collision of unthreatening blimps as a fight for the "World Super-Heavyweight Championship," and booked it for Oklahoma City on September 5, 1972.

Mathis arrived in Oklahoma for a press conference a few days before the fight, and at their first face-to-face meeting Humphrey unaccountably lapsed into a spate of trash-talking. He told Buster he was "going to kick his fat ass," and at one point offered to do it then and there.

Mathis calmly tolerated the smack-talk for as long as he could. Then he quietly displayed his right hand.

"See this fist?" he asked.

"Yup," said Humphrey, his curiosity aroused.

"Well," said Buster, "I knocked out a horse with this fist."

Humphrey's jaw dropped open.

"You *did?*" he asked.

Pat O'Grady slapped himself on the head and groaned.

"The fight," he would later recall, "was over then and there. I could see it all—the shot with Ali, the money, maybe even the heavyweight title—going up in smoke."

But when the two blobs collided in Oklahoma City a week or so later, Humphrey startled the audience, O'Grady, Mathis, and, probably, himself, a minute into the fight, when he landed two successive right hands that sent Buster stumbling backwards into the ropes.

Mathis was dazed, but still on his feet as he floundered there, but instead of jumping right on his wounded quarry, Humphrey stood back to admire his handiwork.

"I could see him thinking, 'Oh, God. *I* did *that?*'" remembered Pat O'Grady.

Buster recovered, and having survived his first-round peril, caught up with Humphrey in the third and knocked him cold with a right hand of his own.

After being counted out, Humphrey was revived with smelling salts, and as he regained consciousness he could hear his friends, many of whom had just lost substantial sums of money betting on him, shouting and booing their fallen former hero from their front-row seats.

Humphrey walked slowly across the ring, leaned over the ropes, and addressed the occupants of the ringside seats in a stage whisper.

"Listen," he told them, gesturing over his shoulder toward Mathis, "he knocked out a *horse!*"

"Yeah. And now he's knocked out an elephant," said Pat O'Grady.

"Really?" Humphrey exclaimed.

"Yeah," said Pat. *"You."*

Mathis fought only one more time and retired after being knocked out by Ron Lyle. Humphrey was so chastened by the unhappy experience that he lost six of his next ten fights. Then, in 1975, he managed to win two in a row and proudly announced to O'Grady that he finally understood this boxing game.

"You big jackass!" O'Grady told him. "If you're so damned smart, how come I've fixed forty fights for you and you *still* lost seven of them?"

By then, of course, Pat had bigger fish to fry. A year earlier he had turned his fifteen-year-old son, Sean, pro, and the boy with the clean-cut Joe College look was packing them in all over the Midwest.

Billed as "The Bubblegum Kid," Sean O'Grady was 29-0 when his father overreached to match the seventeen-year-old against Danny "Little Red" Lopez and nearly got Sean killed. The bout was mercifully stopped after four, and it was back to the drawing board for the younger O'Grady.

Taking the Lopez fight is commonly regarded as having been a major miscalculation on the part of O'Grady *père,* but his son disagrees.

"I could have kept fighting opponents in the Midwest and been 50-0, but I needed a test," said Sean. "I needed to find out where I fit in at that stage of my career. Unfortunately, I did."

Around this time a sportswriter named Dave Wolf came to Oklahoma City to do a profile on Pat and Sean. He spent two weeks following Pat O'Grady around, then flew back to New York, turned in his resignation, and went into the boxing business. He would later achieve some prominence managing a lightweight named Ray "Boom-Boom" Mancini.

By 1980 Sean O'Grady was a remarkable 73-1 and attracting worldwide attention. Following a *Sports Illustrated* profile, he was matched against WBC lightweight champion Jim Watt in Glasgow that November.

Since the title bout would be carried on live television back to the U.S., it was scheduled to start at 2 a.m. in Scotland. At the pre-fight press conference Watt was asked whether the unusual starting time would be a problem.

"No," Watt replied, accurately. "In Glasgow, *everybody* fights at two in the morning."

The bout hinged on a collision of heads that was seen by everyone save the Belgian referee, Raymond Balderoux. Both fighters were cut, although O'Grady's was the more serious of the wounds. When it was finally stopped in the 12th, Watt was ahead on all three cards, but O'Grady had proved this time that he belonged in such heady company.

The following spring, his cuts having healed, Sean was matched against Emanuel Steward's WBA lightweight champion Hilmer Kenty. This time

O'Grady pulled off the upset and won a unanimous decision.

I was in Ireland that summer when Pat, Jean, and Sean O'Grady turned up in Dublin, ostensibly to explore the possibility of Sean attending the College of Surgeons there. They were accompanied by Sean's new attorney and business representative, Jimmy Walsh—no relation to Joe Palooka's manager Knobby Walsh—who was also Joe Namath's lawyer and onetime roommate.

We spent several days in the Irish capital, with Pat so charming to the locals that they might as well have been paying customers back in Oklahoma City.

Asked about the possibility of Sean defending his title against Belfast lightweight Charlie Nash, who had lost to Watt just a year earlier, Pat diplomatically replied that his son "would never fight a fellow Irishman."

Sean O'Grady says he wasn't just blowing smoke about attending medical school in those days.

"I also explored the possibility of going to school down in Guadalajara," he said. "It just didn't work out."

But the storm clouds were already gathering. The WBA had Claude Noel of Trinidad rated as its top contender. When Pat O'Grady balked at making a high-risk match against a low-profile opponent, the WBA stripped Sean and vacated the championship.

Reasoning that Sean's marquee value was more valuable than the WBA title, Pat arranged for a televised fight against Howard Davis Jr. to be held in Hartford. When the network asked about a title, he supplied one: The fight would be for the World Athletic Association lightweight championship of the world.

The WAA's first title bout found itself in some jeopardy when Davis withdrew with a knee injury, but Pat salvaged the TV date by moving the fight to Little Rock, Ark., and bringing in Andy Ganigan, a Hawaiian with a 33-3 record, as a substitute opponent.

Ganigan caught O'Grady cold in the second round, knocking him down with a punch that stunned him so severely that he never recovered. Sean was down twice more before the fight was stopped at 2:06 of the round. The first WAA champion had lost his title in his first defense.

"I can't even remember what he hit me with. A Hawaiian punch, I guess," said Sean. "I try not to think about that fight too much."

That wasn't quite the end of the WAA, but it was close. Pat had also arranged titles in several other weight divisions and had designated his daughter's husband, a latter-day Humphrey McBride named Monte Masters, the organization's heavyweight champion.

When Masters and Rosie O'Grady divorced in 1984, O'Grady promptly stripped his erstwhile son-in-law of his title.

In the meantime, Jerry "Wimpy" Halstead had become the world's first super-middleweight champion (Pat called his 168-pound division "junior light-heavyweight") by knocking out Ronnie Brown in Denver.

Wimpy shortly outgrew the division and campaigned thereafter as a heavyweight. Once his usefulness on the Oklahoma circuit had been exhausted, Wimpy went on to a lucrative second career as an Opponent, losing all over the world to the likes of Pierre Coetzer in South Africa, Tommy Morrison in Las Vegas, Alex Stewart in New York, Herbie Hide in London, Yosuke Nishijima in Tokyo, Brian Nielsen in Denmark, and Wladimir Klitschko in Germany.

"When I look back on it, I don't regret the influence my father had on my career," said Sean O'Grady. "When he took his stand against the WBA he was doing what he philosophically and morally felt was right. Like some other things, it just didn't work out. Andy Ganigan was a dangerous puncher, he had his one chance, and he made the most of it.

"I don't regret the things my father did in terms of my own career, but I would have to say that success changed things for both of us. I mean, when I was back in Oklahoma City fighting bums, we didn't have any money but it seemed like we were a lot happier than we were later on. It didn't change our *boxing* relationship, but it changed our personal relationship—and my father never seemed to be able to separate the two."

Pat O'Grady moved with his family to Castaic, Calif., in 1982. He still ran the odd show here and there, including one (Sean against Pete Ranzany) for which his partner and co-promoter was Sylvester Stallone.

As he had during his more active promotional days, he continued to phone friends and acquaintances around the clock. It wasn't unusual for Pat to call at 3 or 4 in the morning.

"What you doing?" he'd ask. Hanging up was out of the question, because you knew he'd just call back. A long (and entertaining) conversation would usually ensue, and an hour later you'd find yourself lying in bed wondering "*why* did he call?"

"Once he phoned me at four in the morning," recalled Sean O'Grady. "I was in college and living on my own, but he said he needed to talk to me, so I got up, got dressed, and drove over to my parents' house. When I got there he just wanted to shoot the breeze."

By 1983, a year-and-a-half after the Ganigan fight, Sean O'Grady had retired from boxing at the age of twenty-four. He went on to a career as a top-flight color analyst, whose broadcast partners addressed him without a trace of irony as "the champ."

"I still broadcast fights for FOX, but it's a nonexclusive contract, so I do a lot of freelance television work as well," said Sean O'Grady. "The odd part of it is that a whole generation of boxing fans has grown up who don't even realize that I fought myself. Kids today only know me for my television work. I guess that's flattering."

Pat died on March 30, 1988. He was sixty years of age. A whole generation of boxing fans has grown up who don't remember him, either. It is their loss.

BoxingTalk.com
2007

Mississippi Riverbank Hustle

MEMPHIS—This old slave-trading center on the banks of the Mississippi might be a comparative neophyte when it comes to professional boxing, but it would be inaccurate to say Memphis has no history or tradition of memorable fights.

On October 18, 1956, a sometime guitar player named Elvis Aaron Presley pulled his Lincoln Mark II into a Gulf station on Second Street for repairs. His presence soon attracted a crowd, and an attendant named Ed Hopper ordered him to move the vehicle.

When Presley didn't respond quickly enough for Hopper's liking, the attendant, according to testimony of the day, took a shot at Elvis, belting him in the chops through the open driver's side window, at which point Presley stepped out of the car and belted him back.

"Both men were charged with assault and disorderly conduct," reads the *Memphis Commercial Appeal*'s account of the fracas. "When asked for his name, Presley told police: 'Maybe you'd better put down Carl Perkins.'"

The winner: Presley, by decision. He was let off the next day. Hopper was fined $26. A witness said Hopper's eye "looked like a travelling bag."

Apart from the night when the present mayor, the Honorable Willie Herenton, scored a one-punch knockout over a circuit court judge in a downtown saloon, Presley's TKO of Hopper stood as the most famous fight in Memphis history.

That is about to change tonight, when heavyweight champion Lennox Lewis and Mike Tyson, the self-proclaimed "baddest man on the planet," meet for a scheduled 12 rounds at the Pyramid, the 19,000-seat home of the NBA Memphis Grizzlies.

When Tyson was greeted by gay-rights pickets at his Cordova training site last week, he leapt out of his car and hugged a startled protester, assuring the fellow: "I'm not homophobic." When he showed up the next day and the pickets were gone, Tyson asked: "Where are all my homosexual friends?" So when Iron Mike arrived for Thursday's weigh-in at the Memphis Convention Center, it was to find a swarm of *pro*-Tyson gay demonstrators.

Thanks, Mike, for saying gay is OK, read one placard. Tyson opposes homophobia. Thanks, Mike! read another, while a third proclaimed: We support Tyson's step up to tolerance.

Tonight's adversaries even took different routes to and from the venue lest they run into each other going and coming. The last time Lewis and Tyson had been in the same room together, back in January, a melee had broken out and Tyson took a bite out of Lewis' thigh.

The pro-Tyson demonstrators weren't the only ones espousing their cause in Memphis on the day of the weigh-in. Some religious zealots marched outside the media center wearing T-shirts that read: "Jesus Christ is the real heavyweight champion of the world." They found themselves competing for space with a crowd of travelling Lewis supporters assembled outside the convention center for the first weigh-in.

When the English fans showed their backsides, they had letters printed on the backs of their red-on-black T-shirts spelling out "Fuck Tyson."

On the same day that Lewis, a celebrated chess buff, played a match against a thirteen-year-old member of a local chess club, Tyson's PR minions did their best to salvage their own photo op by having Tyson, who had disdainfully hit the speed bag for 15 minutes and then departed without speaking to reporters a day earlier, invite a group of grade school students to meet the former champion after his workout.

Most of the children were, reportedly, timid, but one of them, ten-year-old Jamal Cornes, marched up to the ring and asked Tyson: "Why did you bite off Evander Holyfield's ear?"

The startled Tyson chuckled uneasily and replied: "That was a long time ago."

Not even the locals seemed to know what to call tonight's encounter: The River Bout. The Rumble on the River. The Showdown in M-Town. The Clinch in the Pinch. The Fight of the Century. Promoters eventually opted for the understated Lewis-Tyson Is On, and placards bearing that slogan line the streets of Memphis, to say nothing of the 40-mile stretch of Highway 61 from here to the Mississippi casino enclaves.

One-hundred-and-thirteen years have elapsed since Mississippi played host to its first and only heavyweight championship fight. When John L. Sullivan, Jake Kilrain, their respective entourages, and a medium-sized regiment of paying customers departed New Orleans at midnight on July 8, 1889, most of the party didn't even know their final destination—which turned out to be a ring set up on the banks of the Mississippi River a hundred miles upstream.

The match-up of heavyweight champion and challenger had been banned from most respectable venues, and the location of the site had to be kept secret lest the authorities intervene.

Back then, it was the notoriety of the sport itself, and not that of one of the participants, that made the fight a pariah in the eyes of civilized society. But a scribe of the day, writing for the *New York World,* might have been talking about Tyson when he assessed Sullivan's chances: "According to all such drunkards as he, his legs ought to fail him after 20 minutes of fighting."

Tonight, Lewis (39-2-1 with 30 KOs) and Tyson (49-3, with 2 no-contests and 43 KOs) will properly be fighting across the state line in Tennessee, but for the past week Mississippi loomed large in the proceedings, and the epicenter didn't really shift to Memphis until Thursday afternoon's weigh ins. It was money from the Tunica casinos that eventually pushed the Pyramid backers over the top in the dwindling bidding to stage the fight nobody else wanted, and both champion and challenger were headquartered in Mississippi—Lewis at Sam's Town, where Jerry Lee Lewis (unrelated to Lennox, but a cousin of Elvis) headlined last night, while Tyson was officially assigned accommodation at Fitzgerald's Hotel & Casino, though he showed his face there only briefly last week.

Both contestants flew into Memphis a week ahead of time. Lewis was feted with a parade down Beale Street, while Tyson arrived by private jet and was whisked away to the house he had rented for the week. Promoters carefully orchestrated the week's events, right down to the separate-but-equal weigh-ins, to ensure there wasn't even a chance encounter before the two step into the ring.

The thankless task of refereeing tonight's fight has fallen to Eddie Cotton of New Jersey, the lone American included on a multinational slate of officials. Bob Logist of Belgium, Anek Hongtongkam of Thailand, and Alfred Bukwana of Soweto will be the ringside judges.

The suspicion here is that their services may not be required. If Lewis dominates Tyson as handily as we suspect he might, it wouldn't be surprising to see Tyson do something to get himself disqualified before the fight reaches its midpoint. Put it this way: When was the last fight you saw the bookies post odds of 4-1 on a disqualification?

With the likes of Jack Nicholson and Denzel Washington, Mel Gibson and Britney Spears, Wesley Snipes and Johnnie Cochran already due in town for the fight, you could hardly blame the hotel executives down at Sam's Town Hotel & Casino for their excitement when they learned that Prince William and his entourage would be staying at their hostelry over the weekend.

The Tunica hotel spent the better part of last Tuesday making security arrangements for their new special guest. With Lewis and a small army of his English supporters already in residence there, the hotel had thoughtfully added shepherd's pie and lamp chops to the menu, and were prepared to roll out the red carpet for the royal party when they learned that the Prince William in question wasn't the heir to the British throne after all, but rather the potentate of a principality in Africa so tiny that "I can't even remember the name of it," said hotel general manager Maunty Collins.

Although Lewis and Tyson have managed to avoid one another through an aggregate 94 previous professional bouts, they are not exactly strangers. In 1983, Lewis recalled the other day, in a search for quality sparring as he prepared for the World Junior Championships in Santo Domingo, his trainer drove him to the Catskill, N.Y., gym of the late, legendary trainer Cus D'Amato.

Accounts of those sparring sessions between the teenaged Lewis and the teenaged Tyson vary widely. Tyson trainer Stacy McKinley boasted the other day that Tyson "knocked out Lewis wearing 18-ounce gloves." McKinley, who was certainly not there 18 years ago, said he was in possession of photographs establishing the veracity of his claim. That was three days ago and he still hasn't produced them.

Lewis' recollection is that "we went at it pretty good for four days. Mike Tyson never knocked me out in those four days. He gave me a fat lip. I gave him a bloody mouth, so we were pretty even on that exchange."

What effect the memory of that long-forgotten sparring session 18 years ago might have when Lewis and Tyson climb into the ring at the Pyramid tonight for the richest match in boxing history remains to be determined, but as he held court at Sam's Town Casino yesterday, Lewis revealed that at the conclusion of hostilities between the two youthful boxers, Tyson's wise old trainer took him aside and ventured a prediction.

"One day," D'Amato told Lewis, "you and Mike Tyson will meet in the ring for the heavyweight championship of the world."

"This is a very important fight for me," Lewis reflected this week. "It would have been unfortunate for me if I didn't box the best boxers of my era. Tyson is the best out there right now. This is what the world wants to see: me and Mike Tyson in the ring. I'm glad it's finally come about. I've been waiting for this fight for a long time.

"This fight," sighed Lewis, "is my legacy. I'm getting rid of the last misfit in boxing."

The Irish Times
June 2002

Arm and the Man

As soon as I laid eyes on the Fighting Irishmen exhibit I realized that a prized possession on my wall—a poster-sized photo, signed by Muhammad Ali, taken as he playfully took his cuts with a hurling stick at his training camp at Kiltiernan before the 1972 Al (Blue) Lewis fight— belonged in the show, and curator Jim Houlihan immediately and happily took me up on my offer. After its run at the Irish Arts Center the exhibit moved to the South Street Seaport Museum, and from there to Boston College and to the Ulster Folk Park in Northern Ireland, and in May of 2010 it opened a summer-long run at the GAA Museum in Dublin. Jim is already talking about taking it next to London in the run-up to the 2012 Olympics. I've had to sign a new release every time the show moved, and at this point I'm pretty much resigned to the likelihood that if my photo or Barry McGuigan's shorts ever come home it's going to be to our children.

At the time of his death, Dan Donnelly was broker than Mike Tyson, but 186 years later the legendary bare-knuckle champion finally made it to Broadway.

Which is to say, part of him did.

In anticipation of an exhibit entitled "Fighting Irishmen: A Celebration of the Celtic Warrior," due to open at New York's Irish Arts Center next month, the curators staged a media reception at Gallagher's Steak House in midtown Manhattan yesterday afternoon.

Dan Donnelly was the guest of honor. Or, more accurately, his right arm was.

The timing of the 3 p.m. event was carefully orchestrated to avoid unveiling the boxer's mummified limb in conjunction with the busy lunchtime traffic at the onetime speakeasy at the corner of 52nd and Broadway.

Although the display of a human body part flown in from Ireland sufficed to bring curious members of the Fight Mob flocking to Times Square yesterday, some of us, including myself and Gerry Cooney, were on more familiar terms with the *pièce de résistance*. Over the course of several visits to the Hideout Pub in Kilcullen over the years, I'd met up with Donnelly's arm before.

In 1989 I had helped arrange for Cooney to make his first trip to Ireland, to serve as the spokesman for a boys' boxing tournament Father Joe Young had arranged at Adare Manor, and we flew into Dublin for a press conference at Buswell's Hotel. (Through a chance encounter that morning, Cooney wound up posing for a photo op with another bare-knuckle pugilist of some repute, the late Prime Minister Charles Haughey, the result of which was splayed across the front pages of several newspapers the next morning.)

On the day we were leaving for Limerick, we'd arranged for a taxi-man friend, Brendan Freeman, to drive Cooney around on a sightseeing trip. It was Finbar Furey who insisted that Freeman take Cooney to the Hideout "to visit Dan Donnelly's arm."

Following that introduction, I'd stopped off in Kilcullen on several occasions, usually to surprise visiting American friends. I also recall the wonderment of my six-year-old daughter upon her first encounter with what she called "The Giant's Arm"—although, contrary to legend, Dan's reach wasn't inordinately great, and his arm probably no longer than my own.

(During the tenure of Donnelly's appendage at the Hideout, it was displayed alongside a vaguely simian caricature of the decedent, accompanied by the claim that Dan's arms were of such extraordinary length that "he could button his knee breeches without stooping.")

Having appropriated Steve Collins' *nom de ring,* the Irish Art Center exhibit is also supposed to include everything from John L. Sullivan's punchbag to Jack Dempsey's sports coat, Cooney's ring robe, and John Duddy's trunks. Liam Neeson, a familiar figure at ringside when he's in town for New York boxing shows, is nominally the chairman, while the actual exhibition has been curated by Jim Houlihan, who persuaded Josephine Byrne (the widow of the late publican Jim Byrne, who owned the Hideout and, hence, Dan's arm) to bring the much-traveled relic on its first visit to America.

The legend of how the mummified right arm came to repose a few miles from what is still known as "Donnelly's Hollow" at the Curragh remains a tangled tale, but by most accounts, Donnelly's corpse was "burked" shortly after its interment, and spirited off to the medical college at Edinburgh University.

When a few of his friends learned of this fate, they set sail to Scotland in an effort to retrieve his remains, but by the time they arrived Dan had already been dissected, and they returned with what was left—his right arm. For nearly two centuries the appendage served as the centerpiece of traveling carnivals and medicine shows, and was later put on display in pubs from Belfast to Kildare.

Turning the mummified arm into a souvenir might seem a grisly exercise, but is it really any more grotesque than, say, preserving Einstein's brain? (The last we heard, Albert's cranium was still pickled in a mason jar somewhere in Kansas.)

As every Irish schoolboy should know (although, in our experience, startlingly few actually do), Dan Donnelly was the first Irish-born heavyweight champion of Britain, in an era in which the claimant to that title was the *de facto* heavyweight champion of the world.

Donnelly's two most celebrated bouts took place at the Curragh of Kildare. In the first, in 1814, he defeated Tom Hall from the Isle of Wight for a prize of 100 sovereigns, with upwards of 20,000 spectators on hand.

At Donnelly's Hollow a year later he knocked out George Cooper in eleven rounds. Then, in 1818, Donnelly traveled to London, where he defeated the English champion Tom Oliver at Crawley Hurst. Over £100,000 is said to have changed hands that day, and Dan was subsequently knighted by the Prince Regent (later King George IV), who became his patron.

Donnelly's fame was such that he was "presented" with no fewer than four Dublin pubs, but his celebrity status apparently went to his head, and he had become his own best customer by the time he died in 1820 at the age of thirty-two.

According to accounts of the day, Donnelly's funeral procession through the streets of Dublin was witnessed by 80,000 men, women, and children. He was buried in the Bully Acre at Kilmainham, only to be spirited away by the grave-robbers less than 24 hours later, thus setting in motion a chain of events that would lead Dan, or at least part of Dan, to debut on Broadway yesterday.

The Irish Times/TheSweetScience.com
July 2006

A Catalyst for Consensus?

The Jack Johnson Pardon

Although John McCain and I agree on little outside the world of boxing, the Arizona senator has not only authored some of the most effective and commendable boxing legislation in the history of this nation, he has also made the redemption of the reputation of the first African American heavyweight champion a thankless personal crusade. We spent the 2008 presidential campaign on opposite sides of the fence, but when Senator McCain reintroduced his pardon measure the following spring, I was happy to go to Washington to lend my support. In the summer of 2010, when I traveled to Reno to deliver a lecture as part of the Johnson-Jeffries Centennial, Jack Johnson was still unpardoned. I never really expected George Bush to expunge Johnson's federal rap sheet, but I must confess my dismay at President Obama's failure to do so.

WASHINGTON, D.C.—Now that last fall's elections are a thing of the past, John McCain, Ken Burns, and I can all be on the same side again.

And so, unless the Arizona senator had badly misread his erstwhile foe in last year's presidential sweepstakes, can President Barack Obama.

This wasn't the first time McCain introduced a resolution to pardon the great Jack Johnson, but, the Arizona senator vowed Wednesday afternoon, "we're not gonna do it again."

Not that McCain is giving up on his quest for vindication for "Li'l Artha." It's just that this time he believes he's dealing with a president who will actually sign the measure, which was introduced in both houses of Congress on April 1—one day after the 131st anniversary of Johnson's birth.

Wednesday's announcement was made at the Russell Senate Office Building, where McCain and his House co-sponsor, Representative Peter King (R-NY) were joined by Burns, Johnson's great-great niece Linda

Haywood, and several other descendants.

"We need to erase this act of racism against a great American citizen," said McCain. "Jack Johnson was prosecuted on trumped-up charges—and I have great confidence that *this* president will be more than eager to sign this resolution."

Of course, when McCain introduced an earlier Johnson bill in 2005, he harbored similar optimism that Obama's predecessor would endorse his position. When the senator and I spoke at that time, he had optimistically informed me that, as governor of Texas, George W. Bush had actually proclaimed March 31—the Galveston native's birthday—"Jack Johnson Day" in that state for five consecutive years.

As it turned out, Bush the Governor was somewhat more comfortable about honoring the legacy of the first black heavyweight champion than Bush the President was about expunging the criminal record of the unrepentant icon celebrated in Burns' 2005 PBS film *Unforgivable Blackness.* (The title was taken from W.E.B. DuBois' analysis of Johnson's rise and fall.)

Johnson, unable to compete against any of the succession of Caucasian champions in this country, finally got his chance on Boxing Day of 1908 when Tommy Burns agreed to face him at Rushcutters Bay outside Sydney, Australia. Johnson was awarded the heavyweight title by referee Hugh McIntosh, the lone scoring official when the fight was interrupted by police during the 14th round.

As a potential challenger, Johnson couldn't buy a match against a white fighter, but once he was champion, Great White Hopes were coming out of the woodwork to challenge him. He fought and defeated Philadelphia Jack O'Brien, the light-heavyweight champion. In 1909 he fought Stanley Ketchel, the middleweight champion, in what was supposed, by prior arrangement, to have been little more than a gentlemanly exhibition. In the 12th round, Ketchel, alas, got carried away and knocked Johnson down, effectively abrogating the agreement. Johnson got up and knocked Ketchel out with a single punch that scattered his teeth across the ring. Ketchel's manager later retrieved a couple of them and had them made into a pair of dice.

At the urging of Jack London, among others, the retired James J. Jeffries was lured out of retirement to take up the white man's burden by disposing of Johnson. Instead, Johnson disposed of Jeffries, scoring a 15th-round knockout in their 1910 Fight of the Century in Reno.

It wasn't just the notion of the greatest prize in all of sport belonging to an African American that so galled London and his ilk. Johnson's lifestyle disturbed them even more. He lived flamboyantly, consorted with prostitutes, many of them white, and, worse, he even married two white women. Unable to beat him in the ring, the authorities went after him with a vengeance, first shutting down his Chicago nightclub, the Café de Champion, and then charging him with a violation of the so-called Mann Act, a recently enacted piece of legislation aimed at "white slavery," which made it a federal crime to "transport a woman across interstate lines for immoral purposes."

Nothing in Johnson's conduct suggested that he was remotely culpable of the crime the law was intended to punish, but the authorities were so determined to bring him down that they pushed ahead with their case against Johnson for having allegedly corrupted the morals of a young white woman named Lucille Cameron. The charge had gotten as far as a grand jury when Johnson confounded the prosecution by making Miss Cameron his wife.

So the government went out and created another case under which to prosecute him. This time they found a prostitute named Belle Screiber, whom the Bureau of Investigation (the forerunner to today's FBI) held incommunicado and moved around the country until she finally agreed to testify that the heavyweight champion, a former lover, had wired her money for train fare to move from Pittsburgh to Chicago, where he allegedly assisted her in opening a high-class whorehouse.

On the basis of this somewhat coerced testimony, Jack Johnson was convicted, in 1913, on the "white slavery" charge. He avoided immediate imprisonment by slipping across the Canadian border and making his way to Europe.

In exile, Johnson defended his title twice in Paris, and fought another in Argentina, before agreeing to meet Jess Willard in Havana on April 5, 1915. In a bout that has always been regarded with some suspicion, Johnson succumbed in the 26th round.

There is no question but that the Mann Act conviction not only effectively wrecked Johnson's career but succeeded in its even more insidious aim of destroying his reputation.

He had several more fights in Europe (including one against the surrealist Arthur Cravan at a bullring in Spain), and a few in Mexico, but increasingly homesick, he finally reached out to the U.S. Government and agreed to surrender. In a plea-bargained arrangement, he served less than a year at Leavenworth, and even had a few fights while he was doing time. He fought well into his fifties and had his last fight, in Boston, in 1938, six months after his sixtieth birthday. He was killed in an automobile accident in North Carolina in 1946.

His overall career log was 73-13-9. Over half of the losses occurred after his forty-eighth birthday.

When Burns was making *Unforgivable Blackness* he was so moved by the litany of injustice that he undertook the formation of a Committee to Pardon Jack Johnson. Five years ago he approached McCain about sponsoring the resolution, and the Arizona senator, a onetime Naval Academy lightweight who had authored the two most significant pieces of successful boxing legislation in American history—the Professional Boxing Safety Act, signed into law by President Clinton in 1996, and the Muhammad Ali Boxing Reform Act of 2000—became an enthusiastic accomplice.

Burns had obtained the *pro bono* services of a New York law firm to draft the Johnson resolution, but each attempt met with frustration.

"It got bogged down because of inertia," McCain told me Wednesday. After he and King had announced the introduction of the latest Johnson pardon bid to come before congress, I'd asked about the fate of the earlier attempts.

"It was inexcusable," sighed McCain, "and then, of course, *I* got bogged down with a few other, uh, pursuits . . ."

Like last fall's sparring sessions with Barack Obama.

His White House staff had so thoroughly insulated Bush that Obama's predecessor never had to actually come to grips with any of the Johnson resolutions, because not a single one of them ever reached his desk. When Burns asked what had happened to the carefully crafted petition drafted by the New York law firm, he says he was told by presidential advisor Karl Rove "it ain't gonna fly."

When Representative King, the house's foremost boxing proponent (he works out regularly at a Long Island gym), introduced last year's resolution, it was quickly approved in the lower chamber only to die of attrition, bottled up in a Justice Department review.

The excuse at Justice was that posthumous pardons were all but unheard of. There had only been one in history—that came in 1998, when President Clinton retroactively pardoned Henry Flipper, the first African American West Point graduate, who had been court-martialed on an apparently racially motivated embezzlement charge while serving as a quartermaster at Fort Sill in 1882.

But two days before last Christmas, Bush himself granted a posthumous pardon—to the late Charles Winters, who had been convicted of violating the Neutrality Act for supplying two B-17s to Israel in 1948.

Not that one more precedent is likely to make a big difference. McCain said Wednesday that while he had not personally approached the president, "probably the *last* person I have to convince is President Obama," whom he fully expects to support the measure, particularly since Johnson was a Chicago resident at the time of his persecution.

"It's important that it be done," said McCain. "A grave injustice was done to Jack Johnson, and while a pardon won't correct this injustice, it would recognize it, and shed light on the achievements of an athlete who was forced into the shadows of bigotry and prejudice. Taking such action would allow future generations to grasp fully what Jack Johnson accomplished—against great odds—and to appreciate his contributions to society, unencumbered by the taint of a criminal conviction."

Said King: "We've come a long way, and frankly, wouldn't it be wonderful if the first African American president pardons the first African American heavyweight champion. It's now been over a hundred years since Jack Johnson won the heavyweight title. It's time we restored his reputation with a pardon that is long overdue."

Burns expressed a word of caution lest the Johnson campaign be argued entirely on its racial merits: "This isn't a question of color," said the filmmaker. "It's a question of *justice.*"

Despite the success of his earlier measure in the House of Representatives, King said, "I would never predict that anything is going to fly right through Congress, but I expect that it will. Put it this way: Senator McCain obviously knows President Obama a lot better than I do, and he seems to have every confidence that *this* president will be *eager* to sign the resolution."

TheSweetScience.com
2009

MSG's Loss Is Canastota's Gain

NEW YORK—Before we plunge headlong into nostalgia about Wednesday's "retirement" ceremony for Madison Square Garden's historic, eighty-two-year-old ring, here's something you might want to consider:

The Garden people will tell you that phasing out the ancient (circa 1925) boxing ring was part of a planned obsolescence, but do you think for a moment that if Bob Arum or the Garden honchos had known back in June that Miguel Cotto-Zab Judah would be the last fight ever to take place in the fabled ring, they'd have ever let us hear the end of it then?

The ring that hosted everyone from Jack Dempsey to Joe Louis and Muhammad Ali, from Benny Leonard to Sugar Ray Robinson to Sugar Ray Leonard, is officially a 20-foot square—but that's the outside dimension. Inside the ropes the old Garden ring was 18 feet, 6 inches. And when they got around to reading the fine print on the bout agreement for Oleg Maskaev's October 6 fight against Samuel Peter, a clause inserted by the Russian and agreed to by the challenger specified a 20-foot ring—*inside* the ropes.

In other words, if the Garden still wanted to host Maskaev-Peter they'd have had to go out and buy a new ring whether they wanted to or not. MSG's loss thus became Canastota's gain, as Ed Brophy was only too happy to take the old one off their hands to put it on display at the International Boxing Hall of Fame in upstate New York.

Partly to gain some publicity out of donating the ring, and partly to flog tickets for the Maskaev-Peter show, the Garden assembled a ring-full of dignitaries, close to two dozen former champions who had plied their trade on the old Everlast-built canvas, for a retirement ceremony presided over by Sam Rosen Wednesday afternoon.

Ali wasn't there, but Joe Frazier, who beat him in their 1971 Fight of the Century at the Garden, was. So was José Torres, who in 1965 won the light-heavyweight title from Willie Pastrano in that ring and flew up from Puerto

Rico for Wednesday's retirement ceremony. Joey Giardello was also on hand. Giardello shared a distinction with Torres: they both lost their titles to Dick Tiger in that same Garden ring.

Bernard Hopkins, who unified the middleweight title when he beat Felix Trinidad there in 2001, was there, as were Buddy McGirt, Vito Antuofermo, Gil Clancy and Lou Duva, Emile Griffith and Marlon Starling, and a host of others. (Since the event was in New York and the ceremony was preceded by a free lunch, it would have been a major upset if Iran Barkley hadn't been there.)

Television monitors played tapes of some of the more memorable bouts to have taken place in the ring—including Ali-Frazier I and Roberto Duran-Davey Moore—and countless others were cited. It occurred to us that some of the most epic moments ever to take place in that ring had been utterly ignored, their participants uninvited.

Where, for instance, were Riddick Bowe and Andrew Golota, whose 1996 disqualification produced a full-scale riot that nearly retired Madison Square Garden Boxing, period, never mind the ring?

What about Panama Lewis and Luis Resto, whose prefight shenanigans with the gloves produced a lopsided win over the late Billy Collins and got both Lewis and Resto thrown in jail and permanently banned from boxing?

Antuofermo was there, but nobody mentioned his 1978 fight against Willie Classen, one that produced another riot that was, according to witnesses, at least the equal of the Bowe-Golota denouement—if only because the Mosquito's supporters could fight better than Golota's could. (As beer cans rained down on the ring that night, Vito stood there beckoning his antagonists to climb into the ring with him; on their way out the door, Randy Gordon got his briefcase up just in time to block a whiskey bottle whizzing toward Bob Waters' head.)

And, speaking of Classen, wasn't it at least worth noting that a year later he was killed in that ring? (I know, the Classen-Wilford Scypion fight was next door at the Felt Forum, but the ring was the one now headed for Canastota.)

In another 1978 fight in that ring, Edwin Viruet and the late Esteban DeJesus were battling when a shoot-out erupted in the audience. With gunfire blasting all around them, they fought on, with DeJesus winning a split decision.

Eric Esch was probably off fighting somewhere Wednesday, but it wouldn't have been that hard to find Mitchell Rose, the 1-7-1 Brooklyn pug who sent Arum into apoplexy (and nearly cost matchmaker Ron Katz his job) when he knocked out Butterbean in that ring on the 1995 Oscar De La Hoya-Jesse James Leija card.

And before we bid it a tearful farewell, it should probably also be noted that it was in this ring the late ring announcer Harry Balough was standing when he began his announcement "And Gladys Gooding will now . . ."

"Gladys Gooding sucks!" loudly bellowed a voice from the audience.

Balough paused for maybe half a beat before he resumed his call.

"Nevertheless, Miss Gladys Gooding will now . . ."

BoxingTalk.com

September 2007

The Babylonian Heavyweights

An Unseemly Schism

Those who cannot remember the past are condemned to repeat it.
—George Santayana

In the fall of 2009 my daughter Darcy, her boyfriend, Sam Parisi, and I were vacationing in the South of France, where my friend and tenant, Greg Todd, had given us the loan of his house. The visit to Avignon rekindled memories of what I'd learned of the rogue papacy in school, but if I ever knew the bit about the three-headed pope I'd long since forgotten it. It occurred to me that the concept of three popes back then must have been as ridiculous as having three "world" heavyweight champions is today. "That sounds like a column to me," said Darcy.

AVIGNON, France—We have yet to see David Haye's win over Nikolay Valuev. The day of that fight we were en route to Hartford for Dawson-Johnson II, and travelled to Dublin the following night, only to learn that nobody in Ireland had been able to record the WBA title fight because Sky makes it all but impossible to tape its pay-per-view telecasts.

Americans, 1.25 million of whom shelled out $45,550,000 to watch Manny Pacquiao-Miguel Cotto a week later, find it incomprehensible that that fight was on free home television in Britain and Ireland while Haye vs. The Missing Link went out on pay-per-view.

We will thus reserve judgment on the latest heavyweight claimant, but it is worth pointing out that having three simultaneous popes is still considered noteworthy, even though it occurred some 600 years ago. In boxing it happens all the time.

Sometimes described as the Babylonian Captivity, in Provence they prefer to recall it as the Avignon Papacy.

In March of 1309, Pope Clement V, having fled Rome, set up shop at a Dominican friary in the south of France, and for the next century or so Avignon functioned as the Holy See. (Edicts by Clement and his successors were issued with a "Rome" dateline; in the liberal interpretation of the Avignon Popes, some of whom would later be disparaged as Antipopes, Rome was considered to be wherever the Pontiff happened to be.)

Given the constant political turmoil in the Eternal City, this system functioned fairly efficiently for almost 70 years. Then in 1378, Pope Gregory XI, who had travelled to Rome hoping to patch things up with the boys there, died at the Vatican, which is when things started to get really silly.

Unable to agree on a successor, the Sacred College in Rome elected an Italian, who became Urban VI, while the French-dominated College of Cardinals elected Clement VII, who continued to rule from Avignon.

Both papal claimants died in office and were succeeded, respectively, by popes Gregory XII and Benedict XIII. Gregory and Benedict somewhat exacerbated what had then become known as the Great Western Schism by excommunicating each other—sort of the 15th century version of stripping each other of their titles. In response to this crisis, the Council of Pisa was convened in 1409. Declaring both titles vacant, the council named a new pope, Alexander V, which, needless to say, did not sit well with either Gregory XII or Benedict XIII.

Now there were three popes, each claiming to be the lineal heir to St. Peter. "Have you ever heard anything more ridiculous in your life?" we were asked.

As a matter of fact, we had. How about three men each claiming to be the heavyweight champion of the world?

Although there had previously been championship claimants generally considered the boxing equivalent of Antipopes, what was technically the first three-way split of the heavyweight title didn't occur until the late 1960s.

After Muhammad Ali was stripped of both his title and his license to box, the NBA (the forerunner of today's WBA) conducted an elimination tournament that produced Jimmy Ellis as champion, while New York (and then Pennsylvania, Massachusetts, and a few other states) recognized Joe Frazier.

The World Boxing Council continued to recognize Ali, but back then hardly anyone, least of all American boxing commissions, cared what the WBC thought.

In that pre-José Sulaiman era, the organization, which had been established in 1963, didn't have enough clout to persuade a single jurisdiction to license Ali to box, so the WBC's claim was hollow.

Frazier's win in the 1971 Fight of the Century reunified the title, and it remained thus when George Foreman beat Frazier and Ali beat Foreman.

Today Sulaiman will insist the WBC never stripped Ali, which is technically true: rather, Sulaiman stripped Leon Spinks for fighting a rematch *against* Ali, meaning that in Ali's third go-round with the title he was an anti-champ in the eyes of the WBC.

When Clement V, the original Avignon Pope, died in 1314, the College found itself deadlocked in choosing a successor. Under growing pressure to make some white smoke happen, and fast, the body eventually settled on a compromise candidate.

The investiture of the seventy-two-year-old Bishop of Avignon as Pope John XXII was considered a harmless choice, since, given the life expectancy at the time of the Black Death, his tenure didn't figure to last long. But the Pontiff lived another 18 years, during which power was consolidated at the Palais du Papes.

Delegates to the WBC convention probably didn't realize that they were creating a president-for-life when they voted him into office back in 1975, but Sulaiman has outlasted three popes, seven presidents of the U.S., and seven presidents of Mexico.

During the Babylonian Captivity at least two Avignon Popes—Urban V in 1367 and the aforementioned Gregory XI—travelled to Rome in the hope of a rapprochement that would reunify Christendom.

The past quarter-century has also seen two short-lived reunifications of the heavyweight title. Mike Tyson acquired his titles one at a time, and all three were passed along to Buster Douglas, Evander Holyfield, and Riddick Bowe. Bowe dumped the WBC belt in a garbage can rather than defend against the WBC mandatory, Lennox Lewis.

Lewis also briefly held three titles after beating Holyfield but gave up the WBA version rather than face its mandatory, John Ruiz. History should not absolve Lewis of responsibility for creating a situation that eventually inflicted Ruiz, Valuev, Ruslan Chagaev, and now David Haye on the heavyweight world.

The lavish tastes of Pope Clement VI, the fourth of the French-based pontiffs, resulted in the Avignon Papacy running up annual expenses ten times those of the king of France. This, in turn, forced a correspondingly scandalous increase in papal taxes to stave off bankruptcy.

In another eerie historical parallel, almost three decades back José

Sulaiman was indicted by the Mexican Government for attempting to illegally sell archaeological treasures smuggled out of the country. It's probably just a coincidence, but the name of Clement's successor was precisely the same as José's plea, which is to say:

Innocent.

Despite the odd scandal, not only has Sulaiman been repeatedly re-elected, but on two occasions he has ramrodded through the investiture of his personal choice as heavyweight champion of the world, despite rather persuasive evidence that Vitaly Klitschko probably wasn't even the best heavyweight in Ukraine.

When Klitschko, citing injury, pulled out of several scheduled defenses in 2004, Sulaiman obligingly covered the situation by having Vitaly declared "Champion in Recess," and when the fighter subsequently announced his "retirement," José greased the skids for his return by proclaiming him "Champion Emeritus."

Rejected by the Pisa compromise and abandoned by even the French clergy, Benedict XIII was forced to flee Avignon, and lived out his days as an exile in Spain.

"He died forgotten," says our guidebook from the Palais du Papes, "in 1423, aged ninety-four, still convinced he was the legitimate pope."

Or, at the very least, the Champion in Recess. And you thought all they stole in this part of the world were soccer games?

The Irish Times
November 2009

Chapter II—Bruising as Art

Fat City and *Fat City*

An Appreciation

I'd known Leonard Gardner since 1974, shortly after the Fat City *film came out. We'd met in San Francisco, when he dropped by to visit the poet Ed Dorn at his apartment on Geary Street, and wound up spending a pleasant evening at a joint on the corner called The Pub. We'd lost touch over the years, but I knew Gardner had covered the first Duran-Leonard fight in Montreal in 1980, and while I was working on* Four Kings *in 2007, Ed Dorn's widow, Jenny, was able to track him down for me; having renewed our friendship, we have remained in contact since. In June of 2009, Gardner came to New York to receive the A.J. Liebling Award at the Boxing Writers dinner, and three months later the Film Forum in New York had a retrospective screening of* Fat City, *at which Pete Hamill and I introduced the movie.*

Beginning in the fall of 2010, Stacy Keach played a featured character in the FX Network's boxing-themed series Lights Out. *After the first season of shooting had been completed, Keach had dinner with two friends of mine, and revealed that the series' showrunner, executive producer Warren Leight, had been in the audience that night at the Film Forum, and that our analysis of Huston's 1973 film had led Leight to seek out Keach for the role in his series. "It was because of that, that I got the part," said Keach.*

By almost any criterion imaginable, Leonard Gardner's *Fat City* is one of the two or three very best boxing novels ever written. That it rates among the Top Ten is pretty much beyond dispute. That the 1972 screen version is also considered a classic of the genre and would appear on almost any Top Ten list of boxing films makes it unique. Name another book that appears on both lists.

The Harder They Fall—maybe. It would be on both of mine, but it should also be noted that when Budd Schulberg, who had written the 1947 novel, reviewed the Hollywood version in 1957, he all but warned moviegoers to save their money, so dissatisfied was he with the liberties Tinseltown had taken with his book.

Leonard Gardner had no such reservations about John Huston's treatment of *Fat City*. The author had completed his initial draft of the screenplay before Huston came on board as director, and it is to the latter's credit that so much of the book's original dialogue and story line were preserved intact in the movie. One could make a reasonable case that *Fat City* was such a critical success as a film precisely *because* it so closely reflected the language and cadences of Gardner's novel.

They have in a sense become inextricably intertwined. I couldn't tell you how many times I've re-read *Fat City,* but I can tell you that for the past 37 years it's impossible to get through that first chapter without starting to hum Kris Kristofferson's "Help Me Make It Through the Night," which accompanies the hung-over Stacy Keach's shuffling introduction in the film.

Fat City is one of those films that has continued to grow in stature over the years, and on September 18, Film Forum in New York inaugurates a retrospective two-week run.

Leonard Gardner was a graduate student in creative writing at San Francisco State when he began the novel in the mid-1960s. He learned the lore of boxing from his father, a lifetime devotee of the sport, and fought as an amateur in his native Stockton. Gardner also spent considerable time in the same gyms frequented by the pugilistic *dramatis personae* of the book–journeyman middleweight Billy Tully, welterweight prospect Ernie Munger, and Ruben Luna, the Hispanic gym owner who manages them both.

The book opens with Tully, a once-promising local star who had bottomed out once he hit national-level competition, plotting a comeback–for the worst of reasons, but one that could immediately be appreciated by anyone who's spent much time around professional boxers. Tully, who had retired from the ring because he wasn't confident that he had it any more, had surprised himself by knocking out a guy with one punch in a barroom fight the night before, which he immediately interpreted as a sign that perhaps he may have been precipitate in hanging up his gloves.

The novel took four years from beginning to completion. At one point it was twice the length of the compact, stripped-down version (183 pages in the copy I'm looking at) in which it was eventually published. Gardner had in the meantime published short stories in a number of literary magazines (including the *Paris Review* in 1965), and while his New York agent, Robert Lescher, encouraged the novel, he didn't push its author.

"I never showed [Lescher] any of the book until I felt it was ready," recalled Gardner. "I spent a lot of time cutting, editing, rewriting, polishing."

The result was a book so utterly perfect that for 40 years it has served as a source of discouragement to many a young writer. A dozen years ago the award-winning novelist and playwright Denis Johnson recalled his *Fat City* phase in an appreciation published in *Salon*: "Between the ages of nineteen and twenty-five, I studied Leonard Gardner's book so closely that I began to fear I'd never be able to write anything but a pale imitation." (Johnson's eventual solution was to ban *Fat City* from his house.)

Gardner recalls that despite his meticulous approach to the writing process, it never occurred to him that he might have just written a great book.

"I spent what I guess was considered an extraordinary length of time revising it, initially because I wanted to be sure it wasn't going to be rejected," said Gardner from his California home. "I wanted it to be a book I was *sure* would be published."

But once he had completed his meticulous revisions, he recalled, "I was pretty happy with it. I don't think 'great' is a word a writer should use in describing his own work, but in all modesty, sure, I knew even then that I'd written a pretty damned good book."

Lescher submitted the manuscript to a number of publishers, and in short order had achieved the result every writer dreams of: two houses that each wanted it.

"In the end Lescher said he probably could have gotten a bit more money out of Random House, but he felt Farrar, Straus would be more committed in what it would do for the book," said Gardner.

The 1969 critics were almost unanimous in hailing the book as a triumph, and before the year was out Gardner's novel had been nominated for a National Book Award, along with Kurt Vonnegut's *Slaughterhouse-Five* and Joyce Carol Oates' *Them*. (Oates won.) The *Kansas City Star* was moved to note that "probably there isn't a living novelist who, if he were honest with himself, would not be proud to have written *Fat City*. That's how good it is."

Joan Didion wrote that "*Fat City* affected me more than any new fiction I have read in a long while." Another female admirer wrote Gardner a letter telling him how much she had enjoyed the book, "but if it was any darker, I think I'd kill myself."

David Milch, who taught creative writing at Yale before moving to

Hollywood to create *NYPD Blue* and *Deadwood,* regularly made *Fat City* a staple of his writing classes. Forty years after *Fat City*'s publication, Gardner was honored by the Boxing Writers Association of America with the A.J. Liebling Award, along with fellow recipients Larry Merchant and the late John Lardner.

The success of the book predictably brought Hollywood calling, and producer Ray Stark secured the film rights. It would be nice to say "and the rest is history," but as is so often the case with these tangled tales of cinema, the journey from perfect book to perfect film appears in many cases to have been the result of a series of happy accidents.

Fat City in the hands of another director might have been a very different film. Stark had earlier approached Monte Hellman (*Two-Lane Blacktop*), who eventually backed out of the deal for a more lucrative assignment. Mark Rydell (*Cinderella Liberty*) was the next to be considered, but wavered so long that Stark eventually turned to the sixty-four-year-old Huston.

Besides maintaining his allegiance to Gardner's work in refusing to "go Hollywood" with the film, another Huston stamp on the movie came when he insisted, against the producer's wishes, on retaining cinematographer Conrad Hall's noir recreation of the interior skid-row barroom scenes. Stark, who felt the dark scenes would render the film unsuitable for drive-ins (not an insignificant consideration in 1972), wanted to fire Hall and re-shoot the scenes. Huston told the producer, in effect, "If he goes, I go." If it was a bluff, it worked.

Now imagine *Fat City* with Marlon Brando with all that scar tissue above his eyes instead of Stacy Keach. Huston initially wanted Brando to play Tully, but interpreted his vacillation as a lack of interest, and when Brando wound up taking the eponymous role in *The Godfather,* the director turned to the relatively unknown Keach.

Would Margot Kidder have delivered an Academy Award–nominated performance had she and not Susan Tyrell (who did earn a nomination) been cast as Oma, the philosophical barfly who takes up with Tully?

And one thing we know for sure. Had someone other than Huston been the director, we don't know who would have played Earl, Tully's rival for Oma's affections, but we can tell you with absolute certainty that it wouldn't have been Curtis Cokes.

Huston had been living in Ireland since 1964, and once he took on the project he invited Gardner to his estate in Galway. It was a pretty heady experience for the young writer.

"I'd already written a first draft of the screenplay, and what we did over there was go through it bit by bit," recalled Gardner. "Huston spent most of his time painting, so he only wanted to address one scene per day. Sometimes I could rewrite a scene overnight, sometimes I couldn't, but we'd move on to the next one."

Huston had boxed himself in his youth. His first published short story had been a boxing tale called "Fool," which H.L. Mencken published in his *American Mercury* in 1929. Though authenticity was important, Huston didn't define *Fat City* as a boxing movie at all.

"It's about life running down the sink without being able to pull the plug to stop it," was the director's description.

"But his boxing background was reassuring to me," recalled Gardner. "He knew the sport and he understood it. Particularly back then, every time Hollywood got near boxing they seemed to turn to the same schlock clichés, but there was no danger of that with him.

"And just as he was an 'actor's director' because he gave his cast an extraordinarily free hand in interpreting scenes, I guess you could say he was a 'writer's director,' too. He knew what was good about the book and didn't want to screw it up by changing a lot of things.

"And I'd like to think that I have a pretty good cinematic sense myself," added Gardner, who would later enjoy success writing for film and television (in a five-year run at *NYPD Blue*). "I could visualize the way certain things would work on the screen, and he retained most of that—though I'm not so vain that I'd have argued for keeping something Huston *didn't* think would work once he'd explained it."

Thirty-seven years on, the casting of *Fat City* seems a work of genius, but in 1972 it was very much a crapshoot.

Keach had previously had featured roles in two films, both of which had essentially been cast out of the same New York saloon—the Lion's Head—over the previous year and a half. After starring (with James Earl Jones and Harris Yulin) in the film version of John Barth's *End of the Road,* he played Doc Holliday (to Yulin's Wyatt Earp and Faye Dunaway's Big-Nose Kate) in *Doc,* for which Pete Hamill wrote the screenplay.

Young and relatively unfamiliar to film audiences (though not to viewers of *Sea Hunt,* where since the age of nine he had occasionally appeared with his father, Lloyd Bridges), Jeff Bridges (Munger) had recently appeared in Peter Bogdanovich's film of Larry McMurtry's *The Last Picture Show.* (Susan Tyrell's only pre-*Fat City* role had been in the movie version of Richard

Farina's *Been Down So Long It Looks Like Up to Me.)*

Prior to his portrayal of Ruben Luna in *Fat City,* Providence-born Nicolas Colasanto (who would become familiar as "Coach" on *Cheers*) had played both cops and robbers in television bit roles, but his film resume was almost nonexistent. Candy Clark (Ernie's girlfiend/wife, Faye) had never appeared in a movie before.

Neither, of course, had Curtis Cokes. Remarkably, in a film in which more than a dozen boxers and former boxers appear, the former welterweight champion played Earl, a character who isn't a fighter at all.

Cokes, who had lost his welterweight title to José Napoles a few years earlier, had fought out of Texas for most of his career, but in 1971, nearing the end of the line, he had lost fights in San Francisco and Sacramento. We had always assumed that he must have stumbled into a casting call around this time, but the actual story is even more interesting.

"What happened is that Huston was back east for a fight in New York," said Leonard Gardner. "He was sitting at ringside, and a well-dressed black gentleman a few seats away in the same section caught his eye. According to Huston, he was already thinking 'This is what I want Earl to look like' before he even struck up a conversation. I'm sure he must still have had to go through the formality of an audition, but Huston claimed he'd actually decided he wanted this guy to play Earl before he even realized he *was* Curtis Cokes."

Cokes fought three times in South Africa, winning two, in the year after *Fat City* came out. His first screen role also proved to be his last. He has been a successful trainer (Reggie Johnson, Kirk Johnson, Ike Ibeabuchi) back in Dallas for the past quarter-century.

In Gardner's book, Tully is a middleweight, Munger a welterweight, but for the movie it was more important that opponents approximate the sizes of Keach and Bridges, who were both light-heavyweights in 1972.

Argentine light-heavyweight Gregorio Peralta had been the first choice to play Arcadio Lucero, the fading former main-eventer brought to Stockton from Mexico as the opponent for Tully's comeback fight. In 1970 Peralta had fought George Foreman to a decision at Madison Square Garden, and both Gardner and Ray Stark were in the audience for their 1971 rematch at the Oakland Coliseum. Peralta was approached about the role, but his manager, who felt there was money yet to be made with Gregorio in the ring, didn't like the idea of putting his career on hold for several months.

The inspired choice of Sixto Rodriguez was Gardner's idea. The former California light-heavyweight champion, Rodriguez was by then retired, having finished with a record of 28-13-3. A useful boxer, Sixto had wins over Bobo Olson and Eddie Cotton, but the close of his career seemed to mirror that of Lucero's in the book: He had just 6 wins in his last 20 fights, most of them on the road.

Although he isn't given a lot of lines, Rodriguez' haunting performance as the aging—and ailing—opponent is a memorable one. He alights from the Greyhound bus with the cocksure walk of a matador, despite being hampered by a violent case of the runs. (In the movie the bodily function is somewhat altered; Lucero walks into the men's room and pisses blood. And this is *before* the fight.)

What must be attributed to a bit of prescient casting, Rosales, the opponent in Ernie Munger's first fight, was played by a twenty-year-old Stockton amateur named Alvaro Lopez. So young that he's barely recognizable in the film, Yaqui Lopez engaged in the first of what would be 76 professional fights shortly after shooting wrapped up for *Fat City*. Lopez would go on to unsuccessfully challenge for the light-heavyweight championship on four occasions (vs. John Conteh, Matthew Saad Muhammad, and twice against Victor Galindez), and late in his career fought (against Carlos De Leon) for the cruiserweight title as well.

A couple of other, more familiar, boxing types have roles in *Fat City*. Art Aragon, the original "Golden Boy," works the corner with Colasanto as the trainer Babe. Aragon, who died two years ago, was one of the more popular fighters in Los Angeles history, and was Budd Schulberg's best man at the author's third wedding. The old trainer Al Silvani can be spotted as a referee in *Fat City*.

Both Aragon and Silvani appeared in many boxing movies, but middleweight Billy Walker, a California club fighter, won a speaking part as young Wes Haynes, a boxer in Ruben Luna's traveling entourage.

But in a very real sense, Stockton's legacy as a fight town makes it a co-star of *Fat City* as well. Resisting the temptation to shoot the film in more hospitable surroundings, Huston filmed it on location to capture the actual places, people, and milieu Gardner had so meticulously described in the book.

"Almost every extra you see in the film, from the entourages to the gym backdrops to the crowd scenes and what have you, came from the gyms and the boxing scene in Stockton," said Gardner. "The local promoter even gets a scene.

"And of course a lot of the fighters back then would have moonlighted in the fields, just as Tully and Munger do together later in the book. Some of them worked as longshoremen, too."

That's right, longshoremen, as in *On the Waterfront*. Nearly a hundred miles inland from San Francisco Bay, Stockton is uniquely situated. Its geographic location to the rich farmlands of the San Joaquin Valley made it a haven for migrant workers—Chicanos, Okies, and boxers. The river and a ship channel also conspired in the 19th century to make it one of California's two inland deep-water ports, and since the days of the Gold Rush, ships bearing canned produce and lumber sailed from Stockton in such profusion that it was for a time the pirate capital of California.

"Some time after the movie came out, my mother was taking a cruise on a ship that sailed out of Stockton to Europe," said Gardner. "The day I took her down to the ship I ran into a couple of ex-fighters who were working on the docks. Those same two longshoremen had been in the film, where they played the guys working Lucero's corner when he fought Billy Tully."

Gardner went on to high-profile journalistic assignments, covering Foreman-Norton in Caracas for *Esquire,* Ali-Chuvalo in Vancouver for *Sport,* and Duran-Leonard in Montreal for *Inside Sports.* Gardner (b. 1933) also adapted his short story "Jesus Christ Has Returned to Earth" for the film *Valentino Returns* and created nearly two dozen episodes of *NYPD Blue,* but his first novel turned out to be the only one he would write. Although he has dropped hints from time to time of another, 40 years have elapsed since his masterpiece. From time to time you wonder whether looking back at *Fat City* had the same effect on its author as it did on the young Denis Johnson.

His oft-cited rejoinder "sometimes you only get to win one championship" would seem to have been an adequate explanation, but, says Gardner, "I don't think I actually ever *said* that. For one thing, it implies that I won a 'championship' in the first place, which I think would be presumptuous on my part. I don't want to go into all the reasons things turned out the way they did, and I guess it's inevitable that some people are bound to categorize me as a one-book novelist. That isn't what I set out to be, and it wasn't always by choice, but it's hard to call that unfair."

TheSweetScience.com
September 2009

The Reinvention of the Ambling Alp

At the time of the premiere of Walking Mountain, *F. Murray Abraham, who portrays the notorious French fight manager Leon See in the film, was working in an off-Broadway production of Ethan Coen's* Almost an Evening. *Abraham had been cast as God in the play, and when I heard him talking about the film at the Garden that day it occurred to me that perhaps he'd gotten the roles mixed up.*

In the autumn of 1929, fifteen-year-old Budd Schulberg accompanied his father, the Hollywood mogul B.P. Schulberg, on a trip to Europe. A fellow passenger aboard the *Ile de France* on the crossing to Southampton was William Lawrence Stribling Jr., a heavyweight boxer who had already, at twenty-five, amassed 227 wins while fighting under the name Young Stribling.

Both Schulbergs, *père et fils,* were devoted boxing fans and became friendly with Stribling, who promised them ringside seats for his upcoming bout at the Royal Albert Hall against an oversized Italian named Primo Carnera.

"Sandwiched among the English fancy I saw the largest fighter I had ever seen win an awkward and unsatisfactory decision on a foul in the fourth round," wrote Schulberg in his memoir *Moving Pictures.*

Persuaded by what he had seen of Stribling in the gym, B.P. Schulberg had made what his son termed "a casually reckless wager," betting £1,000 on the American, but, wrote Schulberg, "the ungainly stray from a small Italian circus had been awarded a most peculiar decision, claiming he had been hit low by what seemed to be an invisible punch. They repeated their act again a few weeks later in Paris, this time with Stribling winning on a foul. By now I had seen enough to learn one of the sad realities of the Sweet Science: Every so often the fix was in."

Some 18 years later Schulberg would incorporate the essential elements of Carnera's tale in his novel *The Harder They Fall,* which in 1956 became the vehicle for what would be Humphrey Bogart's final film. That same year, Rod Serling's award-winning teleplay *Requiem for a Heavyweight* appeared on *Playhouse 90,* starring Jack Palance as a Carnera-like boxer. In 1962, in a somewhat altered form, *Requiem* also became a Hollywood film, this time starring Anthony Quinn, with Jackie Gleason and Mickey Rooney cast in decidedly un-comic supporting roles.

The Harder They Fall and *Requiem for a Heavyweight* are widely ac-knowledged to be among the best boxing movies ever made. And while we had to wait half a century for it to happen, Primo Carnera also turns out to be the subject of the *worst* boxing movie ever made—*Carnera: The Walking Mountain,* which had its American premiere at Madison Square Garden's WaMu Theatre Wednesday night.

The awkward subtitle, *Walking Mountain*—it is, one supposes, what happens when you translate "Ambling Alp" into Italian and then back into English—is illustrative of one problem with Renzo Martinelli's film, which was shot using (mostly) Italian actors whose voices were redubbed in English. The result is that Andrea Iaia, playing an orthodontically-improved version of Carnera, speaks in accent-less American English, while an American actor (F. Murray Abraham, portraying the venal French fight manager Leon See) delivers his lines in a vaguely Gallic tongue.

The *Carnera* webpage describes its protagonist in terms not commonly associated with the Ambling Alp: "A man who endured hardships with dignity and triumphs with humility," and "He led an extraordinary life with extraordi-nary courage. He had principles and values that were never compromised and followed him through his professional and personal life."

You sure we're talking about the same Primo Carnera here, Renzo?

A disclaimer accompanying the final credits concedes that some events have been altered for dramatic license, but that vastly understates the case. The film takes so many liberties with fact and history that its apparent prem-ise—that, contrary to the generally accepted views, Primo Carnera was nei-ther a willing mob stooge nor a naïve victim of boxing's netherworld, but a bona fide Italian hero who, apparently legitimately, became Heavyweight Champion of the World—is vitiated of any persuasive merit.

Take the aforementioned Stribling fights. Only the first of these appears in the film, and while Carnera does go berserk and clubs the referee in his effort to beat Stribling senseless—bringing the occupants of both corners into the ring for a wild free-for-all unseen anywhere this side of the Judah and Mayweather family get-togethers—the result of the fight is somehow not a disqualification, but a knockout for Carnera.

In Primo's first pro fight, against Leon Sabilo in Paris, Sabilo is introduced as "The Champion." Sabilo had in fact had just nine professional fights, and had lost eight of them. His TKO at Carnera's hands became his ninth.

The only hint of chicanery along the path of Carnera's upward mobility, in fact, comes during his European apprenticeship, when F. Murray, as See, admits prearranging some of Primo's early bouts. The film never even suggests that anything might have been amiss once he fell under the spell of Owney Madden in New York, other than the fact that Primo, despite his heroic efforts, keeps discovering that he is broke every time he goes to the bank.

(In a bizarre bit of casting, after the first such episode, Primo demands to speak to the bank manager and is ushered upstairs into a cavernous office where, behind an elegant mahogany desk, he finds the tycoon himself— Burt Young.)

Carnera's actual immersion into the American fight game did not differ markedly from the one Schulberg chronicled for Toro Moreno in *The Harder They Fall,* where the giant boxer is sent out on the road where he can pile up a bunch of wins in the absence of scrutiny—"as far from the wise boys as possible," explained Nick, Schulberg's Madden character, "where the sharpshooters like Parker or Runyon don't knock you off before we get started."

Carnera's first American bout, against Clayton "Big Boy" Peterson at Madison Square Garden in 1931, had attracted unwelcome attention. Although Big Boy obligingly went down for good in a minute and ten seconds, New York newspapers noted that he had displayed "no inclination to fight," thereby inspiring the decision to dispatch Primo off to the sticks.

Carnera's carefully arranged barnstorming tour began in Chicago just a week later, when Elizear Roux fell down six times in less than three minutes on the way to a first-round KO loss. The commission fined Roux $1,000 and revoked his boxing license.

Subsequent opponents were apparently better schooled. In the first nine months of 1930, Carnera "won" 23 straight fights in backwater arenas all over the country, 22 of them by knockout and all them inside the distance, until he ran into Jim Maloney, who accidentally beat him in Boston that October. Primo was sent back to Europe to acquire a few more wins before he was pronounced ready for the big time.

In Martinelli's revised version of history, by the way, Primo apparently never loses a fight, right up until and after his 1933 title fight against Sharkey. (He had in fact at that point already lost on six occasions.)

Some liberties are also taken with Primo's love interests. His first dalliance, with a Soho waitress named Emilia Tersini, is cut short when See makes him choose between her and his boxing career, after which she disappears without a trace. (In fact, the actual Ms. Tersini successfully sued Carnera for Breach of Promise, and in 1933 was awarded the sum of £4,200.)

And, following what appears to be a five-minute renewal of a childhood flirtation, the woman who would become Mrs. Carnera, Giuseppina Kovacic, materializes in Long Island City for the Sharkey fight, whereupon the victorious Primo, still battered, cut, and bleeding, proposes as he stands in the midst of the deliriously cheering ringside audience.

The legitimacy of Carnera's "knockout" of Sharkey is never called into question. (Although Jack swore it was on the level, his wife said it wasn't. Most historians not named Renzo Martinelli are inclined to agree with Mrs. Sharkey.)

In the movie version, they marry before Carnera's first defense, which is against Max Baer. In real life, Primo made two intervening defenses, against Paolino Uzcudun in Rome and against Tommy Loughran in New York, and he and Giuseppina didn't marry until 1939, when he had retired for the first time after losing a kidney.

If Carnera has been badly treated by Hollywood over the years, what of poor Max Baer? In *Cinderella Man,* Baer was portrayed as a malevolent villain, a homicidal maniac boasting of his two ring kills and threatening to add James J. Braddock to his list of victims. In *Carnera,* Italian actor Antonio Cupo turns Baer into a cackling idiot with a performance lifted straight from Jack Nicholson (as The Joker) in *Batman.*

Against Baer—remember, by now the handcuffs were off—Carnera went down 11 times in less than 11 rounds, breaking his ankle somewhere along the way. In the movie, you'd think it was all bad luck.

With Primo still on crutches, Baer knocks on his door to offer him a rematch (there is no evidence that this ever happened), but Primo declines, opting instead to sail for Italy. As the film ends, he and 'Pina are last seen sailing across the sea, returning, apparently, to Mussolini, with whom we had last seen him a few minutes earlier, triumphantly sharing a Fascist salute after the Sharkey fight.

In actual fact, Carnera did set sail after losing his title to Baer, but it was to South America, where he picked up three more wins before returning to New York to be knocked out by Louis.

He made an ill-advised comeback in Italy after World War II, but after three straight losses to the same guy, retired for good. Primo and Giuseppina then returned to America where he had a modestly successful career in a more honest business: He became a professional wrestler.

BoxingTalk.com
April 2008

What Would Liebling Do?

As should anyone who hopes to make his living in this racket, at least once or twice a year I've found it helpful to recharge the mental batteries by revisiting the work of A.J. Liebling, even though those visitations can sometimes prove a two-edged sword. For all the inspiration an encounter with the muse might provide, one will also inevitably encounter a turn of phrase so utterly dazzling that the effect can be daunting.

> Rocky landed a right to his zygomaticus, and he went sprawling down, forgetting to tread water, until he hit the bottom of the pool.

Being presented with that Liebling description (of the effect of Marciano's punch on Ezzard Charles in their second fight) would seem to leave his spiritual descendants but two choices: Should I steal the line for myself, or should I look for another line of work?

The great man, dead for nearly half a century now, has been a particularly palpable presence over the past few days, in which events have conspired to serve up a double dose of Liebling.

Several years ago the Boxing Writers Association of America decided to honor his memory with the presentation of the A.J. Liebling Award. A few weeks ago I was pressed into service as committee chairman charged with selecting this year's recipients.

And just a couple of days ago I had lunch with my friend Pete Hamill, who presented me with a fresh-off-the-presses advance copy of *The Sweet Science and Other Writings,* a massive collection of Lieblingiana he had selected and edited for a new edition, which will be published by the Library of America on March 19th.

(The 2009 Liebling Awards, by the way, will go to Leonard Gardner, whose 1969 novel *Fat City* remains among the greatest boxing novels ever written; to HBO television analyst Larry Merchant, who spent two decades as a top-flight sports columnist in New York and Philadelphia before crossing over to the dark side; and to the late John Lardner, a Liebling contemporary who produced a similarly diverse body of work before his untimely death, at forty-eight, in 1960.)

A few years ago the editors of *Sports Illustrated* compiled a roster of the 100 greatest sports books of all time, and *The Sweet Science,* the collection of Liebling's boxing coverage for the *New Yorker* first published in 1956, headed up the list in the number one position. With one foot in the sophisticated world of Manhattan intellectuals from whence he sprang and the other in the Runyonesque netherworld of boxing lowlifes in whose company he so evidently delighted, Liebling ("pound for pound, the top boxing writer of all time," said *SI*) brought a unique approach to the sport that was never rivaled before or since.

Although he was the unchallenged master of the medium, Liebling's boxing coverage comprised a relatively small percentage of his overall output. While he didn't invent the role of media watchdog, his monthly *New Yorker* column ("The Wayward Press") so defined that role that 45 years later its practitioners seem but pale imitators by comparison.

Liebling himself had been fired from his first job in journalism, as a copy editor with the *New York Times.* (Required to produce box scores of basketball games according to a house template that included the referee's name, he had taken to identifying the official as "Incogno"—Italian for "unknown"—on those occasions the student-manager phoning in the report failed to get the ref's name.)

Hoping that a semester or two at the Sorbonne might kindle an affinity for a more ambitious calling, his father packed him off to Europe for a year, along with a $2,000 letter of credit that appears to have been more or less exhausted in the bistros and bars of the Rive Gauche.

A youth spent in Paris spawned a lifelong affinity with the French that made his World War II coverage the envy of every writer-turned-war correspondent.

He was also an acute and acerbic political analyst, and *The Earl of Louisiana,* his account of the folksy Earl Long's colorful gubernatorial campaign (conducted in part from the mental institution to which he had been dispatched while his reputation recovered from revelations of his relationship with the stripper Blaze Starr) remains to this day as insightful a rendition of the way politics works in the Bible Belt as has ever been written.

As one might have assumed from its title, *The Sweet Science* comprises the first fourth of the collection assembled by Hamill. With notes and appendices, the new book runs over 1,000 pages, and includes selections, many of them previously uncollected, from *The Earl of Louisiana,* "The Jollity Building" (from Liebling's 1942 book *The Telephone Booth Indian*), a section called "Between Meals: An Appetite for Paris," and, of course, a lengthy compendium of "The Press."

"Ironically, considering that he pretty much invented the medium," noted Hamill the other day, "it's the press stuff which is in some ways the most dated. I found myself continually interrupting to explain in a footnote to today's readers what, for example, the *World-Telegram* even was."

Liebling once famously wrote that "freedom of the press is guaranteed only to those who own one," and while some of his ruminations on the subject might, as his editor notes, require translation for members of the X-Generation, others, when viewed in a contemporary light, seem not only timeless but downright prescient:

> News is like the tilefish which appears in great schools off the Atlantic Coast and then vanishes, no one knows whither or for how long. Newspapers might employ these periods searching for the breeding ground of news, but they prefer to fill up with stories about Kurdled Kurds or Calvin Coolidge, until the banks close or a Hitler marches, when they are as surprised as their readers.

The Irish Times
February 2009

The Cut Man's Baby

This column, for **The Sweet Science,** *was written shortly after the Academy Awards ceremony in 2005. Five years later the Boxing Writers Association posthumously presented the A.J. Liebling award to F.X. Toole.*

When *Rope Burns,* the late Jerry Boyd's wonderful collection of boxing fiction (written under the California cornerman's *nom de guerre,* F.X. Toole) was published back in 2000, I wrote a 1,700-word review, exactly one sentence of which was devoted to the third of the six stories included in Boyd's book:

> Likewise, the gripping drama of "Million $$$ Baby," the tale of the rise and fall of a hillbillyish female fighter and her old Irish trainer, begins to build not as Maggie Fitzgerald is fighting her way to the top, but after she has lost her final fight.

Hey, how was *I* supposed to know?

Jerry Boyd died in 2002, in time to enjoy the adulation that accompanied the publication of his first and only book, but three years before a film based upon two stories from *Rope Burns* would win Oscars in four of the six most important categories at the 77th Academy Awards Sunday night.

In addition to being named 2004's best film, *Million Dollar Baby* is also being hailed in some circles as the best boxing movie ever made—which, in some respects, it may well be. On another front, it has also been dismissed for its trivialized-for-the-masses Hollywood version of the sport, a criticism that is not entirely unfounded.

Although most early reviewers conscientiously skirted the denouement in an effort to avoid spoiling its inherent drama for audiences, subsequent attacks from the right which have labeled *Million Dollar Baby* "propaganda for assisted suicide" have rendered that moot. Whether he's seen the film or not, a person would by now had to have spent the past four months in a cave not to know how it turns out.

And while the Rush Limbaugh crowd has been savaging director Clint Eastwood for the film's allegedly political bent, some of our more squeamish friends on the left have simultaneously recoiled in horror from *Million Dollar Baby* on the grounds that it glamorizes a brutal pursuit, to wit: boxing itself.

Be that as it may, Boyd's publishers have now leapt back on the bandwagon by re-issuing *Rope Burns,* except that the book has now been re-titled *Million Dollar Baby: Tales from the Corner.* If nothing else, this may serve to inform future discussions of the film, because up until now most reviews I've seen appear to have been written by people who have either never read *Rope Burns,* never seen a boxing match, or, in most cases, both.

The gritty West Coast gym milieu Boyd captured so well in the pages of his book is what comes across best in the film. Ironically, the character portrayed by Morgan Freeman (who must have spent a lot of time hanging around Don Turner to so perfectly acquire his mannerisms) doesn't even exist in the "Million $$$ Baby" story. Scrap was imported from "Frozen Water," another tale in the book, which was skillfully grafted onto and intertwined with the title story in Paul Haggis' script.

But anybody who's spent much time around boxing is bound to have problems with *Million Dollar Baby,* because so much of it just doesn't ring true. For one thing, the fight scenes themselves are probably *too* good. If women boxers (and we mean Hilary Swank *and* Maggie's opponents) actually fought this well, everybody would be flocking to watch them.

Maggie Fitzgerald's meteoric rise through the ranks is depicted as a pastiche of knockouts. Each and every one of them is accompanied by the act of Eastwood's Frankie Dunn sliding a stool into the ring. Then, instead of going to a neutral corner, Maggie sits down and watches while her opponent is counted out.

Now, anyone who knows the first thing about boxing is bound to wince at the absurdity of this, but apparently some Hollywood type thought it necessary to prepare the audience so that the climactic stool-in-the-ring wouldn't be criticized as a *deus ex machina* contrivance. (The only other fathomable explanation would be that each and every one of Maggie's knockouts occurred just before the bell ended a round, a proposition so far-fetched that it's even more preposterous than what is depicted.)

In the book, the arch-villain opponent (portrayed by Lucia Rijker in the movie) sucker-punches our heroine just after the bell, catching not only Maggie but Frankie (who has just put the stool in the corner) by surprise. This would have been a perfectly reasonable explanation for the presence of the stool, but apparently the filmmakers thought audiences wouldn't buy it in the absence of all the heavy-handed foreshadowing.

Presumably for dramatic effect, the notion of Maggie's "title" quest as Frankie's Holy Grail has also been introduced into the story. Jerry Boyd would have laughed out loud. The idea is supposed to be that in decades of developing boxers in the gym, actually taking a fighter to a world championship is the one thing that has always eluded Frankie, and that Maggie offers him the hope of fulfilling that lifelong dream. It comes across as the tritest of clichés, and a silly one at that.

The truth of the matter is that on today's boxing landscape women's titles are even more plentiful than men's. "Championships" are cheap and so easily come-by that they don't have much relevance even to the women who win them, and while a fight against Billy "The Blue Bear" Astrakhov on HBO was big enough for the book, that Frankie Dunn (or Jerry Boyd) would have attached much importance to any belt involved is a dubious proposition indeed.

For all its unrealistic flaws, *Million Dollar Baby* is a terrific film, and if one moviegoer in ten is inspired to buy and read *Rope Burns* (or, in its new incarnation, *Million Dollar Baby,* the book) it will have served an even greater purpose. The real pity is that Jerry Boyd wasn't around to enjoy Oscar night.

TheSweetScience.com
May 2005

Trying on the Glass Slipper

Jeremy Schaap's Cinderella Man

Jeremy Schaap had told me about his book project a year earlier when we sat together at an NBA game at the Boston Garden, and even before the galleys were available we'd shared a long talk about Cinderella Man *over dinner in New York. By the time the book came out, then, I had accumulated a wealth of background material not available to most reviewers.*

When he sat down with Mike Tyson last month after the Washington press conference announcing his June 11 fight against Kevin McBride, ESPN's Jeremy Schaap mentioned that he'd just returned from Reykjavik, Iceland, where he'd interviewed "another former world champion from Brooklyn."

Tyson wracked his brain but couldn't imagine who Schaap could be talking about.

"Bobby Fischer," the reporter finally told him.

"Bobby Fischer?" A look of apparent horror spread over Iron Mike's tattooed face. "Man, that guy is crazy!"

A globe-trotting anchor and correspondent for the all-sports network, Jeremy Schaap is the son of Emmy Award–winning broadcaster Dick Schaap. One of the most revered figures of our time, Dick Schaap was a Renaissance man, a nationally renowned sportswriter who also wrote film and theater criticism, and authored over 30 books before he passed away four years ago at sixty-seven. Following in yet another of his father's many-faceted footsteps, Schaap *fils* is celebrating the publication of his first book, *Cinderella Man: James J. Braddock, Max Baer, and the Greatest Upset in Boxing History* (Houghton Mifflin, 324 pp., $24), this week.

Clearly, Jeremy Schaap's conscious decision to write his first book didn't come because he had too much time on his hands; rather, having reached his thirties, he wanted to explore that side of his creative nature. He and his agent, Scott Waxman (a college classmate from Cornell who had also worked alongside Schaap when both were copy boys at the *Times*), then set about finding a likely subject.

That it would be a boxing-based book came naturally: The subject was as near and dear to Jeremy's heart as it had been to his father's. He had done several boxing features for ESPN (and currently serves as a host for the network's nascent pay-per-view telecasts).

"Boxing people are among the most colorful in sports," said Schaap. "They're usually the best quotes, just because they haven't been coached to withhold themselves the way athletes in team sports have."

That there was a high-profile movie in the works, starring Russell Crowe as Braddock, didn't hurt, either.

"We knew the film would spark a natural resurgence of interest in Braddock," said Schaap. "But the more I looked into it, the more I realized that not only might this be the greatest sports story of all time, but that hardly anything had been written about it: Apart from a casual treatment as part of boxing histories, nothing had been written about Braddock since Lud Shabazian's 1936 biography (*Relief to Royalty*). And, amazingly, considering what an intriguing figure he was, very little had been written about Baer since Nat Fleischer's brief biography *Max Baer: The Glamour Boy of the Ring.*"

Simply put, by the early 1930s Braddock was a has-been. He had been a promising light-heavyweight contender in the 1920s, but lost his only title shot, a decision to Tommy Loughran, in 1929. This precipitated a skid in which Braddock lost five times in six fights, but he had earned a fair share of purses and had invested for his future.

Like those of many of his countrymen, Braddock's nest egg was wiped out by the Wall Street crash of 1929. He continued to box, but a series of hand injuries hampered his effectiveness in the ring.

"He couldn't beat *anybody,*" said Schaap.

He was reduced to fighting for peanuts in backwater venues, and by the time Braddock hung up his gloves and retired from the sport in despair he had won just four of his last eleven fights.

He managed to get longshoreman's papers and went to work on the Jersey docks, but even there jobs were scarce. More often than not, he would arise early and trudge to the docks, only to return empty-handed. With a wife and three children to feed, he increasingly despaired for his family. Late in

1933 he put his pride aside and applied for a place on the county welfare rolls. At one point he and his wife, Mae, even had to farm their children out to their grandparents because he could no longer care for them.

During this dark period at least two remarkable things occurred. One was that the time away from the ring gave his hands a chance to heal. The other was that his stint on the docks transformed Braddock from a 175-pounder into a much stronger, well-muscled heavyweight.

Braddock had given no thought to a comeback, and hadn't been near a gym in months, when his loyal friend and ever-scuffling manager, Joe Gould, crossed the Hudson bearing news of an offer to fight again. Primo Carnera was scheduled to defend his title against Baer at the Madison Square Garden Bowl in Queens two nights later, and an up-and-coming heavyweight named Corn Griffin, whom the boxing powers hoped to groom for the big time, was slated to perform on the undercard, but his scheduled foe had fallen out.

Garden matchmaker Jimmy Johnston needed an Opponent—with a capital "O"—for Griffin, and Braddock could earn $250 for serving as cannon fodder. Because he needed the money—Gould had wangled a $100 advance, which he split with Braddock, out of Johnston—he agreed. On June 14, 1934, Braddock knocked out Griffin in three rounds.

Three fights and 364 days later James J. Braddock was the heavyweight champion of the world—"At a time when the heavyweight champion was, inarguably, the biggest man in sports," noted Schaap.

Or, as the tagline for promotions of the upcoming film puts it: "When America was on its knees, he brought us to our feet."

The *Cinderella Man* film will be released in June—fortuitously, just a month after the book hits the stands. Schaap hasn't seen a minute of Ron Howard's movie, nor has he read the script, which had already been completed by the time he started work on his own project, but because they share the same name, the two will doubtless be intertwined in the mind of the public. Schaap sees this as a win/win situation. It isn't entirely clear what the movie people think about it.

"If I were casting a film, I think Russell Crowe would be a perfect choice to play Braddock," said Schaap. "I haven't seen the movie, but from what I understand Baer [played by Craig Bierko] gets a pretty short shrift. He's portrayed as almost a buffoon. Yes, he was colorful, and ran against the grain, but there are people to this day who'll tell you that he packed the hardest right hand of any heavyweight champion in boxing history. And at the time, it was widely assumed that he'd reign as champion for years to come—which made Braddock's upset all the more remarkable."

If Braddock's accomplishment was among the most inspirational sporting achievements of all time, how did it vanish from the public consciousness?

Schaap reckons that Braddock's "Cinderella" (It was Damon Runyon who bestowed the moniker on Braddock) tale lapsed into obscurity for at least two reasons: The first was that Braddock's immediate heir was Joe Louis, whose own legend grew to such proportions that it quickly obscured that of his predecessor. And the other is that Braddock's accomplishments took place in the bleakest period of 20th-century America: Once it was over, Americans wanted to put the Great Depression, and everything connected with it, behind them.

"But to me the '20s and '30s were a fascinating era for boxing," said Schaap. "Far more interesting than the '40s or '50s or '60s. The NFL was in its infancy; the NBA didn't exist. Baseball and horse racing were the only other games in town. Boxing champions were celebrities, and the heavyweight champion was the biggest celebrity of all."

As he researched the Braddock tale, Schaap found himself increasingly drawn to Baer, whose story had also faded into relative obscurity. Although remembered as almost a caricature, when he is remembered at all, Baer was a sporting icon of his day. He fit perfectly into an era when tennis stars were wont to arrive for a championship match still clad in the previous night's tuxedo and reeking of champagne.

The very epitome of the playboy athlete, Baer cut a swath through Manhattan society that wouldn't be emulated until Joe Willie Namath hit town 30 years later. He married one movie star, dated countless others, even starred in a major motion picture, and his exploits were a staple of the daily gossip columns in the New York papers.

Behind his *bon vivant* façade, Baer was an enormously conflicted man, dogged by the memory of a 1930 California ring tragedy in which he killed an opponent named Frankie Campbell. (Born Francisco Camilli, Frankie Campbell was the older brother of future Brooklyn Dodger Dolph Camilli.) San Francisco authorities arrested Baer and briefly attempted to prosecute him for manslaughter. Although he was cleared, he was haunted forevermore, even as the heavyweight champion continued to send money from his purses to Campbell's widow and orphaned children.

Baer also wore a Star of David on his trunks and engaged in verbal warfare with Hitler, Goebbels, and Max Schmeling. Baer's Hebraic ancestry (he was at best one-quarter Jewish, and that on his father's side—the one that by Talmudic law does not count) appears to have been an afterthought; there is no question that it became economically beneficial once he transferred his base of operations from the West Coast to New York.

Although boxing historians, including Nat Fleischer, always regarded Baer's Jewish claims with some cynicism, Schaap seems to bend over backward to give Baer the benefit of the doubt. Electing to ignore what I've always considered the final word on the subject (the late Ray Arcel's observation that "He wasn't. I know. I saw him in the shower."), Schaap apparently decided that perception was more important than reality: "What is clear is that while Fleischer, Arcel, and others did not accept him as one of the chosen people, the Nazis certainly did."

Indeed, if there's a criticism to be made of Schaap's endeavor to retell the stories of Braddock and Baer, it is this occasional tendency—Baer being Jewish makes for a better story, so let him be Jewish—to selectively sculpt the facts to enhance the narrative.

In an almost parenthetical reference, for instance, to Joe Jeannette, in whose North Bergen gym Braddock trained, Schaap notes that "Jeannette, who was black, was constantly passed over for title shots in favor of white men, as was his black contemporary Sam 'The Boston Tar Baby' Langford. Even Jack Johnson refused to defend his title against Jeannette or Langford, opting instead for less dangerous opponents."

This is technically accurate but somewhat misleading. The fact is that Jack Johnson fought Jeannette *nine* times, the last of them in 1908, the year in which he would win the title at Rushcutters Bay. Jeannette won exactly one of those fights—and that on a foul. (Johnson also fought Langford, winning a 15-round decision in John Ruiz' hometown of Chelsea, Mass., in 1906.) As champion, it seems improbable that Johnson ducked Jeannette because he was afraid of him. It is more likely that he didn't defend his title against him because it made no economic sense. (Were James J. Jeffries and Stanley Ketchel "far less dangerous" than Joe Jeannette?)

But such quibbling is almost insignificant in the face of such a wonderful story. *Cinderella Man* is a mighty tale, and one splendidly told by Jeremy Schaap. Somewhere, Dick Schaap is smiling proudly.

TheSweetScience.com

May 2005

Luis Resto–Billy Collins Redux

Doctored Glove Tragedy Won't Go Away

Eric Drath was somewhat upset when he first read this story, but in the end I think he'd agree that I probably did him a big favor. By the time the film presented that day as **Cornered** *made its HBO debut as* **Assault in the Ring** *a year and a half later, virtually every point to which I had taken exception in this piece for* **Boxing Talk** *had been addressed, so I'm claiming partial credit for its 2010 Emmy Award for Outstanding Drama. As I had anticipated, the federal court denied Marc Thompson's motion to reopen the case.*

NEW YORK–When they hand you a press kit in which boxing is described as "a controversial, dying sport," you might suspect that somebody has an agenda. And when the second paragraph of that press kit describes the attendance for the June 16, 1983, fight between Luis Resto and the late Billy Ray Collins as "a capacity crowd of 25,000 at Madison Square Garden," the alarm bells ought to go off.

The actual attendance that night was 20,061, making it the third-largest audience in the history of Garden Boxing. The all-time record remains the 20,748 for Ali-Frazier II in 1974. While the fudged figure is not particularly crucial to the issues at hand, when someone is willing to take such liberties with readily verifiable facts, it doesn't exactly bolster the case for his subsequent, more theoretical pronouncements.

A quarter-century later, the circumstances of the Resto-Collins fight still render it a low point in the annals of New York boxing. The essential elements of the story are well-known, and, since Carlos "Panama" Lewis and Luis Resto were both convicted and sentenced to prison for using doctored gloves in the bout, a matter of public record.

The purpose of Thursday's press conference at Jack Demsey's restaurant was twofold—to boost interest in *Cornered,* Eric Drath's as-yet unreleased film, and to provide attorney Marc Thompson with a forum to announce his having filed a motion to reopen the case in federal district court.

The agendas of the filmmaker and the lawyer would seem to be at cross-purposes, particularly since Resto, in a surprise appearance, materialized at Demsey's and publicly confirmed for the first time that not only was he aware that Lewis had removed the horsehide padding from his gloves but that the trainer had compounded the offense by applying plaster of Paris to his hand-wraps that night.

At the very least, this revelation is going to require some conceptual tinkering with the footage of *Cornered,* at least as described in the accompanying press release: "*Cornered* reveals the inadequacies of Luis Resto's trial and investigates the circumstances behind his conviction. The film confronts the realities of racism, discrimination, and class struggle that plague not just the sport of boxing, but America as a whole."

Since just about the whole world, or at least everyone not named Eric Drath, already assumed Resto was guilty, his admission that he unfairly beat Collins figured to have all the drama of an announcement that the world was indeed round, and it's hard to see exactly how Resto fessing up is going to help Thompson (or Collins' estate) in court.

Thompson, of the Manhattan law firm Pulvers, Pulvers, and Thompson, represents Mrs. Andrea Nile of Nashville, Tenn.. Twenty-five years ago Mrs. Nile was married to Billy Ray Collins Jr. She was supposed to attend the New York press conference, but did not.

Two previous attempts to make a civil case out of the scandalous events of June 16, 1983, met in failure. The first, a federal suit against New York officials, ended in a hung jury, and the second, before the New York Court of Claims, was tossed out by the judge. It is unclear to me just how Andrea Collins-Nile's fortunes are likely to be enhanced by Resto's confession. To prove actual damages she must not only prove that Resto won unfairly (which everybody already knows) but that by failing to prevent the skullduggery, the New York State Athletic Commission directly contributed to the death of her late husband, who did not die until months later from injuries not directly related to the bout when his car ran off a bridge. There are also statute of limitations issues, meaning there must be a good reason to justify a lawsuit over something that occurred a quarter of a century ago.

Did Luis Resto's loaded gloves in New York make Billy Ray Collins get drunk and drive off a bridge in Tennessee nine months later? Billy Collins

Sr., who described his son's death as "a suicide," always maintained so, but being able to prove that to a jury and, moreover, demonstrating actual damages does not seem promising.

Of the 20,061 on hand at the Garden that night, fewer than a hundred were actually there to see the Collins-Resto fight. Roberto Duran, who was celebrating his thirty-second birthday, was challenging for Davey Moore's WBA junior middleweight title in the main event. Both Duran, who had been fighting in the Mecca of Boxing since 1971, and Moore, a Bronx-born former New York Golden Gloves champion, had substantial New York constituencies, but events of the evening would demonstrate that the allegiance of most of the crowd lay with Manos de Piedra.

Two years after the "No Mas" fight in New Orleans, Top Rank's Bob Arum had taken on Duran as a reclamation project, and a fortuitous confluence of events—chiefly Duran's January knockout of Pipino Cuevas and the arrest of No. 1–rated Tony Ayala on rape charges—had provided the opportunity for a title fight.

Moore-Duran was originally scheduled to take place in Sun City, in the South African "homeland" of Bophuthatswana, in combination with a Ray Mancini-Kenny Bogner lightweight title bout and a concert by Frank Sinatra. Weeks before the scheduled date, Mancini broke his collarbone, and Sinatra—who had agreed to the performance because he was a big-time Boom-Boom fan—also pulled out.

MSG Boxing didn't bid on Moore-Duran. Arum hired the building himself and proceeded to fill it with its third-biggest boxing audience ever.

Moore, making his fourth title defense, was favored by nearly 4-1, and when a newspaper polled two dozen boxing writers in town to cover the fight, only four—including myself—picked Duran.

That Moore might be in for a long night was foreshadowed at the weigh-in, when he struggled for two hours to make 154, while Duran made it with ease.

The fight turned out to be completely one-sided. Duran caught Moore with a stray thumb to the right eye in the first round and spent the ensuing rounds bullying him around the ring, hitting his one-eyed foe with punches and elbows until he knocked him down with a right hand in the eighth, at which point Moore's corner threw in the towel. (Referee Ernesto Magana was widely excoriated for not stopping it sooner.)

The win set Duran up for lucrative fights against Marvelous Marvin Hagler and Thomas Hearns over the next year, and in the giddy atmosphere that

surrounded the Panamanian's upset victory, few were even aware that evening of the disgraceful events that had preceded it in the preliminary bout
between Resto and Collins.

Collins was from Tennessee, an ESPN-level fighter who was 14-0, though
unless you counted Bruce "The Mouse" Strauss, a very young Harold Brazier
was the only recognizable name on his list of victims.

Resto, a Puerto Rican then domiciled in the Bronx, was 20-8-2, but had
faced much tougher opposition. I'd first encountered him in Cleveland two
years earlier when he sparred with Duran before the Nino Gonzalez fight,
and I actually expected Resto to win going in.

So did Resto.

"I didn't really need that [stuff]," said Resto at Demsey's. "I would have
beaten him anyway."

Panama Lewis, alas, wasn't taking any chances.

On the night in question, Panama supposedly kicked the inspector who
was supposed to oversee the gloving out of the dressing room, and then put
the contraband gloves on Resto when the inspector left to tell his superiors.

Resto, in any case, beat Collins from pillar to post all night. Between
rounds, Collins could be heard telling his father in the corner "he's a lot
stronger than I thought," and at the end of ten rounds Billy Ray's face was
a mass of lumps and bruises.

At the final bell, Collins Sr. congratulated Resto, but as he shook hands,
said he felt "only knuckles." He was shortly shouting "Commissioner!
Commissioner!" in an attempt to call attention to the treachery.

The gloves were impounded in the dressing room that night. (The hand-
wraps Resto wore that night were not, but Marc Thompson said that he
believed they still existed, which I rather doubt. Not even Panama Lewis is
that stupid.)

The chain of evidence at one point led to the gloves being returned to
Everlast, which, Thompson pointed out, "is sort of like sending the dope back
to the dope dealer for testing."

Once the gloves were subjected to examination, it turned out that Lewis
had surreptitiously removed the stuffing. Even without the layer of plaster
on his wraps, Resto might as well have been hitting Collins with a pair of
bricks that night.

Resto's win was ultimately stricken from the books and changed to No
Contest. Lewis and Resto were convicted on charges of assault, possession of a dangerous weapon, and, in Lewis' case, conspiracy to influence the

outcome of a sporting event. Both were banned from boxing for life. Lewis was sentenced to six years, but served only one. Resto spent two-and-a-half years in prison.

Collins' injuries included a fractured orbital bone and permanent eye damage that prevented him from boxing again. The following March after a night of drinking, he drove off the bridge.

Neither man ever boxed again. Resto has lived for the past decade in the basement of a New Jersey gym.

If Panama Lewis augmented his surgery on Resto's gloves by doctoring the hand-wraps, it might be noted, there existed an historical precedent, in legend if not in fact. For almost ninety years there have been whispers that Jack Dempsey (the heavyweight champion and not the saloonkeeper) had won the championship using loaded gloves in his 1919 fight against Jess Willard.

Supposedly manager Jack Kearns had used plaster of Paris on the wraps in very much the fashion Resto now says Lewis did with his. One irony here is that as the story grew, Kearns was careful never to deny it, and his legacy became that of an impish rogue, the boxing equivalent of Gaylord Perry winking at the umpires while he continued to throw spitballs.

The other irony is that while both Lewis and Resto were banned for life, Panama has continued to earn a living as a boxing bottom-feeder. Sure, he can't be licensed and he can't work corners, but that hasn't prevented him from turning up as a freelance voodoo-master in gyms from Las Vegas to New York to London over the past two decades. And you can bet he's not doing it for nothing.

Cornered has been selected for the IFP Marketplace and will be screened at the organization's showcase for indie films in September, as well as at the HBO-sponsored New York International Latino Film Festival.

Thompson's bid for a new trial faces a more uncertain future. Copies of the motion were supposed to be available yesterday, but were not. We're just guessing here, but the next time you see it may be when it comes sailing out the judge's window.

BoxingTalk.com
April 2008

Bad Day at the Beach

Kevin Mitchell's Jacobs Beach

When the editors of the Irish Times Weekend Magazine *asked me to review* Jacobs Beach *in 2009, neither they nor I had any preconception about the book. I've never taken any particular delight in savaging the work of a colleague; as a general rule if I don't like a book I'd prefer not to review it at all. The rare exception comes when the work in question is so shoddy and so outrageously bad that it literally begs to be ridiculed.*

The guy who really should be reviewing this book died just over a month ago. In 1950, a year after Mike Jacobs had severed his connections with boxing, Budd Schulberg authored an exhaustively researched piece for *Collier's* magazine in which he detailed at length the saga of the son of Dublin-born immigrants who rose from hustling nickels and dimes on the street to hustling million-dollar gates for a decade in which he was the most powerful figure in boxing.

During the era of his greatest prominence, from roughly 1936–1946, Jacobs' influence was such that the one-block stretch of 49th Street that ran between 8th Avenue and Madison Square Garden down to Broadway was familiarly described as "Jacobs Beach," borrowing the name of an actual beach in Connecticut. The epicenter of Jacobs Beach was the ticket agency out of which Mike operated until 1938, when he assumed control of the Garden's Boxing Department. The use of the term "Jacobs Beach" began to lose its relevance once its namesake departed the scene, and had utterly vanished from the lexicon by the time of his death in January of 1953.

The vacuum created by Jacobs' official departure from the Garden in 1949 had rapidly been assumed by an unholy trio of James Norris, the ostensibly respectable front man for the International Boxing Club, and his even more powerful and ruthless gangster associates, Frankie Carbo and Blinky

Palermo. The result was an era of wholesale corruption that far outstripped anything the "red light district of sports" (as Jimmy Cannon described it) had seen before or since. Although they were dogged by Senate investigations headed up by Senator Estes Kefauver almost throughout this reign of terror, it would be nearly a decade before Norris was forced from office and the IBC dissolved in a consent decree, and Carbo packed off to Alcatraz on conspiracy and extortion charges in a case personally prosecuted by Robert F. Kennedy. (Blinky Palermo got a 15-year stretch in the federal pen about the same time.)

Whether Kevin Mitchell, the chief sportswriter for the *Observer* in London, considered the Jacobs era or the Carbo era or some *other* era to have been "the Golden Age of Boxing" remains unlearned, but since "Jacobs Beach" had ceased to exist during the period of the mob's most malevolent influence, the book's title is at least, curious, if not intentionally misleading. It's rather as if a treatise on English music from Elizabethan times through the Arctic Monkeys had been packaged for the bookshelves under the title *Abbey Road.*

Having come up with a title encompassing Jacobs, the Garden, and the Mob, Mitchell devotes 288 pages to an unsuccessful attempt to prop up his thesis that they represented one and the same. Between some of his rather dubious choices of sources, his persistent inclination for latching onto opinions that support his position while ignoring more widely accepted ones that do not, and some fairly glaring factual misrepresentations, the effect is rather like watching a man persistently trying to drive a square peg into a round hole.

Schulberg, of course, could have disabused him of much of this nonsense. In point of fact, Mitchell did interview the iconic author two summers ago, but in his account of that visit in *Jacobs Beach,* fully eight of 11 pages are spent recounting a chatty conversation about *On the Waterfront* and Marlon Brando. The ostensible subject of the book gets two paragraphs, which can be summed up in one sentence: "[Schulberg] might not have missed Jacobs much, but he was hardly keen to see him replaced by Norris, Carbo, and Palermo."

In point of fact, Schulberg's feelings about Mike Jacobs were essentially conflicted on both a personal and a professional level, but when it came to Jacobs "playing footsie with the Mob," said Schulberg, "there's plenty of evidence both to hang and acquit him." Certainly, Carbo and his ilk enjoyed disturbingly free access to the Garden's boxing offices while Jacobs was running the show, but while he might have tolerated what he described as "those motherfucking thieves," Jacobs, in Schulberg's view, actually kept the mob at bay during his time on the throne—at least until 1946, when he may have occasionally let his guard down following a cerebral hemorrhage and accompanying stroke. (The Carbo-engineered Jake LaMotta dive against Billy Fox, for instance, took place in 1947—theoretically still on Jacobs' watch.)

But presumably since anything Schulberg offered might not have jibed with Mitchell's contention that "the Mob never left boxing," the subject was not allowed to intrude on their conversation.

Mitchell relies heavily on the opinions of Dan Parker, perhaps Jacobs' staunchest enemy among the New York fight writers during the heyday of Jacobs Beach, while completely ignoring the more widely held view of Red Smith, the Pulitzer Prize–winning columnist for the *Herald Tribune* (and later the *New York Times*).

"Although it is certainly true that nobody ever exerted such an absolute dictatorship as his over any sport and while it is probably true that no one else ever made such profits as he from boxing, it is emphatically true that no man ever ran boxing as well as he, anywhere," wrote Smith. "If anyone in the world has run fights on the level, Mike has."

Had the author so much as asked, I've no doubt Schulberg would have gladly agreed to look over the manuscript for *Jacobs Beach*. Though Mitchell probably wouldn't have liked much of what he had to say, a vetting by Schulberg, or almost anyone conversant with American history, might have spared him considerable embarrassment by pointing out some of the baffling inaccuracies that riddle the book.

The venerable New York newspaperman Jimmy Breslin, who celebrated his seventy-ninth birthday last October, is described by Mitchell as "well into his nineties now and still kicking." Babe Ruth, according to Mitchell, "moved from Boston to New York in 1923." (Close; it was 1920.) The attack on Pearl Harbor becomes, in Mitchell's telling, "the day of infamy, as General Douglas MacArthur memorably called it." (We're assuming he means President Franklin D. Roosevelt's radio address, which began "Yesterday, December 7, 1941—a day which will live in infamy.")

And those *unforced* errors. The book is replete with equally gratuitous observations such as the description of Harry Markson as "the Garden's loud PR man." *Jacobs Beach* may be the first place the words "loud" and "Harry Markson" have ever appeared in the same sentence. Schulberg described Markson as "a literate, quiet-mannered college graduate," and on the occasion of his death the *New York Times* obituary began "Harry Markson, a soft-spoken and scholarly type . . ."

Markson would later be named the Garden's Director of Boxing in the IBC era because, Norris explained, "there's got to be somebody around here with clean hands." Mitchell apparently took exception to Markson's observation that under the Jacobs regime "boxing today is immensely more honest than it was fifteen or twenty years ago."

"Nobody else thought so," sniffs Mitchell, dismissing Red Smith, Schulberg, and the countless others who would have agreed with Markson.

The factual errors would not be so damning in themselves, but getting so many known facts wrong doesn't do much for the credibility of a book that otherwise relies so heavily on gossip, innuendo, and secondhand tales from dubious witnesses like Bert Randolph Sugar. A notorious plagiarist and bullshit artist, Sugar is one of two men ever to have been expelled from membership by the Boxing Writers Association of America. Mitchell describes him as "one of boxing's more reliable historians," even though he isn't particularly reliable about even his *own* history, assuming he was the source for Mitchell's glowing characterization in *Jacobs Beach:* ". . . Sugar, who has insinuated himself into every corner of the fight game since coming to New York from Philadelphia as an ad man in the late forties."

Bert Sugar was born in 1936. It seems doubtful that even in 1949 Madison Avenue would have required the services of any precocious thirteen-year-old ad men.

After throwing around several unsubstantiated intimations attempting to tie the heavyweight champion Rocky Marciano to Frankie Carbo and the Mob, Mitchell finally throws in the towel, but then as a consolation prize in lieu of a smoking gun, he finds himself chasing down a bit of cocktail party gossip and, not three paragraphs later, presents it as fact.

Mitchell recounts a conversation with a man named Rollie Hackmere, whom he describes as "an upright and dapper gentleman in his seventies.

"[Hackmere] called me aside one night at a meeting of Ring 8, the New York ex-boxers' association, and said 'I knew Rocky. He was some guy. Do you know he fought his brother, Peter, nine times? Bo, I bet you didn't. How about that?'"

Mitchell then presented the rumor to Lou Duva, the octogenarian cornerman who knew Marciano well: "Yeah, he did," Duva supposedly replied. "He fought Peter. They was fights in the smokers. So what?"

From that "confirmation"—Duva, by the way, denies ever having said such a thing—Mitchell allows himself to wax rhapsodic:

"The night he looked across the ring in the Garden at [Joe] Louis, Rocky might have reflected on those smoke-filled nights and how far he'd come . . . With all the clinical detachment he might have brought to punching brother Peter in the nose back in Massachusetts he set about destroying what was left of Joe Louis."

That, in a nutshell, summarizes what is wrong with *Jacobs Beach*: The prose is facile, but the history is flawed.

On October 26, 1951, when Rocky fought Joe Louis with these memories of beating up his youngest brother supposedly bubbling up in his mind, Peter Marciano was nine years old.

The Irish Times Weekend Magazine
September 2009

Terry Malloy Meets Paulie Walnuts

Garry Pastore's Waiting for Budd

Until he was cast in the role of former light-heavyweight Terry Malloy for last summer's two-night performance of Budd Schulberg's *On the Waterfront* in Hoboken, Jason Cerbone's most noteworthy fight experience had come in the men's room of the Bada Bing Club, where James Gandolfini beat him within an inch of his life in a 2001 episode of *The Sopranos.*

So how convincing is Cerbone as a boxer? It's difficult to tell one way or the other from the brief fight clip included in Garry Pastore's *Waiting for Budd,* but Cerbone seems to show a decent jab, effective enough that despite giving away close to a hundred pounds and clutching a script in his right hand, he still had Big Pussy backing up.

And the best part of it was, Budd Schulberg got to watch him do it.

Waiting for Budd had its debut screening on October 29, the final night of the New York International Film Festival, and was enthusiastically received by a select audience that included several members of the Schulberg family, festival judges, and much of the cast. A splendid little gem, *Waiting* is on one level a documentary about the making of a play and on another a tribute to its iconic author, who attended the second and final night of the star-crossed Hoboken production barely a week before his death. And if one has created the impression that *Waiting for Budd* might be characterized in some quarters as *The Sopranos* meets *On the Waterfront,* in the words of George Foreman, "they're only saying that 'cause it's true."

The four principal male leads—Cerbone (Terry), Vincent Pastore (Johnny Friendly), Al Sapienza (Charlie), and Robert Funaro (Father Barry)—are all veterans of the classic HBO series. Both Cerbone's (Jackie Aprile Jr.) and Vincent Pastore's (Salvatore "Big Pussy" Bonpensiero) characters met unfortunate demises as the victims of mob hits, while Funaro's (Eugene Pontecarvo) hung himself in despair after an unsuccessful attempt to resign from the family business. At least two other *Waterfront* cast members—Garry Pastore (who in addition to directing and co-producing *Waiting for Budd,* played Big Mac in the Hoboken play) and Arthur Nascarella (Pop Doyle)—had also had prior *Sopranos* roles.

(Lest we appear guilty of profiling here, it might also be noted that 11 members of the 19-character *Waterfront* cast, including Robin Paul, who played Edie Doyle, have also been featured in various incarnations of *Law and Order,* whose bad guys are less ethno-specific.)

In another of those serendipitous degrees of separation, in 2001, just a year before, Rod Steiger (the original Charlie) passed away. Sapienza, the Hoboken Charlie, had portrayed Steiger's son in *A Month of Sundays.*

The casting, in fact, appears to have been in many cases the outcome of a series of happy accidents since most of the actors were chosen following open auditions at the Mayfair Hotel on June 25. ("Who wouldn't want to do *On the Waterfront?*" noted Garry Pastore, who was inspired by the response to the casting call to corral the cameras and record subsequent proceedings on film.)

The New Artists Theatre Company had been founded by Vincent Pastore, Licato, and Puccio. Cousin Garry was there to read Father Barry's and Terry's lines back to the other actors. The deaths that day of Michael Jackson and Farrah Fawcett cast something of a pall on the proceedings among the show-biz crowd.

"Then Chuck Zito arrived, insisting that he wanted to play Terry Malloy," recalled Pastore. "Now, Chuck is this huge, muscle-bound guy who's sixty years old [only fifty-seven, actually] and he's gonna play Terry? And I told [*Waterfront* director] Frank Licato, 'We really ought to be filming this.'

"I just found it so hysterical that Chuck wanted to play Terry," Pastore continued. "It planted the seed about shooting footage, because I was sort of amused by the cast of characters who kept coming in to audition. Some were good and some not so good, but they all had heart and gave it their best shot."

Once filming began, the bulk of the task fell to Fokke Baarssen, a Dutch student at the New York Film Academy, who initially hired on as a production assistant/intern with the Hudson Film Group, but proved to be so valuable that he was in the end listed as cinematographer and film editor for *Waiting for Budd.*

Rehearsals took place in New York on July 8th and 15th.

The script used was not Schulberg's Oscar-winning screenplay but a stage version written for an ill-fated Broadway run a decade and a half ago that lasted only slightly longer than the two-night stand in Hoboken last July. In the Broadway version, for which Stan Silverman shared writing credit with Schulberg, the "incidental music" was composed by David Amram. Ron Eldard ("Doubt") played Terry; and David Morse, Father Barry; while Charlie was portrayed by—you gotta love this—James Gandolfini.

When that play closed after just eight performances, the $2.5 million it cost its backers was at the time a Broadway record for non-musicals.

Last summer's concept was to use professional actors in a staged reading, and in a unique setting—on the same New Jersey waterfront where Schulberg's original masterpiece had been set, and where the 1954 movie had been filmed, but it was not without its own difficulties. Pastore's partner, executive producer Deborah Mello, became so ill she was hospitalized a week before opening night.

In advance of the performance, the local media had been invited over for a "press day" at the waterfront stage, where several members of the cast would be made available for interviews. When the appointed time arrived, not a single newspaper or television station showed up. Only later did Pastore learn that they had all been pulled off the story to deal with the bombshell events of the day—that Hoboken Mayor Peter Cammarata had been among those taken down on corruption charges that morning.

"Here we were doing a play about corruption on the waterfront in Hoboken and our press day gets spoiled because the mayor was busted for corruption," Pastore noted the irony.

Following just a couple of weeks of rehearsal, the July 28th opening night *al fresco* performance, with the New York skyline serving as a backdrop, was by all accounts a success. Had the second night proceeded so seamlessly, admitted Pastore, "we probably wouldn't have had a movie," but Mother Nature intervened to provide the dramatic tension necessary to drive the second half of the 30-minute film.

On July 29th, 2009, the entire metropolitan area was besieged by a day-long monsoon of Biblical proportions. Their faces glued to the screen, Pastore and Licato looked like a couple of guys trying to read tea leaves as they hopefully stared at a Doppler radar screen in a fruitless search for a break in the weather.

Waterfowl were already swimming around in what would have been the stage. Puddles several inches deep had formed on the seats from which the audience would have watched, in the unlikely event an audience had braved the rainstorms at all.

"This is not good," Pastore reflected as he watched the ducks swim in the newly formed pools on the stage. "This is not comforting."

By early afternoon it had become apparent that the performance would have to be canceled unless a suitable indoor location could be procured on short notice.

Someone came up with a small auditorium—to be precise, it was the physics lecture auditorium at Stevens—but upon reaching that venue, Licato realized that it would be hopelessly inadequate.

"I hate it. We're going to have to cancel," the play's director sighed to the film's director. At that point Pastore reminded Licato that Budd Schulberg was already on his way to Hoboken.

"*Budd's* coming? He's definitely coming here?" Licato seemed to immediately reconsider. "I guess even if we have to play just to Budd, we have to do it."

There seemed to be little choice in the matter.

"The show must go on, right?" agreed Garry.

At this point Licato asked about sound and lighting equipment. Both, it turned out, had been delivered to the school by truck a few hours earlier, but Vincent Pastore made a unilateral decision to send the gear back to Uncle Junior.

"We'd been setting up the stage, Vin and I, with a few wooden kegs and crates set for dressing, and a sound guy moved the set dressing to put up this big, ugly oversized speaker that looked like it could be used for a Stones concert," recalled Garry Pastore.

Lapsing into his Big Pussy mode, "Vinny pretty much told him to take a [bleeping] hike," said Garry. "Maybe it wasn't in the nicest tone or choice of words, but it was actually very comical. I wished I'd had the camera rolling then, but if I had, Vinny probably would have smashed it at that point.

"The rain was coming down so hard you couldn't even ask anyone to stand there with a sign to redirect the audience," recalled Garry Pastore. "Besides, who would have *seen* it?"

Rounding up the cast proved equally challenging. Some of them had been informed, erroneously, that the performance had already been scrapped. Many of the actors lived in Manhattan, a circumstance which was complicated by the fact that the tunnels were flooding and the George Washington Bridge was hopelessly backed up.

At the Lincoln Tunnel it was even worse than that. With police limiting traffic to a single line of vehicles, all of mid-Manhattan had succumbed to gridlock. Facing a delay of several hours, Funaro resorted to ingenuity. Donning Father Barry's collar, he explained to the cops that he was due to give last rites to Runty Nolan and say a mass in Hoboken. (Which was, in one sense, true.) In light of this clerical emergency, his car was escorted to the head of the line and Funaro was shortly on his way to Jersey.

The lecture hall had a capacity of 200. Somehow, the word got around in Hoboken, and the show was completely sold out, with standing room only. Budd Schulberg, accompanied by his son Benn, was a late arrival and was introduced to a standing ovation by the audience.

"The people were in absolute awe of him," said Pastore.

So was the cast.

"To be able to perform in front of an icon like Budd Schulberg—and to think that it almost didn't happen, wow!" marveled Robin Paul.

"It was like Burbridge reciting the words back to Shakespeare," said Joe Dandry. "The fact that I was able to do that is something I'll never forget."

Word trickled backstage that Schulberg appeared to be "beaming" as he watched the show. When the Oscar winner (and Hall of Fame boxing writer) was later asked about the Hoboken production, he said, "I thought they did an excellent job. I was very pleased."

Schulberg autographed programs for those who had braved the storm to attend that night. One of them had the temerity to ask him to compare Jason Cerbone's Terry to Marlon Brando's.

Schulberg resisted the temptation to answer "he coulda been a contender."

"Well, nobody's ever been as good as Brando," Budd replied with a soft chuckle. "But I liked what [Cerbone] did with it very much."

Eight days later the ninety-five-year-old Schulberg was dead.

"We got to perform *On the Waterfront* in front of Budd Schulberg for the last time," said Garry Pastore, "and what started out as a really incredibly shitty day turned into a night I never, ever will forget, not in my lifetime.

"For some odd reason, this play was meant to be done, and this little film was meant to be made. Where it goes from here is anybody's guess," said Pastore. "As our tagline goes, 'Some things are just meant to be.'"

TheSweetScience.com
November 2009

Ali, Holmes, and Maysles

What's Up with This, Doc?

Earlier this year, ESPN revealed plans to simultaneously celebrate its 30th anniversary and expand its cultural horizons with a season-long film festival that would showcase the work of some of the more acclaimed filmmakers of our time—including but not limited to the likes of Barry Levinson, Ron Shelton, Barbara Koppel, and Albert Maysles.

The 30-on-30 series opened earlier this month with Peter Berg's *King's Ransom,* an examination of the ripple effect throughout the National Hockey League of the 1988 trade that brought Wayne Gretzky, the best player of his era, from Winnipeg to Hollywood. Last week the network premiered its second installment, Levinson's *The Band That Wouldn't Die,* in which the man who made *Diner* looks back at the Colts' 1984 abandonment of Baltimore, a bittersweet paean that affords Levinson one more opportunity to kick Robert Irsay up and down The Block.

The initial airing of the third film, *Small Potatoes: Who Killed the USFL?,* was scheduled for October 20. The work of Mike Tollin (*The Bronx is Burning*), *Small Potatoes* has already stirred up its share of controversy, thanks to Donald Trump, whose name is the answer to the question asked in the subtitle.

The network that built its early success on live boxing turns its attention to the Sweet Science next week, with the debut of Maysles' *Muhammad and Larry,* a quasi-documentary centered around Muhammad Ali's doomed attempt to regain the heavyweight title in what proved to be the penultimate fight of his 61-bout career.

The Maysles brothers had been granted virtually unlimited access to the camps of both champion and challenger in the weeks and months preceding the fight at Caesars Palace, but for various reasons (chiefly rights issues concerning the actual fight footage) the project had remained dormant for the better part of the past three decades. Kick-started by the ESPN agreement, Maysles and his new filmmaking partner Brad Kaplan (David Maysles died in 1987) re-interviewed many of the surviving cast of characters—Holmes, along with Angelo Dundee, Dr. Ferdie Pacheco, Gene Kilroy, and Wali Muhammad from the opposing camp, but not, conspicuously, Ali himself—and augmented their recollections with those of a number of boxing writers in revisiting what had by almost any standard been an incredibly depressing experience for everyone concerned. Including the guy who won the fight.

I was in London for the Marvelous Marvin Hagler-Alan Minter fight the previous weekend, and was consequently one of the few boxing writers in America who wasn't at Caesars Palace on the night of October 2, 1980.

When we'd talked about it over breakfast a few days before Hagler's fight, Goody Petronelli seemed to think Holmes-Ali was such a foregone conclusion that he wondered why they were fighting at all.

"If everything's right," he said, "I don't see how Ali can win."

Even though it loomed a colossal mismatch going in, I was curious enough about seeing it that I'd made sure I'd get home in plenty of time to watch the closed-circuit telecast. Rip Valenti was running a live card at the old Boston Garden that night, followed by the telecast of the fight from Vegas, and my flight to Boston would get me back in plenty of time for both.

Of course, those things don't always work out as planned. Europe had been particularly affected by the worldwide fuel shortage, so the Aer Lingus plane that took off from Dublin first backtracked to Scotland and re-fueled at Prestwick. From there came the obligatory stopover at Shannon, where the plane was emptied so the passengers would shop. By the time I actually landed, it was already dark. A cousin then working at Logan Airport had made arrangements to whisk me through customs and I jumped in a taxi for the Garden, arriving with only minutes to spare before Ali's fight.

We watched from the press room, where they'd set up a few folding chairs. I was joined by the venerable *New York Times* columnist Red Smith, who'd come up from his summer home on Martha's Vineyard with his friend Eliot Norton, the drama critic at my newspaper, the *Boston Herald*. At the time of the Holmes-Ali fight, Red had a bit over a year to live, and at seventy-seven, Eliot was two years older than Red was.

Smith had never been what you'd call a huge Ali fan, and in a column a few days earlier he'd expressed reservations similar to Goody's, all of which were borne out that evening. Ali started with nothing and had less as each round passed. Eliot must have felt as if he were covering some sort of Shakespearean tragedy; it was that sad and pitiful. None of us could understand why Richard Greene was allowing it to go on, and why in the absence of any intervention from the referee, Angelo Dundee didn't stop it himself.

Finally, at the end of ten, Dundee called Greene over to the corner and asked him to stop it. This in turn produced a beef with Bundini Brown, who tried to overrule Angelo, but Dundee reminded the referee that he was the chief second, and he won that argument. Bundini almost immediately burst into tears, and by the time they got him on-camera, Larry Holmes was crying, too.

It was a story we all knew we'd have to write one day, but I was pretty glad I hadn't been there that night. As it turned out, it was a temporary reprieve. I was there the next year when Ali fought Trevor Berbick in the Bahamas, so 14 months later I had to write it anyway.

Albert and David Maysles had pioneered the documentary-as-art-form, going back to the days of *Primary* (1960) and their 1975 classic, *Grey Gardens.* In 1970 they had set out to make the first great rock 'n' roll epic in *Gimme Shelter,* and wound up producing the first commercially viable snuff film when they included footage of the Hell's Angels killing a spectator at the Altamont Festival.

In addition to the aforementioned rights difficulties, the Maysles had another problem with *Muhammad and Larry* 30 years ago, which is that the wrong guy won. Whether they actually believed Ali had a chance, or whether they thought that Holmes would emerge from that fight with an enhanced image isn't clear, but the fact is that what happened that night in Vegas seemed so obscene that distributors were convinced, probably correctly, that nobody wanted to look at it again.

Barely half of the hour-long ESPN version is from the original footage, and some of the latter-day observations seem frankly self-serving. The guy who comes off best, ironically, is Pacheco, who had walked away from Ali's corner in 1977 when his retirement advice went unheeded.

Ali had lost and then regained the title for the third time by outpointing Leon Spinks, and then announced his retirement following his final win. The heavyweight title had been divided, with John Tate and then Mike Weaver holding the WBA version. Holmes, who as a nascent pro had been one of Ali's regular sparring partners, had won the WBC version by beating Ken Norton. (The latter remains the only heavyweight "champion" in history who lost the only three title bouts in which he participated.)

The film contrasts Holmes' storefront training camp in Easton with what looks like a 24/7 zoo in Deer Lake, where Ali seems to be more interested in catering to the tourists than in actual training. (A very young Tim Witherspoon, who sparred with Ali for Holmes, offers some interesting observations about his mentor's regimen, or lack of one.)

In the run-up to the Holmes fight, Ali had grown a mustache (he did shave it off when he got to Vegas) and referred to himself as "Dark Gable." Since this was pretty much the only time he sported facial hair, it's almost like watching a stranger who vaguely resembles Ali speak his lines.

And while the physical problems that would overtake him a few years later hadn't fully manifested themselves, his speech in 1979 was so markedly different from what it had been a decade earlier that one can only wonder why no one save Pacheco seems to have noticed.

Early in the film Holmes recalls being approached by a woman—a total stranger—whose first words were "I hate you!" His crime, of course, had been beating Ali. At that point he began to realize that just as his image had suffered because he was considered an unworthy successor, he would henceforth be blamed in some quarters for his part in turning Ali into what he has become today.

Some would argue that this course had already been set. Pacheco, who describes the Holmes fight as "an abomination," may have gotten carried away with himself when he says that everyone connected with it should have been put in jail, but he, and others, argue persuasively that it probably shouldn't have happened.

With rumors, some of them no doubt emanating from Pacheco, that Ali was evincing symptoms of mental and physical deterioration, the Nevada State Athletic Commission ordered a battery of tests performed by the Mayo Clinic before they would reissue his license. Ali's biographer Thomas Hauser points out that the Mayo tests revealed that Ali had experienced difficulty in performing normally rudimentary functions like touching the tip of his nose and hopping on cue. These might have been considered clear warning signs, but Nevada issued the license anyway, and for reasons best known to itself, the commission declined to make the Mayo test results public.

In footage from a round-table discussion conducted at the Versailles restaurant in Las Vegas last March for the Maysles film, John Schulian—my Library of America anthology co-editor who had covered Holmes-Ali as a columnist for the Chicago Sun-Times—notes that the Mayo Clinic tests had showed evidence of irregularity in Ali's brain function.

"They did not!" Former Ali aide Gene Kilroy nearly leaps across the table as he explodes. "All it showed was that he had some problems with short-term memory loss."

Since the film lets that pass without comment, it is left to us to break the news to Kilroy: Short-term memory loss is usually an early indicator of frontal-lobe brain damage.

In training, Ali probably compounded the problem when he let his sparring partners hammer away at him in the belief that it would toughen him up for the ordeal he expected, but as Pacheco points out, one's kidneys do not bounce back from such trauma. Then, in the weeks before the fight, on the advice of some crackpot doctor and with no apparent medical foundation, Ali received a prescription for thyroid supplements and began using the medicine like so much candy.

Holmes was going to win this fight anyway, but the film effectively makes the point that Ali's chances decreased at almost every turn. Participating in a panel discussion (along with Maysles, Kaplan, Pete Hamill, and ESPN's Jeremy Schaap) after Monday night's New York screening, Holmes complained that by pointing all these things out, the film tended to cheapen his victory by making it appear that Ali had beaten himself.

Even during his long and estimable reign as champion, Holmes was always touchy about living in Ali's shadow, and that has apparently not abated with time. While he didn't specifically complain that the film's title has the winner's and loser's names in reverse order, he might have.

And, interviewed in Easton this year, Larry's long-suffering better half, wife Diane, takes it upon herself to complain that her husband never got his just due.

"It's like he fell off the face of the earth," she tells the unseen interviewer. "Look how long it took you to get here!"

As what had become a ritual beating that night wore on, Holmes on several occasions seemed to be imploring Greene to stop it. Jake Holmes, who was in his brother's corner, says that much of the damage inflicted that night came because Holmes, realizing that the referee would be no help, was trying to knock Ali out in sort of a humane gesture that somehow seemed preferable to 15 rounds of protracted torture.

Pacheco says that when he asked Dundee to join his exodus two years earlier, the trainer replied that one good reason for staying on was that he would be in a position to rescue Ali should a fight need to be stopped.

"No, you won't," Pacheco told him—and it turns out he may have been right. In the Maysles film, both retired Newark scribe Jerry Izenberg and Kilroy confirm that Dundee's intervention came only after Herbert Muhammad had issued the order from his ringside seat.

There may be yet one more reason it took *Muhammad and Larry* 30 years to find an audience. Making a film about a fight billed as "The Last Hurrah" probably sounded like a better idea when it actually looked as if it would be, but once the Holmes fight was no longer Ali's last it may have lost some of its shine as an historical marker.

It wasn't in the rough cut distributed to the media beforehand, but in the final version screened at the Chelsea Theatre Monday, a postscript on the screen notes that in December of 1981 Ali fought for the last time in what the film gratuitously—and inaccurately—describes as an "unsanctioned" fight.

It seemed a curious, albeit deliberate, choice of words, designed to conjure up the image of some backwater bare-knuckle bout, or perhaps a winner-take-all fight to the finish in the basement of a Mafia social club. It struck me that the label was tacked on to foster the impression that the Holmes fight was Ali's last "real" one, and that ten rounds against Trevor Berbick shouldn't even count.

Now, there's no question that a lot of silly, undignified things happened on the card billed as The Drama in Bahama, ranging from the absence of an actual ring bell (a Bahamian cowbell assumed that role) to the failure of the organizers to provide enough gloves for the undercard participants, but almost without exception those were the responsibility of promoter James Cornelius—a rank amateur—and not of the Bahamian Commission that sanctioned the card.

And make no mistake about it, Berbick-Ali took place in the Bahamas specifically because it *was* sanctioned there. If it hadn't been, Cornelius would have no doubt found another jurisdiction that *would* sanction it.

Since Brad Kaplan seemed to have done most of the hands-on work with the ESPN version, I asked him about it after the screening. He initially tried to claim the fight hadn't been sanctioned at all, then that what he really meant was that "it wasn't sanctioned by a U.S. commission."

I asked him if he would have described it as "unsanctioned" had it taken place in Germany. At that point Maysles' partner began to yammer about the absence of recognized officials in the Bahamas. "The referee . . . and the judges . . ."

Actually, I told him, I believed that the referee that night was an American, Zach Clayton. (I double-checked when I got home. The same Zach Clayton who had refereed the Rumble in the Jungle seven years earlier was indeed the referee for Ali's swan song.)

Two of the judges, Alonzo Butler and Clyde Gray, were Bahamian appointees. The third, Jay Edson of Florida, was an official of more than 30 years' experience in world title fights. (Gray returned precisely the same score—99-94—Edson did that night, and Butler may have done a better job than either of them, since his 97-94 scorecard included just one even round, while Edson and Gray were indecisive enough to score three rounds level.)

It will be interesting to see whether the Berbick fight is still described as "unsanctioned" when *Muhammad and Larry* opens for business next Tuesday night.

TheSweetScience.com
October 2009

Irish Thunder

In a bookshop one afternoon in the summer of 2010 I came across a paperback edition of Irish Thunder. *The publisher had just reissued the book, hoping to capitalize on the fact that Micky was the subject of* The Fighter, *co-starring Mark Wahlberg, even though the projects had been developed independently. In the age of computerized layouts, a mistake can be rectified with one click of a button. Incredibly, not one of the errors I'd pointed out in 2008 had been corrected.*

The improbable rags-to-riches story that served as the denouement for Micky Ward's late career is an inspirational tale straight out of Hollywood—which is why, come to think of it, a movie based on the life and legend of the blood-and-guts Lowell junior welterweight is in production right now. While we wait on the film, Boston sportscaster Bob Halloran's new book *Irish Thunder: The Hard Life and Times of Micky Ward* has hit the stands.

A book chronicling Ward's saga ought to be a can't-miss proposition, but unfortunately, this one does. There are so many misspellings, factual errors, conflated memories, and faulty assumptions that the sum effect will likely prove only annoying to most knowledgeable fans. Boxers, who get hit in the head a lot, aren't expected to remember this stuff (that's why God invented BoxRec), but a professional journalist should be capable of checking his facts.

Although it's not all that's wrong with *Irish Thunder,* the problem can be encapsulated with one simple illustration, the recapitulation of the judges' scorecards from Micky's 2000 Foxwoods fight against Antonio Diaz, where the three scoring officials are described as "Tom *Pazmarek, Gwen* Feldman, and *Malvino* Lathan."

Tommy Kaczmarek, Glenn Feldman, and Melvina Lathan are among the most prominent boxing judges in the world, and must have scored close to a thousand title fights between them. The book manages not only to get all three names wrong but transgenders two of them.

Sloppy writing, or perhaps sloppy editing, seems to be the exception rather than the rule. The name of New England's most prominent boxing promoter, Jimmy Burchfield, is misspelled *(Birchfield)* throughout, as are names like Emanuel Steward *(Emmanuel)*, Pernell Whitaker *(Whittaker)*, former Globe sportswriter Ian Thomsen *(Thompsen)*, and even, in the index, the name of New England's most prominent mobster—James (Whitey) *Bulgar*. An episode in which Irish Micky's sister sucker-punched the wife of his manager, Sal LoNano, is correctly placed at Hampton Beach, but Halloran has it taking place before Ward's 2001 fight against Emmanuel Augustus rather than his 1997 bout against Jermal Corbin, when it actually happened.

And in a passage certain to amuse any reader who knows the first thing about boxing, the book describes the circumstances of Ward's fight against Diaz: "At the time, there were five championship belts, and the IBA's was the weakest and least prestigious of the group. Micky's WBU belt was fourth on the list."

Then as now, only four titles, those of the WBC, WBA, IBF, and WBO, were considered at all credible. If one were to expand the list to include every fly-by-night sanctioning body the count would have been closer to a dozen—and neither the IBA's nor the WBU's would have been in the top eight.

Ward's story deserves better. Here's hoping Marky-Mark Wahlberg has better luck when he has a go at it.

The Boston Herald
January 2008

Stallone Takes a Final Crack at Rocky

In 1976, Muhammad Ali engaged in what was arguably the last great fight of his career. Although he would soldier on for another five years, Ali won eight of fifteen rounds on all three scorecards in his memorable Yankee Stadium battle against Ken Norton that summer.

1976 was also the year of *Rocky* (or as we are now wont to describe it, *Rocky I*), Sylvester Stallone's uplifting drama about a down-on-his-luck pug who implausibly finds himself in a title bout and stuns the world by acquitting himself well, taking the reigning heavyweight champion right down to the wire.

If Ali remains the most recognizable boxing figure of the 20th century, Rocky Balboa, at least in the public consciousness, probably ranks a close second.

Stallone had drawn his inspiration for *Rocky,* which won the Academy Award for Best Picture that year (the defeated competition included *All the President's Men, Network,* and *Taxi Driver*), from a real-life title fight in Cleveland a year earlier, when a journeyman heavyweight named Chuck Wepner lasted until the 15th round against the great Ali. Wepner, who was known for reasons devoid of irony as "The Bayonne Bleeder," was even credited with a ninth-round knockdown.

On the evening of that bout, The Bayonne Bleeder presented his wife with a filmy blue negligee and instructed her to wear it later that night when, he promised, "you're gonna be sleeping with the heavyweight champion of the world."

Much later that night, having been taken first to a hospital to have his face stitched back together, Wepner stumbled back to his hotel room, to find his wife sitting up in bed wearing the filmy blue negligee.

"Well," Mrs. Wepner asked her husband, "is he coming up here, or do I have to go to *his* room?"

The success of the first *Rocky* film begat a regrettable series of sequels, each more preposterous than its predecessor. Over the next 14 years, Stallone appeared to be either dangerously deluded or engaged in the practice of self-parody, as Rocky Balboa won the heavyweight title in a rematch and then went on to engage a series of villainous opponents lifted straight from the pages of superhero comic books.

We could but shudder when Stallone announced his plans for a sixth *Rocky* movie, and as *Rocky Balboa*–30 years after *Rocky I* and 16 after *Rocky V*–moved into production in time for a Christmas release, debate raged over which was the worst idea of the year–another "Rocky" film or the O.J. Simpson book.

Just as the initial *Rocky* drew its inspiration from an authentic Ali episode, so did this latest incarnation.

In 1969, while Ali was serving out his three-and-a-half year banishment from the ring, he participated in the filming of what was advertised as a "computer fight" against the forty-five-year-old ex-champion, Rocky Marciano. The two spent countless hours sparring at Miami's Fifth Street Gym, preparing for every possible exigency. (Filming had to be stopped on a number of occasions because Ali repeatedly dislodged Marciano's toupee with jabs to the head.) Ostensibly neither man knew the outcome, which would be determined by the computer.

In its 1970 theatrical release in the United States, the computer had Marciano (who had been killed in a plane crash the previous August) winning on a 13th round TKO. Everywhere else in the world, Ali won.

The genesis here involves another "computer fight." After ESPN airs a virtual video bout pitting a champion of yesteryear (Rocky) against the current heavyweight king ("Mason Dixon," portrayed by then light-heavyweight champion Antonio Tarver), both men, egged on by rapacious promoters, are inspired to do it for real.

Rocky, his life barren and empty (Yo Adrian has joined Mick and Apollo in that big ring in the sky), is seeking fulfillment in a return to the ring. Dixon, though undefeated, has come under criticism for his reluctance to face even remotely dangerous opposition.

Tarver was not the initial choice to portray Mason Dixon, but Roy Jones Jr. proved as elusive in his negotiations with Stallone as he had been with proposed opponents and his television employers alike.

"There were like 31 unanswered phone calls to Roy Jones," recalled Stallone. "I was talking to one of the high-ranking officers at HBO, who said, 'Don't feel bad, we pay him and he doesn't return our calls, so join the family.'

"Antonio," said Stallone, "proved to be more reliable."

Alas, Tarver, in real life as witty a boxer as you're likely to meet, isn't given many good lines in *Rocky Balboa*. He reportedly partied so enthusiastically during the Las Vegas filming, which coincided with last year's Jermain Taylor-Bernard Hopkins middleweight championship fight, that by the time the movie was being edited he'd already lost to Hopkins.

Rocky, circa 2006, lives in the same Philadelphia row house, although over 30 years the turtles have grown somewhat larger. He spends his days pining over Adrian's grave and his nights telling the same tired old war stories to the customers of his South Philly restaurant.

Although there's not a hint of sexual tension, Rocky is provided a love interest in Marie, a barmaid he'd known as a girl. Marie has a son by a Jamaican father ("*Jamaica*," nods Rocky. "*A European, huh?*") and winds up with a job as a hostess at Rocky's restaurant (which serves, notes the aging Burt Young character Paulie, "Italian food cooked by Mexicans").

Muhammad Ali is sixty-four, and the notion that he would be allowed to engage in such a fight is utterly ridiculous. But Stallone (and, presumably, Rocky) is, at sixty, nearly as old.

Rocky is initially denied a boxing license (at a hearing presided over by the Philadelphia lawyer Jimmy Binns) but somehow prevails. (Whether as a result of his impassioned speech or because he crossed the commissioner's palm with silver remains unexplained.)

Although the Rocky-Dixon bout is labeled an "exhibition," nothing about it suggests anything other than a real fight. The participants don't wear headgear, and it takes place before a sellout crowd at the Mandalay Bay. It is presided over by a real-life commissioner (Nevada's Mark Ratner), with a real referee (Joe Cortez), and a trio of real judges, and it is broadcast by a trio of actual HBO announcers, Jim Lampley, Larry Merchant, and Max Kellerman.

It is even presented by a real promoter—Lou DiBella, who in a wonderful stroke of typecasting plays a promoter called Lou DiBella. Other touches of verisimilitude include the artist LeRoy Neiman sketching away at the weigh-in, and Mike Tyson woofing at Tarver from ringside.

The fight itself is every bit as brutal as those in any of the previous Rocky films. (In real life, Cortez would have stopped it at least half a dozen times.)

Both combatants are repeatedly pummeled to the floor. Now, anyone who truly loved a sixty-year-old boxer would have been shouting at him to stay down after each of these, but Rocky's son, Robert (Milo Ventimiglia), keeps encouraging his father to get back up and fight some more.

So, incredibly, does Marie. Portrayed by the Belfast-born actress Geraldine Hughes, Marie proves herself to be the bravest boxing consort this side of Cheryl McCullough as she urges the bloodied Italian Stallion back into the fray.

The judges, by the way, should all have been impeached. Despite the multiplicity of knockdowns, all three of them submit scorecards of 95-94 in a split decision verdict, suggesting that each of them ignored all but one of the knockdowns.

When we pointed out this scoring discrepancy to DiBella, the promoter shrugged and replied "Hey, remember, it's only a movie."

Rocky Balboa, which opened in American theaters last week, isn't very good, but it's probably not among the three or four worst *Rocky* films ever made.

After we attended a screening last week, a few of us repaired to an Irish saloon near Madison Square Garden, where DiBella summarized his acting debut by noting that "the original *Rocky* was an inspiration and drew me to the boxing business.

"I should be pretty decent playing myself, but I'm not planning on quitting my day job," said the promoter, who added that it had been "an honor" to participate in the making of the last *Rocky* movie.

"And what," I had to ask him, "makes you so sure it's the last one?"

TheSweetScience.com
December 2006

Deconstructing the Champ

Two New Films Explore the Metamorphosis from Clay to Ali

Full disclosure here: Not only did I participate in **Muhammad Ali: Champion of the World,** *but the interviews with both me and Thomas Hauser were conducted by my wife's former husband in my New York home. Following the wholesale shake-up at* **Nightline** *occasioned by the 2005 retirement of host Ted Koppel, David Marash signed on with the Washington-based English-language channel operated by Al Jazeera. The never-aired Ali documentary (produced by Dave's present wife, Amy Bowers) is the legacy of that brief association. I'd been trying to figure out how I was going to write about a film no reader was likely ever to see when Chip Namias, a friend going back to his days as a PR man for several NFL teams, phoned to ask if I'd like to see an advance copy of* **PBS'** **Made in Miami.** *The astute reader may note that I evidently liked the Hauser quote that ends this story so much that I recycled it in the* **Irish Times** *piece anticipating Ali's 2009 visit to Ireland that opens this book. My excuse is that since Tom said it to Dave in my living room, I should be able to use it as many times as I want.*

Although Muhammad Ali's 1964 stoppage of Sonny Liston and his Rumble in the Jungle knockout of George Foreman ten years later are both depicted in Dave Marash's *Muhammad Ali: Champion of the World,* the seminal moment of the best Ali film you'll never see doesn't take place in the boxing ring at all.

Rather, moments after the 1966-era Ali is heard to murmur "No, I will not go," Marash's voice-over notes, that singular act "turned a boxing champion into a *moral* champion."

Ali isn't just the most recognizable figure on the planet, but the most written-about. In fact, the most astonishing aspect of the field of contemporary

Ali scholarship isn't that there's so much of it, but that it continues to proliferate. It's been 27 years since the man last took a punch, but a decidedly unscientific survey recently undertaken suggests that Ali has been the subject of at least 100 books, with more new titles forthcoming each year.

The most fascinating personality of his era, Ali has been deconstructed in books by Norman Mailer, Budd Schulberg, José Torres, Wilfred Sheed, George Plimpton, and David Remnick, not to mention five, at last count, by Thomas Hauser, the pre-eminent Ali scholar. Amazon.com lists titles from the German-produced G.O.A.T. (retail price $4,500, but discounted by Amazon to a more reasonable $3,906.65) to a bound copy of the Clay vs. the United States transcript (36 cents).

There are Ali legal studies, Ali biographies, and a whole host of Ali children's books, and when you switch to the DVD section the numbers multiply even further. Ali has not only been the subject of films (2001's *Ali,* starring Will Smith) and documentaries *(When We Were Kings)* but has acted in several of them himself, ranging from his small role in *Requiem for a Heavyweight* (1962, with Anthony Quinn) to his title role in the monumentally silly biopic *The Greatest* (1977, with sixty-year-old Ernest Borgnine playing the forty-year-old Angelo Dundee) to 1979's *Freedom Road,* in which Ali, as an emancipated slave turned Reconstruction-era Congressman, co-starred with former West Point (and Oxford) boxer Kris Kristofferson.

Between instructional videos, old fight libraries, and digitalizations of the aforementioned movies, the number of available Ali DVDs stretches into the hundreds, but just when you think the world could hardly bear one more, two new ones recently came across our desk, each fresh enough in its approach that even Ali scholars would be likely to learn something from each of them.

Preceded by a nationwide publicity blitz, *Muhammad Ali: Made in Miami* debuted last August, when it simultaneously aired on PBS stations around the country. The documentary (the title comes from Dr. Ferdie Pacheco's observation that "Cassius Clay was born in Louisville, but Muhammad Ali was made in Miami") has been shown several times since and, unless we badly miss our guess, is destined to a long shelf life as a pledge-week staple around the country, with the possible exception of Louisville, where they have their own axes to grind. (Back on August 12, the night *Made in Miami* premiered in most markets, KET2, the educational TV outlet in Louisville, in a neat bit of counter-programming, preceded it by showing yet another documentary, one entitled *Louisville's Own Ali.*)

Ali's Miami sojourn commenced not long after his gold-medal triumph at the 1960 Rome Olympics, when the Louisville Group, a consortium of white businessmen who had pooled resources to underwrite his professional career, packed him off to South Florida to train under the aegis of Dundee, the man they had selected for that role.

Although Ali's October 29, 1960, pro debut against Tunney Hunsaker took place in Louisville, his next four fights were on Chris Dundee cards in Miami Beach, as were his 1962 fight against Don Warner and his epochal '64 challenge to Liston.

And while the Fifth Street Gym in Miami Beach was the epicenter of Ali's professional life during this period, his interaction with the black community across the causeway in Overtown also had its profound impact.

While he had been confident in Rome, teammates from that era recall him as shy and self-effacing. His Miami period profoundly affected his development. Patterning himself after the wrestler Gorgeous George, he fashioned a brash public image that offended some boxing purists and resulted in his being rechristened as "The Louisville Lip."

"No boxer," notes Marash, whose film was produced for Al Jazeera but never aired, "has ever been a better salesman."

At the same time, on a parallel track, his experiences in Overtown (described in the Miami film as "Harlem South") helped formulate his identity as a black man in 1960s America.

In Miami Beach, Ali the boxer spent his time with Dundee, his trainer, and Pacheco, his physician and confidante, and it was there that he had his celebrated encounter with the Beatles. In the ghetto, on the other hand, he found himself intrigued by the tenets of Nation of Islam founder Elijah Muhammad, and increasingly under the spell of the man who was at the time Elijah's most visible deputy, Malcolm X.

This formative stage of Ali's life, which would ultimately lead to his conversion—initially to Elijah's Nation, although he would eventually (long after Malcolm's murder) embrace a more orthodox interpretation of Islam more attuned to that of his slain onetime mentor.

While the distinction is less clear in *Made in Miami*, David Remnick notes of the same period to Marash, "I don't think he had his heart in the separatist rhetoric," and Marash himself describes the schism with Malcolm as one "Ali regrets to this day."

Two years later, Ali's newly discovered religious beliefs would directly presage his refusal to participate in the Vietnam War, an act of conscience for which he would pay dearly. Stripped of his heavyweight championship and denied a license to box for nearly three and a half years, Ali would sit on the sidelines as what should have been the prime of his career passed him by. All of this is captured in *Made in Miami,* a 60-minute presentation co-written by Alan Tomlinson and Gaspar Gonzalez.

Having already been widely aired, *Muhammad Ali: Made in Miami* is available for purchase both on Amazon.com and from PBS Films. Its companion 2008 contribution to the Ali oeuvre, Marash's *Muhammad Ali: Champion of the World* has yet to be viewed by audiences in America or anywhere else, and probably never will be.

If *Made in Miami* was conceptually geared toward an American PBS viewership, Marash's film was meant to air worldwide on Al Jazeera's various outlets, where it would have reached a predominantly Islamic audience, and although he dealt with some of the same principals (Hauser appears prominently in both) Tomlinson and Ortega did for the PBS documentary, there are stops in inner-city gyms and mosques in both Louisville and Washington, and interviews with both prominent and ordinary American Muslims in an attempt to place the iconic champion in perspective.

"My concept was to focus on the Ali of most interest to Al Jazeera's audience, heavily weighted towards Middle Eastern, African and Asian viewers for whom his cultural, religious, and moral values trumped his athletic prowess," said Marash. "Part of my intent was to show, in particular, that America has a significant Islamic community, for whom Ali is a figure of adoration, an exemplar in the full sense of the word."

Marash had originally been assigned to produce a pre-obit. One of the dirty little secrets of the news business, the pre-obit is a means of assembling material about a subject so that it can be comprehensively, and almost instantaneously, aired at the time of his demise. It is the media's version of the Dead Pool.

But the more material he collected on his subject, the more Marash was enthralled by it, and he eventually came to realize that the film he was creating would be better suited as a testament to a beloved and living figure, than a tribute to a dead one. He eventually persuaded Al Jazeera to let him expand his labor of love into a half-hour documentary, but just about the time he was wrapping up the piece, Steve Clark, the British-born news director of Al Jazeera English who had green-lighted the project, was sent packing. Within a few weeks he was followed out the door by Marash himself.

"Unfortunately, for bureaucratic reasons of no particular interest to anyone outside the business, its production schedule slipped, and by the time it was ready to air, I was on the banana peel myself. My guess is that our Ali show will never air," said Marash, who along with his wife, Amy, is spending this year teaching journalism at Shantou Technical University in China. "I think [Al Jazeera] would be loath to put anything with my name and face on their air now.

"In the event of Ali's death, AJE might run the show—or lift parts of it and have someone else re-voice my narration," supposed Marash. "But even that strikes me as extremely unlikely."

Although one was made with PBS backing for a domestic audience and the other with Arab petrodollars and geared toward Muslims around the world, Ali's religion is central to the theme of both films.

If the Ali of today is the world's most prominent, and surely most beloved, Muslim, *Made in Miami* confirms that in 1965 his impending conversion was treated as a dirty little secret. The promoters of the Liston fight were concerned that Clay's dalliance with the Nation of Islam might have a devastating effect on the box office, and in his memoirs, fight publicist Harold Conrad recalls that his principal brief became a matter of keeping Elijah Muhammad's and Malcolm X's names out of the papers.

At one point shortly before the Liston fight, Chris Dundee and his co-promoter, Bill McDonald, summoned Cassius Clay to a closed-door meeting, from which the boxer emerged convinced that the fight might be called off.

"They want me to say I'm not a Muslim," Ali told Angelo Dundee. "I can't do that."

Although his brother was one of the fight's promoters, the trainer did not attempt to remonstrate with his charge.

"Do what you've gotta do," he told Clay.

"One thing I learned a long time ago about handling boxers," Dundee recently recalled the episode, "is that you don't get involved with a kid's personal life, and you don't get involved with his religion, 'cause you're gonna lose on both counts."

Despite his hands-off approach to Clay's religious preferences, Dundee admits that on one occasion he tried to have Malcolm X tossed out of the Fifth Street Gym.

"I only saw Malcolm once, when he came to one of the kid's workouts," said Dundee. "There were quite a few people there, but I'd seen his picture in the papers and of course I knew who he was."

Dundee summoned the boxer's brother, Rudy Clay (who would later become Rahman Ali), with instructions to "ask that guy to leave.

"Rudy looked at me and said 'You tell him,'" recalled Dundee. "I wasn't going to do that, so he stayed.

"But," insisted Dundee, "that had nothing to do with religion. I just didn't want to inject some controversy that might backfire on us. I'd learned that years before, when I took Willie Pastrano to Scotland to fight Chick Calderwood. Willie and I were both Catholics, and one day before the fight a local priest came along and had his picture taken with Pastrano. I had no idea how controversial that would be in Glasgow, but after it ran in the local papers, we couldn't have won that fight with a gun."

Ali's performance at the weigh-in prior to the Liston fight in Miami is recalled in both films.

"I never knew if it was an act, or if he was half-nuts," Jimmy Breslin tells Marash.

Both DVDs make reference to Dundee's critical role in the first Liston fight, when Ali, blinking back tears after a mysterious substance materialized in his eyes, wanted to quit and ordered his trainer, "Cut the gloves off!" at the end of the fourth round.

"Cut the gloves off?" Dundee recalled his reaction. "In a pig's eye. This was for the heavyweight championship of the world!"

Although there is no doubt that a foreign substance had caused the fighter's discomfort ("I stuck my pinkie finger in his eye and stuck it in my own eye, and it burned," said Dundee), the trainer was confident that Ali's eyes would eventually clear once he rinsed them out with a sponge.

A common supposition at the time, and one that has persisted in boxing lore to this day, is that the mystery substance was part of a nefarious plot, and had been transmitted to Ali via Sonny's gloves.

"I don't buy that it deliberately came from Liston's gloves," said Dundee. "For one thing, I did have the gloves checked. I told Drew Brown to go check the gloves, but the referee (Barney Felix) actually checked them himself."

Dundee thinks an alternate theory—that the burning sensation was caused by an alcohol-based liniment Liston's corner applied to the champion's shoulders between rounds—is plausible, but his own view is that the root of the problem probably lay in the cut Ali had opened up across Liston's brow earlier in the fight.

"I think it was more likely that Joe Polino (the cut man working Liston's corner with Willie Reddish that night) had used Monsel solution on Liston's cut, and it got transferred to Muhammad's gloves," said Dundee.

Monsel is an iron sulfate—based haemostatic coagulant, initially developed by the military to staunch wounds. Monsel had theoretically been outlawed by 1964, but it would have been the rare cut man who didn't keep an emergency supply in his bag for cuts that did not respond to more conventional treatment.

"It was a nasty cut, and you can see on film that it was more blackish than red, which is an indication that they probably used Monsel on it," said Dundee.

Folklore has it that after rinsing Ali's eyes out with the sponge, Dundee saved the day by literally throwing the reluctant fighter back into the ring, but once again the trainer modestly demurs.

"They say I picked him up off the stool, but I never did that," Dundee insisted. "I made him stand up even before the bell."

Surely there is an irony in the fact that by the dawn of the 21st century, Muhammad Ali had more to say than at any previous time of his life, but between the ravages of Parkinson's and the medication to control the disease, could speak only with great difficulty.

"Now," Howard Bingham tells Marash, "*they* speak to *him*."

For a generation more familiar with the barely auditory Ali of recent years, the fast-talking, wise-cracking repartee of the young Clay of *Made in Miami* may come as something of a revelation.

Although there is no narrator per se in *Made in Miami,* Dundee became the point man in the publicity blitz that preceded its August premiere.

As Ali's career-long trainer noted of his agreement to serve as a spokesman for the PBS documentary, "I'm talking now because the kid can't talk too well these days. But back then, I couldn't get a word in edgewise."

At the same time, noted Dundee, by the time the 1960 Olympic gold medalist came under his wing at the old Fifth Street Gym, his razor-like wit was still a work in progress.

"He was almost completely self-taught," recalled Dundee. "Remember, he barely got out of high school, and probably wouldn't have even graduated if it hadn't been for his accomplishments in the ring. When he'd go to sign an autograph back then, anything over five letters he was in trouble. But he soaked up knowledge like a sponge, and he got glib and sharp being around newspaper guys like Pat Putnam."

Now in his eighty-ninth year and in semi-retirement, Dundee seemed in his element as he revisited old friends in his role as spokesman for *Made in Miami,* and even came up with a few fresh anecdotes for the elucidation of his audience.

At the time he was approached by the Louisville Group to train Ali, of course, Dundee had already made his mark, with Carmen Basilio in New York, Willie Pastrano and Ralph Dupas from New Orleans, and with the Cuban-born champions Sugar Ramos and Luis Rodriguez, whom he trained once he followed brother Chris to South Florida and set up shop there.

"In those early days, as a rule I didn't even let Muhammad spar with heavyweights," recalled Dundee. "He was so much quicker than any other heavyweight that it wouldn't have done him any good. They'd only have slowed him down. So we concentrated on his speed by putting him in with smaller, faster guys."

An obvious exception to this practice occurred in 1961, when heavy-weight champion Ingemar Johansson came to Miami for his rematch with Floyd Patterson. In a celebrated sparring session at the Fifth Street Gym, the nineteen-year-old Clay taunted Johansson, who was unable to lay a glove on him in the two rounds they boxed before the embarrassed Swede's handlers terminated the workout.

In his second pro fight, Clay had knocked out local heavyweight Herb Siler. Siler had bounced back and was 11-3 when Ernie Terrell came to town to face him in the first of their two fights. Terrell also trained at the Fifth Street, but, said Dundee, "I wouldn't let Muhammad spar with him."

Some might suggest that Dundee had other reasons for not exposing his young prospect, but, said the trainer in a recollection that will be of small comfort to Ingemar Johansson, "Ali never won a fight in the gym anyway. He was one of the worst gym fighters in the world."

Dundee's reference was to the Cassius Clay of Miami and 45 years ago. In the other film, the contemporary Ali is described (by Remnick) as "a Buddha," and (by Marash himself) as "a living deity."

Early on in *Champion of the World,* Ali is heard to reflect, "I always said growing up as a little boy I would do things to help my people that other people couldn't do," but, as his biographer points out later in that film, Ali apparently did not anticipate the manner in which his post-career celebrity would endure.

"He always thought that once he stopped boxing, people would forget him," Hauser tells Marash. "He really didn't understand how important he was."

Boxing Digest
2008

A Look Inside Tyson's Head

In the quarter-century I've known him, I've been exposed to the multifaceted creature that is Mike Tyson from every conceivable angle: the raging animal, the frightened boy-child, the sensitive boxer with the soul of a poet.

I've seen the ghetto thug and the sensitive father, the profligate spender who walks into a dealership and orders half a dozen matching Bentleys for his entourage and the victimized boxer who wakes up in the morning to discover that his trusted allies have looted him for a hundred million while he wasn't looking.

I've seen the indestructible fighting machine who became the youngest heavyweight champion in history and the flabby, undertrained specimen who quit on his stool against Kevin McBride two decades later. I've watched him rage against colleagues he called "white faggot motherfuckers" and I've been a guest in his house. I've seen him bawl like a baby at the death of a trusted advisor, and I've seen him rail, years later, at how the same man "exploited" him financially. I've seen the contrite Tyson and the boastful Tyson.

I was there when he was being outfitted in a jeweled crown, an ermine robe, and a scepter for a *Sports Illustrated* photo shoot, and I've been there when he was led out of a courtroom in handcuffs. I've seen him almost breathtakingly eloquent, and moments later evince the naïveté of a five-year-old child. I've seen him parade through Las Vegas casinos trailed by an entourage of 30, and I've sat, alone with him on a balcony, and watched him blink back tears as he told me he "had no friends."

I've also personally watched him bite two people, gnawing on one guy's ears and taking a chunk, with his gold-capped teeth, out of another's leg. This entire range of emotions is on display in the 90 minutes it takes to watch *Tyson,* the James Toback–directed documentary that opened in limited release last weekend. Roughly 90% of the film consists of a sometimes brutally honest monologue in which the one-time Baddest Man on the Planet lays bare his soul.

Four years after he last laced on gloves, Tyson remains an enigmatic, controversial, and polarizing figure about whom almost everyone has an opinion, and my guess is that some of those opinions may even be altered by some previously unconsidered aspect of this tortured soul laid bare in the film.

There were even a couple of surprises for me. One was Tyson's confession that on the night he knocked out Trevor Berbick, at the age of twenty, to win the heavyweight title, he was painfully suffering from an untreated dose of gonorrhea because he was too shy to approach a doctor. The other comes near the end of the film when Tyson, shown walking alone on a California beach, recites "The Ballad of Reading Gaol." I knew Mike's taste in poetry ran the gamut from Chairman Mao to 2 Live Crew, but who would have guessed he'd read Oscar Wilde's, much less committed it to memory?

Tyson was well received at both the Cannes and Sundance festivals, and was critically praised by the *New York Times* prior to its opening last Friday. The early returns at the box office, on the other hand, haven't exactly produced Tysonesque numbers: the weekend of the premiere saw it playing in 11 theatres in New York and Los Angeles, where interest would presumably run higher than in Middle America, and the three-day gross was an underwhelming $85,000.

As genuine as his self-effacing confessional might be, there is also the sense that a guy who learned to cheat and scheme just to survive his Brownsville adolescence may have spent all these weeks in front of Toback's camera just to set us all up for one big con. This comes midway through the film when Tyson addresses the singularly most defining episode of his life. Having confessed almost every imaginable sin and character defect (and claimed that "if I have any anger, and if it's directed at anyone, it's directed at myself"), he then defines himself as the victim in the 1993 rape case that put him behind bars at what should have been the prime of his boxing career.

"I was falsely accused of raping that wretched swine of a woman, Desiree Washington," says Tyson in *Tyson*. Describing his conviction and incarceration as "the most horrible time of my life," he laments that it "took away my humanity and my reputation."

His reputation? The evidence of Tyson's guilt was so overwhelming that at his trial not even his lawyers tried to claim he hadn't done it. Rather, they mounted a defense suggesting that his reputation as a violent sexual predator was so widely known that a woman who would return with him to his hotel room should have expected to be raped.

Describing himself as "coarse and crass," Tyson acknowledges his proclivity for what he euphemistically describes as "taking advantage of women" in the film, but denies having done so in Washington's case.

Tyson's denial here is not persuasive, but you have to suspect that maybe he thinks it is.

But considering that it consists, in essence, of an hour-and-a-half long monologue by one talking head, it's a pretty fascinating glimpse inside that head, and Tyson's description of Don King alone—"he was supposed to be my black brother, but he's just a wretched, slimy, reptilian motherfucker"—is worth the price of admission.

Toback has taken some artistic liberties with chronology that will probably be disconcerting to boxing fans. Footage from old Tyson spots cut back and forth to shots of him conferring with father-figure Cus D'Amato in the Catskill gym, even though Cus was dead and buried when some of the fights depicted took place. If you want to watch *Tyson,* you might have to wait a month or so until the DVD comes out.

The Irish Times
April 2009

Chapter III—At Ringside

Tyson Makes Golota Quit

I'm not sure to this day why anyone actually thought this fight might end any way other than the way it did. Less than a year earlier Golota had quit against Michael Grant when things stopped going his way, even though he had a commanding lead on the scorecards, and it seemed apparent that he was ready to quit against Lennox Lewis even before the first bell rang. A few years later, when John Ruiz came back from two early knockdowns to win a decision, Golota seemed very proud of the fact that he hadn't quit. His disgraceful performance notwithstanding, Golota's record suffered no more than did Tyson's from this fight. When Mike's post-fight specimen tested positive for marijuana the result was changed to No Contest.

AUBURN HILLS, Mich.—An hour after Andrew Golota had walked right out of the ring and, almost certainly, right out of boxing, Al Certo was trying to make sense of it.

"I'd been saying before this fight that one guy was gonna wear the pants in the ring and one guy was gonna wear the skirt," sighed the veteran trainer. "And I hadda wind up with the skirt."

Nigde ventze.

That's Polish for *No mas.*

Those of us who had been calling Golota The Foul Pole had it wrong all along. It should have been the Polish Fowl.

Mike Tyson was even angrier than Certo. Once he realized Golota was running up the white flag, Iron Mike had to be restrained from chasing him out of the ring.

"You little shit," snarled Tyson as trainer Tommy Brooks held onto him.

He had it wrong there. Golota is many things, but "little" isn't one of them—unless you're talking about his heart, which is apparently the size of a proton, or his brain, which may be even smaller.

From the moment the match was made, this was a fight that begged for a bizarre outcome, but who could have suspected that Golota's fragile psyche could have been so easily triggered? Fortunately for the loser, the battalion of security forces on hand at the Palace Friday night had prudently run the crowd through metal detectors and confiscated the obvious weaponry. Otherwise Golota might have been seriously hurt. As it was, the crowd of 16,228 pelted his disgraceful retreat with beer, soda, popcorn, and wadded-up programs, and Golota's Polish supporters, who had shown themselves more than eager to do battle with those of Riddick Bowe in the aftermath of the 1996 disqualification at Madison Square Garden, this time were among the more enthusiastic Golota abusers.

The strange outcome—it can hardly be described as "stunning," since Golota had carved out a well-established pattern of quitting, one way or the other, in the past—left Tyson in a most unaccustomed position: that of the aggrieved party.

"I think Mike was a bit unfulfilled," said advisor Shelly Finkel. "He wanted to knock him out, and he would have if the fight had continued.

"Mike realized this fight had to be controversy-free," explained Finkel, "and he did his part. He held up his end of the bargain."

The two combatants' penchant for controversy, of course, was the very cornerstone upon which the whole promotion was based, but considering that this was Mike Tyson and Andrew Golota at work, the six minutes the fight did last were relatively clean.

And if Tyson wasn't exactly the Tyson of old, he redeemed himself somewhat with his brief ring performance, fighting with more discipline than has characterized his recent outings. He bobbed. He weaved. He turned a six-inch height differential to his own advantage, fighting from a crouch that added leverage to his punches as he sprang forth to land on his cumbersome opponent.

Golota fought back. His one-two combinations might be ungainly, but he is large enough that even when he grazed Tyson, Mike knew he had been hit. Golota also did his best to neutralize Tyson's forward charges by enveloping him in a series of bear-hug clinches.

Golota seemed to be holding his own for most of the first round, even though he had sprung a leak above his left eye midway through the stanza. (A head-butt, claimed Golota; a right hand, maintained Team Tyson.) Then, with seconds left in the round, Golota missed with a lazy jab, and Tyson uncorked a vicious right hand that knocked him on the seat of his pants.

Golota bounced straight back up, and the bell ending the round sounded before referee Frank Garza could complete the mandatory 8-count.

Although it was apparent to neither the crowd nor the ringside observers on press row, Golota had tried to quit even then, and Certo had his hands full just getting him back out for the second round.

Midway through the second, Tyson attempted to dislodge himself from a Golota embrace with a well-placed head aimed straight at Golota's chin. He missed, and the blatant attempt at a butt drew not so much as a stern glance from the referee.

Although Tyson continued to land in the second, he was increasingly wild, and Golota connected with some shots of his own, which is what made what happened next so surprising.

Well before the bell opening the third came due, Golota wandered over to a neutral corner. As it turned out, he had taken refuge there in order to resist Certo's attempts to put his mouthpiece in, but of course none of us knew that at the time.

Neither did Garza. When the referee approached Golota to steer him back to his own corner, the Polish Fowl gave him a shove and said, "I quit."

Golota reluctantly returned to his corner, where ensued the most lively exchange of the evening—a wrestling match between the septuagenarian trainer and the 240-pound heavyweight, as Certo tried to shove the mouthpiece down his throat and simultaneously shove his fighter back into the ring.

"What are you doing? What are you *doing*?" shouted the exasperated trainer as Golota stubbornly turned his head from side to side in the manner of a baby resisting its bottle.

Golota quickly slinked out of the ring and beat a hasty retreat in the direction of his dressing room as the patrons showered him with stale beer. Shortly thereafter, a frustrated Tyson departed with similar alacrity. Neither boxer appeared in the post-fight interview room, although Golota submitted to a brief dressing room Q&A on Showtime, one which proved almost as bewildering as his abrupt surrender.

"It wasn't my day today," stammered Golota, seemingly near tears. "The referee didn't respond as he was supposed to: Boxing is a very tough sport. I'm sorry for all my fans who count on me."

But then Golota, who was shortly packed off to Pontiac-Oakland Hospital to have his cuts sutured, wasn't making much sense. He also claimed that the devastating first-round knockdown had been a "slip."

Golota "should not be licensed in any country on this planet," fumed Showtime boxing boss Jay Larkin, whose network bankrolled the fight and charged customers $49.95 to watch it. "He's a coward, a dog, and he'll never fight on Showtime again."

"I never would have expected this from Golota," said Brooks, whose father-in-law, Lou Duva, once trained the Polish joke. "I think he suffers from anxiety attacks—and I think he was having one tonight."

Tyson had claimed several times in the days preceding the bout that the Golota fight would be his last, and Finkel said afterward "at this moment that holds true."

Whether Tyson was sincere in his feelings is somewhat immaterial. If he didn't fight again, he wouldn't even have the wherewithal to pay the taxes on the $10 million he earned for this fight, and he is essentially indentured to Showtime, which has a lien on virtually everything he owns, for the rest of his natural life.

Besides, as Tyson himself has pointed out, if he quits boxing, what *is* he going to do? Take up rocket science?

Finkel suggested that if Tyson were to keep fighting, his next bout would be for a title, either against the Lennox Lewis-David Tua winner, or a third meeting with old foe Evander Holyfield, but that view may be overly optimistic. While Tyson may have redeemed himself somewhat with his brief performance against Golota, he didn't exactly display the skills one would normally associate with a top-level heavyweight. But then, money talks.

BoxingRanks.com
October 2000

Savage Beating by Lewis
Ends Tyson's Claims as a Pretender

Tyson put up a better fight at the New York press conference than he would in the ring against Lewis. When a melee broke out after Tyson took a swing at one of Lewis' bodyguards at the Hudson Theatre, Tyson took a bite out of Lennox's leg that cost him $335,000, and WBC president José Sulaiman was also injured in the scuffle. (Unfortunately, his injuries were not life-threatening.) In a profanity-laced rant, Tyson called internet scribe Scoop Malinowski a "faggot," and offered to copulate with him on the spot. (Scoop declined.) The upshot of it was that most states, including Nevada, wanted no part of the fight, which is how it wound up in Memphis. The Lewis fight was indeed Tyson's last as a useful boxer. He had just three more fights. In the first of these he knocked out an absolutely petrified Orlin Norris in 49 seconds, but when he lost back-to-back fights to Danny Williams and Kevin McBride, even Mike could recognize that it was over.

MEMPHIS—Once Lennox Lewis took over the fight in Saturday night's second round, it became apparent what a mismatch was unfolding. The heavyweight champion at work was a disciplined master beating the rage out of an unruly pet, and did such a good job of domesticating him that when the end came, a surprisingly civil Mike Tyson appeared dangerously close to having been housebroken.

When closure arrived with Tyson, bleeding from both eyes and his nostrils, stretched out on the canvas being counted out by referee Eddie Cotton, Lewis strutted about the ring, pounding on his chest with his left glove.

"This is my defining fight," he proclaimed. "It's what the whole world wanted."

Perhaps not the whole world, but at least that portion of it which had decided that Saturday night's match-up constituted a morality play.

Lewis had promised to "rid boxing of its last misfit," and he may have done just that. Although the contracts Lewis and Tyson signed for Saturday night's heavyweight championship fight at the Pyramid provided for a re-match, Lewis' performance was so decisive and Tyson's so, well, toothless, that there are few compelling reasons for them to stage a reprise, or for the rest of us to watch it.

Saturday night's fight may not only have ended Tyson's championship pretensions, it may have signaled the end of his career as a useful boxer.

After battering and pulverizing Tyson over the last seven rounds of the eight it lasted, Lewis waved an extended left arm in Tyson's face and crushed him with a roundhouse overhand right, and the onetime "Baddest Man on the Planet" was counted out at 2:25 of the eighth.

From the second round on it was apparent that Tyson was but a shell of the dangerous fighter who burst onto the heavyweight scene 17 years ago.

Lewis, in registering his 40th professional win against two losses and a draw (all three of which were avenged in subsequent rematches), completely dominated Tyson, landing 109 jabs and 84 power punches, most of them right uppercuts that Tyson was unable to avoid.

The upset, if there was one, was that Tyson, in Lewis' words, "took it like a man" and did not resort to the foul tactics many among the announced crowd of 15,327 had come half-expecting to witness. There were no bites, no scratches, no arm-breaking attempts in the clinches, and by the time Tyson aimed a couple of punches at Lewis' scrotum late in the fight, he was too spent to do any damage to even that tender spot.

The one-sided beating may have pleased the more sadistic among Lewis' army of supporters, but it did little to whet the appetite of the public for an-other fight between the two.

Lewis is next obligated to defend the IBF portion of his championship against that organization's top-rated contender Chris Byrd, and assuming he gets past that mandatory defense would then theoretically be free to fight Tyson again. But selling the reprise as a competitive match would tax the imagination of showman P.T. Barnum.

For nearly a dozen years now, Tyson has been more sideshow freak than legitimate threat, and even those who clung to that delusion will by now have been disabused.

Finding a site for Lewis-Tyson II wouldn't be a problem. Some box-ing backwater will always be willing to follow Memphis' example and risk bankrupting its fortunes by underwriting the fight as a civic endeavor, although it is unlikely any venue would match the $12.5 million site fee Memphis posted for this one.

If all else failed, one could always take the fight to Lewis' native Britain, where the boxing public is so gullible they'll believe almost anything as long as it involves one of their own. (See Naseem Hamed, et al.)

The larger problem would lie in selling a rematch to the living-room consumers who pay the freight in the world of contemporary boxing economics.

The pay-per-view telecast of Lewis-Tyson was priced at a world-record $54.95, and while Saturday night's sales were brisk, most viewers grudgingly shelled out to watch what they had been persuaded was a once-in-a-lifetime opportunity.

Fooling them again would take some doing, and the notion of persuading Lewis (who contractually would earn the better end of a 60/40 split in any rematch) to fight Tyson at a reduced price seems fancifully unlikely.

There is no earthly reason to suppose that the outcome would be any different the second time around, but that having been said, in a very odd senso, Tyson, on the strength of bravery alone, probably deserves a second fight more than he deserved the first one.

If his number one ranking (by the World Boxing Council) was demonstrated to be a sham illustrative of boxing politics at its worst, he is at the same time probably no worse than many among today's poor crop of heavyweights likely to come knocking at Lewis' door.

"Anything is possible," allowed Lewis when asked about the possibility of Tyson II. "If the public demands it, we should do it."

If the public demands it, the public should have its collective heads examined.

The Irish Times
June 2002

Duddy—Puddy Smackdown at MSG

While matching a 15-0 boxer against one who was 21-2-1 might have seemed competitive on paper, you didn't need to know a whole lot about boxing to realize how illusory that was. Even though Duddy had yet to be seriously tested, the level of opposition he had faced was several steps above the fare at the Sioux casinos. The result represented another triumph for the ingenious matchmaking of Jim Borzell. The Pudwill "fight" headlined the first card of what Irish Ropes turned into a St. Patrick's Day tradition at the Theatre, and for each of the next three years Duddy headlined a card on the weekend of Ireland's national holiday. The practice might have continued indefinitely, but by 2008 Irish Ropes decided Duddy had outgrown the Theatre, and by 2009 Duddy decided he had outgrown Irish Ropes. Neither turned out very well.

NEW YORK—The Duddy-and-Puddy show itself lasted just 1:31, and most of that minute and a half was consumed by the time it took Shelby Pudwill to repeatedly hoist himself up off the floor.

Much to the delight of a loud, raucous, and overwhelmingly Irish crowd, Ireland's John Duddy made short work of the visitor from North Dakota at the sold-out Madison Square Garden Theatre Thursday night, finishing off his opponent before the stroke of midnight officially signaled the advent of St. Patrick's Day.

And give this to Irish Ropes: These guys sure know how to throw a party. After hooking on with other promoters for Duddy's first 15 fights, they embarked on their own maiden promotional voyage for his 16th, and the result was what rival promoter Lou DiBella enviously estimated to have been "the biggest-grossing club-fight show in New York boxing history."

Duddy came away with rave reviews after his stunning, three-knockdown KO of Pudwill, who had come to New York with a 21-2-1 record and left it an embarrassed young man.

Not thirty seconds into the bout, Duddy caught Pudwill with a solid left hook to the temple, whose effect was multiplied by the fact that he was moving forward when he threw it. Duddy kept moving and walked right over his fallen foe. It was as if he had hit him and then used him for a doormat.

"He done well to get up from that one," recalled the middleweight from Derry. "I could see when he did get up that his legs weren't too good, so I just let my punches go."

In short order Pudwill was down again, but after referee Wayne Kelly administered the mandatory 8-count and allowed him to continue, Duddy smashed him with a right that thudded off the side of his head, and Kelly stopped the fight even before Pudwill hit the canvas.

The abrupt conclusion set off a wild celebration among the audience, but the ease with which he handled his opponent appeared to surprise even the protagonist himself.

"Never in my wildest dreams did I think I was going to walk into Madison Square Garden and knock out a guy with 21 wins in the first round," said Duddy.

Duddy, somewhat overmatched to begin with, could have been forgiven if he was intimidated as early as the introduction, when the audience drowned out the ring announcer with an ungodly din reminiscent of the heyday of Barry McGuigan fighting in Belfast.

His last outing, a lopsided decision over Haiti's Julio Jean in Boston, had left some skeptics wondering if Duddy didn't get hit too much for his own good. That wasn't a problem on this night. Pudwill never laid a glove on him.

The announced attendance was 5,038, capacity in the Garden Theatre, and that count was probably modest. Duddy was preceded into the ring by a pipe band from Donegal. The Sam McGuire Cup—Ireland's version of the Vince Lombardi Trophy—was even paraded into the ring by its current custodians from Tyrone. And, in lieu of scantily clad round-card girls, Irish Ropes saw to it that that duty was performed by step-dancers in native costume.

Pudwill became the 14th of Duddy's 16 victims to have been prematurely dispatched, and the 9th who failed to survive the first round. The Irishman won something called the WBC Continental Americas middleweight championship for his brief night's work, and while the title itself might be insignificant, it is likely to leapfrog him several places in the world ratings.

Not everyone appears to be convinced that is necessarily a beneficial career move.

"No question he can punch, and he's a great prospect," opined DiBella.

"But I'm not sure he's a top ten middleweight right now. That's a problem: They [Irish Ropes] are moving him too quickly without really testing him against better opposition.

"If Duddy fought Jermain [Taylor] right now, it's a one-round fight," said DiBella, who happens to be the world champion's promoter. "But I'll say this: he's the greatest ticket-seller I've ever seen."

TheSweetScience.com
March 2006

04/05/2018

<u>Item(s) Checked Out</u>

TITLEManly art : (they can run but

BARCODE   33029090277724

DUE DATE   **04-26-18**

Woodland Public Library

Dawson Overwhelms Adamek, Wins WBC Crown

I'd been watching Chad Dawson's development since he turned pro in 2001, shortly after his nineteenth birthday, and I'd named him "New England Prospect of the Year" after watching him knock out his first three opponents. I still don't know why the guy was running around a rodeo arena dressed up like a gorilla, but I do know that he got more TV face time than some of the boxers did that night, so the reference in the lead didn't exactly come out of left field. With the passage of time, Chad's win seems even more impressive than it did that night. Both Dawson and Adamek went into this fight undefeated, and three years and ten fights later, the loss to Dawson was still the only one on Adamek's record.

KISSIMMEE, Fla.– Jimmy Lennon is lucky the guy in the gorilla suit didn't start jumping up and down on his head.

After reading the judges' scorecards following Saturday night's WBC light-heavyweight title fight, the ring announcer attempted to milk an extra bit of drama out of the verdict with the words *"and still . . ."*

Chad Dawson, who had just hammered Tomasz Adamek around the ring for the better part of 12 rounds, looked as if he were going to faint on the spot, and his promoter, Gary Shaw, almost had a heart attack before Lennon smirked and continued *". . . undefeated . . . and new light-heavyweight champion of the world . . ."*

When Don King moved his Super Bowl Eve card from the Miami Arena to Kissimmee's Silver Spurs Rodeo Arena a few weeks back, many thought it only fitting that the World's Greatest Promoter would at last preside over an event surrounded by the smell of authentic horse manure, but, Lennon's cheap theatrics notwithstanding, the crowd of 5,270 more than got its money's worth out of the main event, as the twenty-four-year-old Dawson upset the previously unbeaten Adamek to win the 175-pound title.

In a conversation a night earlier, Dawson had not only confidently predicted victory but accurately described how he would do it.

"I'm going to rely on my superior speed, quickness, and boxing skills," Bad Chad had said. "And I've heard he had trouble with southpaws."

That, in a nutshell, proved to be the fight. Adamek, who had struggled against the few left-handed bums he had fought in Europe, seemed utterly baffled in the early going, and when he wasn't being confused by the southpaw stance, he was being dazzled by Dawson's quickness.

The New Haven challenger was able to land his right-handed jab nearly at will, and from the early rounds on, Adamek's right eye was growing puffy. And as the Polish champion grew wary of the right, he set himself up for some lashing left-hand leads that Dawson threw with equal alacrity.

Adamek, who came into the bout 31-0, was fighting in the United States for just the third time, and for the first time here against an American opponent. If he had expected another blood-and-guts war like the two he had experienced with Aussie Paul Briggs, he was shortly disabused.

By the time the fight was three or four rounds old, the chants of *"Polska! Polska!"* had all but vanished from the barnyard, and Dawson, who had been led into the ring by a small posse including one guy in a gorilla costume, by now had an army of supporters 5,000 strong.

Dawson piled up a huge early lead, winning each of the first nine stanzas, flooring Adamek in the seventh along the way. (Adamek complained that he was tripped, but referee Jorge Alonso ruled it a knockdown nonetheless.)

The trip to the canvas came after Adamek moved in to throw a one-two combination. As Dawson stepped in to counter with a left to the body, he appeared to get his right foot behind Adamek's left one, so that when he nailed him with the body shot the Pole was immediately caught off-balance and fell over backward.

After nine, in fact, the fight had become such a rout that, in the champion's corner, trainer Buddy McGirt warned Adamek that he was giving him one more round to turn things around before he stopped it himself.

Adamek must have thought Buddy meant it, because in the tenth he caught Dawson with a perfect left-right combination, knocking him down with the latter punch.

Dawson seemed shaken, though he would later claim that he wasn't.

"He caught me with a good punch," said Dawson. "It was a flash knockdown, but it didn't hurt me at all. I just went right back to the game plan."

In fact, Dawson fought more warily over the final two and a half rounds, which seemed quite prudent, given that he had built up such an insurmountable lead that Adamek could have knocked him down two or three more times and *still* lost the fight.

Dawson coasted to victory, winning by scores of 118-108 (Peter Trematerra), 117-109 (Alejandro Rochin), and 116-110 (Anek Hongtongkam). The Sweet Science card also had Dawson winning 116-110.

"This has been a long time coming," said the happy Dawson, whom we'd spotted back in 2001 when we'd named the nineteen-year-old middleweight "New England Prospect of the Year."

"He was much quicker and I was slower, that's all," said Adamek. "That's why I lost. He's the fastest I've ever seen.

"Chad is a good fighter," added the Pole, "and after I knocked him down [in the tenth] I didn't finish him."

"I knew Chad was a good fighter, but when Tomasz finally threw punches he knocked him down," said McGirt. "[Adamek] was waiting on him, trying to counterpunch, and you just can't do that with a guy that fast."

Dawson also credited new trainer Floyd Mayweather Sr., for whom he dumped Dan Birmingham eight weeks earlier to prep him for the title fight.

"Floyd's the best," explained Dawson, who felt he had been playing third fiddle to Winky Wright and Jeff Lacy in the Birmingham stable.

"I trained my ass off for this fight. Six or seven long weeks, and I reached my potential. I'm just happy."

"Chad dominated him from the start," said Mayweather, suggesting that we have yet to see the best of Chad Dawson. "I liked his speed, but I didn't like his combinations. When Chad had him hurt, he could have finished Adamek. He needs to press more, pick his shots and really dig in."

The win gave the new champion a perfect 23-0 record. (Dawson's ledger also includes one No Contest, a 2004 win over Andaulen Sloan at Foxwoods that was voided when Bad Chad registered positive for marijuana on his post-fight drug test.)

So what does the future hold for a youngster of such apparently limitless potential?

"Whoever they bring to the table," said Dawson. "I'll fight the best fighters. I'll be on top for a long time."

TheSweetScience.com
February 2007

Mayweather Outboxes Oscar for Fifth Green Belt

This was De La Hoya's last chance to strut on the big stage, and it now seems remarkable that he kept it as close as he did. I credit Freddie Roach for much of that—and if he'd just kept jabbing, Oscar might even have won this fight. As he has throughout his career following a loss, De La Hoya needed a scapegoat. Freddie found out he'd been fired by reading it in a newspaper.

LAS VEGAS—If this was, as one national magazine proclaimed, "the fight to save boxing," it probably didn't, and if the world was indeed waiting, it probably still is, but it was, nonetheless, an unexpectedly good fight, one better than we had any right to expect.

Floyd Mayweather won a split decision over Oscar De La Hoya at the MGM Grand Garden Saturday night, and while he walked away with the Golden Boy's WBC 154-pound belt, it was hardly the cakewalk most experts thought it was going to be.

For the sports books in Vegas it doesn't get any better than this—a trifecta of Cinco de Mayo, the Kentucky Derby, and a megafight all on the same day, and after De La Hoya came out with both guns blazing to dominate the first third of the fight, the largely pro-Oscar crowd of 16,200 allowed themselves to entertain fanciful thoughts of cashing their bets on the 8-5 underdog.

Although it produced the richest live gate in the history of Las Vegas and almost certainly, once all the precincts have reported, will have drawn the largest pay-per-view sale as well, Mayweather-De La Hoya is unlikely to claim a spot on anyone's list of the great Las Vegas fights of all time. Hagler and Leonard, Hearns and Duran, Chavez and Tyson can all sleep safely tonight. Their legacies are safe.

It had, nonetheless, a big-fight feel, with A-list celebrities (where else can

John McCain rub elbows with J-Lo, Leonardo DiCaprio with John Madden, Helen Mirren with Joachim Noah, Tom Jones with Fiddy Cent?) and an electric atmosphere that only intensified when De La Hoya bopped Mayweather with an overhand right a minute into the fight.

And for a while, anyway, there was at least the illusion of a competitive fight. Punching with both hands, De La Hoya not only cut the ring off but was able to walk Mayweather straight back to the ropes.

De La Hoya had predicted that he might have to chase the quicker Mayweather around all night long, but argued that if that happened, "you're going to be surprised to see that I may be faster than he is."

And over the first four rounds, which Mayweather fought mostly in retreat, De La Hoya was indeed the quicker of the two. Mayweather was able to sneak in a few uppercuts with his back to the ropes, but he didn't become truly effective—or assume control—until he stopped running and stood his ground five rounds into the fight. Once Mayweather got his own jab going, the pace of the proceedings altered considerably.

Early on, De La Hoya was able to snap Mayweather's head back with his jab on several occasions, but as the night wore on Oscar all but abandoned the weapon.

"For some reason," the Golden Boy offered nonsensically, "it wasn't the night of the jab."

In the run-up to The World Awaits, the assumption had also been that De La Hoya's vaunted left hook would be the equalizer, if there was to be one, but that weapon almost never made an appearance.

Mayweather maintained that he was responsible for De La Hoya taking the hook out of play.

"I saw the shots coming. I stayed on the outside," said Pretty Boy, who modestly proclaimed his performance on this evening "a masterpiece of boxing."

CompuBox punchstats had De La Hoya throwing more punches (587-439), but Pretty outlanding Golden, 207-122. Mayweather's 138-82 advantage in power punches was even more pronounced.

Although much of it was flash and dash, De La Hoya was determined and gave a much better account of himself over the first half of the fight than anyone had a right to reasonably expect.

That probably extends to the ringside judges, who appeared to reward the Golden Boy for many punches Mayweather was catching on his gloves and forearms.

And while on several occasions he was able to bull Mayweather to the ropes and through what he hoped would be flurries of scoring punches, Oscar never seemed to be inflicting any real damage.

And, moreover, Mayweather seemed to be a willing accomplice.

"He was rough, he was tough, but he couldn't beat the best in Pretty Boy," boasted Mayweather.

What seems more likely is that Mayweather's caution may have been inspired by the knowledge that he was for once fighting a man demonstrably larger than he, and prudence suggested he guard against the big shot by allowing Oscar to indulge himself with the non-lethal ones.

Somewhat improbably, De La Hoya led on two of the three scorecards after nine rounds, but Mayweather won the last three rounds on Roth's card (as well as on ours) and two of the three on Giampa's to close the show.

De La Hoya appeared to noticeably weary down the stretch, and all but abandoned his jab. Of course, the fact that by then Mayweather was landing right-hand leads almost at will might also have inhibited the soon-to-be-ex-champion.

Over the first half of the fight, Mayweather whistled right hands past De La Hoya's chin on at least half a dozen occasions. If he was just missing then, he couldn't miss over the last four rounds, when Oscar couldn't get out of the way of the right.

(Pretty Boy claimed that he had hurt his right hand in the fifth, which, oddly, is pretty much the point at which he took control of the fight.)

In their final tallies, Giampa (116-112) and Roth (115-113) favored Mayweather, overruling Kaczmarek's card, which somewhat bewilderingly had De La Hoya ahead 115-113.

Our card had it 116-112, concurring with Giampa's.

Kaczmarek's dissenting opinion, in any case, not only made the fight seem much closer than it was but gave De La Hoya an excuse to quibble over the decision.

"I felt I won," said Oscar. "I felt I landed the harder and crisper punches. You've got to beat the champion decisively."

(The same thing had apparently crossed Mayweather's mind. Although he noted that De La Hoya "threw a lot of punches and they weren't landing," Pretty Boy said, "It's a Golden Boy promotion. Anything can happen.")

The split decision also fueled immediate speculation about another fight between the two.

If the world was awaiting, it may have to wait a bit longer for a rematch.

The winner, who sported a swollen right eye, said afterward he was retiring from boxing, while the ageing loser sounded tempted to fight on.

"I am still retiring," said Mayweather, still unbeaten at 38-0. "I'm going to move on to bigger and better things. I have nothing else to prove."

"I've got to go back to the drawing board and see how my body feels," said De La Hoya, now 38-5. "But this is a game I love, and the fight game is what brought me to where I am."

BoxingTalk.com
May 2007

Abraham—Miranda II

Stomping through the Swamp

Edison Miranda has done most of his fighting in the United States over the nearly six years since he signed with the Warriors Boxing, but he still does his trash-talking in Spanish. That would seem prudent, unless one's opponent speaks the same language, but Edison, no shrinking violet he, doesn't require the services of an interpreter for his oft-repeated press conference party trick, the throat-slashing gesture. As unlovable as Miranda might be, his friends seem like altar boys alongside the loudmouthed German thugs who accompanied Arthur Abraham for his first fight in the U.S.

HOLLYWOOD, Fla.—Two nights before Arthur Abraham would face Edison Miranda in a rematch of their controversial first fight, Abraham's countrymen back home warmed up for the occasion by celebrating Germany's 3-2 victory over Portugal in the European Soccer Championships.

According to police spokeswoman Petra Kirsch, a group of celebrants rampaged through the streets of Bautzen chanting *"Sieg Heil!"* and *"Deutschland Über Alles!"*

If nothing else, the episode presaged the mentality that would be on display at the Seminole Hard Rock Arena on the night of June 21. Moments after Abraham had battered Miranda into submission with three fourth-round knockdowns (but at least an hour after the strains of "Deutschland Über Alles" had echoed through the tribal casino), the IBF middleweight champion's twenty-six-year-old brother, Alex, celebrated King Arthur's win by kicking both Miranda and Dr. Donald Weiss, while El Pantera was still on the floor being treated by the ringside physician.

Fortunately, the younger Abraham was wearing sneakers and not jackboots.

Showtime had primed the pump for the rematch with multiple airings of the controversial September 2006 title fight between the two. Beyond confirming that the fight was mishandled by everyone from referee Randy Neumann to IBF supervisor Lindsey Tucker to the German boxing authorities, the replay probably reinforced the disparate views held by the partisans of both combatants.

Miranda's supporters saw their man as the aggressor for most of the evening, excessively penalized by five point deductions meted out by the referee. Abraham's saw it as confirmation of his bravery, since he battled on for eight more rounds after breaking his jaw in the fourth, and impressed the judges enough that he still would have won even in the absence of the five-point cushion provided by Neumann.

The trash-talking Miranda probably didn't help his cause in either fight. In Berlin he had entered the ring by delivering throat-slashing gestures, and had disrespectfully bad-mouthed his opponent in the run-up to the second meeting as well.

The Florida rematch, fought at a catchweight 166 pounds, only vaguely resembled the earlier meeting. For the first three rounds it was Miranda who did most of the punching, with Abraham covering himself up like a turtle to ward off most of the blows. Although the ringside judges had given Pantera two of the three completed rounds (as had *Boxing Digest*), there was no real damage done, as Abraham took most of Miranda's punches on the arms and gloves.

Moreover, Miranda had already placed himself in peril of further sanctions, having been cautioned twice (once for holding and hitting the back of Abraham's unprotected head, another for a borderline low blow) even before he drew a warning for a second-round punch aimed at the scrotum. Referee Telis Assimenios granted Abraham time to recover and sternly admonished Miranda, but did not penalize him for the infraction.

By the midpoint of the third, apparently persuaded that Miranda had punched himself out, Abraham sprang to life and was belting his opponent all around the ring by the time the bell sounded, setting the stage for a fourth-round onslaught the German would later describe, accurately, as *"Boom! Boom! Boom!"*

Early in the fourth, Abraham went for the body, and when Miranda dropped his hands he was surprised by a short right to the jaw that sent him down.

He had barely regained his feet when he went down again, this time from a big left hook. Seconds later, Abraham missed with a right but landed a left behind it that sent Miranda crashing to the floor, his head coming to rest on the bottom ring rope. This time Assimenios didn't even bother to count, waving it off at 1:13 of the round.

Abraham remained undefeated at 27-0, while Miranda (30-3) failed to pass muster against quality opposition for the third time in a year and a half. It was an impressive American debut for Abraham, who had never before fought outside Europe, but the same could not be said of his entourage.

The small but animated German posse behaved as if they were about to celebrate the second coming of *Kristallnacht,* with Alexander Abraham the most obvious culprit.

After the younger Abraham put the boot to Miranda, one of Pantera's cornermen picked up a folding chair and tried to race around the ring to exact revenge. Spotted by Showtime's Jim Gray, who alerted security, he was tackled by the time he rounded the neutral corner.

Weiss tried to protect the stricken boxer, and was himself rewarded by a kick in return. In an effort to ward off further attacks, the ringside physician grabbed Alex Abraham's leg, with the result that by the time Tribal police arrived to quell the incipient mini-riot what they saw was a guy grappling with another's leg, and briefly attempted to put the collar on Dr. Weiss.

Taken into custody, Abraham was turned over to Broward County Sheriff's deputies and hauled off to the local sneezer. He was released on $100 bail early Sunday morning. (By Sunday night, a Sauerland communiqué laughably claimed that Alexander had been "set free for an administrative fee of 100 U.S. dollars without any further sanctions," and insisted that "the accusations leveled at him have proven to be absolutely false.")

Footage shot by a still photographer and Showtime out-takes seemed to indicate exactly the opposite. Several eyewitnesses also confirmed the kicking episode.

"It's a shame that Arthur's brilliant performance and first fight in the United States was marred by the disgraceful and cowardly acts of his brother," said Warriors executive director Leon Margules. "Arthur is a great person and champion, but he needs to be careful and not let people around him who will hurt his reputation."

Boxing Digest
June 2008

Bute: Saved by the Bell at the Bell

Although the referee's actions in the concluding seconds of this fight were clearly those of a panic-stricken man, the more I thought about it, the more the widely shared contention that they had "robbed" Librado Andrade of a victory seemed to be a lot of hooey. Wright's accumulated irregularities did supply Andrade's promoters with enough circumstantial fodder that they were able to successfully petition for a mandatory rematch. When Bute and Andrade met again 13 months later in Quebec City, an American referee, Benjy Estevez, counted out Andrade at 2:57 of the fourth.

MONTREAL, Quebec—He had dominated the first ten rounds of his mandatory defense against Librado Andrade, but over the final two stanzas Lucian Bute found himself staggering around on *Rue Queer,* and when the IBF super-middleweight champion collapsed to the Bell Center canvas with seconds remaining, there was genuine concern that he might not be able to get back up again.

His adoring Quebecois fans, who had spent the better part of the evening in wild celebration, held their collective breaths as Bute, grasping the ring ropes for support, laboriously hauled himself to his feet at the count of six.

Although referee Marlon Wright at this point interrupted his count to admonish the Mexican American challenger, who had ventured a few steps out of the opposite neutral corner, the outcome was not affected by the attenuated count: although Bute could not have been saved by the bell, since the knockdown had occurred with fewer than ten seconds remaining in the fight, all he needed to do was regain his feet before the count of ten—and he had already done that by the time Wright started hectoring Andrade.

Though Wright's mandatory 8-count probably took 13 or 14 seconds, ShoBox announcer Steve Farhood's contention that "the referee probably cost Andrade the title" was somewhat off the mark. Plainly, Bute was so spent that one more punch would have finished him (indeed, Andrade had barely breathed on him in scoring the knockdown), but there would have been no opportunity to throw one.

Although Andrade had landed several big right hands over the last two rounds, it was not enough to close the gap Bute had fashioned in the early going, and the Romanian-born champion retained his title by scores of 117-109 (Alex Levin), 115-110 (Mickey Vann) and 115-111 (Benoit Roussel). (Our card concurred with Levin's.)

Bute, by the hair of his chinny-chin-chin, remained unbeaten at 23-0 (19 KOs), and while it did not affect the outcome, the referee's bizarre handling of the concluding moments may well result in a rematch. Andrade (now 27-2; 21 KOs) had earned the mandatory challenge by stopping German Robert Stieglitz on the March 22 Casamayor-Katsidis card. His only previous defeat had been a one-sided points loss to WBA champ Mikkel Kessler in Copenhagen last year. Andrade weighed 167 ¾, a quarter-pound less than the champion.

Boxing Digest
October 2008

Calzaghe Tames a Legend

We can only contemplate what might have occurred had these two future Hall of Famers met six or eight years earlier when both were at the top of their game. From the moment this clash of once-great boxers ended it was clear to everyone that one of them was destined to keep on fighting while the other slipped into well-deserved retirement. I'd known Roy Jones for 20 years and couldn't tell you how many times I'd heard him talk about hanging up the gloves before, but by the time I left the Garden that night I think I realized that one of them was going to quit, and it wasn't going to be Roy.

NEW YORK—Since Homeland Security wasn't checking passports at the door, we have no way of knowing exactly what portion of the announced crowd of 14,152 had flown across the ocean for the occasion, but long before he even entered the ring it was apparent that the xenophobic streak that characterized Joe Calzaghe's 15-year career might have been misplaced all along.

What may or may not have been the undefeated Welshman's final bout might have been taking place at Madison Square Garden, but for Calzaghe this was clearly going to be a home game.

Undercard performers earlier in the evening must have been startled by the spontaneous roar that erupted when the overhead TV screen cut to a shot of Calzaghe and his party alighting from their stretch limo in the bowels of the Garden, and as a tedious succession of supporting bouts played out, periodic shots of Roy Jones warming up in his dressing room elicited a chorus of boos that confirmed the allegiance of the preponderance of the audience.

The legions who had traveled from England and Wales to bear witness to Calzaghe's swan song were treated to a virtuosic performance, one in which he won each of the last 11 rounds on the scorecards of every single judge— and, the truth be known, the Welshman won a good two minutes of the first round as well.

Jones, and the minority segment of the crowd backing the nearly forty-year-old legend, had taken heart from a promising episode late in the first, when Jones landed both ends of a picture-perfect combination to put the longtime super-middleweight champion on his backside.

With 45 seconds remaining in the opening stanza, Jones, who to that point hadn't landed a single punch, caught Calzaghe flush on the jaw with a left hook. As Calzaghe instinctively ducked, he brought his head directly into the path of the right uppercut he never saw coming, and the next thing he knew, Super Joe was staring at the rafters above the Mecca of Boxing.

In his only other American experience, his win over Bernard Hopkins earlier in the year, Calzaghe had also been dropped in the first round, but had gotten up none the worse for wear. On this occasion, he was plainly damaged—"I was stunned," admitted Calzaghe afterward—but with barely half a minute remaining, Jones was unable to capitalize on what proved to be his one moment of glory. Calzaghe dominated for the balance of the evening.

"He hit me with a good punch, one I never saw coming," Calzaghe recalled the interlude afterward. "But I composed myself, got back up, and started to fight again. Anyone can go down. It's how you recover that's important, and I got back up and came back stronger."

When he watched a replay of the knockdown moments after the verdict had been rendered, Calazghe found himself wondering what must have gone through the mind of his mother, watching on television back in Wales, at that moment.

"Hey Mum," he said, "I hope that didn't make you too nervous."

Although no recognized world title other than a belt offered by a boxing magazine was at stake, some had worried that Calzaghe might have been making a mistake in agreeing to a 175-pound limit, simply because as the longtime ruler of the division, Jones had had a lot more experience as a light-heavyweight than he had. The career-high 174 ½ Calzaghe carried into the ring proved to be a negligible factor, as the Welshman's pronounced advantages in speed and quickness left him in control throughout.

"I knew I had to make Roy respect my punches," said Calzaghe. "I always felt that I was a step ahead. I knew what he was going to do before he did it."

The bout was conducted on Calzaghe's terms. Able to land his right jab virtually at will, and while the lefts from his business hand rarely connected with full force, the sum effect was to put Roy so thoroughly on the defensive that he was never able to produce an attack of his own.

Jones, who had been embarrassingly knocked out by Antonio Tarver and Glen Johnson, was determined that he wasn't going to be knocked out in this one, and once it became clear that he wasn't going to be able to ward off Calzaghe's insistent attack, he spent so much of the evening protecting his head by blocking punches thrown upstairs that he virtually conceded the midsection to Calzaghe's body attack.

Statistics can sometimes be misleading, but a couple of tabulations from this one were particularly instructive: Over 12 rounds Calzaghe threw over 500 more punches than did Jones, and the 344 of those that found their target were more than any opponent had landed in the 31 previous Jones fights that had been tracked by CompuBox.

Perhaps more critically, while Calzaghe was throwing 362 jabs, and connecting with 120 of them, over the course of the entire evening Roy landed just a dozen jabs. That's one per round, and probably half of those came in the seventh, a brief interlude in which Jones stopped posing long enough to back up Calzaghe with a succession of jabs. For reasons that remain unclear, he abandoned the tactic, and barely threw another jab over the last five rounds.

Even as Calzaghe was painting his masterpiece, Jones resolutely remained in his fighting cock pose, upright, with his hands down, hoping to catch his unbeaten opponent with sneaky right-hand leads, but Joe had plainly done his homework and was rarely taken by surprise.

Just before the bell ended the sixth, Jones did land what may have been his last meaningful punch of the night when he caught Calzaghe with a hard right uppercut. As the Welshman walked back to his corner, Bernard Hopkins, in what was clearly a bit of wishful thinking, directed a throat-slashing gesture toward Calzaghe from his ringside seat. (Hopkins, it must be said, had almost as much of an emotional—and financial—investment in a Jones win as Roy did.)

Any hope that the pendulum might be about to swing after that sixth-round exchange quickly dissipated early in the seventh, when Calzaghe fired a left aimed straight at the middle of Jones' face. Unable to avoid it entirely, Jones swung his head to his right, so instead of taking it squarely in the nose, the punch landed, nearly sideways, on his left eye, ripping open the gash along the eyelid that would bleed, unabated, for the balance of the evening.

Dr. Richard Lucey is a family practitioner back in Pensacola. Since 1992 he had traveled around the country as the designated cut man in the Jones corner. It was a marvelous free ride, since not once during those 16 years had he actually been required to repair a cut in the heat of battle. A bit after midnight on what had by then become November the 9th, he was called upon to do so, and Dr. Lucey discovered to his dismay that repairing a gushing wound in the space of 60 seconds isn't quite the same thing as attending to a patient's boo-boo back at the office.

The cut, on the corner of the eyelid, poured blood into Jones' left eye, effectively blinding him for the rest of the evening. Lucey reported having tried all three substances—adrenaline solution, avetine, and thrombine—permitted under New York boxing regulations, all to no avail. (Since he'd never had to use them before, we found ourselves wondering: Had the meds been old bottles Lucey had been carrying around in his kit since 1992, or had he restocked with a more recent supply that just didn't work?)

Between rounds, Dr. Osric King, the NYSAC attending physician, repeatedly climbed up on the apron to Jones' corner, both to oversee Lucey's handiwork, presumably to ensure that more drastic measures were not taken. (When a cut continues to defy legal remedies, cut men are sometimes tempted to resort to old-school tradition and reach for the Monsel's solution or the Crazy Glue.)

Several frustrating rounds elapsed before trainer Alton Merkerson took matters into his own hands and asked Jones if he could apply pressure to the cut.

"Go ahead," Roy told him.

Pressure had apparently never occurred to the doctor.

The cut man's failings notwithstanding, it was within Dr. King's purview to stop the fight on his own, and it seems likely that had this been any fighter other than Roy Jones Jr., he might have. (King said later that he would have had the eye swollen shut, which seems to miss the point since, by the commission doctor's own admission, the blood was flowing directly into the eye.)

Jones didn't lose the fight *because* of the cut, but it did effectively seal the outcome by dispelling any possibility of a late-round counterattack. By then a one-eyed fighter, Jones was forced to turn his head at odd angles, and was so preoccupied with protecting himself that there was no opportunity for a late offensive.

Although it was the sheer volume of Calzaghe's punches that proved his undoing, Jones conceded afterward that Calzaghe's power had been unexpected, and that what he had derided as "pitty-pat" punches "were a little harder than I thought they'd be."

This may have been a revelation to RJ, but it plainly wasn't to Merkerson. At a trainers' round-table two days before the fight, Merk had responded to criticism of Calzaghe as a "slapper" by noting that the Welshman had "slapped 32 guys hard enough that he slapped them unconscious."

Over those last few rounds, as it became increasingly apparent that Superman had left his cape at home, the rollicking chants segued into a continuous roar that rolled through the arena like an approaching train.

The audible impression was not unlike being at Anfield in the waning moments of a game in which Liverpool had fashioned an unassailable lead over Manchester United. The opponent might not have been the ManU of yesteryear, but beating the bejeezus out of an institutional legend under any circumstances can be enormously satisfying—particularly when notice is being served that there is indeed a new sheriff in town.

Calzaghe's confidence had by then soared to the extent that over the last few rounds he took to mimicking Jones, affecting a posture that saw him frequently drop his hands as he sized up his opponent, looking to punch from odd and unexpected angles.

"I *like* fighting with my hands down; it's just my style," said Joe afterward. (No, it isn't. It's *Roy's* style.) "I love the way Roy fights, and I knew his style would make for a good fight."

It was in fact about as entertaining as a one-sided fight can be. The tabulation of the verdict was but a perfunctory exercise, since even Bert Sugar could have scored this fight and gotten it right. All three judges—Americans Jerry Roth and Julie Lederman and Englishman Terry O'Connor—had it 118-109. So did we—as did every other ringside reporter with whom we consulted.

Despite the decisive loss, Jones will doubtless take heart from the fact that it was he who authored the two or three hardest punches of the evening and convince himself that in the absence of the cut he might have done more. The loss leaves Jones' career mark at 52-5, with four of the losses coming in his last seven fights, but we probably haven't seen the last of Roy Jones Jr.

Although there was a clause in the bout agreement providing for a 2009 rematch at Cardiff's Millennium Stadium, that isn't going to happen. This wasn't a fight anyone wants to see again.

Calzaghe, now 46-0, had maintained all along that the Jones fight would "probably" be his last, and deferred any decision until he's had time to sit down with his family and contemplate the future.

"This year I beat two legends in Hopkins and Dawson, and I came to the United States to do it," he said. "I came to them; they didn't come to me."

Boxing Digest
November 2008

Sometimes the Scale *Do* Lie . . .

The previous September on the Mississippi Gulf Coast I'd spent a couple of agonizing days with Nate Campbell, who was supposed to defend his three lightweight title belts against Joan Guzman in Biloxi. Guzman came in overweight, and given two hours to lose weight, gained it instead, leaving Nate little choice but to pull out of a Showtime main event. At the time he could have used the exposure, but he was teetering on the brink of bankruptcy and could have used the money even more. A lot of people were shocked when Nate himself came in overweight for his fight against Ali Funeka, but no one was more surprised than I.

SUNRISE, Fla.–We have a bit of disconcerting news for those South Florida housewives who have been valiantly fighting the battle of the bulge down at the Sunrise chapter of Bally's Health Club: You may not have lost quite as much weight as you *think* you have.

Nate Campbell made this discovery the hard way. Knowing that he had to shed a few pounds before a scheduled 2 p.m. weigh-in, the three-belt lightweight champion visited the steam room there Friday morning, and after an hour's worth of diligent exercise was pleasantly surprised to learn that he weighed 134.6 pounds.

A few hours later when he mounted another scale, this one calibrated and operated under the auspices of Florida's boxing commission, Campbell learned that his actual weight was 138–three pounds above the lightweight limit.

Oops!

"Nate had been having trouble with those last few pounds," said promoter/advisor Terry Trekas. "So we went over early to the health club. This time it actually seemed to come off with ease–or at least that's what the scale said. We'd planned to skip the HBO fighter meetings [at noontime] to keep him in the steam room, but once he made weight I phoned [manager] Jimmy Waldrop and told him we were coming back to the hotel."

Once the discrepancy between the scales was discovered, Campbell still had two hours to shed the requisite two pounds. He hastened back to the health club.

"He went into the steam room five times—you can't leave him in there too long—and each time he'd shadow-box," said Trekas.

"Nate had absolutely hit a wall," said Waldrop. "I've never seen anything like it. All that exercise, and in two hours all he lost was half a pound."

Campbell glumly returned to the BankAtlantic Center to face the music. When he weighed 137 1/2, he had lost his titles on the scale.

King's St. Valentine's Day Massacre had been troubled from the outset. The site, the home of the NHL Florida Panthers, was settled upon only a few weeks before fight night, and within a matter of days, scheduled headliner Ricardo Mayorga, who was supposed to have provided a test for hard-hitting Mexican up-and-comer Alfredo Angulo, had gone AWOL, never to be seen again.

Campbell's defense against South African Ali Funeka was elevated to the main event. Angulo's prospective opponent changed almost daily. By fight week, King was offering two tickets for the price of one in a desperate attempt to lure a respectable crowd to the Boxing After Dark tripleheader.

Campbell seemed hoist by his own petard, in view of his scathing reaction to an eerily similar circumstance in Biloxi, MS, five months earlier, when Joan Guzman had come in three pounds overweight and declined to shed the excess poundage, resulting in the cancellation of the bout.

"I'm shocked and appalled that a professional fighter could behave this way," said Campbell then. Of course, he hastened to point out, his anger was over Guzman's refusal to participate in an over-the-weight match, which cost Campbell his $300,000 purse and plunged him into bankruptcy.

Campbell gallantly insisted on going ahead with his fight, even though he could not regain his titles. Funeka, on the other hand, could win a couple of them if he prevailed.

In January, caught up in the morass of boxing politics, Campbell had re-signed his WBA belt. A week later, Trekas received a letter from WBA president Gilberto Mendoza, urging him to reconsider. Trekas agreed, although he noted "We're probably going to have to give it up sooner or later."

And although King was initially prepared to foot the bill for Campbell's WBA sanctioning fee, the weigh-in cock-up rendered the point moot, but

Funeka could still have won the IBF and WBO championships by beating Campbell.

Funeka, who brought a 30-1-2 record to the bout, is a gangly 6-foot praying mantis who had never before fought outside South Africa.

Campbell looked as if he might make a short evening of it when he dropped Funeka with a huge overhand right in the third round, but as the bout neared its midpoint, the strength seemed to be sapping out of Campbell, who began to husband his energy and confine himself to fighting in spurts.

Funeka, in fact, appeared to have drawn even with two rounds to go, but Campbell finished the issue in style. In the 11th, he landed two hard rights and then literally ran right over Funeka before he could hit the deck. The two went down together, and once he got them disentangled, referee Tommy Kimmons completed a mandatory 8-count. That, and winning the final round on all three cards, provided the margin of victory in what turned out to be a majority decision in Campbell's favor.

Two judges, American Mike Pernick (115-111) and Canadian Benoit Roussel (114-112), scored it for Campbell, while South African Deon Duarte returned a 113-113 scorecard.

"I had two knockdowns," said Campbell. "Of *course* I thought I won."

Campbell plans to campaign henceforth at 140 pounds, and will be an immediate player in that competitive division, but moments after his hollow victory, he reflected on what he had lost.

"All my life I wanted to be a world champion, to be the best in the world at what I do. And I lost it on the scale. I want to apologize to my fans for that," he added.

ESPN.com
February 2009

Bad Mojo at the Joe

It took Showtime's Super Six unification series to bring Arthur Abraham back to America and a big fight to the Joe Louis Arena for the first time in years. It appeared to be a conscious marketing decision, given Detroit's substantial Middle-Eastern population and the ugly residue of his prior U.S. experience, to subsume Abraham's German citzenship by emphasizing his Armenian roots. Abraham's action plainly merited disqualification, but the inexperience of the supervising Michigan commission and the comportment of Texas referee Laurence Cole combined to make the outcome seem more controversial than it should have been. In the end, Abraham was neither disciplined nor suspended, nor did the Michigan commissioners offer any public criticism of the referee's performance.

DETROIT—Has anybody else noticed how often the bravest guys in the aftermath of these skirmishes turn out to be the non-combatants?

Or, put another way, do you suppose Anthony Dirrell knows—or cares—how close he came to turning the result of Saturday night's fight at Joe Louis Arena into a double-disqualification?

Andre Dirrell was still twitching on the canvas in the blue corner when, amid a total breakdown of security, several members of the American boxer's posse came bounding through the ropes and across the ring. On one hand, it might be understandable that Anthony would be so alarmed that he wanted to immediately ascertain his brother's condition, even though in doing so he was issuing an open invitation to Laurence Cole to invoke a second disqualification.

The referee at that point had yet to officially affirm his intention to DQ Arthur Abraham, and, having summoned the ringside physicians to attend to Dirrell, had his hands full trying to herd Abraham back into a neutral corner, so he may well not have even noticed. But even when another cornerman dragged Anthony Dirrell back across the ring to the red corner he remained in the ring, and occupied himself directing threats and menacing gestures toward Abraham—who at least a couple of times looked ready to take him up on the offer.

And of course by then the ring had become total chaos, with several dozen officials and members of both entourages milling around, presumably while they waited for Cole to make up his mind.

In fairness to the referee, although he once again did not have a good night in the ring (does he ever?), his handling of the DQ appears to have been adequate. He might not have rendered his decision with the decisive authority of a Mills Lane, but the interval between the act and his ruling was marked not, as some subsequently suggested, by indecision, but rather by what seemed to be a process of deliberate contemplation to make sure it was done right. (The tape reveals that even with Dirrell still down, Cole can be heard informing Abraham of the impending disqualification.)

And, moreover, you can take this much to the bank: Had Cole's decision been anything other than what it was, he probably never would have gotten out of the Joe alive. And neither, for that matter, might any of the rest of us seated near ringside.

Abraham sounded even sillier attempting to justify the flagrant foul that cemented his first loss than he looked committing it in the first place. After the fight he tried to tell Showtime's Jim Gray that he was watching Dirrell's eyes and not his feet and, ergo, didn't even realize he was down when he almost took his head off with a right hand.

Drawn to his full height, Arthur Abraham is four inches shorter than Dirrell. Put Dirrell on the floor, with both legs tucked underneath his body, and Abraham was standing a good two feet above his target. And we're supposed to believe he didn't *notice?*

In watching the sorry—sorry for everybody save Showtime, since between Dirrell's performance and the controversial outcome the network will receive a huge boost from the events in Detroit—scene unfold, one could not but recall the post-fight melee that attended Abraham's only other previous fight in the United States.

After King Arthur knocked out Edison Miranda two years ago at the Seminole Hard Rock in Florida, Abraham's brother Alex climbed into the ring to kick Miranda, who was still on the floor, being attended to by the ringside physician. The good doctor attempted to protect the boxer by grabbing the offending foot, which was just about the time the Seminole Tribal police arrived.

What they saw, of course, was one guy in the ring grappling with another's leg, so their first reaction was to slap the cuffs on Dr. Weiss.

To the best of our knowledge American authorities still have an outstanding warrant for Alex Abraham as a result of that little affray, which is probably the only reason there was no brother-against-brother battle in the ring at the Joe Saturday night.

Cole, as we have noted, didn't exactly color himself with glory with his performance in the Dirrell-Abraham bout, but he didn't even come close to committing the worst transgression of the evening by a ringside official. For that, Dr. Hisham Ahmed can stand up and take a bow.

By the ninth round the cut Abraham had sustained in the seventh was bleeding copiously enough that Cole called time and led the German over to be examined by the ringside physician—and the operative word here is, or is supposed to be, *examined*.

Since the episode took place on the opposite side of the ring from our position we hadn't paid much attention at the time, but the tape of the sequence shows that Dr. Ahmed pulled out a square of gauze and proceeded to apply pressure to Abraham's wound for an unbroken period of 40 seconds, by which time it had been staunched to a trickle.

In this action, it should be plain enough that he overstepped the bounds of a ringside physician's duties and was functioning as Abraham's *de facto* cut man. Even when his colleague, Dr. Peter Samet, joined Ahmed on the apron he made no attempt to discourage him from this process, which served to revive Abraham.

Cole? Well, there's no rule against a referee greeting his introduction by Jimmy Lennon Jr. by striking a favored pose recalled from his youth. (In this case, it was Elvis, from an early scene in "King Creole.") But when it comes to ruling on low blows, isn't the referee supposed to make those decisions himself? (Early in the sixth, Dirrell delivered a borderline, belt-high shot to the midsection, and Abraham reacted with a swoon. Although the referee, who was behind the fighters, couldn't possibly have gauged whether it was low or not, and in fact did not seem to have considered it noteworthy when it happened, he opted to take Abraham's word for it and, after the fact, called time.)

Add to that what was a blown knockdown call in the tenth. (Cole apparently claimed that the fighters got their feet tangled up as Abraham floored Dirrell. The replay seemed to show that there may have been slight contact between the shoes, but it had absolutely no bearing on Dirrell going down from what was plainly a punch.)

Did Cole, as has been suggested, initially attempt to pick up a count after the flagrant foul that ended the fight? Having watched the replay over and over, we don't think so. The referee did make one reflexive downward motion with his arm just after the impact, but in this case, he appears to have had his wits about him.

What could be interesting now will be the report on the proceedings the referee delivers to the Michigan Commission and to the WBC (who had sanctioned Dirrell-Abraham as a title eliminator). If Abraham's actions are deemed sufficiently flagrant and premeditated, it remains possible that he could not only be fined but could wind up with a significant suspension as well. (And who is to say which would last longer—an Abraham suspension, or the medically mandated interval Dirrell is obliged to sit out in the wake of a devastating, if illegal, knockout?)

After promoter Wilfried Sauerland added his accusation that Dirrell was "trying to sneak out of a fight" to Abraham's contention that Dirrell is "an actor, not a boxer," Gary Shaw responded by calling Sauerland a "sourpuss."

Didn't he mean sauer *Kraut*?

One more question here: Is, or was, Abraham engaged in some sort of image makeover going into this fight? When he came into the ring against Miranda three years ago, there were dozens of German flags around the arena, and the bout was immediately preceded by a stirring rendition of the Hitler-era national anthem, "Deutschland Über Alles." In Detroit Saturday night there was no anthem, no German flags, but tricolored Armenian banners were visible in great profusion throughout the audience.

Just wondering: Was that *Abraham's* idea? Or Showtime's?

TheSweetScience.com
March 2010

The Wrath of Khan's Army

My introduction to Amir Khan had come half a dozen years earlier in Athens, where I'd watched the seventeen-year-old box his way to the Olympic lightweight final before losing a decision to Cuba's Mario Kindelan in the gold medal match. Back then, of course, he had yet to surround himself with the obnoxious entourage that accompanied him to New York. At twenty-three, Khan was already working with his third trainer (and, if you count the family-owned Khan Promotions, his third promoter), while burdened with the hopes of two nations—and it's hard to say which harbors the more fickle boxing fans. A few years earlier my son, who lives in Brooklyn, had told me of a Pakistani-owned corner shop in Bushwick that had been decorated as a veritable Amir Khan shrine. In 2008, Khan was knocked out in one round by Breidis Prescott. By the next morning the posters and newspaper clippings had all disappeared from the shop's walls.

New York State Athletic Commission Chairman Melvina Lathan was so infuriated by Golden Boy's part in the weigh-in rampage that disciplinary action seemed a certainty, but by the time the commission met, even more serious transgressions had come to light. On July 9, 2010, the NYSAC deemed Golden Boy Promotions in violation of the Muhammad Ali Act and placed the company on a 90-day administrative suspension, barring it from doing boxing business in New York.

NEW YORK—Whether one chose to view it as a bout for the trash-talking championship of the 140-pound universe or as the play-in game for that junior welterweight tournament HBO's Kery Davis has fixed in his mind, if not on his schedule, Amir Khan's American coming-out party was a resounding triumph on both counts.

The WBA light welterweight champion didn't lose a single minute of any of the ten rounds he and Paulie Malignaggi completed in a one-sided rout at the Madison Square Garden Theatre, and more ominously from the hometowner's viewpoint, Khan did it by beating the former IBF champ at his own game, landing more jabs than the loser did aggregate punches in a dazzling display.

Malignaggi has acknowledged more than once over the course of his career that his speed has been the great equalizer in putting some distance between himself and more talented (and almost always harder-hitting) opponents, but on this night he quickly learned he was the second-quickest man in the ring.

Malignaggi would say later that facing Khan had been like fighting "a clone of myself when I was younger." The analogy wasn't entirely inappropriate, but the fact of the matter is that the skills Malignaggi put to use in defeating 27 prior opponents had not deteriorated appreciably. It's just that Khan is *so* much quicker and *so* much more elusive than Malignaggi that he was able to out-magic the Magic Man.

Between Khan's ability to tag Malignaggi with jabs and a straight right hand that rarely missed and his total disdain for anything the challenger had to offer in return, the bout quickly took on the trappings of a one-sided rout, one that could have been stopped at almost any point from the fifth round onward.

Malignaggi's former trainer Buddy McGirt might have intervened on humane grounds much earlier, but Sharif Yunan, the chief second in Paulie's corner, never evinced any inclination to curtail the proceedings. (Sharif's thinking—if he was indeed thinking at all—may have been that if Khan kept hitting Malignaggi's unprotected head long enough, sooner or later he might injure one or both of his hands.)

After each of the last three completed rounds, referee Steve Smoger invited the ring doctors into Malignaggi's corner in the vain hope that one of them might order a stoppage. Once Paulie won his argument with Dr. Osric King that momentarily delayed the commencement of the 11th, Smoger realized that the task would fall upon him alone, and at the first opportunity—a hard left hook from Khan that drove Malignaggi across the ring to the ropes, where the champion jumped on him to land a flurry of unanswered punches—the referee moved in to slap a choke-hold on Malignaggi, signaling that the fight was over.

This in turn set off wild celebrations among those remnants of Khan's Army who hadn't already been ejected from the Theatre by Garden personnel. The security team, beefed up after Khan's posse of British street thugs made a shambles of the previous day's weigh-in, were kept busy throughout the evening as skirmishes continually erupted in the audience. The result was that so many of the Brit thugs had been taken into custody and frog-marched out of the building that by the time Smoger rang down the curtain on the one-sided bout there may not have been enough of them left to produce a decent riot.

Before he even left the ring after the Malignaggi win, Khan, now 22-1 with 17 KOs, revived the prospect of an unofficial "tournament" matching the world's top 140-pounders that had been alluded to by HBO's Davis at a May 12 Garden press conference.

"I'll fight [Marcos] Maidana, have Alexander and Bradley fight, and then the winners fight," volunteered Khan in describing the scenario of a four-man knockout tournament.

As recently as early 2009, the 140-pound division was regarded as so deep that such an exercise could not have been credibly contemplated without at least an eight-man draw. Both Manny Pacquiao and Floyd Mayweather would have been regarded as junior welters then; so would Juan Manuel Marquez, although subsequent events have marked him as too small to realistically contend at the weight. A year ago Juan Urango would likely have been part of the mix as well.

In addition to those four, you can probably eliminate both Malignaggi (now 27-4, with just 5 KOs) and Nate Campbell as prospective tournament entries, too. On the strength of his performance against Campbell on the Khan-Malignaggi card, you could make a case for Victor Ortiz, but last June's loss to Maidana and Maidana's mandatory position vs. Khan, the twenty-three-year-old Kansan could find himself the odd man out. (Ortiz could be waiting in the wings for the new unified champion, but a more likely scenario is that the eventual winner from among Khan/Maidana/Bradley/Alexander—and who's to say it might not be Khan—would find himself in a strong bargaining position vis-à-vis the Pacquiao-Mayweather winner, if there is one.)

The British wunderkind's arrival in Manhattan had been delayed by several days by Homeland Security's handling of his application for a work visa, leading trainer Freddie Roach to move the training camp to a Vancouver gym, where Khan wrapped up his sparring while awaiting the approval of his visa application from the U.S. Consulate in that Canadian city.

Already under extra scrutiny due to a dodgy pattern of vehicular infractions back in the U.K. (Amir behind the wheel of a car is apparently a lot more dangerous than Amir wearing boxing gloves), Khan's already perilous position became more so five days into the wait when a fellow Pakistani tried to blow up Times Square. Eventually, after nearly two weeks in British Columbia, the P1 visa was approved, but Khan faced yet another hurdle when he tried to re-enter the United States. Apparently another fellow named Amir Khan (though for all we know there might be several of them; Homeland Security is unlikely to shed much light on the issue) features prominently on a list of potential Al Qaeda operatives, and as a result the boxer was red-flagged by border agents and detained for another two hours as a suspected terrorist.

Since they arrived on visitor's visas, the members of Khan's Army, alas, faced no such problems, and they were waiting in full force when their hero arrived in New York. For the most part, they spent the days before the fight clustered in packs around Central Park South, agreeably barking like dogs whenever a television camera showed up and making a general nuisance of themselves as they bided their time for the weigh-in. Their comportment was no doubt encouraged by Khan, who from the moment he hit the Big Apple seemed determined to overcome any perceived psychological edge by running his mouth even more than Paulie did.

Because the weigh-in was supposed to be closed to the public, there was an almost total absence of security in the ballroom of the staid old Essex House for the Friday noontime ritual. Having been thus warned, Malignaggi's team had deliberately limited the size of the challenger's entourage, but apparently no one, including NYSAC Chairwoman Melvina Lathan, had reckoned on Golden Boy, a company prone to viewing press conferences as pep rallies and weigh-ins as marketing opportunities. Although Golden Boy CEO Richard Schaefer would later claim that he was taken by surprise by the unexpected turnout of Khan supporters, the truth of the matter is that Golden Boy had a pair of scantily clad Tecate Girls on hand to dispense hundreds of souvenir key chains—and trust us, they weren't there to give them to the press, the commissioners, or the boxers' cornermen.

After the weigh-in—Khan scaled 139 ½, Malignaggi half a pound less—someone made the ill-advised suggestion that the boxers pose for one last stare-down. This devolved into the two yapping at one another with their foreheads literally touching, a recipe for disaster which was quickly confirmed when Khan reached out and shoved Malignaggi backward, and, as if by prearranged signal, Khan's Army rushed the stage and chaos reigned.

Golden Boy matchmaker Eric Gomez quickly wrapped Khan in a stranglehold and hauled him away to safety. The bilingual Schaefer, who can lie in English *or* German with equal facility, would somewhat absurdly claim to the Associated Press that he saw Malignaggi with his hands around Khan's neck. Video footage, of which plenty existed, confirmed that the only one who ever had Khan by the throat was Gomez, who, need we remind you, works for Schaefer. Besides the matchmaker, the only other Golden Boy employee to distinguish herself during this rampage of violence was publicist Monica Sears, who valiantly attempted to intercede in a peacemaker's role before she was overwhelmed in the crush of bodies.

When one of the Khan's Army foot-soldiers was discouraged from mounting the stage by the rather large presence of announcer Joe Antonacci, he reacted by cursing the announcer and calling him a "dirty New York Jew."

"Actually," replied Antonacci, "I'm a dirty New York Italian."

"Just my luck," sighed Malignaggi promoter Lou DiBella. "Why did the guy have to say it to the Italian announcer instead of one of the Jewish judges?"

Since the commission plans to review the episode, Schaefer and Golden Boy can expect to be reprimanded and may face financial penalties. DiBella has also called for Khan to be suspended for his unprovoked aggression on the scale. (It was *physically* unprovoked, anyway, though Malignaggi's body language immediately preceding the trip to the scale was hardly that of a choirboy.)

Put it this way: Whether Amir Khan fights again in New York or not, it will be a cold day in Hell before Khan's Army invades another NYSAC–administered weigh-in.

While Khan's first fight on U.S. soil was by any standard an artistic success, it is by no means clear that he is on the verge of establishing himself as an attraction to boxing audiences on this side of the Atlantic. (Weren't Ricky Hatton and, before him, Naseem Hamed, going to take America by storm, too?)

If British fans sometimes seem positively delusional when it comes to these matters, it is often because the Fleet Street press in its creative approach to facts encourages such folly.

Three days before Khan-Malignaggi, for instance, readers of the *Daily Mail* were treated to this bit of inside information:

> The fight takes place in the Theatre at Madison Square Garden.
> Khan admits he would have preferred to appear in the fabled main

arena, but this was already booked when HBO picked this date. Khan says: "I will make a statement with a spectacular win over Malignaggi that will bring me back here for an even bigger fight in the Garden proper before too long."

For one thing, HBO didn't pick the date, or the venue; Golden Boy did. For another, the only thing playing in the Garden's main arena the night Khan fought Malignaggi was a large family of rats who regularly come out to frolic whenever the building is otherwise unoccupied. Since Khan, facing a New York fighter in New York, could draw only 4,420 customers to the 5,800-seat Theatre, any aspirations of playing the big room would at this point appear to be somewhat fanciful.

Boxing Digest
May 2010

Chapter IV—
The Good, the Bad, and the Ugly

From the Tail of a Pony

Some would say, "Come on, the man's been dead for fifteen years now, don't you think it's time to lighten up?" I don't think so. To this day the very mention of Howard Cosell's name makes my teeth start gnashing, not because he was such a self-important fraud (the late Jimmy Cannon once said, "His name is Cohen and he wears a toupee and he says he tells it like it is") but because those of us who knew him saw how needlessly cruel he could be. When another great sportswriter, Red Smith, proclaimed himself Howard's worst enemy, Irving Rudd interrupted him to say, "Not while I'm alive!" Muhammad Ali—whose relationship with the broadcaster Dave Kindred explored in the book that led to this column—cut to the chase in a poem:

> *Cosell, you're a phony*
> *And that thing on your head*
> *Comes from the tail of a pony.*

Two decades ago I was dispatched by my employers, somewhat against my wishes, to Providence, R.I., where Brown University was conferring an award of some sort on Howard Cosell. As part of the festivities, the laureate himself was to address the assembled student body. Why an Ivy League institution might have chosen to honor Cosell, and why the *Boston Herald* would deem it worthy of a column, are questions that to this day remain shrouded in mystery.

Cosell seemed surprised to see me that day, and appeared to be nearly as uncomfortable over my presence as I was being there, but after assessing the situation he evidently decided that as long as I was in the building, I might make a convenient foil for his address.

Howard's chosen topic that day was Muhammad Ali, and the role he himself had played in correcting the injustice perpetrated when boxing's powers-that-be had stripped the great man of his heavyweight champion-ship and, by denying him a boxing license, deprived him of his right to earn a living for nearly three-and-a-half years as punishment for his refusal to serve in Vietnam.

To hear Cosell tell it, he had been a one-man crusader for justice, fighting a solitary battle on Ali's behalf. And, for the benefit of a young audience that plainly knew no better, he chose to make me his whipping boy, repeatedly jabbing in my direction with his finger as he punctuated his vitriolic screed with claims that "98%" of the nation's sportswriters had lined up against Ali, and that none of them (us) had even begun to comprehend the constitu-tional issues that would eventually result in an 8-0 Supreme Court decision upholding Ali's position.

I had no choice but to sit there and take it, but the moment he finished I confronted Cosell. It had been unfair of him to single me out, I told him, par-ticularly since he himself *knew* he was perpetrating a falsehood by lumping me in with Ali's old antagonists.

"I went to jail over that war in 1965," I reminded Cosell. "And everything I had ever written on the subject was supportive of Ali."

"Maybe not you, but what about your newspaper?" he argued.

"Howard," I sighed, "the newspapers I was writing for back then were the *Boston Phoenix* and the *Village Voice*. Exactly which of them do you mean?"

He had no rebuttal, but neither did he apologize, and for all I know, any Brown students present that day still not only believe that I was part of the witch hunt but that Howard Cosell was the only man in the civilized world to have staked his reputation on the correctness of Ali's antiwar stance back in the 1960s.

Three years ago, just before the Lennox Lewis-Mike Tyson fight in Memphis, I ran into my old friend and golfing buddy Dave Kindred, who in-formed me that he was in the midst of an ambitious book project detailing the complex relationship between Ali and Cosell. He asked me if I had any recollections I might share. I e-mailed him a recapitulation of the aforemen-tioned episode, along with some other equally uncomplimentary remem-brances of Cosell.

When Kindred's book *Sound and Fury: Two Powerful Lives, One Fateful Friendship* was published a few weeks ago, I was initially stunned to see that not a word of the material I'd sent its author had been included. But then the more I thought about it, the less surprised I was. If I'd been the one writing a book about Howard Cosell, I probably wouldn't have included the testimony of anyone who claimed that he was kind to dogs and small children.

Not that Kindred is universally effusive in his praise of Humble Howard. He does take pains to note Cosell's insecurities and many flaws, but for the most part his portrayal is that of a sympathetic but misunderstood figure destined to be unjustly maligned by history. Attempting to demonstrate that (a) "Ali loved Cosell" and that (b) "Cosell was a good and decent man" was an ambitious task enough without cluttering up the narrative with conflicting evidence.

Although Kindred's stated thesis is an exploration of the complex and often mutually beneficial relationship between Ali and Cosell, the author appears to be much more sure of himself when dealing with one or the other. Originally a sportswriter for Cassius Clay's hometown newspaper, the *Louisville Courier-Journal*, Kindred has known Ali since the sixties and is consequently able to draw upon four decades' worth of personal interaction.

At the same time, Kindred was somewhat unique among the sports writing profession in that he was one of Cosell's favored scribes, and was once invited to Howard's Long Island home as a prospective biographer. Kindred recognizes many of Cosell's shortcomings, but in the pages of this book he remains considerably more tolerant and forgiving than most of us might have been.

Nor does he shrink from dismissing Cosell's self-proclaimed reputation as a boxing expert. Kindred recounts an unflattering moment a few days before Ali's ill-fated 1980 challenge to Larry Holmes, when the broadcaster strolled into the arena at Caesars Palace in the company of producer Alex Wallau and supposed, aloud, "You know, Holmes is vulnerable to the right hand, and Ali has always been able to land the straight right. I think the old master is going to do it one more time."

"Howard," Wallau reminded him, accurately, "not only is Ali not going to win the fight, not only is he not going to win a round, he's not going to win ten seconds of any round."

While acknowledging that Cosell had "an uneasy working relationship" with Wallau (now the president of ABC), Kindred never explores the roots of the rift between the two.

That dates back to 1976–77, when Wallau, then an assistant producer and researcher whose field of expertise was boxing, blew the whistle on the Don King/ABC enterprise known as the *U.S. Boxing Championships,* a made-for-TV venture predicated on nonexistent fights and rigged ratings. Even after Wallau had exposed the odoriferous corruption underlying the process, Cosell stubbornly refused to acknowledge it, describing the *U.S.*

Boxing Championships as "an open, honest competition," and did his best to undermine the whistle-blower's credibility.

Only after an in-house investigation that brought down *The Ring* magazine (the so-called Bible of Boxing) and resulted in ABC's withdrawal from the disgraceful project, did Cosell stop trying to defend it.

And he never stopped blaming Wallau. Years later, in 1988 when Wallau was diagnosed with cancer, Cosell's reaction was that (as a "boxing guy") "he deserves it."

By then Cosell had walked away from the sport that had helped bring him to national prominence. Although he publicly traced his disillusionment to the Holmes 1982 fight against Randall (Tex) Cobb, the truth is that Cosell had long since lost touch with the sport—in much the same way he eventually lost touch with all sports.

That Holmes-Cobb served as the catalyst that drove Cosell from boxing never seemed particularly persuasive to me. While that bout did have the trappings of an unconscionable mismatch, Howard had broadcast his share of events in which the deck was even more stacked. What seemed more likely to me at the time, and still does today, is that a sport which had nurtured him had become even more weary of Cosell than he was of boxing.

He was, in any case, by that time often stinking drunk while on the air, and a year after Holmes-Cobb, Howard was making such a mess of *Monday Night Football* telecasts that his longtime benefactor and staunch defender Roone Arledge virtually ordered his banishment from the broadcast booth.

To his credit, Kindred doesn't attempt to sugarcoat this decline. He recounts one episode when, the moment an MNF telecast went off the air, Al Michaels turned to lecture Cosell about his drunkenness, threatening to never share the booth with him again. Then Michaels, deciding that he himself needed a drink, handed the luxury box bartender a paper cup and asked for a glass of vodka. The bottle provided to the booth turned out to be virtually empty: between kickoff and the final gun, Howard had drained it dry.

The final straw that rang down the curtain on Cosell's MNF career, of course, came in 1983, when he described Redskins receiver Alvin Garrett, who was black, as "a little monkey." Then, as the phone lines lit up, Cosell attempted to claim, on the air, that he had never used the word "monkey," an absurd denial in the age of videotape.

Although I was acquainted with him for nearly a quarter of a century, I don't pretend to have known Cosell either—certainly, in any case, not as well as Dave Kindred came to know him. But I crossed paths—and crossed swords—with him often enough to consider him a despicable and contempt-ible excuse for a human being, particularly in his later years when he had become thoroughly embittered and turned on friends and enemies with equal venom.

The mid-1980s saw an all-too-brief revival of *Requiem for a Heavyweight*. The production, starring John Lithgow and George Segal, was based on the original 1950s Rod Serling teleplay, and lamentably closed after just three performances. Several of us, in any case, had been invited to the opening night performance, and when Cosell spotted me, Michael Katz, José Torres, Bert Sugar, and our respective wives, he fairly sneered to his wife, "Look, Emmy, it's the boxing fraternity," before elbowing his way past us without further acknowledgement.

Kindred seems to be on much more comfortable ground when he is dealing with Ali, but in attempting to retrace the boxer's relationship with the broadcaster he allowed himself to be walked up a dead-end alley on at least one occasion. Kindred maintains in his introduction that he relied only on "trusted sources" for otherwise undocumented material, but in revealing details of a previously unreported (and almost certainly nonexistent) 1967 episode, he plainly trusted the wrong source and got merrily led down the garden path for his trouble.

Having been reclassified 1-A and having exhausted other remedies, Ali was ordered to report to the draft board in Houston. When his name was called he was asked to step forward as acknowledgement of his agreement to be drafted into the armed forces.

Ali refused to take that symbolic step in Houston on April 23, 1967, and the boxing hierarchy immediately began to move against him. When, a day later, the New York commission revoked his boxing license and withdrew recognition of his heavyweight championship, according to Kindred, a hast-ily formed committee consisting of several high-powered literary types at-tempted to enlist Cosell in a mission to defend Ali, or at least Ali's right to earn a living:

> That day, six men met for drinks at the Lion's Head Bar in New York's Greenwich Village. They were Jack Newfield, a *Village Voice* reporter; novelists Norman Mailer and Frederick Exley; Jimmy Breslin, the *New York Post* columnist; Pete Hamill of the *New York Daily News;* and George Plimpton, editor of the *Paris Review* and an Ali specialist for *Sports Illustrated* . . .

What this ad hoc Ali committee could do, its members had no idea. They knew only that it needed to be done dramatically . . .

"We need a national voice," someone said.

Someone else said, "How about Cosell?"

"George, you know him, don't you?"

In Kindred's version Plimpton was thus deputized to recruit Cosell, only to be rebuffed: "Georgie-boy, I'd be shot, sitting right in this armchair, by some crazed redneck sharpshooter over there in that building," Cosell allegedly told Plimpton, "if I deigned to say over the airwaves that Muhammad Ali should be completely absolved and allowed to return to the ring. I'd be shot, right through that window."

(Plimpton, says Kindred, at this point reminded the broadcaster, "Howard, no one's going to shoot you from that building. That's the Banker's Trust.")

"Reporting to the Lion's Head literati," Plimpton told them that Cosell had rejected their invitation on the grounds that the committee's ideas were "absurd, amateurish, and impractical," writes Kindred.

Now, this account immediately set my bullshit detector to twitching. While I had yet to meet Cosell in 1967, I was intimately acquainted with the Lion's Head in that era, and it seemed unlikely that a summit meeting of this magnitude could have taken place without my knowledge. Both Cosell and Plimpton are conveniently dead (as are Newfield and Exley), but it immediately struck me that somebody had sold Kindred a bill of goods with their account of this "committee."

Hamill was working at the *Post,* not the *News,* in 1967, and Breslin, I'm pretty sure, was not at the *Post,* but this went beyond a mere conflation of employers. To the best of my recollection, Fred Exley was at that time living in Florida, his initiation into the world of the Lion's Head still a couple of years away.

When I contacted Hamill in Mexico City a few days ago and asked him about the account, he replied that "the scene in the Kindred book almost certainly never took place—and if it did, I was certainly not part of it.

"I only remember Mailer being in the Head on two occasions, probably for book parties, and I never saw Plimpton there at all," said Hamill. "Neither was a regular."

Hamill's recollection, like mine, was that Exley had yet to make his first visit to the Lion's Head at the time in question, but just to be on the safe side, I consulted Exley's own memoir, his seminal story on the Lion's Head entitled "The Last Great Saloon," which appeared in a 1990 edition of *GQ*. In that piece, Exley himself says that his first visit to the bar he would come to call home didn't occur until June of 1969.

"I never thought of Plimpton as an Ali specialist at *SI* [the guy who wrote about him most was probably Gil Rogin]," continued Hamill. "I did see Cosell at the '68 Olympics in Mexico City and remember him [off-camera] being vehement about the treatment of Ali.

"I actually liked Cosell—no doubt a Brooklyn thing," said Hamill, "but it's unlikely that the group Kindred assembles, even if it had existed, would ever have deferred to a TV/radio guy as their leader. Another tip-off [about the 'meeting'] is that the paragraph starts off 'that day.' Nobody met during the day for anything in those days. We were all too busy working."

"I'm not saying it didn't happen," said Breslin when I contacted him. "But if it did, I don't remember it."

But the fact that Kindred's account of the apocryphal Lion's Head summit was hopelessly off-base doesn't diminish the unlikelihood of Cosell agreeing to spearhead such a project. As the author himself acknowledges in *Sound and Fury,* the man who would later proclaim that he had been a one-man voice in the wilderness standing up for Ali was, "on the important questions in Ali's life . . . invisible.

"In his four memoirs, Cosell never takes a position pro or con on Ali's opposition to the Vietnam War, or on the war itself, for that matter," concedes Kindred. "Cosell did a clever high-wire act. He portrayed himself as a brother-in-arms standing with Ali. In fact, he never defended a single Ali position on race, politics, or religion. He defended the fighter's rights to hold those positions. That was a good and brave thing to do in a time when many people's rights were taken from them. But it was a different thing from agreeing with Ali's philosophies and ideologies. Cosell's defense was a narrow constructionist's that excused him from ever taking a stand on the volatile issues in Ali's life."

The author also notes that while their Abbott-and-Costello routine often made for a mutually beneficial relationship, it was hardly a symbiotic one: "As Cosell did not truly know Ali," writes Kindred, "Ali never knew Cosell."

TheSweetScience.com
2006

The Prisoner of Hell's Kitchen

A Shaggy Bag Story

When I start weaving one of these stories from three or four seemingly disparate strands I'll confess that there's a certain mischievous pleasure imagining a befuddled reader wondering "How the hell is he going to get home from here?"

If I've done enough wrong in this life that I'm brought back as a boxing promoter in the next one, first thing I do is abolish press conferences—press conferences announcing fights, post-fight press conferences, photo ops at the Statue of Liberty, the lot of them.

From the standpoint of the working press, they're all but useless, and from the promoter's they represent an unnecessary expense producing little of value in return. For a fraction of what they'd save, promoters could spend their money on something truly useful, like health insurance for their boxers.

There's a wonderful scene in Neil Simon's *The Prisoner of Second Avenue*. Mel (Jack Lemmon), already afflicted with big-city malaise, has endured a rough patch in his life that makes the Trials of Job seem trifling by comparison. When a scruffy-looking kid bumps into him on the street, he reaches for his wallet, realizes it is missing, and takes off in pursuit of a mugger half his age.

After a mad dash across Central Park, a panting Mel runs his quarry down and pounces on him. Cocking his fist, he demands his wallet "or I'll beat your head in." The terrified mugger complies. Mel, his sagging spirits lifted by having finally fought back, returns home to report the adventure to his wife, Edna (Anne Bancroft), who seems unimpressed.

"But I got my wallet back!" he says.

"Your wallet's brown. This one's black," she sighs. "You left yours on the dresser this morning. This isn't your wallet, Mel." `

The excitement drains from Mel's face.

"My God," he says. "I mugged a kid."

In bygone times press conferences were absolutely essential to putting on a fight show. You hired a restaurant, picked up the tab for lunch, poured a bunch of booze down the throats of the assembled newsmen, and they'd return to their offices and dutifully file glowing stories about that week's Fight of the Century. At a time when there were a dozen daily papers in New York and five or six in Boston this made a lot of sense. It eventually got to the point that promoters were so reliant on the practice that they tried to outdo each other. If one of Dan Parker's colleagues thought the other guy's lunch was better, he might write about his fight and forget yours altogether. Promoters learned that this could usually be addressed by slipping favored scribes a cash-stuffed envelope on the way out the door.

By the late 1970s Don King had taken this practice to a whole new level, and when word got out in connection with the investigation of the ABC/Ring *U.S. Boxing Championships* it cost some pretty good writers their jobs. Since newspapers today are more ethically circumspect, overt bribery is discouraged, but that doesn't mean it has disappeared altogether. Nowadays, if the guy owns his own website, the promoter can just write him a check and call it an "ad."

Back in those days, of course, the post-fight press conference did not exist. Even after the biggest of fights, reporters routinely interviewed both winner and loser in their respective dressing rooms. There was plenty of room to handle the working press, and everybody knew who they were.

I'm not sure when the post-fight press conference started, or why, but I can promise you one thing: they're not for the press. If you're writing on deadline, you want to get a quote or two to set the mood (and prove to the boss and your readers that you were there) and get your story written and filed as quickly as possible, not sit around waiting an hour or more for the last undercard fighter's manager to be seated at the dais so a press conference can get started.

The result is that post-fight press conferences are mainly attended by posses, entourages, relatives, and hangers-on. They're all but useless for anyone actually covering the event, and if you see a newspaperman or even a legitimate internet reporter at a post-fight press conference, you can pretty much take it for granted that he's already filed his story. Ninety percent of the people in attendance have no function and no reason to be there anyway, and the bigger the event, the more true that is.

The same is true for press luncheons and their even more ghastly modern-day counterpart, the Golden Boy Media Event masquerading as a press conference. The latter is as a rule open to the public and overrun with shrieking fans; a reporter who actually tries to interview a fighter at one of them might be shot on sight.

At any of the aforementioned, there is a pretty reliable way to determine how many frauds are in attendance: the applause meter.

Reporters don't cheer for fighters or trainers or promoters or television executives, so the more people who break into applause when one of these is introduced, the more interlopers you know are in the room. You don't ever hear members of the working press applauding the police commissioner at his press conferences, do you?

Imagine the reaction if a member of the White House press corps showed up at a presidential press briefing and asked Barack Obama for an autograph. Yet there are people who regularly show up at fight press conferences with boxing gloves, posters, and magazine covers they expect the fighters to sign. These people aren't writers—and if they are they should be drummed out of the profession.

Today's boxing writers—the real ones, anyway—don't care about a free lunch. They're there to do a job, but these things have become so glutted with hangers-on that newspapers often tell their reporters to skip them altogether. It's the very rare New York press conference today when the *Times,* the *Post,* the *News,* and *Newsday* all have a representative there, but the promoter winds up picking up the tab for lunch for sixty, eighty, a hundred people anyway. A promoter could get a lot more mileage out of promising each newspaper, and the four or five internet sites people actually read, ten minutes each alone with each fighter. They'd get more and better coverage out of it, and it sure would be a lot cheaper.

And the perfectly ridiculous part of this is that the promoters know it, too. Just a couple of weeks ago I drove back from Yankee Stadium with Lou DiBella and listened to him moan the whole way about all the lunches he'd bought for people who as far as he could tell had never written a word about one of his fights. Exactly a week later, Lou was buying lunch for ninety at

Gallagher's. There might have been two newspapermen in the whole bunch. The applause meter almost went off the charts that day.

If you've spent much time at all around the fight game, the chances are you know Teddy Blackburn, and even if you're a casual fan you've probably seen his work, which graces the pages, and sometimes the cover, of almost any boxing publication you could name.

He grew up in Ann Arbor, where his father was a professor at the University of Michigan, but Teddy's interests veered away from academia when he started to hang around a growing enterprise called the Kronk Gym. He hung around there with the young Thomas Hearns, and boxed a bit himself, but if getting knocked out by Booker T. Word in the Detroit gloves wasn't enough to convince him that his vocation lay elsewhere, a sparring session with the late Mickey Goodwin did. Mickey was trying to take it easy on him but he still broke Teddy's nose, and when they toweled off Mick told him he really ought to stick to taking pictures.

Beyond his professional credentials, Teddy enjoys a reputation as one of boxing's truly good guys. This status was officially recognized in 2001, when the Boxing Writers Association of America presented him with the Marvin Kohn Good Guy Award in recognition of what was essentially a one-man campaign to raise funds and build a support system for Gerald McClellan, the former middleweight champion who has been blinded and brain-damaged since his 1995 fight against Nigel Benn. It was one of those boxing tragedies everybody remembers, but boxing people don't like to be reminded that things like this can happen, so apart from Teddy and a few guys like Roy Jones, Gerald doesn't get many visitors.

Over the years Teddy and I have shared rides to fights, bunked together at casino hotels and out of the way flophouses in club-fight towns, and before I went on the disabled list we used to get up two or three mornings a week for a 6 a.m. round of golf at one of the city courses.

Teddy is one of those friends who's always eager to help and never asks anything in return. So a few days ago, as the aforementioned press conference at Gallagher's was breaking up, I saw the baleful look on his face and asked him what the matter was and he said, "Somebody stole my camera bag." I knew it was a long shot, but I was determined to help if I could.

He quickly described the bag, one I knew well because he's had it for years—a black North Face backpack, the principal contents of which on this day consisted of two Nikon cameras and the results of a day's work, stuff he was supposed to get down to the Reuters office so they could move the photographs of Carl Froch and Jermain Taylor on the wire for the papers back in England.

Since the room was still half full, there seemed at least a chance that the culprit hadn't yet made good his escape. Our quickly formulated plan called for me to station myself on the sidewalk outside, where anyone exiting the press conference would have to leave from one of two doors, while Teddy circulated among the crowd, hoping to spot somebody who looked as if he'd recently acquired something he hadn't come in with.

Security at boxing events, and at boxing press conferences, can be pretty lax, but theft is surprisingly rare. This has less to do with the integrity of the guests than the fact that even the posse thugs realize that if anything depreciates faster in value than last week's cell phone, it's last month's laptop or last year's pre-owned camera. Some of these people wouldn't think twice about swiping, say, a press kit right off your seat if you turned away for a moment, but the two cameras in Teddy's bag had set him back $5,000, and a thief would be lucky to get $200 for the pair of them on the street. It would be a lot less trouble to just sneak out the door with somebody else's signed boxing gloves.

I'd been out on the sidewalk for about five minutes, swiveling my head from one door to the other as I clocked the clientele exiting the restaurant. Then, in mid-swivel, I found myself staring at Teddy's backpack.

I hadn't actually seen the kid come out the door, but he was standing right in front of Gallagher's. His face was shrouded by a hoodie, and he seemed to sense me staring at him, because he looked around nervously and quickly crossed the street, where he was joined by an accomplice. The crooks headed west on 52nd Street. I spotted them half a block, and, keeping them in sight, followed at what I hoped was a discreet distance while I simultaneously tried to phone for backup.

To my chagrin I discovered that Teddy's number had vanished from my latest phone. It presumably didn't survive the data transfer after I dropped its predecessor into a fountain at Caesars Atlantic City. DiBella's was switched off. I eventually managed to reach *Boxing Digest* editor Sean Sullivan, who was still at Gallagher's, and told him I had the perps in sight, but by then I was a few blocks away. Sean couldn't find Teddy, but said he'd go look for him. Over and out.

I'm not sure when the perps realized they had a tail, or even if they did at all, but they seemed to cast increasingly furtive looks back over their shoulders as they continued in the direction of the river. By now Times Square was well behind us, and we were in the heart of Hell's Kitchen, between 10th and 11th Avenues, when they made the drop.

The two perps were joined on the sidewalk by the rest of their posse, so now there were at least half a dozen of them. I ducked behind a delivery truck and watched the one with Teddy's backpack enter a building while the other gang members stood sentinel outside.

When he emerged a few minutes later he no longer had the backpack. Now I was in a real quandary. There couldn't have been more than five or six apartments in the building, and the cameras were in one of them. Should I keep the drop under surveillance, or follow the perps?

As I was trying to calculate Popeye Doyle's advice when Frog One and Frog Two split up and went in opposite directions, the delivery truck abruptly pulled away and left me standing there exposed. Across the street, the kids seemed to think this was pretty funny.

I rang Sean's phone again.

"Oh," he said. "Teddy was just looking for you. He said to tell you he found his camera bag under a table at Gallagher's."

I couldn't tell you how many black North Face backpacks I saw on the long walk back to Broadway, but there were a lot of them. For all I know I had just followed some Stuyvesant honor student on his way home to drop off his school books.

"But he had a backpack that looked just like Teddy's," I tried to tell my wife.

"I don't care." She was unmoved. "You were profiling."

I was about to offer in my own defense the fact that they had behaved so suspiciously while they were leading me on this wild goose chase when I remembered another pearl of Neil Simon wisdom.

In *The Prisoner of Second Avenue,* as he rationalizes his mistake, Mel recalls that he was certain he'd nailed his mugger when the guy abruptly took flight.

"Why did he run?" wonders Mel.

"You *chased* him, didn't you?" says his wife. "You get chased, you run."

Although it may have produced a wild-goose chase through the streets of New York, Teddy Blackburn weighed in with the information that the mission wasn't predicated entirely on false assumptions: "I found my bag at Gallagher's, all right, but it wasn't where I'd put it. It was hidden under a table on the other side of the room, so I've got to assume that somebody did plan to take it later."

The Pac-Man Politician

Does PPV Stand for Pay-per-Vote?

Pacquiao became the Martha Coakley of the 2007 Philippine elections, blowing his double-digit lead down the stretch as Representative Antonino-Custodio retained her seat. Bob Arum, who had as promised gone to General Santos City to campaign for his star attraction, blamed the loss not on Pacquiao's failure to identify substantive issues but rather on what the promoter called "a pervasive fear among the voters that if Manny was elected he would stop boxing." So what were we to make of the fact that three years later Manny ran for Congress again—and this time was elected in a landslide?

SAN ANTONIO, Texas—Under normal circumstances it's asking a bit much of a boxer to prepare for two opponents simultaneously, but we'll actually be surprised if Manny Pacquiao doesn't have two fresh scalps on his wall a month from now.

The 2006 Fighter of the Year is a 10-1 favorite to beat Jorge Solis, an undefeated but largely untested Mexican, in Saturday night's non-title fight at the Alamodome.

And the latest polls emanating from the Philippines show the Pac-Man with a 20-point lead in his quest to unseat incumbent Representative Darlene Antonino-Custodio in his race for a Congressional seat in his homeland.

You might expect that a boxing promoter trying to sell tickets for the former event might be somewhat annoyed by the distraction presented by the latter exercise, but whether he has developed a genuine concern for the impoverished Tagalogs of South Catobato or is, as some suspect, merely humoring his star attraction, Bob Arum has thrown himself headlong into the Pacquiao-for-Congress campaign.

"I believe in Manny's issues," Arum told a San Antonio boxing audience

Wednesday. "I have decided to accept his invitation to go to General Santos City to stump for him."

Arum plans to fly to the Philippines to campaign for Pacquiao once Manny disposes of Solis, but in the meantime he has neatly folded the May 12 Filipino elections into this weekend's Texas promotion. Pacquiao for congressman posters double as advertisements for the fight, and buttons advertising Arum's "Blaze of Glory" card at the Alamodome read, simply,

Vote for MANNY!
April 14
LIVE ON PPV

"What does PPV stand for?" asked one pressroom wag. "Pay-per-Vote?"

Solis says he is "here to beat Manny Pacquiao." Back in the Philippines, Darlene Antonino-Custodio appears to be somewhat less confident. The two-term congresswoman, in fact, attempted to have the telecast of Saturday night's fight card blacked out in Pacquiao's constituency, on the grounds that its airing would violate the nation's equal-access election laws.

(The Philippine Commission on Elections met in en banc session yesterday and ruled that the fight could be broadcast.)

Pacquiao is hoping to make the smoothest transition from the ring to government since Idi Amin, the former heavyweight champion of Uganda, proclaimed himself that nation's president.

But what, we wondered, is Manny's platform? I mean, the Filipino government did the right thing and pulled its troops out of Iraq three years ago, eliminating *that* controversy.

"The way the political system works there, the power is in the hands of entrenched oligarchies," campaign manager Arum explained yesterday. "Two or three designated members of one family run for office and then band together to kill all progress. They only serve to protect the interests of the family business.

"Manny's opponent is a member of a family that runs the whole economy in that part of the Philippines," claimed Arum. "Her record is that anything the president proposes to do for the people, she opposes it.

"So Manny's platform is very simple. He won't represent special interests. He'll represent the people. It's one thing if a politician says that, because they're all full of shit anyway, but when somebody like Manny says it they believe it because *he* believes it.

"Now, whether he can really effectuate change is another question," admitted Arum, who is no stranger to politics himself, having served in the Justice Department under Robert F. Kennedy. "But one thing I know about Manny: He really cares about people. You won't have to worry about *him* being a dishonest politician."

"If he wins it will be a great example for the other boxers of the world," said WBC president José Sulaiman, who knows a bit about winning rigged elections. "I'm going to support him."

If it strikes you as curious that Sulaiman would travel from Mexico to Texas for a fight with only his organization's meaningless "International" 130-pound belt on the line, there are at least two good reasons why he is here.

One is that there are two authentic WBC title fights on the undercard—Jorge Arce-Cristian Mijares for the 115-pound championship, and Brian Viloria-Edgar Sosa for the vacant light flyweight belt.

The other? "The WBC has a convention scheduled in the Philippines," said Sulaiman. "We really need a Filipino champion."

Arum, already looking past Solis (as, one suspects, is Pacquiao), hopes to match Manny later this year against Marco Antonio Barrera, whom he stopped in the 11th round of a one-sided fight here four years ago.

This would necessarily obviate a Barrera rematch with Juan Manuel Marquez that had been thought to be on the drawing board for August. Marquez, said Arum, would instead fight Umberto Soto in the fall. "Those are the fights I want to get done, and the winners can fight each other," he said of an arrangement that, it might be noted, appeared to have the blessing of Sr. Sulaiman, who nodded happily as the scheme unfolded.

"Of course," said Arum, "we'll have to schedule those fights when the Philippine legislature isn't in session."

BoxingTalk.com
2007

Baghdad's Friday Night Fights

Although this column is clearly a spoof, the news item prefacing the piece and the quotes attributed to Don King are all completely factual and are repeated verbatim. Five years later Saddam Hussein is no longer with us; Valuev had lost the WBA title to David Haye (who made his first defense against John Ruiz) but the implicit point remains unchanged: The notion that a public boxing event could safely be staged in Iraq is as absurd today as it was in 2005.

> NEWS ITEM: Legendary promoter Don King said he would like to host a morale-boosting boxing exhibition in Iraq featuring world champion boxers he represents. King made his comments to CNN's Wolf Blitzer while appearing on *The Situation Room* last week. Major General Thomas R. Turner II of the U.S. Army's 101st Airborne Division told King earlier this year he would welcome such an event.

BAGHDAD—Arabic translators monitoring the ongoing trial of Saddam Hussein report that in testimony this week the former Iraqi dictator claimed to have been tortured by his American captors. Hussein asserted that he was subjected to cruel and inhumane treatment in violation of the Geneva Accords when he was forced to watch all 12 rounds of a World Boxing Association heavyweight championship fight between Nicolay Valuev and John Ruiz.

Saddam charged that President George W. Bush had entered into a conspiracy with boxing promoter Don King to beam the telecast of the Berlin fight into his jail cell.

"Bush would never do this to his own people," the erstwhile despot told the court. "The fight was banned by United States television networks. Not a single American had to watch this fight."

Hussein claimed that prison authorities, with the connivance of Bush and

King, had not only secretly ordered up the German pay-per-view telecast of the bout between the plodding, 7-foot Russian giant and the U.S.-born former champion but had stolen the remote control from his cell to prevent him from switching it off.

In voicing his outrage, Saddam pointed out that not even Al Jazeera, a network which routinely televises live beheadings, had been willing to subject its viewers to the King-promoted fight.

In a related development, The World's Greatest Promoter announced plans to stage a boxing exhibition, possibly including a world championship fight, in Iraq next year.

"Major General Turner and President George W. Bush are absolutely right about helping the troops," King told CNN's Wolf Blitzer. "I intend to answer the President's call and do all I can to support our troops. Our men and women in uniform around the world are defending our freedom and liberties. They need to know that we appreciate their service and will make sacrifices to honor their bravery and dedication."

Although King traveled to Germany in his role as Ruiz's longtime promoter, by the time the December 17 fight at Berlin's Max Schmeling Halle took place he had Valuev under contract as well. Ruiz's attorneys, noting the controversial nature of the widely booed Berlin decision, intend to petition the WBA to order an immediate rematch. While no venue in the Western world is likely to offer a site fee for that bout, King, in a masterful stroke, has reportedly informed the White House of his willingness to stage Valuev-Ruiz II before the troops in Iraq.

"I intend to stage exhibition matches in Iraq displaying the skills of many great champions from the boxing world," said the flag-waving promoter. "I want to entertain the troops, raise their morale and let our soldiers know that the American people are one hundred percent behind them. It will be an unforgettable, historic event. I'll even stage a true championship match if I am allowed."

"Don," Blitzer reportedly sighed off-camera, "haven't they suffered enough already?"

TheSweetScience.com
2005

Paulie's Hair

The Kojak look didn't last much longer than Paulie's junior welterweight title, which he had already given up by the time he lost to Hatton that November. Since he lost three of his next five fights, maybe it's time to bring back the hair extensions.

His fellow passengers probably didn't even recognize the young fellow with the freshly shaved head on Tuesday morning's New York-to-Boston Acela.

Suffice it to say that the length of Paulie Malignaggi's hair isn't going to be an issue any time in the immediate future. He doesn't have any.

When he came to his senses and realized that wearing a head full of corn-row extensions into the ring against Lovemore N'Dou had nearly cost him the fight, Malignaggi went to the opposite extreme. When Malignaggi was growing up in Brooklyn, if a kid turned up looking like he does right now it usually meant the teacher had sent him home with a note asking the parents to do something about the head lice.

Paulie flew back to New York from Manchester on Sunday. He shaved his head on Monday evening, and by the next morning he was en route to Boston to consult with Dr. Steven Margles of the Lahey Clinic about the right hand he damaged on N'Dou's head in England Saturday night.

"I think Paulie realizes now that he's not a little boy any more, and he shouldn't do stuff like that," said promoter Lou DiBella, who had unsuccessfully argued against the coif in the dressing room even before the near-disaster in the ring at Manchester City Stadium.

"Manchester is a working-class town. There were 58,000 people in the stands and he managed to alienate most of them before the fight even started, so he was not only dealing with a hostile crowd, but it didn't sit too well with the judges, either. A couple of them admitted afterward that it had been a factor. Every time Paulie would feint, the hair would fly in front of his face, so if one of the judges couldn't see exactly what had happened he probably wasn't going to give Paulie the benefit of the doubt. Ultimately he had to overcome the crowd, the disapproval of the officials, and a probably broken hand to beat N'Dou."

Malignaggi (25-1) got the nod on the cards of two judges to pull out a split decision on Saturday night's card, retaining his IBF 140-pound title and preserving the possibility of a November megafight against Ricky Hatton, who won a unanimous decision over Juan Lazcano in the other half of the Versus-telecast doubleheader.

Malignaggi's 'do began to unravel almost the first time he got hit, and a few rounds into the fight it was in such disarray that referee Mickey Vann ordered him back to the corner to be bound up with adhesive tape.

And once that stopgap measure proved inadequate, cut man Danny Milano began snipping away at the dreads between rounds with a pair of shears. Over the last couple of rounds, Paulie's head looked like a partially plucked chicken.

"It was," said Malignaggi afterward, "a really hairy situation."

When he got home he took one look in the mirror and reached for the razor. Less than half an hour later he looked like a contestant in a Lou DiBella look-alike contest.

Dr. Marglos, who had earlier performed several surgeries on Micky Ward's brittle hands, first operated on Malignaggi four years ago, grafting a bone from his pelvis onto the damaged paw, and has performed several subsequent repairs to the oft-injured hand.

"We won't know for a fact that it's broken until he sees the doctor," said DiBella Tuesday morning, "but Paulie thinks it probably is, and I'm inclined to agree."

Whether the injury will require surgery or just rest, it would seem to rule out an intervening fight, so Malignaggi almost certainly won't fight again until his proposed meeting with Hatton in November.

Saturday night's card was supposed to build interest in that one, but neither winner's performance seemed exactly calculated to bring them running to the box office. In his first outing since December's dismantling at the hands of Floyd Mayweather, Hatton (44-1), amusingly, came into the ring looking like the Pillsbury Doughboy, wearing a fat suit that teased his "Ricky Fatton" nickname, and although he won handily on the scorecards, Lazcano did appear to wobble him late in the bout.

"Unless the news [from Dr. Margles] is something truly catastrophic, it shouldn't affect the November timetable at all," said DiBella.

BoxingTalk.com
2008

Golden Boy's Gold Rush

If the **New York Times** *bought the rights to the Pulitzer Prize, how much credibility would those annual awards retain? What if a top studio like MGM got to pick the Academy Award winners? Or, say, the Dallas Cowboys got to fill in the network TV schedule before any other team even thought about its dates? It's inconceivable that the position Golden Boy Promotions enjoys in the world of boxing would be tolerated in any other field. In fact, if it were anything but boxing, there would have been a congressional investigation long before now. When future historians look back at Richard Schaefer's lasting impact on the sport, they'll probably say, "Well, yeah, but he made the trains run on time."*

Early in his political career, the young Lyndon Baines Johnson served as a congressional aide to Representative Richard Kleberg, the wealthy owner of the King Ranch who was elected to seven consecutive terms in the House of Representatives because, at least in part, he often ran unopposed.

One year an upstart rival politician we'll call Joe Bob had the temerity to challenge Kleberg in the Democratic primary, resulting in the convocation of the Texas congressman's staff to plot an election strategy. Several ideas were kicked around before Kleberg himself came up with a brainstorm.

"Why don't we start a rumor that he [copulates with] sheep?" proposed the politician.

This was a bit over the top, even for Lyndon Johnson. The future president leapt to his feet and said, incredulously, "But you *know* Joe Bob *don't* [copulate with] sheep!"

"Yeah," replied the congressman, "but watch what happens when the son of a bitch has to stand up and *deny* it!"

Events of the past week or two have seen the Floyd Mayweather camp adopt a similar tactic with regard to Manny Pacquiao. But if introducing what would appear to be a red-herring issue—the debate over drug-testing procedures—to the negotiating process was intended as a negotiating ploy, it would appear for the moment to have backfired. The idea might have been to force Pacquiao to go on the defensive, but Pac-Man instead responded with his stock in trade, the counterpunch—in this case the multimillion dollar defamation suit he filed against the Mayweathers, *père et fils,* with the U.S. District Court in Las Vegas on Wednesday.

In boxing even more than in life, you never say never, but you'd have to say that Pacquiao-Mayweather is a dead issue right now, at least in its March 13 incarnation.

In the midst of all the posturing that's gone on, you'd be a fool to accept at face value anything coming out of any of the parties' mouths. And if you had absolutely no desire to actually get in the ring with Manny Pacquiao but were still looking to save face, you'd do pretty much exactly what Mayweather has done. Which is to say, talk tough while you get others to run interference with a series of actions seemingly calculated to ensure that the fight doesn't come off.

But left almost unscathed in all of this heretofore has been the convoluted role played by Golden Boy—by CEO Richard Schaefer; by the company's namesake, Oscar the Blogger, by GBP's subsidiary enterprise, *The Ring*; and by at least a few of the lapdogs and lackeys whose favor GBP has cultivated elsewhere in the media.

In late March of 2008, Shane Mosley and Zab Judah appeared at a New York press conference to announce a fight between them in Las Vegas two months later. As it happened, the BALCO trial had gotten underway out in California that week. That day I sat with Judah and his attorney, Richard Shinefield, as they explained that they intended to ask that both boxers agree to blood testing in the run-up to the fight. Citing Mosley's history with BALCO and its products The Cream and The Clear (which Shane claimed Victor Conte had slipped him when he wasn't looking), Shinefield and Zab, noting that Nevada drug tests were limited to urinalysis, proposed that the supplementary tests be administered by the World Anti-Doping Agency.

Want to know what Richard Schaefer's response to that was?

"Whatever tests [the NSAC] wants them to take, we will submit to, but we are not going to do other tests than the Nevada commission requires," said Schaefer. "The fact is, Shane is not a cheater and he does not need to be treated like one."

But the fact is that Mosley had a *confirmed* history as a cheat. Manny Pacquiao does not. Yet in the absence of a scintilla of evidence or probable cause, less than two years later Schaefer was howling that the very integrity of the sport would be at risk unless Pacquiao submitted to precisely the same sort of testing he had rejected for Mosley.

And you thought it was *Arum* who was famous for saying "Yeah, but yesterday I was lying. Today I'm telling the truth!"

Schaefer, by the way, defended his 180-degree turnabout by saying he is now better educated on the issue. He couldn't resist aiming a harpoon at the media by adding that many sportswriters "don't know the difference between blood and urine testing."

Don't know how to break this to you, Richard, but sportswriters, who have had to deal with this stuff for the past twenty years, probably know more about drug-testing procedures than any other group you could name.

Now, the reasonable assumption would be that by assuming the role of the point man in this unseemly mess, Schaefer was insulating his boss (De La Hoya) and his fighter (PBF) by keeping their fingerprints off it while he made a fool of himself publicly conducting this snide little campaign.

And yes, Money Boy would have stayed out of the line of fire had not a two-month-old, expletive-filled rant, in which he described the Philippines as the world's foremost producer of performance-enhancing drugs, exploded on the internet at the most inopportune moment. That the lawsuit was filed less than 24 hours after "Floyd Meets the Rugged Man" overtook the Tiger Watch probably wasn't a coincidence.

And we're assuming that this Dan Petrocelli, the lawyer who filed Pacquiao's suit, knows what he's doing, because if there were an even one-zillionth chance that somebody could credibly link Manny to PEDs, then it was a pretty dumb thing to do. You could ask Roger Clemens about that. Clemens' transformation from Hall of Famer-in-waiting to nationwide laughingstock didn't come from the Mitchell Report. It came from his wrongheaded decision to file a lawsuit against Brian McNamee, which in turn threw everything open to the discovery process.

De La Hoya, in the meantime, was playing both sides of the fence. He let Schaefer play Bad Cop as he distanced himself from the negotiating process, but simultaneously was sniping away at Pacquiao from his First Amendment–protected perch as a ring.com blogger.

"If Pacquiao, the toughest guy on the planet, is afraid of needles and having a few tablespoons of blood drawn from his system, then something is wrong . . . I'm just saying that now people have to wonder: 'Why doesn't he want to do this? Why is [blood testing] such a big deal?'" wrote Oscar the

Blogger. "A lot of eyebrows have been raised. And this is not good."

Ask yourself this: Exactly what *caused* those eyebrows to be raised, other than the innuendo coming straight from Oscar's company?

Providing De La Hoya with a forum from which to dispense propaganda only begins to illustrate the hopelessly compromised position from which *The Ring* continues to operate. They might as well give Schaefer a column, too, while they're at it.

Nearly seven months have elapsed since we last visited the *Ring*/Golden Boy relationship, and at the risk of winding Nigel up, it might be useful here to note that in the midst of last June's discourse, *The Ring*'s editor offered a laundry list of the magazine's covers since the De La Hoya takeover as a demonstration of Golden Boy's restraint.

After listing them, Nigel Collins wrote "that's 28 covers over the course of 21 issues, of which Top Rank had 12 fighters, as opposed to eight for Golden Boy and eight for other promotional entities. Obviously, *The Ring* has shown no bias to Golden Boy when it comes to magazine covers."

It had never even been suggested that the conflict of interest extended to the magazine playing favorites in choosing its cover subjects, but since Nigel brought it up it is probably worth noting now that of those eight covers given over to "other promotional entities," two were of David Haye, whose promoter was properly listed as "Hayemaker," but who had also signed a promotional deal with Golden Boy in May of 2008. (Just last month GBP issued a release in De La Hoya's name in which it described itself as "Golden Boy Promotions, the United States promoter of World Boxing Association Heavyweight World Champion David Haye.")

And even more to the point, in four other issues Nigel Collins offered in evidence, the cover subject was Floyd Mayweather (Independent), although what has transpired with regard to the Pacquiao fight doesn't make Money look very independent at all, does it?

We don't regularly keep track of these things, but in making sure we didn't misquote Oscar's Blog we also came across a representation of the January 2010 issue on *The Ring*'s website. The picture on the cover of the Bible of Boxing is of the Golden Boy himself, and the cover story "De La Hoya: The Retirement Interview."

Wow! Now there's a hot topic for crusading journalists.

High Blood Sugar and Sour Excuses

As a rule I'd prefer to leave investigative pieces in the hands of younger journalists who are not only better suited to the task but seem to enjoy the process a lot more than I do, but the litany of excuses that followed the younger Klitschko's 2004 loss to Lamon Brewster simultaneously aroused my curiosity and insulted my intelligence.

On the night of April 10, 2004, Lamon Brewster had climbed off the floor in the fourth, and a round later was beating the piss out of Wladimir Klitschko when referee Robert Byrd intervened to take Klitschko into protective custody. Although Wladimir's performance was consistent with—indeed, redolent of—his prior boxing history, a day later he and his camp were fanning the flames of a conspiracy theory, charging that the beaten fighter had been mysteriously drugged.

A few years ago George Foreman recalled his reaction to his loss to Muhammad Ali in their 1974 Rumble in the Jungle as one of the most shameful episodes of his boxing career. "By saying I'd been tricked or that my food might have been poisoned I detracted from Ali's victory," said Foreman. "The man beat me that night. I should have given him credit for a great performance. Instead I was so embarrassed I started looking around for excuses."

Wladimir must not have been paying attention. After wilting before Brewster's fifth-round onslaught in their WBO heavyweight title fight at the Mandalay Bay, the Ukrainian tried to alibi away his performance by claiming that his food had been tampered with, and trainer Emanuel Steward subsequently claimed that his fighter was suffering from "unusually high blood sugar."

"It wasn't the water in Wladimir's eyes," said Brewster's promoter Don King a few days later. "It wasn't no soup he ate at the Mandalay Bay. It was Lamon Brewster's punches that knocked him out. *That*'s what happened to Wladimir Klitschko."

On May 3, attorney Judd Burstein undertook the representation of the Brothers Klitschko. Two days later, to great fanfare, Burstein posted a letter demanding a federal investigation into the circumstances surrounding the Brewster-Klitschko fight, copies of which he sent to every media outlet on his Rolodex.

Burstein must have coveted the Klitschko account badly. The circulation of the letter might make the younger Klitschko look like a crybaby, but it makes his lawyer look just plain silly.

The public release of Burstein's missive to Daniel G. Bogden, the United States Attorney for the District of Nevada, was accompanied by a press release that included this bizarre sentiment voiced by the defeated Klitschko: "I have thought long and hard about requesting an investigation because I am concerned that the public, and particularly my fans, will see me as making excuses instead of taking responsibility for a loss."

What makes this apologia so laughable is that in the month since getting whipped by Brewster, Wladimir has done nothing *but* make excuses. And there's not the slightest suggestion anywhere that he has even remotely accepted responsibility for his loss. The Klitschko camp even fired cut man Joe Souza, claiming that his liberal application of Vaseline had "trapped body heat" inside the fighter. If that were true, Souza would have an entire century's worth of co-conspirators, including virtually every man who ever hefted a spit-bucket.

When his brother fought Corrie Sanders at the Staples Center two weeks later, Wladimir Klitschko was the representative dispatched from Vitali's camp to Sanders' dressing room to oversee the gloving of the opponent. Sanders later recalled that Wladimir (whom he himself had knocked out in two rounds last year) spent virtually his entire time in the dressing room that night offering a litany of excuses for the Brewster fight.

Dr. Margaret Goodman is the chairwoman of the Nevada State Athletic Commission's medical advisory board and has, since the appointment of Dr. Flip Homansky to the NSAC, served as Nevada's chief ringside physician. She was in the ring and attending to Klitschko seconds after Byrd stopped the fight.

Although there are obviously some doctor-patient confidentiality issues involved, Nevada Attorney General Ken Kizer has assured Dr. Goodman that by placing their inflammatory charges in the public domain, Klitschko and Burstein have essentially waived confidentiality on the particulars they have discussed.

Burstein's letter to the U.S. Attorney claims that:

> Mr. Klitschko has also confirmed that his head was completely
> clear after the Brewster fight was stopped; yet he could not speak
> or move his body with ease. It is also important to note that Mr.
> Klitschko's blood sugar level after the fight was 230—almost
> twice the normal level. Medical experts have confirmed to the
> Klitschko team that such an elevated count may well indicate that
> Mr. Klitschko was given a foreign substance.

But Dr. Goodman's recollections of events paints a very different picture.

"When I got to the ring Wladimir initially seemed alert and responsive," recalled Goodman, "but then back in the corner he began to exhibit changes. He seemed increasingly lethargic, and within a few minutes became less responsive to questioning."

Dr. Goodman ascribed this to a "transitory loss of consciousness"—in layman's terms, Wladimir was "out on his feet."

Burstein's letter also claims that Klitschko's "pupils were dilated," which isn't precisely correct, either.

"There was an inequality in the pupils," said Goodman, who recognized this as another cause for concern.

"My immediate concern was that there might be a cerebral injury—either bleeding or swelling on the brain," she said. "Or possibly, he had been hit directly in the eye."

Under Goodman's instruction, Klitschko was immediately transported by ambulance to the trauma center at the University Medical Center in Las Vegas. He was accompanied on this journey by EMTs; a neurologist, Dr. Albert Capanna; Vitali Klitschko; and Emanuel Steward (whose name is somewhat bewilderingly spelled "Emmanuel" in Burstein's letter to the U.S. Attorney's office).

On the short trip to the hospital Klitschko was fitted with an IV—a standard precautionary measure in emergency-room situations like this simply because, should the worst happen, the IV will already be in place; were the patient to, just for instance, suddenly go into convulsions, it would be much more difficult to hook him up to an IV.

Under normal circumstances the standard IV would be a D5½NS, which includes a glucose solution. Dr. Goodman was not in the ambulance but noted that "we usually don't use glucose" in connection with potential brain injuries. Still, it is entirely possible that Wladimir Klitschko was either given D5½NS, or, if the EMTs feared a hypoglycemic reaction, they might have pushed an ampule of an even more heavily concentrated glucose substance called D50 to replenish Klitschko's blood sugar. It may well have been that the EMTs, who are *not* brain surgeons, administered the most handy available IV. Either would certainly explain the subsequent—and temporary—elevation in his blood sugar.

"We don't know what was in the IV," said Dr. Goodman.

At the hospital Klitschko was administered a full battery of tests, including a CAT scan, and the pupil inequality resolved on its own. Goodman's initial diagnosis of a Grade 3 concussion was confirmed, but to her relief, her fears of more serious cerebral injury were not. Following the brain examinations, several other routine procedures were followed. All were normal save the blood-sugar level, which was 232, which physicians uniformly agree was "elevated, but not dangerous."

Despite having ruled out their gravest fears, attending physicians wanted Klitschko to remain in the hospital overnight for observation—for the concussion, *not* for the blood sugar, which at that point wasn't even a concern. Dr. Wladimir Klitschko at this point conferred with Dr. Vitali Klitschko and decided to check himself out of the hospital. After signing a form that he was doing so "against medical advice," the two Klitschkos left, accompanied by Steward.

By the next morning they had contacted an independent lab called Quest and had repeat blood work done. Everything was normal, including the sugar level. They requested the specimens from UMC and were given the proper phone numbers and instructions for the protocol involved in obtaining these. Although this information was repeatedly provided to the Klitschkos and their representatives over the next several days, they never followed through.

Although blood work and lab specimens which have yielded positive results would be preserved, samples whose results were unremarkable and normal would routinely be disposed of in a week to ten days. The Klitschko camp was provided with phone numbers and ample warning, but in the absence of a response the samples were destroyed.

Burstein apparently sees this as evidence of a conspiracy:

> Incredibly, though, all of the specimens, with the exception of one milliliter of urine (too small an amount to permit meaningful testing), had been destroyed by UMC and Quest. To date, no

rational explanation has been presented for this failure to deliver the specimens which UMC and Quest had in their possession at the time Mr. Klitschko requested that they be transferred to Dr. [Robert] Voy. Of course, there are a number of possible explanations, some innocent, for what occurred. However, one of those possible explanations—and an eminently reasonable one—is that those specimens were destroyed in order to hide the truth of what happened to Mr. Klitschko.

"The truth of what happened to Mr. Klitschko" is that he got smacked upside the head by Mr. Brewster. And what would have been highly irregular would have been the preservation of the specimens after the normal expiration period.

The independent lab work done for the Klitschkos by Quest tested for over 100 substances, and even included a toxicology scan on Wladimir's boxing trunks, which were thoughtfully provided to the lab the next day. (Which technician got to check out the brown stains remains unlearned.)

Between Quest's tests and those done at UMC after the fight, the only remotely abnormal result was the blood sugar level drawn after the CAT scan had been completed, and that had resolved by the next morning. The 232 level—again, "elevated but not dangerous"—could have several possible explanations, but the IV in the ambulance remains the most likely one.

In other words, if Klitschko (and Burstein, who ought to know better) are going to throw around charges of "foul play," let's hear some specifics. What mysterious substance is this that would cause Wladimir to get his ass kicked and then disappear altogether?

"How come all of the screens have been normal and nothing has come up?" said Dr. Goodman to the *Las Vegas Review Journal*'s Royce Feour last week after Burstein went public with his letter.

Noting that Klitschko had nearly knocked Brewster out in the fourth round, she asked, "How could a drug be that transient? Why wouldn't the tests be more abnormal? How come nothing is showing anything?"

"What is it," Goodman asked us over the weekend, "that they *think* he was given?" The assembled evidence suggests that Wladimir Klitschko ought to be grateful for the medical assistance with which he was provided and thankful for his physical safety. Instead he continues to whine like a child.

And it's not as if this hasn't happened before. Did somebody slip Wladimir a mickey before the Corrie Sanders fight? Was he drugged against Ross

Purrity? Was it some mysterious substance that made Vitali "Quitschko" against Chris Byrd? Was Lennox Lewis able to bust up Vitali because his gloves were loaded?

Oops, sorry. Forget that last one. Judd Burstein represented *Lennox* back then.

What about the other particulars cited in Burstein's missive demanding a federal investigation?

First of all, Burstein noted that the sportsbook odds tumbled from 11-1 to 7-2 in the days before the fight. He claims that it "is virtually unheard of for them to change so dramatically in such a short period of time."

Well, it's *not* unheard of, for openers. What it more probably means is that there was very little action on the fight up until the weekend, and that when there was, most of the money that came in was on Brewster.

This seems entirely reasonable. Think about it: Given his history, would *you* have bet $110 on Klitschko to win $10?

Burstein also made much of the case of the vanishing credential. Supposedly somebody scammed his way into the fight by picking up a credential reserved for an unnamed member of the Klitschko posse. Despite promoters' elaborate precautions, we can assure you that this is not unheard of, either. Since whoever was in possession of the *faux* credential was never spotted, we can probably assume that either somebody miscounted on the initial allotment, or the interloper, if indeed there was one, just found a seat and watched the fight. There is no evidence that any unauthorized person ever got near the Klitschko corner, but Burstein's letter to the U.S. Attorney leaps, incredibly, in a single paragraph, from this allegation, to Robert Mittleman, to Arnold Rothstein and the 1919 Black Sox.

Even more preposterously, Burstein attempts to use as "evidence" a comment made by an employee of the Palms sportsbook to the *Las Vegas Sun*'s Deane Juipe that the Vitali Klitschko-Corrie Sanders fight two weeks later had been taken off the board "because the other Klitschko [Wladimir] looked like he was poisoned or something in the fight with Brewster."

Of course, when this decidedly unscientific view was elicited (on April 19), the Klitschkos had been howling to anyone who would listen about Wladimir having been "poisoned" for eight days already.

Could it be, rather, that the gambling industry came to the same wary conclusion much of the boxing world did? To wit: if you've seen one Klitschko, you've seen them all.

The notion that Wladimir was defeated by foul play and not by his own inadequacies would neatly fit into the agenda of at least one major player on the boxing scene. A few days before the Brewster-Wladimir Klitschko fight, an HBO insider said to boxing author and attorney Thomas Hauser, "How can we go wrong with four Klitschko title fights a year?"

And in a report on the *other* Klitschko's Los Angeles fight two weeks later, *Sports Illustrated*'s Richard Hoffer somewhat preposterously claimed that "Vitali is the sole bona fide heavyweight champion."

Would we risk stooping to a Judd Burstein–level low here to point out the authors of those two statements draw their paychecks from the same company?

And on the basis of exactly *what* does Vitali rate as "the sole and bona fide heavyweight champion"? Beating an out-of-shape, thirty-eight-year-old Corrie Sanders? In point of fact, Vitali had more trouble with Sanders than Hasim Rahman and Nate Tubbs did in Corrie's two previous defeats. Would Sanders have been the "sole and bona fide champion" if *he*'d won? Or would Judd be demanding another investigation?

Even if one accepts the proposition that Lewis was the legitimate heir to the mantle of John L. Sullivan, Joe Louis, and Muhammad Ali, as far as we can see the retired champion and *SI*'s "sole and bona fide" one have at this point just one thing in common. Their lawyer.

TheSweetScience.com

May 2004

Semper Fi or Swift Boat Redux?

Reconsidering the Late Pat Putnam

Yes, sometimes it is personal. That a guy I'd known for more than 30 years turned out to have been conning even his closest friends when it came to an elaborately constructed fictitious past wasn't something I was prepared for, but that so many of his former colleagues—most of them his professional inferiors—would jump on the runaway bandwagon to savage Pat Putnam's memory was something I found even more unsettling.

He was the finest boxing writer of his generation ("Maybe the best since [A.J.] Liebling," says Michael Katz), and the unfortunate part of it is that in the eyes of people who never knew him, the late Pat Putnam's enduring legacy could turn out to be not his lifetime body of work but as the creator of an alternate universe in which he represented himself to have been a Marine Corps veteran of the Korean War who spent 17 months as a POW.

Putnam, who died in 2005, wrote for *Sports Illustrated* for 27 years and was the 1982 recipient of the Nat Fleischer Award for Excellence in Boxing Journalism.

Within the past few days, Putnam's alleged military background has been revealed to have been an elaborate fiction. Veterans' groups have condemned what they termed a "fake" and a "disgrace," and the Boxing Writers Association of America appears to have leapt aboard the same bandwagon, hastily distancing itself from Putnam with the announcement that it would remove his name from an award for perseverance that it had bestowed in his honor in each of the three years following his death.

(Since the BWAA couldn't take Putnam's name off the award fast enough, it should probably be noted that we're talking about an organization that routinely bestows annual awards named for crooked politicians and boxing officials of dubious ethics.)

"He had us all fooled," BWAA president Bernard Fernandez, who labeled Putnam's tale "totally bogus," told the *Navy Times.*

It now appears that Pat Putnam's fate will be to take his place in sporting lore alongside the likes of former Blue Jays manager Tim Johnson and (briefly) erstwhile Notre Dame coach George O'Leary, whose falsification of their resumes brought them into disrepute and cost them their jobs.

There is no doubt that Pat made the claims he stands accused of making. He recounted them in my presence at the Galleria Bar at Caesars and the lounge at the Flame in Las Vegas, and like many others who were taken in, I had little reason to doubt them, but there is an important distinction to be made here.

Pat's wartime adventures might have been tall tales, but he never attempted to make them part of his official resume. They were never a consideration in helping get him a job. They weren't included in his official biographies at the Miami *Herald,* at *Sports Illustrated,* or at TheSweetScience. com, for which he wrote following his retirement from *SI.*

He never publicly represented himself as either a veteran or a POW. He never attempted to join groups representing either. He never applied for veterans' benefits, he didn't ask to be buried with military honors, and he certainly didn't ask the BWAA to label him a war hero or to name an award after him. He didn't even attempt to tell these tall tales to his children.

"Never, ever, ever," said his daughter Colleen Putnam, who was herself surprised by the accounts of his Korean experience that emerged at the time of her father's death.

In short, if Putnam is going to be posthumously convicted of anything, it should be of slinging bullshit in a bar. If that were a hanging offense, we'd all be in trouble.

That the BWAA has chosen to view this as a scandal exposed is, to say the least, interesting, because any public accounts of Putnam's wartime experiences were never promulgated by Pat himself, but almost exclusively by fellow BWAA members—by myself, by Katz, and by Bernard Fernandez, among others—following his death. References—obviously, unchecked—to Korea, the Marines, and POW camps were also prominent in obituaries circulated by both *Sports Illustrated* (Richard O'Brien) and the Associated Press (Ed Schuyler).

In other words, if we're going to question somebody's journalistic principles here, should it be Pat Putnam's or ours?

When BWAA vice president Tom Hauser contacted me with the revelation on Friday morning I was, like virtually everyone else who knew Pat well, stunned, but when asked for my reaction, I replied that since Putnam's journalistic career was an open book that would hold up to scrutiny, the episode should not reflect on his professional accomplishments.

Hauser wondered whether his having been unmasked as an accomplished teller of tall tales on one front might cause some to wonder whether he had similarly embellished his reportage.

For most of his writing career, in fact, Putnam operated under journalistic constraints more rigid than the rest of us had to endure. His stories were combed over by armies of fact-checkers, and *SI* minions routinely phoned his subjects to verify the accuracy of quotes. Moreover, because of *SI*'s status in the sporting world of his era, he almost always had better access to his subjects than the rest of us did. (While the rest of us made do with press conference quotes, Pat usually had a private post-fight audience with the fighter in his hotel suite.)

And whether it was Muhammad Ali or Sugar Ray Leonard or Mike Tyson, there has never been the remotest suggestion that Pat Putnam fabricated a single word in any of his stories. He didn't have to. He could write circles around the rest of us anyway.

It seems plain enough—plain enough to me, anyway—that Pat's fictitious past simply represented saloon banter that eventually took on a life of its own, and I imagine he expected the truth would be revealed once he died and his colleagues began to check the facts of his life against the public record. If so, his confidence in the journalistic process may have been naïvely optimistic.

Still, it must have become at times an unsettling burden to carry around. In the past 24 hours, three different colleagues have recalled the widespread apprehension at the 1988 Seoul Olympics when Pat would have ostensibly been returning to Korea for the first time since the war.

"I remember everybody being so nervous about how Pat would do in the situation," said Leigh Montville. "He pretty much did fine."

"That was my first year at the magazine," recalled Rich O'Brien, "and I too remember quite vividly his distress at being 'back in Korea.' It's very strange to reassess that now."

"I spent a day in Seoul with him when he pointed out the places he was under fire before his capture," said James Lawton of the *Independent* in London.

Judging from its seemingly precipitate reaction in wiping his name off the former Pat Putnam Award, the BWAA has reacted as if the organization itself had been dishonored. Since the move itself came within hours of his denunciation by the veterans' groups, it is interesting to note how that process worked.

Earlier in the week Fernandez had written a story about this year's recipients, Lamont and Anthony Peterson, for the Philadelphia *Daily News,* in which he described Putnam as a "rawhide-tough Marine" who "came back from Korea with four Purple Hearts and the Navy Cross."

Which of these Google-able phrases triggered the interest of Mary and Charles Schantag remains unlearned, but pownetwork.org was shortly on the case.

Although they have no official status, the Schantags operate their investigative resources out of their home in Missouri. Described on a rival website as "a mom-and-pop Columbo team," the Schantags were themselves the subject of an investigation by the office of the Virginia Inspector General for having exercised excessive zeal in outing what they describe as "phonies and wannabes," at least some of whom turned out to be neither.

(In this regard, pownetwork.org would appear to share a spiritual kinship with Swift Boat Veterans for Truth, the sham organization hastily assembled four years ago to undermine the candidacy of John Kerry.)

"It is a disgrace that somebody allowed this to go on for so long," Mary Schantag told ABC News after the Marine Corps had confirmed that they had no record of Putnam having ever served. "I have no sympathy for someone that told lies like this and goes to the grave this way."

Well, they were lies, no doubt about it.

"What made my father such a great writer was that he was such a great storyteller," said Colleen Putnam. "I think this one just got away from him, but what concerns me most is that this is what people will remember him for. That would have been devastating to him.

"I guess until this I never realized," added Ms. Putnam, "that the award they named for my father was associated with all that stuff about Korea."

"But since the Putnam Award is supposed to be for 'courage,' I can see the problem," said Leigh Montville. "Maybe they should just give out another award for writing or reporting and name it after him."

Richard O'Brien pronounced himself "gobsmacked" by the news, but added, "it really doesn't change how I felt about Pat as a friend, and certainly not as a writer."

The revelations may have been surprising, said James Lawton, "but it doesn't take a fig away from his tremendous achievements professionally. But, hell, why would he need to invent extra heroism?"

"It still doesn't change who he was," said Katz. "He'll always be a hero to me."

Me, too.

BoxingTalk.com ·
2008

Termite: A Pest by Any Other Name

As a card-carrying member of the organization, I found the decision by the Boxing Writers Association to honor Termite Watkins troubling for a couple of reasons, not the least of them that it would inevitably be construed as an endorsement of the Bush-Cheney invasion of Iraq.

I can't have been the only one to have felt uncomfortable when Najay Ali walked into the Peristeri Boxing Hall last August. The light flyweight had the slogan "Iraq is Back!" emblazoned on the back of his jacket, and he was accompanied not only by Iraqi coach Maurice "Termite" Watkins, but by Basheer Abdullah, the head coach of the U.S. Olympic boxing team, who didn't always work the corners of his *own* fighters.

I had the feeling I was watching the sporting equivalent of George W. Bush landing on an aircraft carrier to proclaim "Mission Accomplished."

That Ali and, in a sense, Watkins were pawns in a propaganda game is undeniable: the message was, apparently, "Iraq is Liberated—and here's *proof.*"

The Bush administration also attempted to make political hay of the Iraqi soccer team, running campaign ads taking credit for their successes in Athens.

"At this Olympics there will be two more free nations—and two fewer terrorist regimes," said the narrator in the voiceover, as footage of the Iraq team rolled on the Bush-Cheney spot.

When word of this reached the Iraqi players they were uniformly indignant. One of them even told *Sports Illustrated* that if he weren't in Athens playing soccer he'd probably be back in Fallujah fighting against the Americans.

Whether you consider Termite Watkins a great humanitarian or a shameless self-promoter, there can be no doubt that this was the crowning moment of his life. Fighting mainly in his native Texas, he had compiled an admirable 59-5-2 record as a pro, but in his only fight for a world championship he came up on the wrong end of a decision in a WBC 140-pound title bout against Saoul Mamby.

Watkins had originally gone to Iraq as an exterminator, volunteering to work for a subsidiary of the Halliburton corporation. Although he would later describe his decision to travel halfway around the world to kill bugs as "a calling from God," another recollection of his decision sheds more light on his motivation: "It was my time to do my part in serving the country and helping the military," Watkins told reporters in Athens.

In other words, Watkins went because he believed the invasion of Iraq to be justified, and he went to make money.

It was Mike Gfeoller, a regional director for the Coalition Provisional Authority, who first envisioned the potential propaganda value of getting an Iraqi boxer to Athens. Having learned of Watkins' pugilistic background, he approached him with the idea of re-forming a boxing team that hadn't competed in the Games since 1988.

Initially working with equipment nearly as rudimentary as the skills of his pupils, Watkins assembled an 11-man team, but once the word got out, a donated ring, gloves, and protective cups quickly materialized.

Given what he had to work with, there is no question Watkins did a tremendous job, but the greatest coach in the world couldn't have transformed the Iraqi boxers into bona fide world-class competitors overnight.

None of them qualified for the Olympics. In qualifying matches, Najay Ali went 0-3. But pressure was exerted on the International Olympic Committee to extend a "special invitation" to one member of the Iraqi team. Ali got the nod and traveled with Watkins to Colorado Springs, where he spent six weeks training with the U.S. team.

Many of my brethren scribes felt Watkins should have gotten a medal in Athens, if only for his storytelling prowess. There can be little doubt that Termite relieved much of the tedium of what may have been the dullest boxing tournament in Olympic history.

No reporters had to track Termite down. He found *you*. And, if you had a moment to spare, he would regale you with, mostly, war stories—his awakening in the middle of the night to discover that his bunkhouse was under a mortar attack, being a passenger in a gas-laden Humvee that flipped over doing, or so he claimed, 100 mph.

The tales grew more grandiose with each telling. Ten days into the Olympics you'd have thought Termite had single-handedly put Saddam

Hussein to flight, but nobody protested. In the midst of some truly awful boxing, Termite made for great copy, whether you believed everything he said or not.

And few did. Even the most sympathetic of Termite's chroniclers described him as "a raconteur and boaster," which is a kind way of saying "bullshit artist." He was plainly as much snake oil salesman as snake exterminator. Before getting back into the pestilence game, Watkins had been working in Texas as a used-car salesman. Need we say more?

Only a cynic would suggest that the same sporting politics that got Najay Ali into the Olympics were also responsible for his first round draw. The Iraqi may have been the second-most inept boxer in the Olympics, but in his opening match he met the first. After Ali defeated North Korea's Kwak Hyok Ju 21-7 to advance to the second round, Basheer Abdullah conceded as much when he noted, "I don't want to say anybody is easy in the Olympics, but we thanked God we had that type of draw to get him some confidence."

After Ali was eliminated by Armenia's Aleksan Nalbandyan in the next round, Termite Watkins ensured that he would remain available for interviews by attaching himself to the American team as a spit-bucket carrier.

Even boxing writers who had devoted reams of copy to Watkins' improbable Olympic quest often joked about it over dinner. As far as I could tell, *nobody* believed everything he said, and some didn't believe *anything* he said.

Which is why I found it somewhat startling last week when I received a communiqué from the Boxing Writers Association of America proclaiming Termite Watkins a "hero" and announcing that he would receive a Special Achievement Award at next month's BWAA dinner in Las Vegas.

Having been a member of the organization for over a quarter-century, I've dutifully cast my vote whenever such awards were presented, but I didn't recall this having appeared on any ballot I'd seen. Moreover, I couldn't imagine any boxing writer who had endured prolonged exposure to Termite Watkins voting for it.

BWAA president Bernard Fernandez replied to my query, explaining that Termite had been "nominated and approved by a vote of officers and board members."

As it happened, I found myself seated in the presence of several BWAA officers at Don King's John Ruiz-James Toney press conference at Madison Square Garden the next day, and when the subject came up, not a single one of them could recall having voted to honor Watkins.

Ron Borges said he'd never heard of the vote. Tom Hauser couldn't remember, but said he would likely have abstained in any case. Steve Farhood and Tony Paige had no recollection of any vote for a special achievement award. Most of them did remember that Watkins had been proposed for a "long and meritorious service to boxing" award, but had failed to get enough support to even be placed on the ballot for that honor.

When I suggested to Fernandez that the episode seemed uncomfortably redolent of the previous year's balloting for the Nat Fleischer Award for Distinguished Boxing Journalism, in which the 2003 award was embarrassingly vacated when it was revealed many eligible voters—i.e., past recipients—had never been polled, it appeared to strike a raw nerve. The e-mail I got back went into a rant about "Iraqi boxers who had been routinely tortured by Uday Hussein." (Najay Ali never claimed to have been tortured by anybody. Moreover, the BWAA press release refers to the "triumph" of his having "qualified" for the Olympics, which he did not.)

My suggestion that honoring Watkins could be perceived as legitimizing the invasion of Iraq was predictably challenged by the contention that "even those who oppose the war usually speak of supporting the troops," and that "Watkins initially did go over there to serve as an exterminator at U.S. military installations, which probably made living conditions a little more comfortable for our servicemen and servicewomen."

Now, personally, I think that the best way to "support our troops" would be to bring them home forthwith, but that is beside the point. They had no choice in the matter. Termite Watkins did. He went to Iraq voluntarily, and he was well paid for it. I told Bernard if he wanted to name Watkins Exterminator of the Year, I wouldn't have a problem with that, but this didn't sit well with me.

Bernard did say, "I'd like to see our involvement [in Iraq] quickly lessened if not ended outright," but added, "I do not support politicizing the BWAA one way or the other."

But to me it should seem obvious that honoring Termite Watkins *is* a political statement.

"I refuse to be casually categorized, and neither should you, or anybody," argued Fernandez. "Watkins coached some athletes who were in need of a coach, and had suffered under an oppressive regime. Even the *New York Times* appears to think he did a good job of it. Now, is he a self-promoter hyping himself now? Yeah, probably, and that doesn't sit well with me. But his doing what he did was fairly courageous, and I for one am not going to penalize him for his personal politics."

Bernard also suggested that I "check with Steve Farhood and Tom

Hauser again. They were at the December meeting when Watkins was nominated and confirmed by vote for this award."

I did. Hauser is certain that he wouldn't have voted one way or the other
at the time, but that upon reflection, probably wouldn't have approved the
award for the reasons under discussion here.

"I'm not saying there wasn't a vote taken," said Farhood. "I just don't remember one having taken place."

Watkins, alas, will probably have the last word. *Termite,* his autobiogra-
phy, co-written with Suzy Pepper, will hit the bookstores in two weeks' time.

TheSweetScience.com
2005

Forbes: The New Bible of Boxing?

Brett Pulley was hardly the first journalist to be snookered by Don King, but given the promoter's well-chronicled history of taking liberties with facts, Forbes' *reputation in its field, and the almost limitless fact-checking resources available to a magazine of its stature, wouldn't you have thought that it might have occurred to somebody to vet this story before publishing it?*

If you thought you knew all about boxing, you are about to be disabused. Just pick up a copy of the May issue of *Forbes* magazine—that's the one with Don King on the cover—when it hits the stands next week, and you're bound to be embarrassed by the depth of your ignorance.

We'll bet you didn't know, for instance, that "currently five different punchers lay claim to five different World Heavyweight champion titles, and two other major titles are vacant."

Author Brett Pulley never makes clear exactly which seven sanctioning organizations he considers "major," but then he may have been so busy verbally fellating King that he never stopped to write them down.

Pulley's cover story is at once a paean to The World's Greatest Promoter and a lament for what he considers the sport's decline.

Like many another ill-informed chronicler, Pulley appears to think that the principal deficiency posed by the current heavyweight landscape is that Mike Tyson is no longer part of it: "Boxing's biggest problem—and Don King's ready-made solution—lies in the fact that it hasn't found a flamboyant and dangerous new heavyweight champion since Mike Tyson went to prison [for the first time] in 1992," writes Pulley, conveniently ignoring the fact that when Tyson went to the sneezer in '92 he hadn't been the champion for over two years.

Pulley goes on to demonstrate a serious case of Tysonitis, noting that "since Tyson's exit in 1997, after a disqualification for biting Evander

Holyfield's ear, the sport has been better known for one-round letdowns, mismatches, bums and embarrassments."

Exit? Exit from *what,* exactly? Tyson was the *challenger* in that fight. He'd already lost his title a year earlier when Holyfield knocked him out—and he had ten more fights *after* the 1997 ear-biting incident.

Here's Pulley's version of the origin of the King-Tyson relationship:

> In 1988 Tyson was the youngest heavyweight champion in history and one of the most fearsome fighters ever. But he was vulnerable: His manager, Jim Jacobs, had just died; his trainer and father figure, Cus D'Amato, had died three years before; and his marriage to actress Robin Givens was coming to a volatile end. King seized the moment, convincing Tyson he would make him richer and help fill the void in his life.

Not a word, you'll notice, about Bill Cayton, the co-manager from whom King actually stole Tyson that year.

But then this Brett Pulley clearly comes to praise Don King, not to bury him. He writes, for instance, that "in 1979 King brought the fledgling HBO pay-TV channel its first heavyweight fight and three years later sold another bout to the network for $2 million, putting the now huge Time Warner outlet in the boxing business."

This revelation is apt to come as a major surprise to the people at HBO, who for all these years have been laboring under the delusion that they put *themselves* in the boxing business with George Foreman-Joe Frazier in 1973, and that *that* was their first heavyweight title fight.

The King portrait is framed around last January's Zab Judah-Carlos Baldomir card in New York. Judah is described as "a Brooklyn-bred, gazelle-like welterweight at less than 150 pounds." (As opposed, presumably, to those less-gazellelike welterweights who weigh *more* than 150 pounds.)

And from Pulley's account you'd think that night's defeat of Jean-Marc Mormeck by O'Neill Bell was an upset that made Buster Douglas-Tyson pale by comparison.

But what is most maddening about the *Forbes* story isn't Pulley's boxing ignorance, for which he can be forgiven, but his deliberate propensity for misleading distortion when it suits his purposes. He notes, for instance, that "the Garden has played host to some of the great fights in boxing's history," and even names some of them, but at no point in his story would the reader discover that King's Baldomir-Judah card took place in the 5,000-seat Madison Square Garden *Theatre* and not in the 20,000-capacity main arena.

And he buttresses his point about the sorry state of contemporary boxing by noting that "even a reality show on NBC—*The Contender,* hosted by Sugar Ray Leonard and Rocky actor Sylvester Stallone—didn't help; it got canceled after one season. By contrast, a reality series for Ultimate Fighting Championship, whose bare-knuckled, full-contact fights draw legions of young viewers, soon begins its third season on Viacom's Spike TV."

Which is, strictly speaking, true enough. We're no great fan of *The Contender,* but the fact is that the show was picked up by ESPN for its second season and is now headed for a third. Does one season on NBC and two more on ESPN render that show an abject failure while a three-year run on Spike makes UFC an unqualified success?

Although *Forbes* is ostensibly a financial magazine, Pulley seems at his most befuddled when he's dealing with fiduciary matters. He seems utterly aghast, for instance, when he notes that "Tyson grossed more than $400 million in his career but kept only 25%. During the years he was represented by King, he paid 30% to the promoter, 20% to two managers, and half of what was left to taxes."

Except for the part about the two-headed manager, those figures aren't especially uncommon for a boxer in Tyson's tax bracket. The astonishing part is, or ought to be, what happened to the $100 million he *did* get?

And there's this baffling non sequitur: "Each sanctioning entity takes a 3% cut of the gross purse, and three or four can profit from a single fight when a title is being 'unified.'"

Which is once again true, or would be if it ever happened. Off the top of my head I can recall exactly one fight in which all four major titles were involved—Bernard Hopkins-Oscar De La Hoya in 2004. And Don King wasn't the promoter of that one.

And in what appears to be an attempt at warts-and-all balance in his otherwise fawning portrait of The World's Greatest Promoter, Pulley concedes that "in the early 1980s he got sued by Muhammad Ali, who accused King of shortchanging his purse from a fight against Larry Holmes. King settled for less than $100,000."

Which is once again, sort of true, but doesn't begin to tell the whole story, in that it makes it sound like some civilized, out-of-court accord hammered out by the lawyers. What actually happened is that after Ali sued King for the $1,170,000 the promoter had shortchanged him for the Holmes fight,

King arranged for a suitcase containing $50,000 in cash to be delivered to Ali. It was a forerunner of a similar ploy he would use years later in spiriting Hasim Rahman from beneath Cedric Kushner's nose: When Ali got a look at that much flash-cash, he obligingly signed a release absolving King from paying him the rest of what he owed from the Holmes purse.

When Ali's attorney learned what he had done, he reportedly burst into tears.

So what does Don King make of Pulley's brand of hard-hitting journalism? Well, the *Forbes* issue won't hit the stands until April 18, but the promoter's publicists are already e-mailing copies to anyone willing to sit still long enough to read it.

TheSweetScience.com

2006

Bring Back the Titans

By the time they finally got around to fighting each other, neither Roy Jones nor Felix Trinidad was exactly a "titan" of the sport, but in New York, where "Titans" occupies a special place in sporting history, it seemed almost a clever double entendre. The ticket-pricing ruse employed for the fight was actually a variation on the "accordion" technique pioneered by "Uncle Mike" Jacobs three-quarters of a century earlier. Jacobs routinely had duplicate sets of tickets printed for entire sections at the Garden and allowed the law of supply and demand to determine which price to use. In that pre-computer era, Jacobs carried around the information in his head. The trick, of course, was to avoid having the guy who'd paid $50 for his "ringside" ticket wind up in a seat next to a guy who had a lesser denomination printed on his.

NEW YORK—There wasn't a speck of snow on the street and the sun was shining outside, but when Roy Jones shuffled into the WaMu Theatre lobby for Tuesday's pre-fight press conference half an hour ahead of Felix Trinidad, he was bundled up like he was Quinn the Eskimo and he'd just emerged from his igloo.

At least he was there.

As a host of frustrated promoters would attest, there was a time in the not-too-distant past when you couldn't have gotten Jones to New York at gunpoint four days before a January fight, but that was then and this is now.

"Hey," explained RJ with a shrug. "Global warming."

Jones was also in winter plumage, having grown a full-length beard, which he promised would disappear once he makes weight (170 pounds) Friday afternoon.

Don King and Madison Square Garden have labeled Saturday night's exercise in nostalgia "Bring on the Titans," but what they probably should have called it was "Bring *Back* the Titans."

For a generation un-steeped in New York sporting lore, the "Titans" handle hearkens back to an era that only slightly antedates the primes of Jones' and Trinidad's boxing careers.

The New York Titans were, of course, New York's original entry in the old American Football League. The team's publicist was Murray Goodman, whose son Bobby is now director of boxing for Don King Promotions.

When the late Sonny Werblin bought the cash-strapped franchise from Wismer in 1963, he changed the name from Titans to Jets, and a year after that he signed Joe Namath. Several years later, Sonny also headed up a group that bought Madison Square Garden (which makes him one of Jim Dolan's immediate predecessors) and proceeded to pretty much run the Garden's Boxing Department into the ground, but that, as they say, is a story for another day.

Since pretty much everyone concerned, including the competitors themselves, agree that Jones-Trinidad (or Trinidad-Jones, if one goes by the billing on the fight posters) is happening at least six years too late, you have to wonder just why, beyond making the participants a bunch of money, it is taking place at all.

Whatever the outcome, it isn't a fight that is likely to dramatically alter the boxing landscape. Neither man owns a title, nor is any championship at stake. Jones, who turns thirty-nine on Wednesday, has been knocked out twice in losing three of his last five and hasn't held a title for more than three years. Trinidad just turned thirty-five, but he's 2-2 since 9/11 and hasn't been a champion since he lost to Bernard Hopkins six-and-a-half years ago. In other words, the winner will be able to claim superiority over the loser, but not much else.

To give credit where credit is due, King's people and the Garden didn't try to insult the intelligence of the public by trying to sell the meeting of these two old codgers as something it is not—i.e., a championship fight, though God knows it would have been easy enough to persuade, in exchange for a small tribute, one of the sanctioning bodies to create some sort of extra-terrestrial championship and bring another meaningless belt into the ring Saturday night.

Not that the idea of making it a title fight wasn't discussed.

"We actually thought about it," said Bobby Goodman. "I think Roy might actually still have some kind of bullshit belt [RJ's fight against Anthony Hamshaw last summer was for something called the 'vacant IBC light-heavyweight title'] but then we said 'Aw, what would be the point?' This is a fight between two legends. It should be able to sell itself."

Or should have been, anyway. All signs point to half-a-house at the Mecca of Boxing Saturday night, but that is due at least in part to some cockamamie marketing techniques on the part of MSG Boxing, which elected to pay King a site fee in exchange for the gate, only to undermine itself by trying to gouge the ticket-buying public right out of the box.

Much has been made, for instance, of the $15,000 price tag on front-row ringside seats. The Garden tried to "auction" the choice seats at that price, but when it found precious few takers began to drop the "minimum bid," so those same tickets can now be had for a third of the original cost.

The most pissed-off guy in New York won't be the loser of Saturday night's fight. Rather, it's going to be the guy who paid $15,000 to sit at ringside and finds himself seated next to somebody who paid $5,000 for his seat.

If Jones-Trindad isn't a title fight, why is it being contested at 12 rounds?

"If you're going to charge people $49.95 for the pay-per-view you have to give them their money's worth," said Jones. "You can't ask them to spend that much money for a 10-round fight."

If Jones seems more concerned with the PPV cost than the live gate it is with good reason. RJ is working with no guarantee in this one; his purse will come from the PPV upside. Jones has also noted on several occasions that "there's no way this is going more than six anyway."

And trust me, if it does go 12, the public will not have gotten its money's worth.

Instead of calling it Bring on the Titans, they might also have called it Bring on the Juniors. We'll leave it to the promoters to explain why Roy is billed on the posters as "Jones Jr." while Tito, who is also a junior, is not.

For all of that, Jones-Trinidad is what it is: a reasonably competitive fight between two Hall-of-Famers-in-waiting who figure to be more well-matched than they might have been when they could still fight. (And think about this for a moment: while it might have been an intriguing matchup when they were in their primes, it was never even seriously entertained back then, because at the top of their games Jones and Trinidad were separated by a good 20 pounds.)

If it is what it is, it is also not what it's not. In what appears to have been a well-intentioned attempt to defend Jones-Trinidad against its skeptics a few days ago, espn.com's Eric Raskin plainly stretched the bounds of credulity in noting, "Cashing-in on nostalgia is a time-honored tradition in boxing. Ray

Leonard spent 1989 fighting a rematch with Tommy Hearns and a rubber match with Roberto Duran."

This argument conveniently overlooks the fact that both of those fights matched reigning world champions. Leonard was thirty-three and Hearns thirty-one when they met for the second time; Ray was the WBC super-middleweight champion and the Hit Man held the WBO title. And while neither was at the prime of his career, events of that evening showed that if they had slipped, they had slipped to the same place and were more competitive than ever, as witness the result—a 12-round draw.

Duran might have been a Jones-like thirty-eight, but he was the reigning WBC middleweight champion when he challenged for Leonard's 168-pound title in '89, and was, moreover, still the only man to have defeated Leonard, which more than justified a rubber match in the eyes of the public. (Manos de Piedra miscalculated and came in at 158 for Leonard III; when Ray weighed in at 160 for what was supposed to be a 168-pound title fight it put Duran's title in jeopardy as well, and provided Los Bandidos with a pretext for relieving him of same.)

Please spare us those comparisons, then. It would be surprising indeed if Jones-Trinidad turned out to be even as good as Leonard-Duran III—and if it turns out to be half as good as Leonard-Hearns II it will be absolutely shocking.

The fact that no title awaits its winner does not mean there's nothing in it for the winner. As Jones slyly pointed out Tuesday, the 170-pound limit for Saturday night's fight is "just two pounds more than 168."

"I've already made history by winning the middleweight title, then the super-middleweight title, then the light-heavyweight title, the heavyweight title, and then went back and won the light-heavyweight title again," pointed out Jones with a twinkle in his eye. "What if I went down and won the super-middleweight title again?"

It has already been speculated that a Jones win over Trinidad could eventually position him for the Joe Calzaghe-Bernard Hopkins winner, but RJ noted that negotiations between those two appeared to have hit a recent snag.

"They'd better hurry up and get it done," warned Jones, "because if they ain't got it done by next Sunday morning, I'm out of here. I'm going straight to Wales."

BoxingTalk.com
2008

Hopkins–Wright

"Title Fight" or Flim-Flam?

The question posed in the headline isn't one I'd have asked without already knowing the answer. Despite another bald-faced attempt by the Schaefer/Golden Boy/Ring magazine nexus to cast themselves as an arbiter of championships, HBO's Ross Greenburg assured me on this day that his announcers would make no attempt to represent B-Hop vs. Winky as a title fight. They didn't—but everyone tuned to the HBO broadcast heard Michael Buffer (whose introduction is scripted by the promoter signing his paycheck) describe it as a fight "for the light-heavyweight championship of the world."

NEW YORK The philosophy that "a lie repeated often enough will come to be accepted as the truth" is generally believed to have originated with Josef Goebbels, who, although he was obviously born to be a boxing promoter, eventually went into another line of work.

His spiritual descendants, on the other hand, were out in force at lunchtime Thursday, when the Bernard Hopkins-Winky Wright traveling circus hit the ESPN Zone in Times Square.

Publicist Kelly Swanson described Hopkins as "the current light-heavyweight champion of the world."

In promotional literature distributed to the press, MGM/Mirage sports boss Richard Sturm called the July 21 encounter "a great championship fight."

Hopkins' bio in the press kit said he would fight Wright for "the 170-pound *Ring* magazine belt."

Gee. If so, they've not only created a title, they've created a whole new division.

Make no mistake about it, Hopkins-Wright is an intriguing matchup. It could turn out to be an extremely entertaining fight. Its hype may not match the buildup for Mayweather-De La Hoya, but this Golden Boy promotion could be far more competitive. ("I just love beating up on these Florida boys," said Hopkins. "All they do is sit out in the sun all day.")

But anyone trying to sell it (at $49.95 a pop) to the public as a "world championship fight" should be arrested for violating the truth-in-packaging laws.

HBO, whose pay-per-view arm will televise the July 21 matchup in Las Vegas, says they won't be a party to the deception.

"Does either guy have a title?" HBO Sports president Ross Greenburg asked rhetorically. "Then it isn't a title fight, and you won't hear our people describe it as one."

Look, Hopkins was a great middleweight champion and he is a future Hall of Famer. (So, for that matter, is the Winkster.) But his claim to being a "current" champion is utterly specious.

Seven months after losing to Jermain Taylor for the second time, he fought Antonio Tarver, who hadn't held a recognized title in over two years. He won that fight convincingly and announced his retirement thereafter.

The only "title" at stake against Tarver was that of the IBO—you know, those people in Florida who will give a belt to anyone willing to wear it. And not even *they* are recognizing Hopkins-Wright as a championship fight. (The IBO has promised its belt to the winner of Tarver's June 9 bout against Elvir Muriqi.)

Right now the only belt at stake will be that awarded by *The Ring*. Do you think Nevada is going to let Nigel Collins appoint the Hopkins-Wright judges?

Or is Richard Schaefer going to take the next logical step and start looking around for Dean Chance's phone number?

Think about this for a moment: July 21st will be the 53rd bout in Bernard Hopkins' career, but he is 1-1 as a light-heavyweight. B-Hop made his pro debut as a light-heavy, and lost a four-round decision. By the time he got out of Graterford, the prison diet had turned him into a super-middleweight.

This isn't to cast aspersions on the forty-one-year-old Hopkins' career, but you *would* have to say that when it comes to his light-heavyweight credentials the jury is still very much out.

And even at the 170-pound catchweight, Winky will be ten pounds bigger than he's ever been before. That makes for an interesting betting proposition, but it doesn't make it a world title fight, no matter how many times its promoters call it one.

Although HBO maintains that it will describe Hopkins-Wright as a "12-round, non-title fight," Golden Boy CEO Schaefer was adamant in his insistence that it is the real goods.

"Yes, it is a world championship fight," maintained Schaefer. "*The Ring* belt is as credible as any other—and it may be more difficult to earn."

That is precisely the logic Don King used three decades ago when he hoodwinked ABC into bankrolling his U.S. Boxing Championships based on *The Ring*'s ratings, but Schaefer & Co. seem confident that if they call Hopkins-Wright a title fight enough times, people will begin to believe them.

Bernard Hopkins, a student of boxing history who made it a point to solidify his undisputed middleweight title by collecting all four recognized titles, seemed almost embarrassed by hearing this fight described as "for a championship," but he did call *The Ring*'s "the belt most boxing writers and experts give the most credit to."

Really? And here we thought all one had to do to get a *Ring* belt was be named Klitschko.

BoxingTalk.com
2007

Pretty Boy: Money Boy

The Irish Times *had asked me to bring its readership up to speed on the Mayweather phenomenon on the eve of his 2008 bout against Ricky Hatton; by the time it ran, I was in Belfast, where several of us stayed up until nearly six in the morning to watch the Mayweather-Hatton telecast from Las Vegas. Floyd stopped Hatton in the tenth round of a pretty one-sided fight. It did occur to me, though, that guys like Mayweather, who seem otherwise attuned to the Age of Twitter, will readily say things into a cell phone they'd know better than to say into a live microphone. The truly amazing thing is that Mayweather seems genuinely surprised every time one of his indiscretions comes back to bite him after surfacing on YouTube.*

Charles Arthur (Pretty Boy) Floyd, a Depression-era Oklahoma bank robber and murderer, was romanticized as a sort of Robin Hood of the Great Plains by, among others, Woody Guthrie. (Guthrie's composition "Pretty Boy Floyd" included a line—"Some will rob you with a six-gun / and some with a fountain pen"—that could have been a paean to a boxing promoter.)

In the 73 years since Pretty Boy's demise, every American whose misfortune it was to have been christened Floyd has at some point in his life answered to the name "Pretty Boy," but Floyd Mayweather Jr. makes the unique claim that his *nom de ring* has nothing to do with the outlaw.

"My amateur teammates gave me that name," insists Pretty Boy Floyd the boxer. "I got the nickname because when my fights finished, I never came out cut or bruised."

At thirty—the age of the original Pretty Boy when he was gunned down in a 1934 FBI ambush—Mayweather has won world titles in five weight classes and is widely considered the world's most accomplished pound-for-pound boxer.

In the process of defeating 38 of 38 professional opponents, he has earned upwards of $100 million in the ring—a figure that could swell by another $20 million when the receipts from tonight's blockbuster fight against Ricky Hatton are tallied. And he isn't shy about letting you know it.

As viewers of HBO's *24/7* promotional series learned last spring, Mayweather routinely walks around with $30,000 in flash-cash in his pockets.

"I got money longer than train smoke," boasts Mayweather. "I been riding Bentleys since the '90s."

He has suggested his nickname be replaced by a new one, "Money," and when he founded his rap-music label, he called his firm "Philthy Rich Records."

Although Philthy Rich has yet to produce a commercially successful album, Pretty Boy's connections in the world of gangsta rap run deep: when he fought Oscar De La Hoya last May he was escorted into the ring by the entertainer 50 Cent, who serenaded the crowd with his rendition of "Straight to the Bank."

That he is universally admired as a boxer has not translated into personal popularity. When he preceded his training camp for the Hatton fight with a stint on the television program *Dancing with the Stars* he was summarily voted off by the viewers.

And while just 3,000 of Hatton's British compatriots will be among the 17,000 at the MGM Grand Garden Arena tonight, it is a safe bet that at least half the audience would consider a Hatton upset a triumph of justice.

In the ring, Mayweather has not tasted defeat since his controversial loss to the Bulgarian Serafim Todorov in the featherweight semifinal of the 1996 Atlanta Games. He turned pro that October, and two years later won his first world championship, at 130 pounds, by stopping the Mexican champion Genaro Hernandez.

He has subsequently won titles at lightweight (from José Luis Castillo in 2002), light welterweight (knocking out Arturo Gatti in 2005), and welterweight (Zab Judah, 2006), and this May outpointed De La Hoya for the WBC light middleweight title, a belt he relinquished in order to maintain the 147-pound championship he will defend against Hatton tonight.

Along the way, Mayweather has kept his name in the news outside the ring as well. He pleaded no contest to assault charges after putting his boot to a bouncer in a 2004 Michigan barroom fight, and later that year was convicted of misdemeanor battery for punching two women at a Las Vegas nightclub. He was also arrested, but later acquitted, on domestic violence charges brought by a former girlfriend.

And the odd part of it is that Pretty Boy may be the most normal member of his family. These Mayweathers are a case study in dysfunction. Pretty Boy's father, Floyd Sr., was a useful welterweight of the 1970s who lasted into the tenth round of a 1978 fight against Sugar Ray Leonard.

Things began to fall apart for Floyd the Elder once he began to train on cocaine, and the demise of his ring career was further hastened when he was shot by a drug dealer named Tony Sinclair, the brother of Pretty Boy's mother. (The bullet struck him in the leg. Uncle Tony's aim may have been thrown off when his target used the infant Floyd Jr. as a shield.)

In 1994, Floyd Sr. received a five-year sentence for cocaine trafficking. Two years later, Mayweather Jr. wrote a letter to Bill Clinton, unsuccessfully imploring the president to let his father out long enough to watch him box in the Olympics.

It is probably significant that for all his transgressions, Floyd Sr. was awarded custody of the boy who became Pretty Boy. Junior's mother, a crack addict named Deborah Sinclair, was deemed an even *less* fit parent.

Although Floyd Sr. trained his son for a time (and has continued to train many top-flight boxers, including, for a while, De La Hoya), the two no longer speak. Roger Mayweather, who began to work with Pretty Boy while his elder brother was in jail, has trained him for several years.

Roger, who billed himself as "the Black Mamba," was once the WBC junior welterweight champion. In a scrum in the ring after a 1988 title fight I saw him punch Lou Duva, his opponent's then-sixty-six-year-old trainer.

In 2006, Roger received a one-year suspension from the Nevada State Athletic Commission for his part in a brawl that erupted after Floyd Jr.'s win over Judah—though the suspension was somewhat moot since Uncle Roger was concomitantly doing six months in the pokey for beating up the grandmother of his infant son.

"I fought from the bottom to the top," Mayweather Jr. reminded a gathering of reporters in Las Vegas last week. "Ricky Hatton never saw his father being shot. He never saw his mom on drugs or his father in prison."

At press conferences and in his adversary's presence, Mayweather has been respectful toward Hatton, but in a remarkably profane, self-involved, four-minute rant recorded at the Philthy Rich studios he dismissed tonight's adversary as "a faggot motherfucker from England."

The snippet is (or was) available via YouTube. If you're going to play it on your home computer you might want to get the kids out of the room first.

The Irish Times
2007

Freddie vs. Ugly Boy

The Subtext

This piece was written for the 2008 BWAA Journal, the program distrib-uted at the annual Boxing Writers Dinner. Roach won his third Trainer of the Year Award that night, and he won it again for 2009. The trophy is named for Roach's old mentor, the legendary Eddie Futch, and when I presented it to Freddie I remarked that some day the membership might have to add his name to the award. Wouldn't it be wonderful if at some time in the future Floyd Sr. was elected Trainer of the Year and had to come to New York to receive his Freddie Roach Award?

Freddie Roach will admit it now. It might have begun as some good-natured woofing enacted primarily for the benefit of the 24/7 cameras, but by the time last month's weigh-in finally rolled around he was ready to rip Floyd Mayweather's lungs out.

"[Floyd Sr.] had said some things that got a little personal, and I guess I let it get to me more than I should have," recalled Freddie. "The day of the weigh-in Manny even had to pull me aside and remind me to act like a gentleman."

Still, when they met face-to-face at the scale that day Roach and Ugly Boy were eyeing each other like a pair of pit bulls. It took the sanest member of the Mayweather family to defuse the situation: "Why don't you both just shut up and let the best man win," snapped Floyd's mother.

"Ma'am," Freddie replied, "that's the smartest thing anybody's said around here all week."

Freddie Roach was going to be the 2008 Trainer of the Year no matter what happened in the May 2 fight, of course, but he did get the last laugh when Manny Pacquiao destroyed Ricky Hatton in less than six minutes.

Freddie, who had predicted that his man would knock out the Mayweather-trained Brit inside three rounds, says he was never even worried about the outcome, but I'm probably not giving away any secrets here by telling you that BWAA president Jack Hirsch was more than a little relieved by the result.

As professionals, we're not supposed to have a rooting interest in fights, but there's always an inherent danger in scheduling events like tonight's six months into the calendar year—mainly, the possibility that one of your award-ees gets knocked off on his way to the dinner. One of Jack's predecessors, Barney Nagler, the longtime BWAA president, used to roll his eyes when he told the story about getting a 1963 press release out announcing that Emile Griffith had won the Edward J. Neil trophy just in time to coincide with Hurricane Carter's first-round KO of our Fighter of the Year.

Mr. Pacquiao, obviously, is the most prominent of his clients today, but Freddie has trained two dozen world champions since taking over the reins from his longtime mentor Eddie Futch more than two decades ago. The for-mer lightweight from Dedham, Mass., is busier than ever. So busy, in fact, that immediately after tomorrow night's fight at the Garden he will hop a flight for London, where another of his fighters, Amir Khan, faces Andriy Kotelnik in a WBA 140-pound title fight at the Millennium Dome two weeks hence.

Khan, in fact, is one of a trio of Roach-trained fighters who will be in ac-tion on the night of June 27, in three far-flung arenas. Since Freddie can't be everywhere, his principal assistant, former heavyweight champion Michael Moorer, will work the corner of Roach's undefeated junior middleweight Vanes Martirosyan on the Pavlik-Mora undercard in Atlantic City, while an-other Roach understudy, Aaron Brown, will work that of heavyweight Andrei Arlovski as the UFC fighter makes his legitimate boxing debut on the Chris John-Rocky Juarez bill at the Staples Center.

Whether it's due to his booming stature in the boxing world, his Trainer of the Year hat trick, or the result of his exposure in the two most popular 24/7 series of the past two years, 325 new customers have beaten a trail to the door of Roach's Wild Card Gym in Hollywood since the first of the year. Some of them are seasoned professionals, some of them raw amateurs, but, says Freddie, "I've never turned anyone away." He remains obliged to devote most of his time to his top pros, but he now oversees a staff of eight assis-tants to work with the other boxers and would-be boxers.

In the run-up to last month's fight it was often suggested that Moorer had been hired to pick up the slack because of Freddie's ongoing battle with Parkinson's disease. Nothing could be further from the truth, says Roach. The Parkinson's tremors are more evident when the body is at rest. Once he climbs into the ring and gets to work, the symptoms are barely noticeable.

"I heard people were claiming that I'd brought in Michael because I was sick or because it was getting worse," said Freddie. "I brought him in because he was broke and he asked me for a job. Sure, he's helped me, but I've helped him even more.

"I still get up in the ring and do all the mitt work myself," added Freddie. "Michael watches from outside the ring and makes his suggestions. He's got a good eye for picking up details and he's been very helpful that way, but believe me, his being there has nothing to do with my illness."

The Futch-Condon Award Freddie takes home tonight is his third in a decade, more than any man living or dead has captured in the two decades since a separate category for Trainer of the Year was established by the BWAA, and breaks a logjam he had shared with four other two-time winners—Emanuel Steward, Dan Birmingham, George Benton, and the great Eddie Futch, the man who taught Freddie to box and then taught Freddie to train, and for whom the award is jointly named. Winning more Eddie Futch awards than Eddie Futch himself is a remarkable achievement. 2009 has more than half a year to run yet, but you'd have to say that off what you saw in Vegas last month, Freddie might be the leader in the clubhouse for a *fourth* trophy.

BWAA Journal
2009

Hailed As "Brilliant,"
Bradley's Move Wasn't

Once Showtime's announcers labeled Tim Bradley's take-a-knee strategy a game-changer, the boxing media took up the refrain like a pack of trained seals. I had my doubts, and when I began to ask around, found that several of the game's most respected cornermen agreed with me.

Since boxing is a sport that trades on its legends, we're generally not disposed toward debunking myths, particularly those that support an otherwise plausibly good storyline, but since this one appears to be taking on a life of its own it might be a good idea to nip it in the bud, lest it spawn an entire generation of pugilists suddenly disposed to crawling around on their knees for all the wrong reasons.

In the first round of last Saturday night's 140-pound unification fight in Montreal, Kendall Holt unleashed a left hook that looked capable of taking Timothy Bradley's head off. Bradley went down like he'd been popped with one of those stun-bolt guns they use in slaughterhouses, but then, amazingly, bounced right back to his feet.

A second later he reconsidered that hasty rise and deliberately took a knee while referee Michael Griffin continued to count. At "eight," Bradley sprung back to his feet, and not only lasted the round but went on to win a unanimous decision, despite the knockdown and a later trip to the canvas in the bout's waning seconds.

Al Bernstein, calling the fight for Showtime, credited Bradley's "quick thinking" after the knockdown as a critical factor in the eventual outcome. A quick survey of that night's coverage reveals that the boxing media seems to have bought wholesale into the notion that Bradley's decision to take a knee either won, or helped him win, at the Bell Center that night.

Depending on whose account you're reading, "some quick thinking by

Bradley in the first round saved his night," or Bradley "intelligently took a knee," or "the Californian wisely elected to get back down." Another on-line scribe–the same guy who called me "stupid," by the way–referenced Bradley's "clever" move.

But it occurred to us that night that, far from being a brilliant tactic, it may well have been a foolish one, and that at best it was irrelevant. Bradley, after all, was going to get a mandatory 8-count from the referee. Once he was up, it seemed self-evident that it required a greater expenditure of energy to (a) go down on his knee and (b) get back up again than if he'd simply composed himself while he took the count on his feet.

When I brought this point up at the post-fight press conference, Bradley; his trainer, Joel Diaz; and his promoter, Gary Shaw; all looked at me like I had two heads. Bradley confirmed that he had gone back down at the direction of his corner. Shaw waved the query away, dismissively grunting his assurance that Bradley "did the right thing."

By then it was nearly 2 a.m., and since there obviously wasn't going to be a dialogue on the matter, I allowed it to drop, though in a report filed that night I did note that since Bradley was going to get a count either way, "it didn't seem particularly material whether he did it on his feet or on his knee."

No one else seems to have given it much thought at all, judging from the almost universal praise heaped upon Bradley for his "brilliant" move, but a random survey of top trainers and officials undertaken over the past few days confirms that far from being "the right thing," it was almost assuredly the wrong thing.

That it came at the behest of his trainer only compounds the transgression. To be sure, in an earlier age of boxing–one that had ended before Joel Diaz was even born–the trainer's directive would have been meritorious, but you have to wonder about a trainer who would dispense that instruction in 2009. Does he also feed his boxers steak and raw eggs for breakfast–after they've finished chopping all their wood for the day?

The ancient axiom upon which this time-honored theory relied was summarized by Rocky Marciano's trainer Charlie Goldman, as quoted by the great A.J. Liebling in *The Sweet Science:* "If you're ever knocked down, don't be no hero and jump right up. Take a count."

Goldman's logic was impeccable–under the rules of the day. In the absence of a mandatory 8-count, as Liebling put it, "hostilities were *de règle* as soon as the fallen man got to his feet."

And since a boxer was penalized no more for a knockdown that lasted nine seconds than one that lasted two, it made perfect sense for a man who might be buzzed to stay down and take advantage of the respite while he gathered his wits. A guy who jumped up at "three" marked himself as a novice, since he would be fair game a second or two later.

But the theory was already edging toward obsolescence even in Liebling's day. The New York commission, for instance, had already adopted the mandatory 8-count by the mid-1950s. Liebling, incidentally, was no great fan of the then-new regulation, which he described as "a foolish, though well-intentioned rule." Wrote Liebling:

> Whenever a boxer is knocked down, the referee must stop the fight for eight seconds, even if the man is back on his feet by "One." This is designed to protect boxers from the effects of their own imprudence, but has resulted merely in atrophy of their estimative powers. Formerly boxers stayed down as long as they could when they were truly hurt. When they were undamaged, they got up as quickly as possible, in order to minimize the seriousness of their mishap. Now they all bounce to their feet as if conscious, secure in the knowledge they will get the eight seconds anyway. This substitutes a reflex for the exercise of reason. It is also hard on the fellow who, after staying on the mat until "eight" or "nine," might have decided to remain there.

More than half a century later, the mandatory 8 is with us to stay. It is incorporated into the rules of the WBA, the WBO, and the IBF, and while the WBC does not specifically require it, it obtains in virtually all of that sanctioning body's title fights as well. The mandatory 8-count is used in every state jurisdiction, and is incorporated into the Unified Rules that obtained last Saturday in Montreal.

Whether Bradley might have just stayed down in the first place is at best a debatable point, but once he was up, the experts seem to agree, taking the knee was just plain dumb.

Three-time Trainer of the Year Freddie Roach, who is training Manny Pacquiao for his May 2 encounter with Ricky Hatton, watched Bradley-Holt with some interest, since Bradley looms a future rival for the winner, and had the same reaction we did.

"Why would you go back down again?" wondered Roach. "He was already up, so he should have stayed up."

"Taking a knee after getting up is a bad idea," said Randy Neumann, a top-echelon New Jersey referee. "It involves too much activity, at what is not a good time."

"With the mandatory eight, I'd rather have all my boxers get to their feet if they can," said Hall of Fame-trainer Emanuel Steward. "But once he was up, getting down on his knee was, as you say, not only a big waste of time and energy, but it could have been dangerous. What if his legs had been shaky when he got back up? The referee might have stopped the fight."

(How many times have you seen that happen? A boxer goes down from a punch, stays there to collect his thoughts, gets up late in the count, and then when the referee asks him to step toward him he lurches ever so slightly and all of a sudden the ref is waving his arms.)

"How is a fighter going to even know if his legs are all right if he's still on the canvas?" asked Steward. "The legs recover best if he's on his feet."

"If a guy looks like he might be dazed when he gets knocked down, you might want him to stay down a little rather than struggle to get right back up," said Goody Petronelli, who trained Marvelous Marvin Hagler. "But going back down when he's already up? I agree; it sounds like a rookie move. It makes no sense at all."

One other point might be made about the efficacy of the tactic. Freddie Roach recalled an episode at Foxwoods half a dozen years ago. Mohamad Abdulaev, the 2000 Olympic champion from Uzbekistan, was unbeaten as a pro and well ahead in his bout against Emmanuel Clottey when he was decked in the tenth and final round. Abdulaev got to one knee and looked over at his corner, where his trainer was motioning him to stay down while Mike Ortega administered the count.

"Trouble was," recalled Roach, "he didn't speak English, so he just stayed there on his knee and got counted out."

TheSweetScience.com

2009

What's This? A Boxing Promoter with a Conscience?

I'd been aware since Lou DiBella returned from Germany following Jermain Taylor's knockout there that he would no longer promote the former middleweight champion if he continued to box. Lou got a lot of mileage out of his principled stand, but trust me, the timing of the announcement could have been better. The wife of a Taylor associate had apprised me of Jermain's decision earlier that day, and when Taylor confirmed it to another website on the eve of Malignaggi-Diaz II in Chicago, DiBella wound up upstaging his own fight.

Whether Showtime responded to my suggestion by insisting on additional testing remains unlearned, but four weeks later came the announcement that although he intended to keep fighting, Jermain Taylor was dropping out of the World Championship Tournament. His place was taken by Allen Green. In the end, wiser heads may have prevailed. Seven months after announcing his intent to resume his ring career, there has been no indication that Taylor actually intends to fight again.

CHICAGO—Sometimes even more than its eponymous president himself, Jermain Taylor was the veritable face of DiBella Entertainment.

He might not have been Lou DiBella's first world champion—Bernard Hopkins was—but he was the first he'd developed from square one. DiBella had signed Taylor straight out of the Olympics and promoted his entire career, watched a kid who'd never had a pro fight become a man who won the undisputed middleweight championship of the world, and if their personal relationship wasn't exactly father-son, it was at the very least uncle-nephew, and when Lou said he "loved" Jermain, you believed him.

This is a sport in which the term "bloodsucking promoter" often seems redundant, but when DiBella severed his relationship with Taylor on a cold

Friday afternoon in Chicago yesterday, it was a move borne of conscience alone. Rather than be a party to what he considered the "unnecessary risk" of Taylor's continuing to box, DiBella walked away and left more than half a million dollars on the table.

Ask yourself this: How many other promoters would have done the same?

It has been clear since the night of October 17 that DiBella would never promote another Taylor fight. After sitting up all night watching his fighter wander in and out of consciousness in a Berlin hospital, the promoter extracted a promise from Taylor that he would hang up his gloves. No announcement was made at that time because DiBella wanted to give the guy who had once been the middleweight champ the opportunity to retire gracefully, on his own terms, and with any explanation he wanted to offer.

The two have not met face to face since they parted in Germany. DiBella flew back to the states. Jermain Taylor stayed behind. It was announced that he wanted to spend a week touring Europe with his wife. The truth of the matter is that the German doctors who treated Taylor for the concussion administered by Arthur Abraham warned that it would be dangerous for him to get on an airplane.

Make of that what you will. Once Taylor got to the hospital that night, the staff neurologists—as opposed to the boxing buffs with kit bags who pass for "ringside physicians" in that country—were sufficiently concerned that they put him on a round-the-clock watch. It is our understanding that Taylor underwent multiple MRIs. We know he passed the last one, else he would not have been released. But what about the others?

By the time they parted company in Berlin, DiBella's mind was already made up that this was it. If Taylor ever boxed again, it would not be under the aegis of his company. This understanding was as clear to Taylor that morning as it was to DiBella.

In the nearly two months since, there had been increasing rumblings emanating from Little Rock that Taylor was wavering on his pledge. The rumors were a matter of sufficient concern that in Atlantic City last Saturday night, DiBella found himself huddled together with Taylor advisor Al Haymon as they tried to figure out a means of heading off the comeback plans without embarrassing Taylor.

The matter was already producing a schism within the camp. Manager Ozell Nelson, who had returned to the corner as trainer after the tenures of Patrick Burns and Emanuel Steward, was working with Taylor in Arkansas, and of course the Little Rock homeys who comprise Jermain's inner circle down there were foursquare behind their man—for pretty much the same reasons that Muhammad Ali's entire entourage—with the exception of Dr. Ferdie Pacheco, who had walked away—not only abetted but encouraged Ali's participation in that ill-fated 1980 fight against Larry Holmes.

On the way from O'Hare to downtown Chicago yesterday, the wife of one of Taylor's closest friends confirmed to me that Jermain had decided to keep boxing and would reaffirm his place in the ongoing "Super Six" super-middleweight tournament, and hours later, Taylor repeated that intention to another website.

So by five o'clock Friday in Chicago, DiBella was making an announcement of his own—that he was recusing himself as Taylor's promoter. When he had signed him out of the 2000 Olympics, DiBella had promised the fighter that he would leave the game with his faculties intact, and he had promised the same thing to Jermain's mother two months ago in Berlin. Now that that prospect had assumed proportions of an unacceptable risk, DiBella felt that he could not in good conscience function as an enabler.

It should probably be noted that even today, Taylor would probably be DiBella Entertainment's most marketable client, and that by walking away right now, Lou DiBella is out between $500,000 and $600,000 he stood to collect just for passing "Go."

Obviously, DiBella could use the money, but after what he has seen he seems to feel that he can't comfortably condone the notion of Jermain Taylor continuing to box.

All of us, of course, have seen Taylor lose four of his last five fights and get knocked out in three of them. But what we haven't seen is Taylor's alarming behavior in the locker room once he regained consciousness—behavior so erratic and so indicative of possible frontal lobe damage that an ambulance was summoned.

And what we haven't seen, either, are the results of the several MRIs administered in the hospital that night. While that information is shrouded in medical confidentiality issues, Taylor's post-concussive state should be a matter of extreme concern for whatever jurisdiction considers licensing him again.

As of last night, Al Haymon planned to fly to Arkansas in a last-ditch effort to discourage Taylor's comeback plans. If he is unsuccessful, it will be interesting to see whether he follows DiBella out the door.

The current Super Six schedule calls for Taylor to fight Andre Ward in April. No site has been named, but it is a reasonable assumption that a pairing of two Americans would take place in the United States. Whichever commission winds up with this one in its lap needs to take a long, hard look at the situation.

And so, for that matter, does Showtime. Before this tournament even began, we had expressed our reservations about the whole concept of a "knockout bonus" and suggested that it could lead to something like this. We'd even noted that if they were going to award one point for a knockout, why not two for putting the opponent in the hospital, and three if you managed to kill him.

That had been intended as sarcasm, but now we may get a chance to find out.

As the creators, sponsors, and bankrollers of this enterprise, the people at Showtime have an opportunity, and perhaps even an obligation, to stake out an ethical position of their own. If Jermain Taylor can pass a brain scan in March, even the most circumspect boxing commission might legally have difficulty denying him a license, but Showtime can, and should, go one step further.

The network can't demand that the Germans hand over confidential medical information, for instance, but they can, and should, take Jermain Taylor aside and ask that he obtain the neurological reports from that night and make the information available to them. They could, and should, make that a condition of his continued participation in the tournament.

And it they don't, they must share in the responsibility for the consequences.

TheSweetScience.com
2009

Debbies Do New York

Manny Pacquiao's headline act at Cowboys Stadium before a crowd of more than 50,000 proved one of the more refreshing boxing stories of 2010. When an anticipated fight against Mayweather blew up on the launching pad, Bob Arum joined forces with Jerry Jones to simultaneously showcase the world's best fighter and Jerry's spectacular new stadium—an event called, simply, "The Event." While many boxing people unfamiliar with Jerry Jones took him for just another Texas blowhard about to be separated from his money, I knew better, and the fact that I had something of a history with the Cowboys' owner gave me a leg up in this story. Jones and Arum announced The Event with back-to-back press conferences in Dallas and New York. I found it more than slightly amusing to see grizzled fight-game veterans who don't even look up when scantily clad round-card girls parade around the ring absolutely bedazzled by the presence of authentic Dallas Cowboys Cheerleaders.

NEW YORK—Boxing history is littered with the carcasses of guys with more money than brains who, having watched their intellectual inferiors accumulate cash, decided that if it was that easy for some dope to get rich out of boxing, then they themselves might as well get even richer.

Whether they were financiers who fancied themselves possessed of the Midas Touch (see Trump, Donald), consortiums of local banks (see Shelby, Montana), despotic third-world dictators (see Mobutu Sese Seko), or embezzlers in search of a creative outlet for their ill-gotten cash (see Ross Fields, a/k/a Harold Smith), since the earliest days of the sport they have shared a common experience: When the box office receipts were counted they were left holding an empty paper bag as the real boxing guys got out of town with all the dough.

A word to the wise here (not that Bob Arum doesn't know it already): Yes, there's a sucker born every minute. Just don't count on Jerry Jones being one of them.

Arum, in New York Wednesday to announce the Manny Pacquiao-Joshua Clottey fight at Cowboys Stadium, called the March 13 site "the greatest venue ever to host a boxing event," and then went on to sing its praises in terms we hadn't heard in fifty years since another generation of Texans described the Astrodome.

On the other hand, when Arum described Jones as his "partner" and suggested that Jones might revolutionize boxing—or at least the marketing of boxing—in the immediate future, he may not have been far off the mark.

I found myself reflecting on a conversation in a bar at Caesars Palace a few days before the 1987 Ray Leonard-Marvin Hagler fight. Leonard's lawyer/advisor Mike Trainer had brought Jim Troy, the NHL goon-turned-WWF-marketing-guru, on board in a consulting role to Team Leonard, and Troy had in turn introduced Trainer to his boss.

"Bob Arum and Don King and the rest of them had better pray that Vince McMahon doesn't get interested in boxing," Trainer said that night, "because if he ever did, he might put them all out of business."

Vince McMahon never did. But Jerry Jones has been thinking about it for the past quarter-century.

Madison Square Garden might be the Mecca of Boxing, but even stuffed to capacity it can only accommodate half of the 40,000 Arum and Jones anticipate passing through the gates at Cowboys Stadium come March 13. On the other hand, the 5,000-capacity WaMu Theatre was just about the right size for the press conference.

The wording on the schedule—"lunch will be served at 11 a.m., with the news conference beginning promptly at noon"—pretty much guaranteed a substantial early crowd. Press conference veterans knew they could spend a leisurely hour gorging themselves on the usual Madison Square Garden fare (pausing only to throw an extra wrap or two into the briefcase while nobody was looking) before Pacquiao and Clottey even showed up.

The first sign that this might not be business as usual came around quarter past 11, when the first Debbie approached a table filled with masticating boxing writers, placed a full-color glossy photo of the Dallas Cowboy Cheerleaders in front of one, and asked him if he'd like her to autograph it.

The expression on the guy's face was the look of a man who'd just been offered a free lap dance.

Similar occurrences took place around the Theatre as other Debbies worked the room in this campaign to win the hearts and, uh, minds of the media. Batting her eyes, one Debbie even told a grizzled fight writer she hoped she'd see him in Dallas when he came for the March 13 fight.

"Boy," he sighed as Debbie Three moved on to the next table. "Getting these cheerleaders here was a great idea!"

Yeah, but with the Cowboys out of the playoffs and Tiger Woods in rehab, it wasn't as if they'd have been real busy that day anyway.

Promoter Bob Arum revealed that the initial plan had called for four Debbies to fly to New York. At the Texas stop on Tuesday it emerged that another of the Cowboy cheerleaders was of Filipino extraction. Invited to join the Pacquiao-Clottey traveling entourage, Debbie Five raced home to pack an extra thong and was shortly on her way to the Big Apple.

"Jerry Jones is one of the shrewdest men I've ever met," says Arum of his new partner. "He told me that even before he bought the Cowboys he'd learned that the most important number in the NFL is nine. If you can maintain eight solid allies you control nine votes. And since the rules require a 75% approval to do anything, they'll never be able to go against your wishes."

The extension of this logic is that a guy with nine votes and five Debbies at his disposal could make for a truly formidable ally—and an even more dangerous enemy.

Jones bought the keys to the last-place Cowboys in 1989. The new owner promptly fired the iconic Tom Landry, the only coach America's Team had ever known, replacing him with his lifelong friend and former college teammate Jimmy Johnson. Four years and two Super Bowl titles later, he fired Johnson and replaced him with Barry Switzer. By ownership standards he is considered meddlesome to a Steinbrennerian degree, but justifies his extraordinary involvement by pointing out that he is also the Cowboys' General Manager, having appointed himself to that position.

How his employees—and ex-employees—feel about him may have been aptly illustrated late in the telecast of last Sunday's playoff loss to the Vikings. As the waning minutes ticked off the clock in the embarrassing 34-3 loss, the Fox broadcasting team speculated on the future of coach Wade Phillips.

"Jerry Jones," said former Cowboys quarterback Troy Aikman with all the diplomacy he could muster, "is not a patient man."

Jones appears to regard Cowboys Stadium as the crowning achievement of his career. Built as a monument to himself at a reputed cost of a billion dollars, the ultramodern playpen opened for business this year. The cost alone may be precisely why it is also being touted as a multi-use facility. A team could sell out every football game for eons and not make a dent in the debt service.

But as Jones has pointed out on more than one occasion over the years, "I didn't buy the Dallas Cowboys looking to make money. Fortunately, I already had some of that."

Robert Kraft's $172 million offer to purchase the New England Patriots had been approved on January 21, 1994. Two days later I flew to Atlanta. Jerry Jones, whose team would play the Buffalo Bills in Super Bowl XXVIII a week later, was there too. (O.J. Simpson, who would cover his last Super Bowl as a sideline reporter, was also there, but that's a story for a different day.)

When I ran into Jones in Atlanta he almost immediately launched into effusive praise of Kraft, whom he predicted (correctly) would be a great NFL owner. At this point I was still trying to encourage Kraft to come down to the Super Bowl. He had initially been ambivalent about the idea, since he wasn't sure he'd exactly be welcomed with open arms. He had purchased Foxboro Stadium out of bankruptcy court in 1988 and then wielded the Patriots' lease like a hammer, not only heading off at least two attempts to relocate the franchise but successfully beating back an NFL-backed attempt to build a new stadium in downtown Boston, and for the previous half-dozen years he and then-commissioner Paul Tagliabue had communicated only through their respective lawyers.

I then told Kraft what Jerry had said about him.

"Gee," he said, "that was awfully nice of him, but Jerry Jones doesn't know me from Adam!"

"I know a lot more about him than he probably thinks I do," said Jones, a twinkle in his eye. Jerry sat on the league's finance committee, one of whose functions was to quietly vet the credentials and financial status of prospective members of the world's most exclusive club. When rival suitors for the Patriots had leaked rumors questioning Kraft's financial suitability to their favored columnist at the other newspaper about town, the NFL's stony silence had been taken by some as a suggestion that the league shared that view.

Jerry Jones, on the other hand, not only knew pretty much to the penny what Kraft was worth, but his politics as well. (He's a Democrat.)

"Tell him to come on down," said Jones. And, when I relayed that message, Kraft did.

"Robert," I remember telling him just before I hung up that day, "I realize that up until now this has all been a series of business decisions, but I don't think you have any idea how much you're going to enjoy it."

By the time of the Commissioner's Party that Friday night, Jones and Kraft might have been joined at the hip. As the pair of them staggered from table to table, the Cowboys' owner introduced his new friend to his old ones, pausing intermittently to refill Kraft's glass from the whisky bottle Jerry was clutching in his left hand. They were trailed by a somewhat anxious-looking Jonathan Kraft.

"But Dad," the present-day Patriots' president kept trying to remind his father that night, "you don't even *drink!*"

That Bob Arum has also fallen under the Jones spell was evident. By all accounts the pair were on their best behavior in Dallas on Tuesday—and while Jones had to pull out of the New York trip the next day, as a gesture of good faith he did place the five Debbies under the promoter's care.

And just wait till *next* week.

"Jerry and I are going to Mexico together," said a beaming Arum, who hastened to add that it would be a business trip. "Monterey and Mexico City have some of the greatest fight fans in the world—and they're all Dallas Cowboys' fans!"

There was another wonderful moment in New York when Arum introduced Freddie Roach as "the greatest trainer in boxing." No one was arguing with the promoter's description, but it does illustrate just how ephemeral boxing's ever-shifting alliances can be.

The last time Arum promoted a Pacquiao fight in Texas—Manny vs. Jorge Solis at the Alamodome three years ago—Roach was off in Puerto Rico training Oscar De La Hoya for his fight against Mayweather and didn't fly into San Antonio until the night before the bout, leaving his assistant Justin Fortune in charge of Pacquiao's day-to-day preparations.

Arum was still furious at Roach, whom he blamed for Pacquiao's attempt to jump ship to Golden Boy. (Freddie proclaimed his innocence, maintaining that all he'd done was introduce the two, at De La Hoya's request, which was kind of like Oscar saying "I didn't do anything wrong. All I did was hand Manny a satchel full of cash in the back seat of a limo.")

When the fight was over, Arum made out the check for the trainer's end of the purse to Fortune, who promptly cashed it and pocketed the dough, pausing only long enough to stop by the Wild Card, where he cleaned out all of his stuff and some of Freddie's.

It was one of those little twists of the knife Jerry Jones would have appreciated.

Jones had involved himself in boxing even before he involved himself with the Dallas Cowboys. In January of 1983 he teamed up with the late Pat O'Grady to promote a card at the Little Rock Convention Center. The main event saw Anthony Davis (13-1) knock out Otis (Hardy) Bates (9-3-2) to win the cruiserweight title of O'Grady's short-lived World Athletic Association.

Even as club-fight shows go, that one would seem singularly unattractive, but Jones' promotion produced the largest crowd in the history of Arkansas boxing—a record that stood for more than twenty years until Jermain Taylor won the middleweight title and came back to Little Rock to defend it.

In 2010, Jerry Jones wasn't just looking to get back into boxing and he certainly wasn't thinking about Pacquiao and Clottey. He wanted to make the biggest splash possible for his new stadium, and the prospective Pacquiao-Floyd Mayweather Jr. fight loomed the biggest attraction boxing had ever seen. Jones was so anxious to land it that he ponied up a $25 million site fee offer—a fairly ostentatious pre-emptive strike, since unlike the places he was bidding against, Jerry couldn't count on hijacking the paying customers to a roulette table on their way out of the stadium.

In early December Arum, HBO's Ross Greenburg, and Golden Boy CEO Richard Schaefer were due to fly to Dallas to meet with Jones. Schaefer, who was presumably operating at Mayweather's direction, telephoned his regrets at the last minute, and the trip was canceled. Since the blood-testing issue had yet to surface, it was the first indication that Money might not be quite as anxious to fight Manny as he kept telling people he was.

Arum, for his part, was livid, particularly over what he considered the dismissive slap at Jones. Then, two weeks ago, after things had fallen apart with Mayweather, Arum, a lifelong Giants' fan, flew to Dallas at Jones' invitation and watched the Cowboys' playoff win over the Eagles from the owners box. By the time the game was over the two were partners.

"You know how long it took us to make a deal?" recalled Arum. "Fifteen minutes."

"Yeah," noted Top Rank matchmaker Bruce Trampler. "Good thing Schaefer didn't get on that plane. Maybe none of this happens if he does."

Or maybe that's exactly why it is happening. Those with a cursory understanding of Texas assume that football is the guiding obsession among its natives, but the truth of the matter is that while Texans do spend their Friday nights watching high school football played under the lights and their Sundays are devoted to the Cowboys, the other five days of the week are generally devoted to the pursuit of the real state game: Revenge.

TheSweetScience.com
2010

The Accidental Trainer

When Umar Farouk Adnulmutallab tried to ignite his underwear en route from Amsterdam to Detroit on Christmas Day of 2009, he set in motion a chain of events that led to Lenny DeJesus' promotion from obscure New York cut man to the head trainer's role in the biggest fight of 2010. Let it be noted that DeJesus actually acquitted himself well on the night of March 13th. Not that Joshua Clottey had much of a chance against Manny Pacquiao to begin with, but if he'd listened to Lenny he might have made a better show of it.

NEW YORK—You don't hear much about it otherwise, but the Kingsway Gym periodically gets its moment of fame whenever there's a big fight in New York—and sometimes even when the big fight is in, say, Dallas. Its location, at Fifth Avenue and 28th Street, makes it easy to reach for Manhattan-based media types, many of whom are prone to developing allergies at the very mention of words like "Bronx" and "Brooklyn," and, as boxing gyms go, you'd have to say that it borders on the hygienic, in that the toilets flush and nobody spits on the floor. The interior is sufficiently bright that photographers and TV crews know they won't have to hump in a bunch of lighting equipment up a flight of stairs from street level, so they like it too.

Of course, the very factors that make it an ideal location for these Media Day extravaganzas are counterintuitive to boxing tradition. A boxing gym is supposed to be dark and dank and, if not foul-smelling, exude that blend of forty-year-old cigar ash, human body odor, rodent excreta, and backed-up plumbing that provides a gym with its own distinctive aroma.

In that respect the Kingsway can only function as an impostor. It doesn't smell like a gym, feel like a gym, or even *look* much like a gym in any traditional sense.

On the other hand, on this day at least, Lenny DeJesus looks every inch a trainer: As he waits for Joshua Clottey to go to work he is wearing clean dungarees, a zippered jacket over a T-shirt, a jaunty black Kangol cap on his head, and a white towel draped over his left shoulder.

DeJesus is a sixty-four-year-old boxing lifer, one of those guys most boxing fans have seen climb up and down the steps for years without ever knowing his name. On the other hand, you've probably read his name a lot in the last two weeks. That was when the March issue of *ESPN: The Magazine* hit the stands, with a story ("The Substitute") on Clottey that described DeJesus as a "part-time locksmith and long-time boxing satellite" and conveyed the distinct impression that as he heads into the biggest fight of his life against Manny Pacquiao, the supervisory role in Clottey's corner had been entrusted to the Village Idiot.

Now it looks like one of the PR minions had instructed Lenny to drop by the wardrobe department and pick up a trainer's uniform.

1:15: Josh is in the ring

DeJesus stands off to one side and watches Clottey go through the motions while a large Ghanaian named Bruce wields the mitts. The other one-third of the corner DeJesus will be running, an even larger Ghanaian named Kwaku Gyamfi, keeps time. Lenny just watches. He seems to be paying attention, but he issues no instructions.

"Look," says one member of the fight mob as he watches Clottey's workout, "Clottey is thirty-two years old. He's had almost 40 fights. There's nothing you can tell him now that's going to turn him into a different fighter. You just wind him up and let him go.

"And what's the corner going to tell him during the fight—other than 'Get up, Josh!'"

Maybe "Josh! Stay down!"?

1:35: Josh hits the double-end bag

Irish middleweight John Duddy has had a place on the Pacquiao-Clottey undercard since its inception, but he was just added to the Media Day lineup this morning. Half the photographers and most of the print guys seem more interested in Duddy, and they keep watching the door behind Clottey.

In December of 2007 DeJesus was in Duddy's corner at the King's Hall in Belfast when the Irishman beat former Commonwealth champion Howard Eastman. Irish Ropes had just begun to shake up the Duddy corner; Don Turner had replaced Harry Keitt, and Lenny was the cut man, taking George Mitchell's place. Both Keitt and Mitchell are back, and DeJesus long since moved along. That is the life of a vagabond cornerman. Hell, earlier in the Filipino champion's career he even worked as *Pacquiao's* cut man.

"There are five things you can do in a corner and I've done all of 'em," says Lenny. "Not even Freddie Roach can say that. I've been the bucket guy, the stool guy, the advisor, the cut man, and I've been the head guy before, too. But mostly I've been a cut man."

It has been nearly 22 years, in fact, since the last time DeJesus was the chief second in a world title fight. He was in charge of Miguel Santana's corner and led the celebration when IBF lightweight champ Greg Haugen, his face bloodied from a deep cut to his right eyebrow, failed to answer the bell for the 12th round.

"We had the title for about 15 minutes," he recalled. "The fight was in Seattle [Tacoma, actually], and after they'd raised Santana's hand they decided that the cut had come from a butt, so they went back to the scorecards."

The referee that night, Jim Cassidy, said that he was aware of the rule, but assumed that Santana was ahead on all three cards anyway. As it turned out he was ahead on only one of them, and, long after most of the crowd had gone home, a "stunned" Haugen was awarded the decision. The headline in the local paper read "Santana 'robbed' as Haugen gets bizarre win," and the story noted that

> Santana's trainer, Lenny DeJesus, of New York City, thought his fighter had been robbed. "My fighter's hand was raised in victory, and my fighter was awarded this fight!" said the distressed DeJesus.

"They never looked at a replay or nothing. Even the referee told us he knew it was a punch and not a butt," adds Lenny. "The reason they did it was everybody knew Haugen had already signed to fight Jim Watt in London—for a lot of money."

Lenny has been doing pretty well until he says that. And here we thought cut men didn't have to worry about taking too many blows to the head.

Watt had retired after his 1981 loss to Alexis Argello—seven years before Haugen-Santana.

1:40: Josh hits the heavy bag

When the gloves are pulled off Clottey, the towel comes off Lenny's shoulder for the first time all day. He vigorously sets about drying the fighter's forearms and hands, sending out a spray of sweat that glistens beneath the lights. Joshua is wearing a dark red T-shirt with a baseball on the front. On the back it says *"Baseball."*

Does Clottey play baseball? DeJesus is asked.

"I don't think so," says Lenny.

After a January press tour that opened at Cowboys Stadium and moved on to New York, Clottey returned to Accra, where he hoped to secure a visa that would have allowed his trainer, Godwin Nil Dzanie Kotey, to work his corner against Pacquiao. Kotey's previous visa expired in December of 2009, and the security regulations involved in the process had changed dramatically between then and the time he applied for a new one; over Christmastime a Nigerian passenger had attempted to turn himself into a Roman candle on approach to Detroit, and the State Department was no longer rubber-stamping visa applications from West African nations.

So when Clottey flew back in February to open camp in Fort Lauderdale barely a month before the Pacquiao fight, DeJesus had more or less by default become his trainer.

"I guess I'm it," he told ESPN's Chris Jones at the time. Jones did not, it should be noted, seem exactly bowled over when Lenny explained that his "first job will be getting this kid up those stairs and into the ring."

Lenny assumes that Clottey must have worked while he was back in Ghana. DeJesus, in any case, was there to meet him in Florida, and claims that over the last several weeks the challenger has sparred close to 90 rounds.

"I got the sparring partners," he says. "They was all left-handers, too."

1:45: Josh hits the speed bag

John Duddy shows up, in street clothes, and announces that he is not going to work out.

"Nobody told me about this until it was too late," he explains. "I already did all my work this morning."

He does pose for a few pictures with Clottey, and chats amiably with boxing writers. Around the gym, grumbling photographers begin to pack away their equipment.

Over on the other side of the gym, Media Works' Ed Keenan describes the Clottey camp in Florida.

"I finally went to Lenny and said 'Look, you have to give me your phone number. I keep setting up these interviews with Clottey, but then he won't answer his phone.'

"Lenny tells me 'Aw, mine won't work either. A few days ago I fell in the swimming pool with my clothes on and my phone was in my pocket.'

"That was last week. He *still* hasn't gotten a phone."

This might mark Lenny as old school, or maybe just stubborn. Just imagine for a moment Emanuel Steward, for instance, having to make a split-second decision which to carry out of a burning building, his training mitts or his cell phone. It wouldn't even be close.

But Lenny, we felt like asking him, doesn't a locksmith need a phone, too?

1:50: Josh talks

Albeit briefly.

For the past month the question has been whether DeJesus or anyone else actually had enough time to get Clottey ready for this fight. The groundwork in Florida was by all accounts preliminary jousting, and from a preparation standpoint, the dog-and-pony show at the Kingsway has largely been a wasted day.

Now Joshua Clottey says, "I have done all the work I need. I wish I did not even go to Texas for the next eight days. I want the fight to be now."

Is the tail wagging the dog here, or what?

1:53: Josh done talking

Josh says he's ready. Lenny says he's not.

"But that's not exactly what I'll say to him," says Lenny. "Dealing with fighters is like dealing with little kids sometimes. If you don't want them eating candy, you can try to show them how it's harmful, but if you give them an order—*Don't eat candy!*—the first thing they're gonna do is go eat even more when you're not looking.

"Sure, he needs more work between now and March 13th. He's fighting *Manny Pacquiao!* I just gotta figure out a way to make him think it's *his* idea."

TheSweetScience.com
2010

Johnny, They Hardly Knew You

He was in his own way as unlikely a heavyweight champion as James J. Braddock and Buster Douglas, and neither of those came close to the decade-plus he spent at the top of the heap. His style was neither entertaining nor crowd-pleasing—Budd Schulberg, who likened watching a John Ruiz fight to some form of medieval torture, once accused him of boring his opponents to death—but he was a blue-collar fighter, a classic overachiever, and on a personal level, probably the nicest fellow ever to wear the heavyweight crown. He hadn't gotten much respect over the course of his career, including from me; hence this appreciation of The Quiet Man as he walked out the door.

I wasn't even in Atlantic City on the night of March 15, 1996. Mike Tyson was fighting Frank Bruno in Las Vegas the following evening, and Don King had dressed up the undercard with four other world title fights (plus Christy Martin-Dierdre Gogarty), so even though I worked for a Boston newspaper and Johnny Ruiz, who lived across the river in Chelsea, was one of ours, there was never any question in *my* mind where I should be that weekend, even though there might have been in Stoney's.

But a bunch of us did get together to watch Friday night's HBO show, a unique event the network's then-vice president Lou DiBella had cooked up called "Night of the Young Heavyweights." Not many of the 16 guys who fought that night were especially well known then, though several of them would be later. There were heavyweights from six different countries, and while six of these unknowns would eventually fight for world titles, only two would actually win one—and they both lost that night. Shannon Briggs got stretched in three rounds by Darroll Wilson, and Ruiz was counted out by Tony Perez exactly 19 seconds into his fight against David Tua.

It was about as devastating a one-punch knockout as you'll ever see.

Nobody, or at least nobody in Boston, was exactly gloating about it, but the long-range implications were obvious. Even though Ruiz and his manager Norman Stone were saying "he just got caught; it could have happened to anybody," anyone who'd spent much time around boxing could have told you that a knockout like this one usually turns out to be the first of many.

As an amateur Ruiz had been the best light-heavyweight in New England, but never quite made it to the top in national competition. In the 1992 USA Boxing Championships he lost to Montell Griffin. In the Olympic Trials in Worcester that year he lost to Jeremy Williams. You wouldn't term either loss a disgrace—those two met in the final of the Trials, which Williams won, but then Griffin came back to beat him twice in the box-off and earned the trip to Barcelona—but it did sort of define Ruiz' place in the amateur pecking order.

As a pro Ruiz had already lost twice. Both were split decisions (to the late Sergei Kobozev in '92 and to Dannell Nicholson a year later) and controversial enough that Stone could scream "We wuz robbed!" on both occasions, but now they, coupled with the Tua result, appeared to have defined his place in the heavyweight picture as well.

Three months later at the Roxy in Boston, Ruiz TKO'd Doug Davis in six. Davis was 7-17-1 going into that one and lost 16 of the 17 fights he had afterward. Davis was a career Opponent from Allentown, Pa., a little guy built like a fireplug who lost to nearly every mid-level heavyweight of his era, so the only real significance to this one was that back then he usually tried very hard to finish on his feet so that he'd be available the next time the phone rang.

To watch Stoney's reaction, you'd have thought Ruiz had just knocked out Lennox Lewis at the Roxy.

As soon as the main event was over I'd glanced at my watch and realized there was an edition I could still make if I filed my story in the next 20 minutes. I was already pounding away at my laptop before the fighters cleared the ring.

Next thing I knew, a red-faced Norman Stone was directly above me, bent over and shouting through the ropes, which was about as close as he could come to getting in my face without falling out of the ring.

The invective consisted for the most part of a stream of disconnected expletives, but from the few decipherable words in between I gathered that he hadn't much enjoyed my interpretation of what the Tua loss might portend for Ruiz' future.

Since I was on deadline, I just ignored him and kept writing. Trainer Gabe LaMarca and Tony Cardinale, Ruiz' lawyer, finally dragged him away.

Seated next to me was a young boxing writer named Michael Woods, now the editor of *The Sweet Science*.

"What," asked Woodsy, "was *that* all about?"

"Nothing." I shrugged without looking up. "He's just a fucking psychopath, is all."

I finished my story and filed it, and then raced upstairs to Ruiz' dressing room. Stone was still there.

"I don't come up in the corner and interrupt you between rounds," I told him. "If you want to act like a jerk [though I don't think 'jerk' was actually the word I used], fine, but don't try and drag me into it when *I'm* working."

Having gotten that off my chest, I added, "Now. Is there something you want to talk about?"

Actually, there wasn't. He'd just been blowing off steam. The point of the exercise had been to remind Ruiz that he was standing up for him.

But I'll have to admit two things. One was that John Ruiz had 27 fights after the Tua debacle, and he never got knocked out again. (Even when he was stopped in what turned out to be the final bout of his career, it was Miguel Diaz' white towel and not David Haye's fists that ended it.)

The other is that if somebody had tried to tell me that night that John Ruiz would eventually fight for the heavyweight championship of the world, let alone do it a dozen times, I'd have laughed in his face, so on that count maybe Stoney got the last laugh after all.

No boxer ever had a more loyal manager. Stone was a hard-drinking Vietnam veteran who eventually kicked the booze and replaced it with another obsession. He had enough faith in Ruiz' future that he twice mortgaged his house to keep the boxer's career afloat, and was so protective that he eventually convinced himself, if not Ruiz, that it was the two of them against the world.

At that point in his career Ruiz was still vaguely aligned with London-based Panix Promotions, the same people who were guiding the fortunes of Lewis. It is unclear exactly how beneficial this might have been to Ruiz—who between 1993 and 1996 flew across the ocean to knock out obscure opponents in some fairly obscure U.K. cards—other than giving him the opportunity to boast that he knocked out Julius Francis a good four years before Mike Tyson got paid a fortune to do the same thing.

Working with Panix' other heavyweight client was also supposed to be part of the arrangement, but Ruiz' actual time in the ring with Lewis was brief. As Stoney and he'll say, Lennox wanted no part of him after "Johnny kicked his ass." Ask Lewis and he'll laugh and point out that sparring with Ruiz was pretty much a waste of time anyway unless you were getting ready to fight a circus bear.

In any case, a few fights later Cardinale and Stone made what turned out to be a pivotal career move by enlisting Ruiz under Don King's banner. (Panos Eliades seemed utterly shocked that a fellow promoter would poach a fighter from under his nose. "Ruiz isn't *Don's* boxer, he's *my* boxer," exclaimed Eliades.)

If Cardinale and Stone get full marks for aligning Ruiz with King, matchmaker Bobby Goodman deserves credit for the next critical phase of Ruiz' career.

In January of 1998, Ruiz fought former IBF champion Tony Tucker in Tampa and stopped him in 11 rounds. For his next three outings, Goodman was able to deliver opponents who, despite each having but a single loss on his record, posed little threat to Ruiz, and, moreover, to strategically place the bouts on high-profile cards, which provided national exposure to The Quiet Man.

In September 1998, on the Holyfield-Vaughn Bean card at the Georgia Dome, Ruiz fought 19-1-1 Jerry Bailey and stopped him in four.

In March 1999 on the Lewis-Holyfield I card at Madison Square Garden, he scored a fourth-round TKO over 21-1 Mario Crawley.

In June 1999, on a Showtime telecast topped by two title bouts in an out-of-the-way Massachusetts venue, Ruiz was matched against 16-1 Fernely Feliz and scored a seventh-round TKO.

Ruiz at this point had been working his way up the ladder of contenders, and by the time Lewis beat Holyfield in their rematch that November, Ruiz was rated No. 1 (making him the champion's mandatory challenger) by both the WBC and WBA. Ruiz, who at that point hadn't fought in five months while he waited for the title picture to sort itself out, needed to beat an opponent with a winning record to maintain his position.

Enter Thomas "Top Dawg" Williams of South Carolina (20-6). Ruiz knocked him out a minute into the second round.

Was it on the level? Hey, I was ten feet away that night in Mississippi, and I couldn't swear to it, but I can tell you this much: three months later Williams went to Denmark where he was knocked out by Brian Nielsen, and then when Ruiz fought Holyfield at the Paris in June of 2000, Williams and Richie Melito engaged in an on-camera fight before the doors to the arena had even opened, with Melito scoring a first-round knockout that was the subject of whispers before it even happened. Having cut a deal and been flipped into a cooperating witness, Williams' agent, Robert Mittleman, testified under oath that he had arranged for Top Dawg to throw both the Nielsen and Melito fights.

The government had extensively prepped its witness before putting him on the stand. If the Ruiz fight had been in the bag, isn't it reasonable to suppose that Mittleman would have been asked about that, too?

In any case, when Lewis ducked the mandatory, the WBA vacated its championship and matched Ruiz and Holyfield for the title. Holyfield won a unanimous decision, but under circumstances so questionable that Cardinale successfully petitioned for a rematch.

The return bout at the Mandalay Bay in March of '01, produced Ruiz' first championship, along with another career-highlight moment. Like so many of The Quiet Man's other highlights, this one also involved Stone.

Stone had been foaming at the mouth since the fourth, when a Holyfield head-butt had ripped open a cut to Ruiz' forehead. Then in the tenth, Holyfield felled Ruiz with what seemed to be a borderline low blow that left Ruiz rolling around on the canvas. Referee Joe Cortez called time, deducted a point from Holyfield, and gave Ruiz his allotted five minutes to recover.

No sooner had action resumed than Norman Stone, loudly enough to be heard in the cheap seats, shouted from the corner, *"Hit him in the balls, Johnny!"*

So Johnny did. And at that moment, not only the fight and the championship, but the course John Ruiz' life would take for the next ten years were immutably altered.

The punch caught Holyfield squarely in the protective cup. Holyfield howled in agony, but didn't go down. He looked at Cortez (who *had* to have heard Stone's directive from the corner), but the referee simply motioned for him to keep fighting.

But Ruiz had taken the fight out of Evander Holyfield, at least on this night. The next round, he crushed him with a right hand that left him teetering in place for a moment before he crashed to the floor, and once he got up, Holyfield spent the rest of the night in such desperate retreat that he may not have thrown another punch.

Inevitably, the WBA ordered a rubber match. The only people happier than Holyfield himself were Chinese promoters who had been waiting in the wings after the second fight. They seemed to be only vaguely aware, if they were at all, that Holyfield was no longer the champion, but when King announced the August fight in Beijing, they seemed to have gotten their wish after all.

This particular Ruiz highlight *doesn't* include Stoney, nor, for that matter, does it include The Quiet Man himself.

Despite sluggish ticket sales, the boxers were both already in China, as was King, that July. I had already gotten a visa from the Chinese embassy in Dublin a few weeks earlier, and then after July's British Open at Royal Lytham had driven up to Scotland for a few days of golf.

St. Andrews' caddies can often astonish you with the depth of their knowledge, but I guess if a man spends a lifetime toting clubs for the movers and shakers of the world he's going to pick up a lot through sheer osmosis. And on this occasion I'd come across one who was a boxing buff as well. We'd repaired to the Dunvegan Pub for a post-round pint to continue our chat, and when the subject of Ruiz-Holyfield III came up, I told him I'd be on my way to China myself in a few days.

"Oh, I wouldn't count on that," he said ominously. I asked him why.

"Ticket sales are crap," he said. "Ruiz is going to hurt his hand tomorrow. The fight's not going to happen."

The next day I got an emergency e-mail from Don King's office announcing that John Ruiz had incurred a debilitating back injury and would be sidelined for several weeks. The Beijing fight was indefinitely "postponed."

At least the paper didn't make me fly home via Beijing.

The third bout took place at Foxwoods that December. When the judges split three ways, Ruiz kept the championship on a draw. He then beat Kirk Johnson, who got himself DQ'd in a fight he was well on the way to losing anyway, and then decided to cash in, agreeing to defend his title against Roy Jones for a lot more money than he could have made fighting any heavyweight on earth.

It was as clear beforehand as it is now that if Jones just kept his wits about him and fought a disciplined fight, there was no way in the world John Ruiz could have outpointed him. The only chance Ruiz had at all was a pretty slim one—that of doing something that would so enrage Jones that he took complete leave of his senses and succumbed to a war, where Ruiz would at least have a puncher's chance.

The trouble was, Ruiz' basic decency would never have allowed him to stoop to something like that. But Stone gave it his best shot.

The Jones-Ruiz fight took on such a monotony that it's difficult to even remember one round from the next, but Stone's weigh-in battle with Alton

Merkerson was pretty unforgettable. Merkerson is big enough, and agile enough, to crush almost any trainer you can think of, and even at his advanced age I'd pick him over some heavyweights I could name. He's quiet and reflective and so imperturbable that I've never, before or since, seen him lose his temper, and it's fair to say that's not what happened that day, either. When he saw Stoney flying at him, he doubtless thought he was being attacked (albeit by a madman), and reacted in self-defense.

Stone was in fact so overmatched that even he must have expected this one to be broken up quickly. Instead, boxers, seconds, undercard fighters, and Nevada officials fled in terror for the twenty seconds or so it took for Merkerson to hit Stone at least that many times. It was a scene so ugly that even Ruiz seemed disgusted. It wasn't the end of their relationship, but it was surely the beginning of the end.

The public reaction to Jones' win was an almost unanimous outpouring of gratitude. "At least," they were saying, "we'll never have to watch another John Ruiz fight." But they were wrong.

He beat Hasim Rahman in an interim title fight that was promoted to the Full Monty when Jones affirmed that he had no intention of defending the WBC title. (Referee Randy Neumann, exasperated after having had to pry Ruiz and Rahman apart all night, likened them to "two crabs in a pot.") He stopped Fres Oquendo at the Garden six years ago, and then in November of 2004 came back from two knockdowns to outpoint Andrew Golota.

The Golota fight produced yet another Ruiz moment when Neumann, wearied of the stream of abuse coming from the corner, halted the action late in the eighth round and ordered Stone ejected from the building.

Most everyone found the episode amusing, Ruiz and Cardinale did not. LaMarca had retired, and while Stone was now the chief second, he was also the only experienced cut man in the corner. Having forced the referee's hand, Stone had placed Ruiz in an extremely vulnerable position of fighting four rounds—against *Andrew Golota*—without a cut man. Strike two.

Ruiz was reprieved when his 2005 loss to James Toney was changed to No Contest after Toney's positive steroid test, but he bid adieu to the title—and to Stoney, it turned out—for the last time that December, when he lost a majority decision to the 7-foot Russian Nikolai Valuev in Berlin.

Already on a short leash, Stone had openly bickered with Cardinale the week of the fight, but his performance in its immediate aftermath sealed his fate. When Valuev was presented with the championship belt after the controversial decision, he draped it over his shoulder in triumph. Stone tore out of the corner and snatched it away, initiating a fight with an enemy corner-man. With Russians and Germans pouring into the ring bent on mayhem, Stone had to be rescued by Jameel McCline, who may have saved his life, but couldn't save his job.

Four days later it was announced that Stone had been dismissed. Ruiz seemed bittersweet about the decision, but the two have not spoken since.

All of Ruiz' significant fights over the past four-and-a-half years took place overseas, and while he was well compensated for all of them, they might as well have taken place in a vacuum. Few American newspapers covered them.

I didn't cover them either, but Ruiz and I did get together for a few days last fall out in Kansas, where we appeared with Victor Ortiz and Robert Rodriguez at a university boxing symposium. He'd brought along his new wife, Maribel, and his young son, Joaquin, and the morning we were to part company we got together again for coffee and reminisced a bit more.

Neither one of us had seen Stoney, though I would hear *from* him, indirectly, soon enough. Newspapermen don't write their own headlines, and a few months ago the lead item in my Sunday notebook for the *Herald* reflected on Ruiz' upcoming title fight against David Haye in England representing this country's last best chance at regaining the championship for what could be years to come.

When somebody at the desk put a headline on it that described Ruiz as an "American Soldier," word came back that Stoney—who had, remember, *been* an American soldier—was ready to dig his M-16 out of mothballs to use on me, Ruiz, or both.

Few Americans watched the telecast of Ruiz' fight against Haye earlier this month, which is a pity in a way, because his performance in his final losing cause was actually an admirable one. In his retirement announcement he thanked trainers Miguel Diaz and Richie Sandoval "for teaching an old dog new tricks," and while the strategic clinch hadn't entirely disappeared from his repertoire, it was not the jab-and-grab approach that may be recalled as his legacy.

And while Haye was credited with four knockdowns in the fight, three of them came on punches to the back of the head that would have given Bernard Hopkins occasion to roll around on the floor for awhile. If somebody had decked Ruiz with three rabbit punches back in the old days with Stoney in the corner, the city of Manchester might be a smoldering ruin today.

When Ruiz officially hung up his gloves on Monday he did so with a reflective grace rarely seen in a sport where almost nobody retires voluntarily.

"I've had a great career but it's time for me to turn the page and start a new chapter of my life," he said. "It's sad that my final fight didn't work out the way I wanted, but, hey, that's boxing. I'm proud of what I've accomplished with two world titles, twelve championship fights, and being the first Latino Heavyweight Champion of the World. I fought anybody who got in the ring with me and never ducked anyone. Now, I'm looking forward to spending more time with my family."

In his announcement he thanked his fans, Diaz and Sandoval, Cardinale and his brother Eddie Ruiz, and his conditioning coach. He thanked everybody, in other words, except you-know-who.

Oh, yeah, one more thing. Ruiz, who has lived in Las Vegas for the past decade, now plans to move back to Chelsea. He hopes to open a gym for inner-city kids. "With my experiences in boxing, I want to go home and open a gym where kids will have a place to go, keeping them off of the streets, so they can learn how to box and build character."

I guess the question is: Is Metropolitan Boston big enough for Ruiz *and* Stoney?

While no one will ever confuse it with the Riviera, Chelsea today is a markedly different place from the one in which Ruiz grew up, and as economic conditions have steadily improved, the murder rate has declined.

So far.

TheSweetScience.com
2010

A Bronx Tale

The Selling of Cotto–Foreman

For the better part of four decades I've marveled at Bob Arum's marketing techniques. His principal competitor for most of that time is inclined to employ a more straightforward approach: Don King will hand you a plate of chicken shit, tell you it's chicken salad, and hope you don't notice. Arum's style is usually more nuanced and subtle, but in analyzing the task at hand for this fight he may have allowed himself to be dazzled by both the astonishing success of the Manny Pacquiao-Joshua Clottey fight in Texas earlier that spring and by his own youthful recollection of the House That Ruth Built. They're not quite so gullible as their boxing-starved Texas counterparts, so persuading hard-core New York fight fans that Miguel Cotto might not be a shot fighter and that Yuri Foreman was the next Leonard—Sugar Ray or Benny, depending on the audience—was always going to be a tough sell. Cowboys Stadium itself was the real star of the Dallas show. But when you came right down to it, not only was the Yankees' new ballpark not Cowboys Stadium, it wasn't even Yankee Stadium.

At some point over the past half-dozen years it must have crossed that invisible plane between tradition and ritual, one now fixed in the minds of New York boxing fans as a celestial phenomenon more reliable than the summer solstice. The onset of Daylight Savings Time might be a date subject to the whims of Congress, but you could set your clock and plant your gardens based on the comings and goings of Miguel Ángel Cotto. Like the swallows returning to Capistrano, on the second Saturday in June each year Cotto would swoop into Madison Square Garden and beat the living bejeezus out of his highly touted opponent as sort of a tuneup for the next day's Puerto Rican Day Parade.

When they sat down to prepare their calendar for the fiscal year, it was the first date HBO boxing executives penciled in, and Bob Arum's bankers became accustomed to receiving a large annual deposit on the Monday morning *following* the second Saturday in June.

In 2005 it was Muhammad Abdulliev, 15-1 at the time, and the following June it was Pauli Malignaggi (21-0). The year after that it was Zab Judah, who was 34-0 and still considered dangerous. Last year it was Joshua Clottey (32-2).

The lone interruption to this time-honored June rite came in 2008, when the MGM waved so much site-fee money under Arum's nose that Cotto allowed himself to break with tradition for a July fight against Antonio Margarito, an opportunity both he and his promoter envisioned as a long-term investment that would elevate his national profile to the status he already enjoyed on the East Coast.

Instead he came away with the first defeat of his professional career. There is no way of proving that Margarito, who would be caught using doctored hand wraps in his next fight, loaded up his gloves against Cotto as well. It might have been close on the scorecards, but Cotto's bewildered face by the time it was stopped in the eleventh round looked like that of a man who'd been bludgeoned with the business end of a claw hammer.

The June tradition was to have continued this year. Arum had already placed a hold on the Garden for the second Saturday in June, but two developments occurring just a couple of hours apart on the night of November 14 intervened: Cotto once again got beaten silly—and this time it *wasn't* close on the scorecards; no judge had given him more than two of the eleven completed rounds. And Yuri Foreman, an undefeated but light-punching junior middleweight whose resume includes almost as many countries of residence as it does knockouts, looked as if he'd borrowed Margarito's gloves for the night as he battered usually durable Daniel Santos, whom he knocked down in the final round to cement a runaway lopsided decision to win the WBA 154-pound title.

That Cotto was manhandled by the world's best fighter was not an upset of the highest order, and with Pac-Man apparently headed for a lucrative, winner-take-all showdown with Floyd Mayweather Jr., the logical course of action seemed obvious: Give Cotto time for his wounds to heal, rehabilitate him with a spring tuneup against another Michael Jennings type (maybe even for another vacant title), bring him back to New York in June, and then sit back and count the money.

Possibly because he was still as stunned as the rest of the boxing world by the nature of Foreman's win, the newest world champion in his stable does not appear to have figured into the promoter's plans back then. In fact, once Pacquiao-Margarito began to unravel over the red-herring blood-testing issue, Arum's initial inclination seems to have been throwing Foreman to the wolves by offering him to Pacquiao as a consolation prize.

It must have been at roughly this point that Arum's mind kicked into overdrive. Cotto needed an opponent—preferably one who couldn't punch hard enough to hurt him. Foreman, having won a title, was looking for a payday worthy of a champion—preferably one who, like Santos, had absorbed enough punishment over time that he might be vulnerable. Arum couldn't rehabilitate both guys through such an arrangement, but a fight between them would surely validate the stature of the winner, who was going to be a Top Rank fighter either way.

Cotto's drawing power was a matter of record. Foreman's, since he had never headlined a card in his adopted hometown, was not. But Arum, a native New Yorker, knew that while boxing today held little interest for most of the nearly two million Jews in the metropolitan area, the prospect of watching a wholesome, Torah-toting, yarmulke-wearing rabbinical student defend his title in the ring might convert some of them back *into* fight fans. Why, if just a *fraction* of one percent of them enlisted in the Yuri Foreman Army for just one *night,* the Garden wouldn't be big enough to hold them all . . .

Last fall Arum had hired Yankee Stadium for a day to host the New York edition of the Pacquiao-Cotto press tour, and he came away impressed with the facility. His March venture with Jerry Jones for the Pacquiao-Clottey fight at Cowboys Stadium was a triumph for all concerned, conclusively demonstrating that a modern, outdoor arena was a viable alternative in the age of casino-bankrolled boxing. Thirty-four years earlier, Arum had promoted Ali-Norton III, the last fight to be held at the old Yankee Stadium. Now he found himself contemplating the possibility of promoting the first in the new one.

The first item on the Top Rank agenda was to check the stadium's availability on June 12th. *Negatory.* The Yankees were hosting the Houston Astros in a three-game series that weekend. But, it was pointed out, the Bronx Bombers would be on the road the *previous* weekend.

Top Rank provisionally booked the date, but didn't cancel its June 12 Garden reservation. (The date eventually went to a card at the Theatre, headed up by WBO light-flyweight champ Ivan Calderon, a Puerto Rican, who will defend his title against Jesus Iribe on Arum's usual parade-eve show.)

There remained one significant obstacle: A Wall Street lawyer named Jonathan Ballen had booked one of the Stadium's luxury lounges for his thirteen-year-old son Scott's bar mitzvah on the night of June 5. Both Top Rank and the Yankees could spare the seating capacity of a lounge on the night of the fight, but Ballen's contract also included a stipulation that part of the festivities would be shown on the Stadium's giant scoreboard screen. The scoreboard, the Texas Stadium fight had demonstrated, *would* be an essential component of the fight-night experience for the live crowd.

If there's one thing a Wall Street lawyer loves even more than a good bar mitzvah, it's a good lawsuit, so brokering a settlement became a priority for all concerned. In boxing it is called a step-aside fee, and Arum would prefer to describe it as a "negotiation"—as, no doubt, would Jonathan Ballen. Whatever name might have been applied to it, stripped to its bare bones, the ensuing process consisted of Arum (whose press kit biography once described as "an outstanding Talmudic scholar"), on behalf of his rabbi-in-training fighter, sitting down with a fellow member of the tribe to determine what price would constitute an acceptable bribe for Ballen to alter the conditions of his son's bar mitzvah.

The terms of the settlement were not disclosed, but we're assuming Ballen did not demand Mayweather numbers. Once the hurdle had been overcome, it was pointed out in some newspapers that the main event would probably start past Scott's bedtime anyway, since the devoutly observant Foreman wouldn't even leave his house until darkness had signaled the end of Shabbat.

Now part and parcel of his appealing image, Foreman's religious devotion is a comparatively recent phenomenon. In a 2004 profile for the website SecondsOut.com, Thomas Hauser noted that "Yuri has little religious training and admits 'I don't really follow the traditions.'"

In an updated story three years later, Foreman ascribed the spiritual journey that led to his rabbinical aspirations to the influence of Rabbi Dov Ber Pinson, at whose Iyyun Institute in Gowanus the boxer receives his instructions. Pinson, who represents what is apparently a splinter brand of Orthodox Judaism, describes himself as "a modern mystic," which makes him sound a bit like the rabbinical equivalent of Panama Lewis.

· · ·

There was a time when being a Jewish boxer in New York was considered such an economic asset that even *goyische* fighters tried to pass themselves off. In the 1970s the fighter born Michael DiPiano adopted his mother's surname as his *nom de ring* and, as Mike Rossman, briefly held the light-heavyweight title. And when onetime heavyweight champion Max Baer moved from California to New York, he widened his fan base by stitching a Star of David on his trunks and claiming to be Jewish.

"He wasn't," said the late Hall of Fame–trainer Ray Arcel. "I know. I saw him in the shower."

In his 1988 memoir *The Facts,* the novelist Philip Roth reflected on his boyhood fascination with a sport that in almost every respect seemed the utter antithesis of the Jewish mindset: "I could no more smash a nose with a fist than fire a pistol into someone's heart," wrote Roth. "And what imposed this restraint, if not on Slapsie Maxie Rosenbloom, then on me, was my being Jewish. In my scheme of things, Slapsie Maxie was a more miraculous Jewish phenomenon by far than Dr. Albert Einstein."

Or, as Arcel told Hauser when the author interviewed him for *The Black Lights* a quarter-century ago, "punching people in the head isn't the highest aspiration of the Jewish people."

Which is not to say that "punching people in the head" accurately describes what Yuri Foreman does for a living.

"Boxing is an art form to me," says Foreman in a statement with which few who have endured watching him go the distance 20 times in 28 fights would disagree. Monet displayed more unbridled aggression approaching a lily pond with a watercolor brush in his hand than has Foreman in some of his masterpieces.

His skills in the ring are impressive, but Foreman bouts have taken on such a predictable cadence that New Yorker fight regulars time their bathroom breaks to coincide with them. Even though everybody in the joint might have the same idea, they can be secure in the knowledge that no matter how long the lines are, the fighters will still be in the ring when they get back. There must be at least three dozen *rabbis* in New York who punch harder than Yuri Foreman.

"But I'll tell you something, the kid is surprisingly tough," says promoter Lou DiBella, who featured the developing Foreman on many of his shows in the Big Apple and at the Connecticut casinos. "Coming up he fought the same usual suspects the other guys did, and you *expected* him to win those, but there came a time when he was in so tough that he seemed to be consistently overmatched against guys like Anthony Thompson and Andrey Tsurkan and

Saul Roman. But he not only hung in there with those guys, he figured out a way to beat *all* of them."

Foreman says he learned to be tough at an early age, first back in Gomel, Belarus' second-largest city, and even more so after he moved with his family to Israel less than a year after Belarus declared its independence from the USSR.

In Haifa, according to Foreman, his immigrant status precluded access to the facilities and equipment normally available to Israeli youth of his age, so he made do by showing up at a gym that had previously been the exclusive province of Arab kids.

"I needed to fight." He shrugs at the recollection. "And boy, did they want to fight *me!*"

He graduated from this school of hard knocks with honors, winning three national age-group titles by the time he departed for the United States, stepped off the plane, and went straight to Gleason's Gym. He won the Daily News Golden Gloves the year he arrived, and then turned pro.

It is commonly supposed that Foreman was following a well-trodden path familiar to boxers from many other nations, and had come to Brooklyn because America offered the prospect of a professional career. That is partially true, but, Foreman confessed to Hauser in an interview for SecondsOut.com half a dozen years ago, his departure was hastened by the fact that he had been put on notice that he was about to be inducted into the Israeli Army.

Whether it was a matter of conscience or mere common sense, it's difficult to find fault with this position, roughly the equivalent to that of the tens of thousands of Americans who crossed the Canadian border for approximately the same reasons four decades ago. But one does have to wonder if all those Israeli flag-waving rooters who show up for Foreman's fights are even aware of the circumstances of his departure and self-imposed exile.

"Someday, I hope to go back to Israel to visit," Foreman told Hauser in 2004. "But I cannot go now because the army wants me."

Miguel Cotto and his adherents maintain that the loss to Pacquiao was the first legitimate defeat of his career, a position not without validity.

Cotto's detractors, on the other hand, maintain that there should be at least three losses on his record—and that's just in the last two years. In addition to the stoppages by Margarito and Pac-Man, many (including one of the three judges) felt Clottey did enough to merit the win in their fight at the Garden last June.

At the very least, Clottey *looked* more like a winner after twelve rounds than did Cotto, who fought the last nine rounds with a nasty cut above his left eye.

But beyond the question of wins and losses, there is the matter of how much punishment any boxer can reasonably absorb over the long haul without being adversely affected. Not only has Cotto endured wars with the aforementioned sluggers, his 2007 wins over Judah and Mosley weren't exactly cakewalks, either.

Three years ago a matchmaker proposing a fight between Miguel Cotto and Yuri Foreman would have been reported to human-rights organizations, but the issue is no longer as clear-cut.

There is also the matter of weight. Cotto made his pro debut at 135 and won titles as a junior welter and welterweight. That progression did not appear to trouble him, but he has never fought above 147, and weighed 144 for his last bout. Foreman, who weighed 154 for his pro debut, and was 154 on the nose for each of his last three may be, at twenty-nine, as "natural" a junior middle as any man who ever donned gloves.

There is a legitimate question, then, of how much of Cotto's once-vaunted power will survive the journey to yet another weight class. At 140 he had knocked out all but two of his opponents, but in his welterweight incarnation stopped just four of nine and two of those (Judah and Oktay Urkal) came in the penultimate round.

A promotional free agent for most of his career, Foreman fought on cards promoted by DiBella, Cedric Kushner, Joe DiGuardia, Leon Margules, New England Ringside, and Don King before he performed on his first Top Rank bill, but never had a problem finding work. His ethnic appeal would sell enough tickets that promoters were happy to have him, and, aware that he couldn't break an egg with his fists, few opponents ducked him. They all thought they were going to be the first guy to put an L beside his name.

Santos undoubtedly shared the same confidence going into their November title fight. He had won his first title ten years earlier, and while he had been TKO'd by a big right hand from Kofi Jantuah back in 1999, Santos had never been stopped since—and that interval included two fights with Margarito, a 2001 No Contest halted in the first round after Margarito was cut by an accidental clash of heads, and the 2004 rematch, in which a similar injury in the tenth round sent the decision to the scorecards; Santos, who led on two of them after nine, retained his WBO title on a technical decision.

Apart from a three-round No Decision with Cornelius Bundrage occasioned by another head-butting injury, Foreman went into the Santos fight
having stopped just one of his twelve previous opponents—and in the exception it wasn't as if Foreman exactly bludgeoned Jimmy LeBlanc to death
in that fight in Boston back in 2006; LeBlanc went to the canvas the first
time Foreman so much as waved at him, and before the first round was out
retired by announcing to referee John Zablocki, "I'm all done."

That LeBlanc was there just to collect a paycheck seemed so apparent
that the Massachusetts Boxing Commission decided not to give him one
and withheld his purse.

Foreman didn't stop Santos, either, but he might as well have. The accumulated wear and tear of too many hard fights and a less-than-Spartan
existence in between them caught up with the thirty-four-year-old champion
in one night, but the extent of Foreman's domination and twelfth-round knockdown still seemed such an aberration that "modern mysticism" may be the
only plausible explanation.

An April 2009 argument outside their Caguas gym led to a knock-down,
drag-out fight between Miguel and Evangelista Cotto that irreparably rup-
tured the relationship between the boxer and his uncle, onetime confidant
and career-long trainer. Although Uncle Evangelista was the clear-cut loser
in the fistic battle—when he accompanied Juan Urango to a DiBella press
conference in the Bronx a week later he wore dark glasses to mask the damage—he did manage to score a TKO of sorts when he put a cinder block
through the windshield of Miguel's Jag.

Despite the availability of a whole host of better-known (and better-
qualified) candidates, Cotto ultimately filled the position by promoting within
the ranks of his own team, elevating nutritionist Joe Santiago to chief second
for the Clottey fight; more surprisingly still, Santiago remained his trainer for
Pacquiao.

No trainer was going to survive what happened in those two bouts, but
both Cotto's choice of a replacement and the timing of the announcement
seemed almost calculated to produce disruption in the opposite corner.

Foreman's advisory team was engaged in negotiations with Emanuel
Steward about joining the new champion's corner in an advisory role.
(Manager Murray Wilson claims that Steward himself initiated the talks; the
trainer maintains that he was approached by the Foreman camp.) The essential details had been all but agreed to when Wilson began hearing that

Steward was simultaneously engaged in talks with Cotto's people.

"Manny Steward is uninvited," said Wilson, who decided that since Foreman had gotten this far without a Hall of Famer in the corner there was little to be gained in fixing what was not broken. Shortly thereafter Cotto and Steward formalized an arrangement for the latter to take over as chief trainer.

When he was queried on the matter, Foreman insisted that Steward was "not a thought. I have a wonderful corner. My team has all my confidence and my loyalty."

In this case, Foreman probably wasn't just whistling in the dark in proclaiming *L'affaire Kronk* a non-factor; it seems unlikely that the boxer would spend much time fretting over the absence of something he never had. The principal impact of the contretemps on the June 5 bout will be that Steward will not be part of the HBO PPV team.

When Arum trotted out the principals for the press and the cameras at Yankee Stadium in April, Cotto, even though he had been through this before, appeared more in awe of his surrounding than did Foreman, who seemed to be vaguely aware of the role the older version of the House That Ruth Built had played in boxing history. But then Cotto had grown up in a baseball-oriented environment.

"I just hope nobody asks me to bat," joked Foreman, who may yet wish he *had* a Louisville Slugger available on June 5th.

Foreman was at his gracious and disarming best with the media that day. He insisted that his daily lifestyle had been wholly unaffected by his acquisition of the championship belt. When he stepped into the training ring at Gleason's he was still treated no differently than any other boxer. He still made his way around the streets of Brooklyn on his bicycle. He still took out the garbage on trash days.

Somebody even asked him about his Shabbat observance and the resultant 11:30 bell for the main event. Foreman explained that once the lights went back on, Top Rank had arranged for a police escort from Brooklyn to the stadium.

Arum's last Yankee Stadium event in 1976 took place in the midst of an NYPD strike that turned the venue into a sometimes terrifying hotspot of lawlessness. Some patrons were beaten and robbed despite the presence of picketing cops just a few yards away. When the crowd rushed the ring at the announcement of the verdict—Ali, by the narrowest of decisions—the plywood tabletops installed for the ringside press were smashed and splintered. Red Smith, whose pocket was picked under the noses of striking patrolmen, wondered the next morning what the thief might decide to buy with his Brooks Brothers card.

Which is not to say that the cops won't be a factor this time, too: we can already envision what it's going to look like shortly after dark when a phalanx of squad cars, red lights flashing and sirens wailing, creeps along the streets of the Bronx at the pace of Yuri Foreman's bicycle.

Boxing Digest
2010

The Ref Strikes Out

Cotto Beats Foreman at Yankee Stadium

I was hardly alone in questioning Mercante's handling of the Yankee Stadium fight, but most critics focused on the issue of whether the referee had compromised Yuri Foreman's safety by prolonging it. As it happens, I actually like Arthur Mercante Jr., who can break down a production at the Metropolitan Opera as knowledgeably as he can a world title fight. I think this one got away from him in that he allowed himself to become the story. If my judgment seemed harsh, I don't think I said anything here that his late father wouldn't have himself told his son if he'd had the opportunity. Apart from the italicized portions, which come from that night's ringside report and are included for context, this column was composed the day after I'd had an opportunity to review a tape of the telecast and balance that with my more immediate impressions.

NEW YORK—*Miguel Cotto won a ninth-round TKO when a gimpy Yuri Foreman, injured two rounds earlier, was unable to maintain his footing. The Puerto Rican star captured Foreman's WBA junior middleweight title in a bizarre fight before more than 20,000 at Yankee Stadium Saturday night.*

The last fight at a Yankee Stadium had taken place 34 years earlier when Arthur Mercante refereed the controversial third fight between Muhammad Ali and Ken Norton. Mercante's son Arthur Jr. was the third man in the ring Saturday night, and played several important roles. Not only did Mercante take Foreman into custody, but a round earlier the referee had refused to accept a flag of surrender when Foreman trainer Joe Grier fired a white towel out of the corner.

Foreman, who had come to Yankee Stadium with a well-deserved reputation as one of the nicer fellows ever to lace on boxing gloves, demonstrated himself to be among its bravest as well. Foreman's gritty attempt to fight Cotto on one leg for the better part of two rounds Saturday night may not have been particularly wise, but it certainly earned him newfound respect and a legion of new admirers that will probably translate into further television opportunities for the rabbi-in-training.

And for his part, Cotto conclusively demonstrated that those who were prepared to write his boxing obituary may have been more than somewhat premature. In winning Foreman's WBA junior middleweight title, the Puerto Rican star added a world championship at a third weight class to his resume, and raised his personal record to a perfect 7-for-7 in New York main events.

He may still be no match for Manny Pacquiao, but then who is? In this age of multiple champions, Cotto proved that he belongs among them, and in the process revived his own prospects as a box office attraction.

On the other hand, in placing his own personal stamp on the proceedings at Yankee Stadium, Arthur Mercante Jr. seemed less to be laying claim to a lineal birthright as the heir to the legacy of his illustrious father than to be staking out his own turf as the East Coast version of Mills Lane.

Employing a tough, no-nonsense approach to his enforcement of the rules, not a few of which he seemed to be making up as he went along, Mercante may have ensured that long after boxing fans have forgotten the names of the participants in the first (and, possibly, only) main event ever fought at the new Yankee Stadium, they will almost certainly remember who refereed it.

Although its termination came directly as the result of a freakish injury, it would be inaccurate to claim that Foreman lost the fight advertised as the Stadium Slugfest *because* of the seventh-round slip on the canvas that deprived him thereafter of the one demonstrable advantage he enjoyed over Cotto—his foot speed.

But on Saturday night at Yankee Stadium, and probably on any other night, Yuri Foreman wasn't going to beat Miguel Cotto on *two* good legs. By the time fate intervened the bout had already passed the halfway point, and it had long since assumed a well-defined course that seemed unlikely to change.

By the time he took his unscheduled tumble to the canvas, Foreman had a bloody nose, was cut around both eyes, and had been solidly outboxed. Cotto was not only beating him, but beating him at his own game. All three ringside judges (Steve Weisfeld, Don Ackerman, and Tony Paolillo) had scored the fourth for Foreman but, with the exception of Paolillo—who for some unaccountable reason also scored the fifth for the champion—hadn't awarded him any of the other eight completed rounds.

Although Cotto was supposedly the competitor with balance issues, Foreman had to scramble to recover his footing after being knocked from his moorings by Cotto jabs in each of the first two rounds—and one of the two occasions, a Cotto punch that sent Foreman's mouthpiece flying across the ring, occurred *before* the seventh-round slip.

The evening did, on the other hand, include several controversial points, and footage of Foreman's unprovoked tumble alone may provide grounds for an eventual rematch. (And since the fight did not in any sense produce a potential opponent for Pacquiao, a return bout may well be the direction post-mortem activity will take.)

Most reasonable pre-fight analyses had cast Cotto in the puncher's role, and the question going in seemed to be whether he could cut off the ring on the elusive Foreman, and if and when he did, whether his once-potent power would have survived the journey up to 154. All of that wisdom had gone out the window before the first round was over.

The most significant impact of the addition of Emanuel Steward to the Cotto corner in the trainer's position came not in terms of fight strategy (though Steward had correctly predicted that Cotto's hand speed might prove to be at least the equal of Foreman's), but in the temporizing role the Hall of Fame trainer played once Cotto had seized a clear-cut advantage. In some of its more recent incarnations, an excitable Cotto corner might have pushed him to go for the kill once it became clear that he was dealing with a badly wounded quarry. Steward, on the other hand, wisely counseled patience, recognizing that what was by then a certain win could only be undone if an overanxious Cotto exposed himself to unnecessary danger from his by-then desperate foe.

Thirty-four years earlier the late Arthur Mercante had been the third man in the ring for the last fight at the old Yankee Stadium. His principal impact on the outcome came not in his handling of the bout, but in his scoring of it. The Hall of Fame referee awarded eight of the fifteen rounds to Ali, as did judges Harold Lederman and Barney Smith, resulting in a razor-thin unanimous decision that allowed Ali to retain his title.

The decision to assign his son to Saturday night's main event of the first boxing card at the New Stadium was, then, in a sense a symbolic tribute to the seamless nature of the sport's history.

In retrospect Mercante Jr. may also have viewed his first high-profile as-signment since his father's death (two weeks before Cotto-Foreman, Junior did work an off-TV card at the Mohegan Sun) as his opportunity to reinvent himself as his own man, with a distinct style incorporating the cult of per-sonality into his strange concept of a referee's duties.

It was also evident that at least one aspect of Mercante Sr.'s guiding credo (to wit: "stay out of the picture") did not occupy a high priority in his son's vision of the referee's role, in which he seemed to view himself less as an honest broker there to enforce the rules than as a co-equal participant whose high-profile function was at least as important to the proceedings as that of the boxers themselves.

Cotto, of course, had lost his own father in the year since he and Mercante last shared space in the ring, but while the referee's nod to the recently departed (*"Miguel Senior and Dad, Rest in Peace!"*) just before the fight commenced might have seemed a compassionate touch in some quarters, it could easily have been interpreted as inappropriate in others. Referees aren't supposed to be influenced by ghosts—their own, or those harbored by the men whose conduct they are administering.

Mercante's interaction with the boxers (particularly with Foreman, both before and after the pivotal injury) was overly chummy throughout the eve-ning. On at least four different occasions he addressed Foreman as "champ," and his encouragement of the latter may well have crossed the line of pro-priety as well, particularly when it strayed into an area in which he seemed to be evaluating the boxer's performance in a fight that was still in progress.

How much difference is there, really, between Arthur Mercante Jr. ask-ing Yuri Foreman, "Want more time?" and telling him, "You're a game guy!" or "Suck it up, kid!" and Laurence Cole advising Juan Marquez that it would be propitious to quit because "you're winning the fight"?

Not much, it says here. And, it might be noted, the latter was both fined and suspended for *his* actions.

The immediate cause of the seventh-round injury remains open to ques-tion. When it initially occurred, a startled Jim Lampley suggested on live television that Foreman might have tripped over a ringside photographer. Once that was demonstrated to have been inaccurate, the broadcast team proceeded on the assumption that, since Foreman wears a knee brace as the result of an old injury, he had aggravated a pre-existing condition and that his knee "just gave way." (Our view at the time was that Foreman's legs seemed to shoot right out from underneath him exactly as if he'd hit a wet patch on the canvas. Having watched it repeatedly, it *still* looks as if he slipped, perhaps on a logo painted on the mat. In other words, until presented with testimony to the contrary, the assumption here is that when Yuri slipped and fell he aggravated the prior injury, not that the old injury caused the slip in the first place.)

Mercante properly informed Foreman that he had five minutes to recover, but even though he was at this point hopping about on one foot, the boxer elected to resume action almost immediately. When the leg collapsed yet again before the round was over, Mercante once again intervened to chase Cotto away and allow Foreman time to collect himself and survive the round.

All of the confusion attending Saturday's eighth round could have been avoided, of course, had Foreman's corner done the right thing and stopped the bout after the seventh. At that point their man had been reduced to a one-legged boxer, was bleeding from at least three places, and was pretty hopelessly behind on the scorecards to boot.

The chance that a hobbled Foreman might be abruptly transformed into a 2010 version of Willis Reed or Kirk Gibson was approximately zero.

We're talking, after all, about a guy who had been able to stop only 8 of his 28 victims when he had *two* legs underneath him. Sending him back out for the eighth was so wrong-headed that it bordered on the sadistic, and a minute or two later Joe Grier apparently realized this when he tried to stop the fight by throwing in the towel.

A bit of explanation is in order here. A referee is under no obligation to recognize a towel thrown into the ring as a legitimate indication of surrender. In fact, commission guidelines, including New York's, commonly suggest that the referee ignore that time-honored gesture unless he's absolutely certain *where* it came from, and that, moreover, the towel-tosser is someone with the authority to actually stop the fight.

For the same reason, a boxer's seconds are advised not to try to end a fight by throwing in the towel, but rather, to communicate their decision to the corner inspector assigned by the commission, who is in turn supposed to inform the referee of the desire to surrender.

The problem is, Foreman's cornermen had followed these guidelines to the letter of the law. When Grier told Ernie Morales, the NYSAC-appointed inspector, he wanted to stop the fight, Morales started up the corner stairs to so inform Mercante. The referee pointed to the inspector, and rather heatedly directed him to climb back down the stairs and stay away from the ring.

(Whether Mercante, in the heat of the battle, didn't recognize Morales, or was refusing to submit to his authority, remains unlearned.) It was only then that Grier went into a full windup and heaved the towel as far as he could throw it. (Turns out Joe has a pretty good arm. The towel actually hit Cotto, who was on the opposite side of the ring.)

The interaction between the inspector and the referee occurred off-camera; of the HBO broadcast team, only Roy Jones Jr. appears to have even noticed it. RJ did speculate for the benefit of HBO viewers that when "the commissioner" started up the steps, Mercante "didn't recognize him" and hence shooed him away. None of Jones' broadcast team partners so much as alluded to the episode.

The irony here is that when the evening's assignments were initially handed out, Morales had oversight of the Cotto corner and Felix Figueroa, Foreman's. For reasons that remain unexplained the roles were switched before the main event. Our guess is that the commission may simply have wanted the senior inspector in the opposite corner as a safeguard against Steward throwing his weight around had things gone badly for the challenger.

The entourages of both boxers, in any case, swarmed into the ring, as-suming the fight to be over, but Mercante, who assumed the towel had come from the guy he had just chased out of the ring and not from Grier, immediately ordered the ring cleared. Morales pitched in to help herd Grier & Co. out of the ring, though he didn't look especially happy about it. (Our interpretation of the withering glare the inspector cast in Mercante's direc-tion was, "anything that happens now, it's on *you*.") After giving Foreman another pep talk, Mercante directed that action resume, and while Foreman somehow remained erect for the balance of the round, he absorbed even further punishment.

During that five-minute eighth round, by the way, Mercante's dialogue with Foreman included such cheerleading gems as *"You're fighting hard! I don't want to see you lose like that!"* and *"You all right, Champ! Come on, walk it off!"*

Think about this for a minute: Just suppose by some miracle Foreman had come back from all of this and somehow *won* the fight. The tape of Mercante's ongoing chatter with Foreman would have been Exhibit A in any review of the proceedings. Doesn't it seem possible that the referee's litany of encouraging *mots* to the guy he kept addressing as "champ" might have been considered evidence of misconduct?

HBO's assessment of the referee's bizarre actions?

"What a take-charge job by Arthur Mercante!" exclaimed Lampley.

Before the ninth, Michael Buffer was instructed to announce that the towel was not recognized because it had come from an "outside source," which was particularly laughable since at that very moment HBO viewers in their living rooms and those watching the scoreboard at Yankee Stadium alike were treated to a replay clearly showing that the "outside source" had in fact been Foreman's chief second.

The end, in any case, came just 42 seconds later. Cotto landed a left to the body that drove Foreman backward into the ropes, at which point his right leg once again splayed and he went down again. This time Mercante stopped it on his own.

There were constant reminders that Saturday night's card was destined to be Bob Arum's second-most successful ballpark promotion of 2010. At Cowboys Stadium back in March the atmosphere had been positively electric from the moment the gates were opened to the public, and the Dallas card managed to sustain that high-energy air of expectation throughout the night despite what turned out to be a relatively tedious Pacquiao-Joshua Clottey main event.

There seemed to be little juice among the crowd during the early bouts at the Bronx. The same Top Rank representatives who had claimed an advance sale of 30,000 voiced their expectation that, like Foreman himself, significant portions of the audience would be late in arriving, but that never happened. Cotto-Foreman was preceded by three anthems. (It could have been worse; somebody with an eye for strict historical detail could have insisted on the Soviet and Belarus anthems being played as well.) By the time the final note of the last of these faded away, it was clear that what you saw was what you were going to get.

The final tally of 20,272 was a number that could have been accommodated with a lot less trouble at Madison Square Garden, and it suggests that the fight's exotic locale, the sometimes heavy-handed attempts to bolster its appeal with sometimes tenuous historical connections, and the hard-sell push to tap into metropolitan New York's two million–strong Jewish population by appealing to Foreman's tribal affiliation had all in the end been non-factors.

As the crowd response to Buffer's introductions of the main event principals made clear, by fight time Cotto fans may have outnumbered Foreman fans by as much as five or six to one. (If the latter were no match for the former vocally, their presence was somewhat more conspicuous in that most of the Israeli flag-wavers seemed to be concentrated in the more expensive sections nearest the ring. The Puerto Rican fans, on the other hand, were *everywhere,* from ringside to the $50 nosebleed seats in the upper deck.)

But then Cotto's hard-core New York audience was a known factor. In six prior headline appearances at Madison Square Garden and its Theatre adjunct, he had attracted an average of nearly 15,000. Throw in the small but enthusiastic bands of supporters the likes of Foreman, Joe Greene, Pawel Wolak, and James Moore might bring to, say, the Hammerstein Ballroom on a routine night, and you'd come up with a number pretty close to 20,000.

In other words, almost nobody came *because* the fight was at Yankee Stadium, and it could be reasonably argued that many boxing fans stayed away precisely because of the venue. So much for the House That Steinbrenner Built.

TheSweetScience.com

2010

Chapter V—The Final Ten-Count

Chico Goes Down for the Last Time

Diego Corrales, 1977–2007

Nevada

In the tenth round of their memorable slugfest on the night of May 7th, 2005, Diego (Chico) Corrales was knocked down twice by the Mexican champion José Luis Castillo. Chico climbed off the floor on both occasions, and before the round was over had improbably knocked out Castillo.

It was a stunning and thrilling conclusion to what many consider to have been the most spectacular fight—and surely the most spectacular round—in lightweight annals.

Corrales-Castillo was a near-unanimous choice as the 2005 Fight of the Year.

Who could have guessed then that it would be the last fight Chico Corrales would win? Or that, two years later to the day, the two-time world champion would be dead, killed in a high-speed motorcycle accident at twenty-nine?

The answer to both questions is, apparently, a lot of people.

I spent the better part of last week in Las Vegas, where he lived, but never ran into Corrales. The closest I came was a secondhand conversation on Saturday afternoon. Four of us—myself, Michael Katz, Budd Schulberg, and his son, Benn—had gone to a Vegas pub where we could have a late lunch and watch the Kentucky Derby.

Benn, considerably closer in age to Corrales, was a close friend, and phoned him on his mobile from the restaurant. Chico told him that, since he didn't have a ticket to that evening's Floyd Mayweather-Oscar De La Hoya fight at the MGM Grand, he probably wouldn't see us that night.

Two years earlier, it's safe to say, any number of promoters, managers, and television or casino executives would have been tripping over one another in an effort to have Corrales as a ringside guest, but over the past few months he had so effectively burned his bridges that nobody much cared whether he was there or not.

And 48 hours later he was dead.

The first Corrales-Castillo fight naturally begat a rematch, and a few days before that October's scheduled return bout I interviewed Chico on radio. My assumption was that Corrales, who could have boxed circles around the strong but plodding Mexican, would have learned his lesson and would approach him differently this time.

No, replied Corrales. He wasn't being paid a million bucks to engage in a tactical chess match. If boxing fans wanted to see another war, then a war they were going to get.

As it turned out, Castillo somewhat disgracefully didn't make the weight for the rematch. Corrales could have collected his show-up money, taken his lightweight championship belts, and gone home. Instead, he agreed to proceed with a non-title fight despite the obvious physical disadvantages. And when he was knocked out in four rounds, he refused to use the weight issue as an alibi.

I was in Dublin for the Bernard Dunne-David Martinez fight last June when the shocking news arrived that Castillo had failed to make the weight yet again, this time for the rubber match scheduled in Las Vegas that same evening. This time trainer Joe Goossen refused to let Corrales go through with the fight. Corrales left approximately $1.2 million on the table that night.

His next defense was to have been against the Cuban Joel Casamayor last October. This time, ironically enough, Corrales himself came in over the lightweight limit and forfeited his title before he even stepped into the ring. He wound up losing a split decision in any case.

Joe Goossen had contributed significantly to the Castillo win. (When Chico spit out his gumshield after the second knockdown, the trainer took such a long time cleaning it that referee Tony Weeks docked him a point, but it allowed Corrales to recuperate to the point that he could finish the job.) Now he couldn't even get Corrales to pick up the telephone.

Goossen, who had yet to be paid for the Casamayor fight, went to court last month and was granted an attachment on a house Corrales owned. Goossen made sure it wasn't the one Chico's estranged wife and kids were living in. Michelle Corrales was six months pregnant, and Joe didn't want to see her tossed out on the street.

Chico was not a bad kid, but his life seemed to have been a litany of bad decisions. Shortly after suffering his first loss, to Mayweather six years ago, he was jailed for 14 months on a domestic abuse charge, and more recently he had lost his driver's license following a conviction for driving under the influence. Many of his ill-fated decisions appear to have been alcohol-related, although at this point there is no evidence of booze or drugs having been involved in the mishap that took his life.

Despite having earned millions, he was by most accounts nearly broke, and the government was hot on his tail for back taxes. He signed a promotional contract with De La Hoya's Golden Boy Promotions and used the signing bonus to get the IRS off his back. When it turned out he was still under contract to another promoter, Gary Shaw, Golden Boy took him to court. To avoid fraud charges, Corrales recently stipulated to an agreement to return the money.

Last month he returned to the ring, this time as a welterweight, and on April 7th at a Shrine Mosque in Missouri he was unanimously outpointed by Joshua Clottey of Ghana.

Two weeks later, according to the bill of sale that was found on his body, he went out and bought himself a new Suzuki racing bike.

"He had an X-Games lifestyle," said Shaw, who viewed the body before the medics had even been able to pry the helmet off what had once been Chico's head. "He did everything hard and fast."

Indeed, in an interview with the *Las Vegas Review-Journal* that appeared the day of the ill-fated Castillo III weigh-in, Corrales recounted to scribe Kevin Iole tales of jumping from airplanes, daredevil skiing, and scuba-diving in the midst of sharks.

"I'm only young once, and unless somebody hasn't told me something yet, I only get to live once," Corrales told Iole. "If I couldn't do this stuff now, stuff I always wanted to do, I would never get a chance to do it."

According to Las Vegas police, Corrales was going at least 100 miles an hour when he lost control after hitting a speed bump and clipped the back of a 1997 Honda Accord. He was thrown into the air and landed in the path of a Mercedes coming the other way.

This time he wasn't getting up. He was pronounced dead before the police even figured out who he was. Corrales' manager, the rap mogul James Prince, was first of his acquaintances to arrive on the scene and identify the body on Monday afternoon.

It was almost as if it were destined to end this way. And while many were saddened, few seemed surprised.

"Diego was not immune to the pitfalls of life, especially as a young man

surrounded by the fame and fortune of this game," said Goossen, his estranged trainer. "His better times in boxing were behind him. I'm sure he felt
he was in a bad spot. It's too bad Diego couldn't stay in the top place he
once was. Now, we'll all say prayers for him."

Joshua Clottey phoned in his condolences from Africa. In Mexico, where
he is training for next month's fight against Ricky Hatton, Castillo said: "We
had what I would call a friendly rivalry when we got into the ring. We had
two amazing fights, and our names will be linked forever."

The Irish Times
2007

Vaya con Dios

José Torres, 1936–2009

Puerto Rico

PONCE—"I only wish," Pete Hamill was saying, "that José could have lasted just 48 more hours, so he could have seen Obama's inauguration."

José Torres, the former light-heavyweight champion of the world, had passed away less than two days before the 44th president of the United States was sworn in. Hamill recalled that their last conversation had taken place on the telephone a few days earlier, as Barack Obama set out on his Lincolnesque train journey to Washington.

"It had been 41 years since José and I had ridden on another train over the same route, with Bobby Kennedy's body in the back car," said Hamill. "I said to José, 'Can you even believe this is *happening*?'"

"Pete, I know," said Torres. "I've got tears in my eyes just *thinking* about it."

José Torres and I had been friends for 40 years, and Hamill had known him even longer.

In 1958, the twenty-three-year-old Hamill was working as the art director of a magazine called *Atlantis,* which published a Greek-language newspaper of the same name. One afternoon, a barroom conversation with the editor's son produced the novel suggestion that circulation might benefit from a few pages in English.

"Yeah," said Jimmy Vlasto. "But who would write them?"

"I said 'Well, I'd like to try,'" recalled Hamill. "I mentioned this hot young fighter named José Torres, who was starting to knock people out at the St. Nicholas Arena, and Jimmy liked the idea.

"So I went to the Gramercy Gym on 14th Street, where I found José. My friend Billy Powers came along and took some photographs. We talked and cracked jokes, I made some notes, and then I went home and wrote it up."

The *Atlantis* story on Torres was the first ever to carry Pete Hamill's by-line. He was paid $25 for the piece, and more important, it was the beginning of a lifelong friendship.

Not long afterward, Torres moved in with Hamill, sharing a tenement flat at Second Avenue and 9th Street near the gym, and when José moved out to marry Ramona in 1961, Hamill was the best man.

José's manager, Cus D'Amato, footed the bill for the wedding.

"José loved D'Amato," recalled Hamill. "Back then Cus was at war with the people who ran Madison Square Garden. José turned pro in early 1958, and he didn't have a fight at the Garden until 1964. That probably cost him tens of thousands of dollars in purses, but he stayed loyal to Cus."

Pete was with him at the Garden in 1965 when José stopped Willie Pastrano to win the light-heavyweight title, and he was with him in Spanish Harlem the next morning when Torres climbed a rickety fire escape at 110th and Lexington to address a crowd of his deliriously happy countrymen still celebrating the win.

Now, two days after his death at seventy-two, Hamill and I were on a plane to Puerto Rico to say good-bye to our old friend.

By the time we drove across the island from San Juan to Ponce and checked into our hotel it was well into the evening. We headed off to find the wake, which Ramona had promised Pete would not be difficult ("just look for all the people"), and it wasn't. As we passed the wonderfully named local saloon, La Taverna de Moe's Spot, a voice called out, and José's son Cheguito came out to welcome us.

A cluster of smokers stood on the sidewalk outside the Funeria Gonzalez, and half of Ponce seemed to be gathered inside. Gerson Borrero, the broadcaster/journalist for NY1 and La Prensa, greeted us in the reception area, and we passed a small kitchen, where another group of mourners huddled around a steaming coffee urn. The next room had been decorated as a veritable shrine to José's career, with mementos dating from his amateur days in Ponce to photos of him battling Laszlo Papp, the Hungarian legend, in the gold medal match at the 1956 Melbourne Olympics, and of the 1965 fight at the Garden in which he won the light-heavyweight title by stopping Pastrano in nine rounds.

The champion lay in peaceful repose in an adjacent third room, as mourners filed past to pay their respects. Ramona maintained a vigil in a nearby chair, where she was joined by an ever-changing rotation of family members.

Hamill knelt before the casket, silently communing with his friend of 50 years. When it came my turn, I placed my hand over José's.

"It's almost like he's taking a nap," marveled Hamill. "He looks like he could wake up at any moment."

"Yes," agreed Ramona. "And he'd look around and say 'My *God!* What are all these fucking *people* doing here?'"

The mortician had done a marvelous job. Even in death, José looked as if he could spar a few rounds. Or maybe, as he had in the Max's Kansas City game 40 years earlier, come out of the bullpen to retire the side.

We were heavy underdogs that day in 1969. The team from Max's, after all, played in a regular league and wore uniforms, while the Lion's Head was once accurately described as a haven "for Jewish drunks and Irish intellectuals." But once the challenge for the grudge match had been accepted, there was no shortage of volunteers from among a rag-tag collection of Lion's Head regulars: newspapermen, folksingers, poets—and at least one practicing pugilist.

Hamill played right field, I played left, and Vic Ziegel manned the short field position that afternoon. To compensate for the limited range of our starting outfield, our centerfielder, a nephew of *Post* scribe Joe Kahn, was a kid who'd played a couple of years in the Cleveland Indians' farm system and could presumably cover our defensive liabilities. Novelist David Markson played third base.

The starting pitcher was poet Joel Oppenheimer, who claimed that during his days at Black Mountain College he'd been the star of a team that included Charles Olson at first base. Joel figured to be somewhat rusty, since to the best of anyone's knowledge he had spent the intervening fifteen years more or less glued to a bar stool in the Village.

"But Joel," I tried to dissuade him, "these guys play a very serious game. There'll be an umpire calling balls and strikes."

Oppenheimer was resolute, and we agreed to let him open on the mound. "But," I warned him, "if you walk so much as one batter, you're coming out of the game."

When the poet walked the first Max's hitter on four pitches I called time, walked in to the mound, and signaled to José, who was already warming up.

The prospect of facing the former light-heavyweight champion of the world must have been intimidating to all those painters. They certainly didn't argue any ball-and-strike calls, and Chegui got us out of the inning.

• • •

Budd Schulberg knew Torres almost as long as Hamill did, and wrote the foreword to José's 1971 book, *Sting Like A Bee*. Budd's son Benn was born eight years later.

"I knew him my whole life, and I can still hear his laughter when I think about him," said Benn Schulberg. "Every few years he'd look at me and ask 'How old are you now?', and when I'd answer he'd always shake his head and say the same thing:

"Ho-ly shit!"

"Want to know how my brother became as strong as he was?" Jaime Torres reminisced. "When he was a boy he used to walk around the Barriada del Caribe—on his hands. Upside down, he would go around the neighborhood, up and down the sidewalks that way. People would come out of their houses just to watch him. Of course he got a lot of attention by doing it, but he also developed tremendous upper body strength, and sometimes he'd walk around the Barriada on stilts, which also developed his leg muscles and gave him great balance.

"By the time José was twelve years old he was the strongest kid in the neighborhood, and as a result he became everyone's protector. If an older boy bullied one of his friends, the friend would turn to José, and no matter how big the other kid was, José would find him and kick his ass."

Young Chegui might have been the toughest kid in Playa de Ponce, but he wasn't the toughest guy in his own home. Andres Torres Morel was a trucker by trade, an old-fashioned disciplinarian never in danger of spoiling the child by sparing the rod.

"When some kid's father complained to the old man that José had beaten up his son—and that happened a lot—then our father would turn around and beat the shit out of José, no questions asked," said Jaime. "Back in those days we never thought of it as 'abuse'; it was common and almost expected when a kid misbehaved. But later on it was almost as if José came to appreciate those beatings. He was never intimidated by anyone he faced in the ring, because no opponent could be more intimidating than his own father, and I guess it gave him some excellent, if unintended, boxing training. He learned at a very early age that he could take a punch."

José left Ponce when he enlisted in the U.S. Army at seventeen, and began to box shortly thereafter, initially, he once recalled, because members of the camp boxing team were excused from KP duty.

Three years ago he and Ramona had moved back to Ponce, primarily for health reasons.

"I missed having him around," Cheguito Torres, a lifelong New Yorker, reflected, "but being here in Ponce I can understand why my father wanted to come home. It's nice to think about how much he must have enjoyed being back here those last few years."

On Thursday morning José's casket was taken from the funeral home and, accompanied by a small procession of family and friends, driven over the mountains to San Juan, where the champion's remains were displayed for several hours at La Casa Olimpica. For over half a century Chegui had been considered a non-person by the Puerto Rican Olympic Committee because when he won his Silver Medal in Melbourne he had boxed under the colors of the United States. (Since 1948, Puerto Rico has fielded its own Olympic teams.)

Now, three days after his death, he was posthumously inducted into the organization's Hall of Fame. David Bernier, the president of the executive committee, asked Ramona's permission to affix a pin bearing the Puerto Rican Olympic logo to his jacket.

"This is something Pops always wanted," said one of the kids. "I just wish they'd done it when he was alive."

An honor guard stood vigil as a veritable Who's Who of Puerto Rican boxers—Felix Trinidad, *père et fils,* Miguel and Evangelista Cotto, John John Molina, Ángel Espada, Ivan Calderon, Juan Manuel Lopez, Sammy Serrano, and Manny Siaca—paid their respects. Late in the afternoon José was loaded back into the hearse and returned to Ponce. By nightfall the wake had resumed in earnest.

José Torres fought five times in 1966, the year after he won the title from Pastrano. In May he won a decision in an outdoor bout at Shea Stadium. His August win over Eddie Cotton in Las Vegas was named Fight of the Year. And that October he knocked out Chic Calderwood, the Commonwealth Champion from Scotland, in five.

Then, just before Christmas he was back at Madison Square Garden, to face former middleweight champion Dick Tiger of Nigeria. José lost a unanimous decision that night, as well as a rematch the next year.

"Even *I* thought he lost the first Tiger fight," said Hamill, "but I thought he won the second one."

The split decision could not have been closer. Two scorecards had it 8-7, Tiger, the other 8-7 Torres.

But an almost forgotten 1965 bout may have had more lasting impact than any of the aforementioned. As the new champion, José wanted to pay homage to his homeland and arranged a non-title fight against former heavyweight challenger Tom McNeeley at Hiram Bethorn Stadium. Fighting as a heavyweight for the only time in his 45-bout career, he was giving away 22 pounds.

"José won the fight, but he was in the hospital for two weeks afterward, with damage to his pancreas," recalled Hamill. "That may have been the cause of the diabetes problems he had later in his life."

The Plaza Las Delicias was just a few hundred yards away—a long block, really—from the funeral home, which was in turn just across the street from José's home. As the casket was loaded into the hearse on Friday morning, it occurred to me that in his final years Chegui had made this same journey nearly every day, but this time he wouldn't stop to chat with at least a dozen people along the way.

The casket was placed on the steps of the Parque de Bombas, an old 19th-century firehouse built by the Spanish, which now functions as a civic museum. There were speeches from Maria Melendez Altieri, the Mayor of Ponce, and from Representative Nydia Gonzalez. The Brooklyn Congresswoman, the first Puerto Rican–born woman elected to the House of Representatives, was an old friend, and choked back tears as she struggled through her tribute.

For the next couple of hours the people of Ponce queued up to pay their last respects at the firehouse. There were still people standing in line when it came time to reassemble the procession and head south toward the coast and the Playa de Ponce.

When Torres climbed off the canvas after two first-round knockdowns to stop substitute opponent Charley "Devil" Green in 1968, nobody had to tell him he'd just fought for the last time.

"When one of your sparring partners starts knocking you down, it's time to get out," said José.

Encouraged by his new circle of friends and mentored by Hamill, Schulberg, and Norman Mailer, Torres turned his hand to writing and became very good at it—in two languages.

He authored two books. (*Sting Like A Bee* was a biography of Muhammad Ali, and *Fire and Fear* [1989], about fellow D'Amato protégé Mike Tyson.) He wrote a column for the Spanish-language dailies *El Diario* and *La Prensa,* and when he signed on with the *Post* he became the first-ever Latino to write a column for an English-language New York daily newspaper.

The best I could tell there had been no public announcement of the funeral itinerary, but there were people lining the streets all the way to the Playa. There came a particularly touching moment when we reached Ruiz Belvis Elementary and Santiago Gonzalez Intermediate, the schools where Mrs. Cordero had taught José in his youth. The kids, in uniform, had assembled outside, as the hearse passed by they waved from behind a twenty-foot banner that read *José Chegui Torres, El Campeón. We Will Never Forget You.*

At the Playa the pallbearers brought the casket to a gazebo in the large, open-air plaza, and for more than an hour yet another group of mourners, many of them the families of José's boyhood neighbors, filed past.

There was yet another round of speeches from another batch of dignitaries, and music from the Ponce Municipal Band, who performed in their uniforms despite the sweltering midday heat.

The procession then moved on to La Iglesia de la Virgen del Carmen for a funeral service that seemed, considering the solemnity of the occasion, almost upbeat, a folk mass with the congregation joining in to a lively guitar accompaniment. The noted Puerto Rican musician Antonio Cabán Vale (more familiarly known, for reasons devoid of irony, as "El Topo"), accompanied himself on Spanish guitar as he performed a poignant *danza* version of his composition "Verde Luz."

The plan had been for José's children to each speak at the mass, but the night before, Cheguito, Mona, José, and Brenda had jointly asked Hamill to be their surrogate.

"We've talked it over and decided we'd like you to speak for all of us, Uncle Pete," Cheguito told Hamill. "You were Pops' best friend. I'm sure you'll know what to say."

Among those sending their condolences was Dr. Wilbert McClure, the respected Boston psychologist. Forty-five years earlier Torres had won a unanimous decision over "Skeeter" McClure in a main event at Madison Square Garden. At the time the fight was advertised as a battle of former Olympic medallists. (McClure had won the gold at Rome in 1960.) Nobody would have guessed it at the time, but it also turned out to be a ten-round fight between two future boxing commissioners.

In 1983, Governor Mario Cuomo appointed Torres chairman of the New York State Athletic Commission, making him the first Latino ever to hold the position. José hadn't exactly lobbied for the job, and took it in part because he was afraid that if he didn't, his old D'Amato stablemate Floyd Patterson, already a commission member, would, and José told me at the time, "The last thing this commission needs is another Republican."

Torres remained not only a spokesman for the Latino community but also a passionate activist in political, social, and environmental causes. In 1999 he was arrested at the United Nations for his participation in a demonstration against the U.S. Navy's practice of using Vieques Island, just off the Puerto Rican coast, as a bombing range.

"José spent more than 50 years of his life in New York," said Hamill. "He was very proud to be a Puerto Rican, but he was a New Yorker, too."

As the funeral procession departed the church and pushed its way through the narrow streets on the three-mile journey to El Cementerio de la Playa, the ranks of the cortege almost immediately began to swell, as the throngs lining the streets for one last glimpse at the departed champion fell into step and joined the parade. By the time they got within a mile of the cemetery the crowd had completely enveloped the vehicles, bringing the entire procession to a halt.

Some of them were banging on the sides of the hearse, and others took this as a signal to strike up a *plena*.

A time-honored tradition along the southern coast of Puerto Rico, the *plena* is an African-influenced art form dating to the days of slavery when, Jaime Torres explained, "the tasks of the day were finished and people met around the community fire or common ground with their drums and began chanting a spontaneous refrain that is repeated by the people gathered there."

In this case the refrain was *"Chegui el Campeón seguira vivendo en nuestras corazones."* Bongos and conga drums had by now materialized, and the chant was interspersed with impromptu verses shouted out by members of the chorus.

Inside the black limousine, Ramona Torres decided to surrender to the will of the proletariat, who plainly wanted to say good-bye on their own terms.

"He belongs to the people," she sighed, at which point the casket bearing José Torres' body was removed from the hearse. Several men hoisted the coffin above their heads and carried it the rest of the way up the hill to the *cementerio* in a swaying procession guided by the rhythms of the *plena*.

"I can't recall the improvised verses," Jaime Torres told me a few days later. "My emotions were so elevated that I got caught up in them. Even Ramona was singing along."

The military honor guard was waiting at the gravesite. They prudently shouldered their weapons, and the formal ritual was deferred until the conclusion of the *plena*.

"As I looked down into the coffin I pointed to Ramonita [José's daughter Mona] to look down, too," said Jaime, "so she could see the smile on José's face. It was as if he was enjoying all the festivities and gaiety."

There were more tributes back in New York, including one in the ring at the Garden just before the February 21 Cotto-Jennings fight, a moment that fittingly took place before thousands of Puerto Rican fans.

A couple of weeks after the funeral I'd fallen asleep watching a fight, and awoke at three in the morning with the television still on. Showtime was airing a twenty-six-year-old movie called *Exposed* that night, and when I opened my eyes, it was like being visited by an apparition: The ghost of José Torres was looking back at me from the TV screen.

Actually, in the film he was looking at Nastassja Kinski while he made small talk at an art gallery opening. When he said something about boxing, she said something about murder, and then she walked away to find Rudolph Nuryev, leaving José with a look on his face I'd seen a thousand times before.

As Nastassja disappeared into the crowd, José Torres shook his head and said, *"Ho-ly shit!"*

Boxing Digest
2009

Arthur Curry, Come on Down!

Artie Curry, 1960–2009

New York

As several hundred boxing and television types filed out of his memorial service at Madison Square Garden's WaMu Theatre Wednesday afternoon it occurred to me that Artie Curry's worst fears had been realized. For us it had been a poignant and often uplifting celebration of his life, a tribute to a departed friend, but Artie, well, he might not have *hated* it, but he would have squirmed uncomfortably through almost every minute of it.

Once I recovered from the shocking news of his death five weeks earlier, I'd inquired about arrangements. There were none, I was told. Artie had left express wishes that he be cremated without fuss, privately and quietly interred without a formal funeral service.

I wondered then whether he had had some vague premonition of his impending demise, because men in their forties don't commonly devote much thought to these matters. As it turned out, his death had been preceded less than two months earlier by that of a beloved sister, who'd succumbed to cancer. Her burial struck Artie as such a gut-wrenching, grief-stricken experience that he determined that he didn't want to be the focal point of a similar exercise. He'd told Lise Curry that, and lest his mother be tempted to override his wishes, he'd told several friends as well: no body, no funeral, no tears.

Of course he could have anticipated that with HBO showing Paul Williams-Winky Wright in Vegas just a few nights later there would be the inevitable 10-count before the main event. And as they attempted to convey their sense of loss even while attempting to explain just who Arthur Curry was and what he did to a television audience that had probably never heard of him, first Michael Buffer, then Jim Lampley, and finally Larry Merchant each flubbed his lines, bursting into tears on-camera.

The concept behind Wednesday's gathering was that it wouldn't violate

Artie's proscription. The well-intentioned idea was that his friends, his family, and his HBO family would come together at the Mecca of Boxing to exchange some light-hearted reflections, share a few memories by telling stories in which Artie would often be the butt of the joke—in his self-deprecating humor he was used to that—and everyone would go home happier for the experience.

They even managed to retrieve footage of the high point of his non-HBO television career—his appearance as a contestant on *The Price Is Right.*

When Bob Barker looked to Row 18, fourth seat from the right, and said, *"Arthur Curry, come on down!"* recalled his old friend and HBO mentor Carl Veibranz, "Artie sprang up like a jack-in-the-box and bounded down the stairs like a boxer entering the ring." In his subsequent conversation with the host he was in the process of bonding with a spellbound Barker when there came a voice-over:

"We interrupt this program to take you to the White House . . ."

And for the next 25 minutes Ronald Reagan addressed the nation over the troublesome issues in Afghanistan (back then, we were defending the rights of our friends, the Taliban), and that was the end of Artie's career as a game-show contestant.

But despite such moments of levity, and the fact that a decent interval had elapsed, close to a dozen speakers shared their memories of Artie at Wednesday's gathering, and almost without exception they were unable to get through their remarks without succumbing to tears. Whether it was HBO Sports President Ross Greenburg or Time-Warner CEO Jeff Fewkes or Lou DiBella, whose tenure as an HBO executive paralleled Artie's eventual role with the network, or Kery Davis, the VP to whom Artie allegedly reported (though as Davis made clear, the opposite sometimes seemed to be the case), or Roy Jones Jr., not a man normally given to sentimental reflection, at some point they all found themselves crying, and when they cried, the rest of us did too, and somewhere Artie was saying *"Damn!* I *told* you this was a bad idea!"

It wasn't a bad idea at all, and we all left the better for it. But it clearly wasn't what Artie would have wanted, because in his mind it was never about himself. But they all turned out for him Wednesday—boxers great and small, past and present, promoters, sportswriters, judges, officials, trainers, sanctioning body officials. There were even a couple of what looked suspiciously like round-card girls.

In the just over an hour it took for a dozen people to fill in the gaps of a life story, interspersed with some uplifting—but inevitably emotionally over-whelming—live musical performances from Tracy Adams, Fabian Spady, and Chaz Perry, it became clear that while both Artie's life and career over the past three decades had been the product of a series of happy accidents, in each instance it had been he and he alone who had seized the moment and made the most of every opportunity to arrive at the indispensable position he held at the time of his untimely end.

Essentially an abandoned child from Brownsville who barely knew his natural parents, he grew up in a series of foster homes and at seventeen was about to be discharged from the system. Lise Curry and her husband, a sometime jazz singer, were looking to adopt a small child, but a social worker passed along word about Artie Sheppard, whom he described as "a diamond in the rough."

When DiBella phoned Lise Curry a day or two after Artie's death, he'd never met her.

"You're going to be surprised," she told him. "I'm a little white lady."

"Yes," said DiBella, "but I also understand that you're a strong black woman."

Artie finished high school as a member of the Curry family, and eventually took their name. A few phone calls through friends of friends resulted in a pro-forma "job interview" and a place in the mailroom at the Time-Life building, whose rounds included the offices of subsidiary HBO.

"He never took anything for granted, not even the smallest kindness," recalled Mary-Ellen Simonnin, who arranged his job interview back then. "He'd thank me and tell me how thrilled he was to be working at such a great job, and I'd be thinking 'Great job? As a mailroom boy?'"

And, if you went strictly by the job description, he wasn't even very good at that. "It quickly became apparent that getting the mail delivered on time was not among Artie's priorities," recalled Veibranz. But as he made his rounds and stopped to chat in each office, he brightened the day of each and every occupant with his infectious conversation, and along the way he absorbed everything he came in contact with, and learned the way this intricate company operated by mentally connecting its individual components.

Always a sports fan (and as footage shown at his service attested, the owner of a deadly jump-shot from three-point range well into his forties), Artie had naturally gravitated to the HBO side of the Time empire, and after seven years in the mailroom was offered the chance to join HBO sports as a production assistant. On the surface this could have been a job holding even less promise for the future than the mailroom, but he plunged into it with such enthusiasm that it eventually became clear that his people skills might make him useful in an even more important role, that of a go-between coordinating relations between the network, its sometimes contentious roster of boxers, and the public that represented the constituency of both.

The role has been described as "ambassador," but it was more and less. Officially at the time of his death Artie's title was "Manager of HBO Sports Talent Relations." He had his own expansive office, and he told Veibranz in a recent visit, "You wouldn't believe how much money I'm making now." (He was right about that part. Veibranz, who had been an HBO VP when he was ushered out the door a decade ago, couldn't.)

The job was a two-way street, of course. Artie managed to maintain the trust and loyalty of both his employers and the boxers because he never favored one over the other and never tried to bullshit either one of them. His friendship with Jones appears to have been one of the more enduring, and while Roy deliberately avoided citing past examples, one can almost imagine a conversation between the two, whether on the grounds of the farm in Pensacola or in a Vegas hotel suite.

"An HBO jacket for your cousin? What size does he wear, my brother?"

"Smoke on *another* HBO undercard? I can pass it along and see what they say."

"You headlining as a rapper at Radio City Music Hall? Get real, my brother. No chance."

"But how about you *fighting* at Radio City Music Hall? Now, there's a chance to make history."

"Artie," said Bewkes, "would come up with all these ideas that shouldn't have worked, but you'd be surprised how often they did."

Kery Davis recalled a meeting when Artie reported for his annual job review. The network, of course, hadn't a single complaint, but Artie did: "I don't think I've been giving enough back," he told Davis, and proposed a program that would send HBO boxers out into the community to speak at schools and social agencies. Somehow the concept had never occurred to his superiors, but as Artie outlined it to Davis that day, Kery found himself thinking, "He's absolutely right."

He truly carved out his own job description, one that made him so irreplaceable that the notion of a single successor has not even been contemplated. As Merchant noted on the broadcast the weekend Artie died, he was not only the bridge between the fighters and the HBO suits, but between them and the guys in the tuxes at ringside, too.

"His job was so unique and he was so good at it that he actually had better access to the seats of power at HBO than the guys in the boardroom did," said DiBella. "Artie was HBO royalty."

And he rubbed shoulders with boxing royalty as well.

"I can't begin to tell you the basis for our relationship because it doesn't even make sense to me," said Jones. "He's from the North, I'm from the South. He's from the big city, I'm from the country. It's not like we had a lot in common, but we hit it off right away and stayed that way for years."

When he spoke to Artie just before his death, Jones recalled, he had mentioned that he wasn't feeling well but said he had medication and had things under control. RJ had been worried enough to offer to fly to New York. Given his well-documented history of Big Apple xenophobia, this was, Artie had to know, a reflection of the utmost concern, but he discouraged the visit. Within a day he was dead of a heart ailment.

"Sometimes an angel just appears in your life," said Jones. "But don't ever take anything for granted, because in a spark that angel might just fly off without warning."

Even as he choked back his own tears, Jones expressed his confidence that "wherever Artie is right now, he's happy and he's smiling."

One can only hope so. Peace, my brother.

TheSweetScience.com
2009

The Kronk's White Shadow

Mickey Goodwin, 1958–2009

Michigan

If Emanuel Steward seems burdened with a heavy heart when he arrives in Ireland with Andy Lee this weekend, it is understandable. Few circumstances can be more painful than a man's outliving his own children. The charter members of the Kronk Boxing Team he founded more than three decades ago might as well have been his sons, and when they laid Mickey Goodwin to rest on Monday, they buried Steward's first professional star.

When he established an after-school program at the dank, inner-city Detroit gym in the early 1970s, Steward spent half a dozen years developing a cadre of mostly ghetto-bred adolescents into the top amateur program in the United States.

"I always knew they would turn pro eventually, and when they did, I would too," Steward recalled a few years ago.

On the evening of November 25, 1977, four Kronk boxers made their professional debuts on a card at Detroit's Olympia Stadium. Among them was nineteen-year-old Thomas Hearns, who stopped Jerome Hill in two rounds. The main event featured another Kronk teenager, Goodwin, who knocked out Willie Williams in the first round.

In those days the Kronk Gym was located in the midst of an urban jungle considered so dangerous that most white kids were afraid to walk down the street, making Mickey's presence there something of an anomaly. Ebullient and wise-cracking, he wore his hair in a tousled mop-top and had a perpetual grin on his face, presenting an aura of civility belied once he stepped between the ropes.

Given the subsequent successes of many of his contemporaries, a mythology has developed holding that Goodwin's prominence on those early Kronk cards owed as much to his pigmentation as to his fighting ability, since his visible presence would supposedly attract Caucasian boxing fans.

Not so, says Steward. At this stage of their respective careers, Goodwin's development was probably ahead of Hearns'. "Mickey was the best natural puncher I ever worked with," recalled Steward. "The first time he sparred in our gym, he knocked out a kid with the very first punch he threw."

Between that November debut and the following February, Goodwin and Hearns jointly performed on six shows. Goodwin was the headline act in all of them, and five of his fights didn't get beyond the first round.

Steward had arranged a card for the night of March 17, 1978. Noting that the date coincided with his school's spring break, the fun-loving Goodwin asked out and spent the week on a trip with his friends. Hearns got top billing on the St. Patrick's day show.

"We advertised him as 'Tommy O'Hearns,'" recalled Steward. "Mickey came back for the next show, but Tommy was always the star after that point."

Although he regularly sparred with half a dozen teammates who would become world champions, Goodwin never fought for a world title, though he came close.

In early 1982 Steward had signed a unique three-bout contract with Bob Arum, who promoted Marvelous Marvin Hagler, that called for the middleweight champion to defend his title against a trio of Kronk boxers—Goodwin, followed by William (Cave Man) Lee, and, eventually, Hearns.

Mickey's challenge to Hagler was supposed to take place that March in San Remo, Italy. In a sparring session at the Kronk a few weeks before the scheduled title bout, Goodwin broke his right hand. To keep the television commitment, the date was preserved, but the venue was shifted to Atlantic City, and Lee was moved up in the rotation to take Mickey's place against Hagler.

A few days before that fight in New Jersey, his hand in a plaster cast, Goodwin cheerfully described the new challenger by saying, "Cave is the only black guy I know who likes rock 'n' roll and can swim!"

Cave Man lasted but 67 seconds with Marvelous Marvin, and subsequent contractual complications would put off the Hagler-Hearns fight for another three years. Mickey Goodwin never came close to fighting for another title.

His most formidable opponent became the scale. Making 160 pounds was a struggle, but at barely 5'7" he found himself at a distinct disadvantage against the larger light-heavyweights he boxed for the second half of his career. He retired in 1994, with a career record of 40-2-1.

I last ran across Goodwin a year ago October, when he materialized at ringside in a Michigan hockey rink the night Andy Lee knocked out Marcus Thomas. He told me that in recent years he had, in emulation of the Steward he had known as a young man, been training young amateurs at his River Rouge Boxing Club.

"Mickey was maybe the only boxer out of the original Kronk team who had really gotten involved with the amateur program, working with those kids in the downriver area," Steward said last week. "That had become his passion over the last four or five years. He was totally wrapped up in amateur boxing."

Mickey and I made vague plans to hook up again that night in Plymouth, but we never did.

Teddy Blackburn had been better about keeping in touch. The noted boxing photographer, who grew up in nearby Ann Arbor, recalled a 1981 visit to the Kronk in which he sparred with Goodwin.

"Even though he said we 'were only going light,' he sent me to the doctor and the dentist that day," said Blackburn. "He advised me to keep out of the ring and stick to taking pictures. But every time I saw him after that he was always there with a big hug, and I got a Christmas card from him every year."

Goodwin was fifty-one when they found his body, early on the morning of March 3, at the home he shared with his parents in Melvindale, Mich.. Facial contucions led the small-town cops who were first on the scene to leap to the conclusion that he'd been bludgeoned to death, and that erroneous report circulated all over the globe. An autopsy undertaken a day later confirmed that after returning home that night, Mickey had taken a shower just before he suffered a stroke and fell down a flight of stairs.

Confirmation of the actual cause of death didn't do much to ease the pain of his passing, but it did bring a measure of comfort in answering two questions that had been weighing on the minds of those of us who knew him for the previous 24 hours: (a) Who in the world would want to bludgeon Mickey Goodwin, who hadn't an enemy in the world, and (b) Who *could*?

The Irish Times
2009

Counting the House in Wise-Guy Heaven

Vin Vecchione, 1945–2009

Massachusetts

He'd be the first to tell you he made his share of mistakes in the sixty-four years he spent on this earth, but rescuing Peter McNeeley that night in Vegas wasn't one of them.

For most boxing fans the enduring image of Vinnie Vecchione remains the night in August of 1995 when he climbed through the ropes at the MGM and deliberately forced Mills Lane to disqualify McNeeley just 89 seconds into his fight against Mike Tyson. The seemingly precipitate haste of his intercession was widely criticized elsewhere, and to those who didn't know better it created the impression that the fight had been a prearranged charade.

It was, but only in the sense that the scenario he had anticipated had materialized before Vecchione's eyes.

The night before the fight Vinnie had confided his intentions in me. "People are saying Tyson might kill Pete, and he probably could, but I'm not going to let that happen," he said. "Believe me, if I see he's in any danger I'm going to stop the fight before he gets hurt."

Vinnie knew how outgunned he was. He knew his heavyweight couldn't fight a lick and that the only chance he had lay in the element of surprise.

"Pete is going to charge out of the corner and crash right into Tyson, and maybe we'll get lucky," he said.

When McNeeley did exactly that, Tyson was indeed startled.

"You came right after me, White Boy," he smiled wryly when he spoke to McNeeley afterward. "You were trying to knock me out!"

In most newspapers the next day Vecchione was widely criticized for having abetted a scam: Not only had the paying customers been defrauded and a pay-per-view audience that had shelled out $49.95 a whack been ripped off, but McNeeley had collected almost $10,000 a second for his participation.

Personally, I thought Vinnie deserved to be named Manager of the Year. And at least one respected scribe, Bob Lipsyte of the *New York Times,* agreed.

"I would fight Tyson myself if Vecchione would manage me," wrote Lipsyte. "He did the right thing. If, as St. Cus D'Amato often said, the first obligation of a manager is to make sure his boy doesn't get hurt . . . That's the moral bottom line in boxing."

The Ring magazine did join the *Boston Herald* in making Vinnie the Manager of the Year for 1995. The BWAA gave the award to Roy Jones' management team of Fred and Stanley Levin. The Brothers Levin had also done a commendable job on behalf of their client that year, but you'd have to admit they had a bit more to work with.

Vinnie was a boxing guy through and through, a Runyonesque character who looked as if he'd modeled his image on that of Joe Palooka's manager, Knobby Walsh. It was as if he'd been born in that white cap he wore into the ring when he saved McNeeley, and for all I know he slept in it too; I don't think I ever saw him without it. The other constant was the stubby remains of a cigar he kept clenched between his teeth. You never saw him light up a new cigar, and I always wondered whether Vinnie had found a good deal somewhere on half-smoked stogies.

He didn't like to fly on airplanes because it always required some fairly complicated explanations when the metal detector went off. For most of his adult life he carried around a bullet slug in his shoulder, a souvenir of a shooting he described as "a case of mistaken identity."

Sports Illustrated described him as a "former mobster," and Vinnie never tried to discourage that notion. "I used to be in organized crime," he once told me, as if a guy could resign, or be expelled, from the Mafia. He never elaborated, but it was my impression that any criminal activities in his earlier incarnation weren't very organized at all and must have been at the club-fight level of the hoodlum world.

He learned the business side of boxing in the footsteps of the legendary promoter Subway Sam Silverman, and 40 years ago he was operating a gym in Brockton. One day a kid who'd never even put on a pair of gloves walked in. He sat around for three days and nobody said a word to him, so the kid finally got up and walked across the street to another gym, this one run by Goody and Pat Petronelli, who turned out to be more welcoming and took the kid on.

Not bothering to say hello to Marvin Hagler that day may have been one of the more costly miscalculations of Vecchione's life.

In those days the star of Vecchione's gym was a Massachusetts middleweight named Paul Poirier. Poirier was unbeaten, 18-0, when Vinnie signed him for a fight in Italy. The execution of the contract more or less coincided with Poirier's religious conversion; when he joined the Seventh-Day Adventists he took a vow not to fight again. Rather than welsh on the contract, Vinnie flew to Italy and, under Poirier's name, lasted three rounds before he was stopped by a guy named Enzo Cornetti. Years later Poirier decided to make a comeback, and it took him a dozen years to convince people he hadn't lost to Cornetti and to get that "L" expunged from his record. (Box.rec now lists two Paul Poiriers. The first was 31-3, and retired for good after his 1993 loss to Larry Holmes. The other Paul Poirier [0-1] was actually Vinnie.)

But he understood how the game was played, and when he spotted a raw amateur named Peter McNeeley, Vinnie could have been Michelangelo eyeing a slab of marble. It was a chance to create his masterpiece.

By then he had migrated to Cliff Phippen's South Shore Boxing Club in Whitman, Mass., not far from Medfield where McNeeley had grown up. The boxer's father, Tom, had played football at Michigan State before turning to a boxing career. The high point of McNeeley *père*'s career had come when he earned $40,000 in a title fight against Floyd Patterson. McNeeley knocked the champion down once. Patterson knocked Tommy down eleven times before Jersey Joe Walcott stopped the fight at 2:51 of the fourth.

The creation of McNeeley's resume was indeed a work of art. His first five opponents had never won a fight. In fact, up until the time he fought Tyson he fought 13 winless opponents, a couple of them twice. Eight of these were guys who never *did* beat anybody; they finished with an aggregate record of 0-49-1. Five others (including John Basil Jackson twice) wound up 11-179-4. He fought Jimmy (Lurch) Harrison three times in the space of six months in 1992. Lurch was 6-28-4 when this rivalry commenced, 6-31-4 when it ended, and 6-35-5 by the time the Commonwealth of Massachusetts took his boxing license away. The only mistake along the way came when Vinnie matched Peter against Stanley Wright, a 6'10" former basketball player, for the New England heavyweight title in Boston. McNeeley got cut and was bleeding so copiously that the referee stopped the fight.

Not long afterward Vinnie and Peter presented themselves at the offices of Don King and signed a promotional contract, and shortly after that miraculous things began to happen. McNeeley was still fighting bums, but every time he'd knock one of them out he'd move up another notch in the ratings.

This process took a few years, but Vinnie's timetable knew only one limit: the date of Tyson's release from the Indiana Youth Center, where he was serving out his rape sentence.

Vinnie was a promoter without peer. He never actually held a promoter's license, but he always knew somebody who did, and he staged shows at the Whitman Armory and Plymouth Memorial Hall and at the racetrack in Foxboro or the dog track in Revere, while he continued to chisel away on his work-in-progress. By then he had reached out for some help. Al Braverman seemed to have an endless supply of beatable victims, and Beau Williford, the Louisianan who aligned himself with Vecchione in the early 1990s, was on speaking terms with more bad heavyweights than any man in the country. When Beau wasn't bringing them up to New England to lose to McNeeley, he was bringing McNeeley to places like Louisville and Raleigh and Fort Smith to beat them.

Boxing audiences can be notoriously gullible, but sometimes Vinnie seemed to be underestimating even their collective intelligence. I'd look up the record of the latest bum he'd lined up for the Hurricane and ask him, "Vinnie, are you sure this guy even has a fucking *pulse?*"

"Shlih," he'd whisper, holding a finger to his lips, and slyly wink.

The relationship with King oven brought the promoter to New England for a nationally televised card. Julian Jackson-Augusto Cardamone and Orlin Norris-Adolpho Washington were the fights Showtime was willing to put on television. On the undercard, Francois Botha fought Brian Sargent, while Williford had disinterred Danny Wofford for McNeeley. The corpulent Wofford was 15-41-2 when he faced McNeeley at the Worcester Auditorium, and he didn't last a round. Beginning with the McNeeley fight, he would lose 61 of his last 63 fights.

The high point of the Worcester card occurred not in the ring but at the weigh-in the day before, when Botha made some disparaging remark about McNeeley, the Hurricane bitch-slapped the White Buffalo in front of a room full of people, and you were thinking, "Even if he *can't* fight, the kid's got some stones."

The Tyson fight let the rest of the world in on Vecchione's dirty little secret, which is that the WBC's third-ranked heavyweight could barely fight at all, but Vinnie even managed to turn *that* to his advantage, negotiating a lucrative deal for a nationally televised commercial in which McNeeley, by then a nationwide joke, got knocked out by a slice of pizza. McNeeley, alas, went quickly off the rails, plunging into a drug habit so severe that the Pizza Hut money followed the same trail as his end of the $850,000 Tyson purse, which is to say it went straight up his nose. There were periodic comeback attempts, whenever Vinnie could get McNeeley back into the gym for a few weeks, and there were also a few side trips to jail and to rehab. (In the most famous of these latter, somebody at Hazelden with a great sense of humor assigned the late Chris Farley to be McNeeley's roommate.) In 1999 the Hurricane was knocked out in back-to-back fights by Brian Nielsen and Butterbean Esch, heavyweights as useless as he was. Vinnie could only sigh.

A year after the Tyson fight Vinnie had another chance to cash in. Cliff Phippen's brother Danny had been built, on the McNeeley pattern, into an 18-0 junior middleweight. An undefeated fighter can be like a company ripe for a hostile takeover. In this case, Sugar Ray Leonard, who hadn't fought since losing to Terry Norris four years earlier, was plotting another comeback and looking for a tuneup against a soft touch with a deceptively good record. Danny Phippen seemed to fit that description, and in the summer of 1996 Leonard dispatched his matchmaker and boxing advisor, J.D. Brown, to Boston to have a look for himself. If the fight came off, Danny stood to make more for one fight against Leonard than he had in his other 18 put together, and Vinnie's end for brokering the deal would have been his biggest payday in the year since Tyson-McNeeley.

J.D. and I spent the early evening at my son's Little League game before driving down to the Whitman Armory for that night's card, where Phippen was fighting the main event. By the time we got there Vinnie and Cliff Phippen were a pair of nervous wrecks. Danny had gone AWOL and was nowhere to be found. His fight was eventually scrapped. He turned up, days later, in a local crack house and was packed off to rehab. He didn't fight for another year. J.D. Brown flew back to Washington, and Leonard decided to go straight to the Hector Camacho fight without a tuneup. Fighting on a bum leg, he was stopped in five.

"Christ," said Vinnie. "*Danny* coulda beat Leonard in that one."

Vinnie didn't completely lose interest in boxing after that, but the Leonard-Phippen flirtation was his last dalliance with the big time. He periodically rang up to excitedly tell me about his latest club show. Invariably they sounded as if they had been calculated to lose money.

When he heard I was ill, Vinnie was one of the first to ring up and called periodically to ask about my health. Every time he called he unfailingly asked about my son, whom he'd known since he was a small boy attending McNeeley fights in Foxboro and Whitman. Vinnie had a soft spot for kids, and that was in part because his own son, Vinnie Boy, was handicapped and had been institutionalized for virtually his entire life. It was an enormous emotional burden as well as a financial one for his father.

Our last conversation was a couple of months ago. After the usual pleasantries he cut straight to the chase. Judy, his lady of many years, was suffering from cancer. The medical bills were piling up and neither of them had insurance. He was looking to make some quick but substantial cash, and it had dawned on him: "Why don't I write a book?"

I carefully explained the realities of the publishing world, circa 2009, particularly when it came to boxing books, and provided a reasonably accurate representation of what he might realistically expect as an advance in the unlikely event he actually did manage to interest a publisher. Even in the best case it would have represented a small fraction of what he was hoping to get, and as far as I know that was the end of the book idea.

Even in his anguish I don't think it had ever occurred to him that Judy might outlive him, but this past Thursday he suffered a heart attack and now he's gone. Next Tuesday evening his friends will gather at a funeral home in Braintree to say good-bye, and I'll be there too. He was an original, a boxing character, but most of all, Vinnie was my friend.

TheSweetScience.com
2009

The Human Highlight Film

Arturo Gatti, 1972–2008

Brazil

JERSEY CITY, N.J.– There's something inevitably tragic when a man's life is snuffed out before he's spent half his allotted time on this earth, but Arturo Gatti's approach to life so mirrored his approach to the ring that you almost expected it would end badly. Gatti's legendary capacity for absorbing punishment might have made him a likely candidate for eventual evidence of brain damage somewhere, but there was always the sense that the chances of his actually reaching old age were somewhat remote. I don't think there's a man who knew him who actually expected that the Human Highlight Film would expire of natural causes in a nursing home forty years down the road.

The gathering at St. John the Baptist Church in Jersey City Thursday night was intended to have been a celebration of his life. Nearly three weeks had elapsed since his tragic death in a seacoast villa in South America. Since the Brazilian authorities did not release his body, it wasn't until ten days later that he was interred in Canada. Many of his colleagues, friends, and admirers from his adopted New Jersey had been unable to attend the service at L'Église de Notre-Dame-de-la-Défense (reports of the funeral may have been the first time in 37 years that "Arturo Gatti" and "defense" appeared in the same sentence) in Montreal, so the New Jersey memorial mass was scheduled for Thursday. No one had anticipated the bombshell news from Brazil that arrived scant hours before the service to cast an unsettling pall over the entire proceeding.

The boxing community had turned out in force. There were more than half a dozen former world champions (including Mark Breland, Bobby Czyz, Paulie Malignaggi, and Tracy Harris Patterson—from whom Gatti won his first title) as well as one reigning one (Tomasz Adamek). There were boxing officials (Larry Hazzard, under whose aegis Gatti had performed in his last nine fights—all at Atlantic City's Boardwalk Hall—as well as countless others be-fore, and Benjy Esteves, the referee for Gatti's bouts against Gabriel Ruelas, Joey Gamache, and Ivan Robinson), promoters and matchmakers (Kathy Duva, Lou DiBella, Carl Moretti, Dennis Dueltgen, and Cedric Kushner), and Gatti's devoted manager, Pat Lynch. There were former fighters (rang-ing from Chuck Wepner to Brian Adams), trainers (Ronnie Shields), televi-sion executives (Kery Davis and Mark Taffett), celebrities (Oscar nominee Mickey Rourke), and even a celebrity bodyguard (Chuck Zito), along with reporters, television talking heads and cameramen, and at least a hundred fans who'd probably never even met Gatti in the flesh but wanted to be there to say good-bye.

And—this would be the hard part to explain to people unfamiliar with box-ing who don't understand the bond that comes from the shared experience of combat—there was a trio of Gatti foes: Micky Ward, Ivan Robinson, and Joey Gamache.

Ward's and Gatti's names will be forever linked as a result of the three brutal wars in which they engaged between 2002 and 2003, but these two men who participated in 30 rounds' worth of what seemed a near-death experience for both became fast and lifelong friends. What had begun as mutual respect turned into a genuine friendship, one that traced its origins to the night they wound up sharing the same emergency room in a Connecticut hospital following their first fight. Micky and Arturo became golfing bud-dies and mutual confidants, and when Buddy McGirt walked away after the Carlos Baldomir fight, it was Ward who trained Gatti for his boxing swan song against Alfonso Gomez two years ago. Ward had already attended the funeral mass in Montreal, but he took the train down from Boston for this one, too.

And though they were subsequently somewhat eclipsed by the trilogy against Ward, Gatti's two 1998 fights with Robinson were cut from the same cloth. Robinson won a split decision in the first, and the encore would have been a majority draw had not Esteves deducted a point from Gatti for an eighth-round low blow. Robinson-Gatti II was not voted Fight of the Year only because that award was already taken by Robinson-Gatti I.

Gamache, a former two-time world champion, was knocked out in his final fight by Gatti under circumstances so unseemly that it remains the subject of a lawsuit nine years later. Following testimony undertaken less than two weeks ago, Gamache's suit against the New York State Athletic Commission was being deliberated by Court of Claims Judge Melvin Schweitzer the same day as the mass in Jersey City. In the view of most, Gatti (who was given a pass and never actually weighed in, but who outweighed Gamache by 15 pounds the following night) might be considered the villain of the episode, or at the very least an accomplice, but Joey has never looked at it that way and he was there to pay his respects along with everybody else.

No one had previously suspected Dueltgen of harboring a past as an altar boy, but the Main Events Chief of Boxing Operations appears to have coordinated the service as meticulously as he does fight cards. Serving as a veritable aide-de-camp to the presiding priest, Father Michael Santuro, Dennis provided the first scripture reading (from Deuteronomy) and introduced the first post-communion speaker—his boss, Kathy Duva.

What no one had expected when they planned this event was that it might be upstaged by a thunderbolt from Brazil.

The initial result of the police investigation there had resulted in the 20-day imprisonment of Amanda Rodrigues, a/k/a The Black Widow, who had been the only suspect in what the Porto de Galinhas constabulary had determined to have been a homicide. Upon arresting the most recent Mrs. Gatti, the police said that she had first attempted to kill the comatose Gatti by stabbing him in the back of the head with a knife (as we have noted previously, anyone who'd watched the way Arturo Gatti reacted to punches to the head could have told her that was a good way to ruin a knife) before strangling him with the strap of her handbag.

"[Amanda Rodrigues] could have tried to make it appear as if Gatti had committed suicide. The death may even have been premeditated. Rodrigues may have encouraged Gatti to drink excessively so she would be able to overpower him later. He was very drunk and that made it easier for her. He was sleeping when she did this. She waited for the moment when he was drunk enough for her to do it." (The above-quoted conclusions were not ours, but those of the Brazilian police.)

But then Thursday afternoon the *polícia* effected a 180-degree turnabout, announcing that Gatti's death had been the result not of a murder but of a suicide, and by the time the first candle had been lit at St. John the Baptist, Amanda Rodrigues had walked out of jail, a free woman with all charges dismissed.

The reversal was so abrupt and unforeseen, and the alternate theory advanced so preposterous, that most of Thursday's supplicants assumed it to have been the result of some well-placed bribery.

"It's just unbelievable," said a shocked Pat Lynch. "Are they trying to say he stabbed himself in the back of the head and then strangled himself with her purse strap? It's ridiculous."

The new theory doesn't account for the lengthy delay before the cops were summoned. The earlier police version assumed that it had taken a bit of extra time to rearrange the crime scene. Ms. Rodrigues had previously explained that she had slept until 9 a.m., and that only then had she discovered Gatti's body. Since the couple's ten-month-old son was sharing the bedroom with her, this would also make Arturo Jr. the world's best-behaved baby.

Suffice it to say that there wasn't a soul in the church Thursday who was buying it—and up in Montreal, where they have possession of Gatti's body, Arturo's brother Joe was already talking about an exhumation for an independent autopsy.

DiBella, whose address to the congregation followed Duva's, noted that Gatti had approached every facet of his existence with the same passion he brought to the boxing ring and echoed Duva's plea for justice.

"Arturo Gatti loved life," said DiBella. "Let me repeat that: *Arturo Gatti loved life!*"

It may have been the first time in the 125-year history of St. John the Baptist Church that a message from the pulpit produced a standing ovation.

TheSweetScience.com
2009

Pal Joey

Joseph G. Roach, 1962–2009

Nevada

"Listen, I got a story for ya!" Anthony (Rip) Valenti sounded excited, but that wasn't unusual.

Every time the octogenarian boxing promoter called to relay the details of his latest project there were two things I could count on him telling me. One was that this was the biggest story yet. The other was "ya gotta get this in the paper right away, 'cause I ain't giving it to nobody else—yet."

By the early summer of 1982 I'd been dealing with Rip for a while, so I knew enough to listen to what he had to say before I phoned the composing room with orders to stop the presses.

"Never happened before in the history of the Boston Garden," I could hear him saying on the other end. "All three of them!"

"All three of them?" I asked. "Don't tell me. You've got Magda, Eva, and Zsa Zsa coming to Boston?"

"Naw. The Roach kids," he said. "Freddie, Pepper, and Joey. They're all gonna be back here and fight on the same card."

As amateurs, the three brothers had achieved almost legendary status in New England boxing circles, winning everything from Silver Mittens to Golden Gloves titles. Even their mother had followed them into the family business. When her sons headed out West to turn pro, Barbara Roach underwent a seamless transition from AAU volunteer to professional judge. At a time when female judges were a rarity, she was already the best in Massachusetts—of either gender.

Freddie, the oldest, had just turned twenty-two. He had turned pro at eighteen, signed on with Eddie Futch, and moved to Phoenix, later relocating with the Hall of Fame trainer to Vegas. Rip had continued to nurture a relationship with Freddie. In January of '81 he brought him back to the Garden where—on the undercard of the first Hagler-Obelmejias fight—he beat Joe Phillips to win the New England featherweight title that had once belonged to Willie Pep. A month later Rip had flown Freddie and Futch back for a headline performance on an ESPN card he staged at the old Hotel Bradford Ballroom, the site of today's Roxy.

By early '82 Freddie's brothers had followed him to Las Vegas. Pepper had already had a couple of fights that spring. If memory serves, Rip had hoped to have twenty-year-old Joey turn pro on his Boston show in June, but Joey beat him to the punch and made his debut in Vegas a couple of weeks earlier, fighting a guy named Alex Silva to a draw at the Showboat.

Although they enjoyed something of a local following, Rip Valenti didn't think for a moment that the three Roach brothers were going to fill the Boston Garden. Back in those days big fights were routinely shown on closed-circuit television, and boxing venues like the old Causeway Street building were often augmented by live cards that might attract a few thousand extra customers.

Larry Holmes was defending his heavyweight title against Gerry Cooney at Caesars Palace that night. Joey, fighting a pro for just the second time, made short work of Joe Vanier, knocking him out in the first round. Pepper did his part, outpointing Jaime Rodriguez in the six-round co-feature. But in the main event, Freddie, who had come into the bout 26-1, had problems with Rafael Lopez, a decent prospect from Pawtucket, and wound up on the wrong end of a unanimous decision.

It was the first and last time all three Roaches fought together on the same bill, though they came close: On November 10, 1983, Marvelous Marvin Hagler won a come-from-behind decision over Roberto Duran at Caesars. Joey Roach fought a six-round draw with Manny Cedeno in one of the undercard bouts, while Freddie dropped a ten-round decision to his old nemesis Louie Burke in another. Pepper didn't fight that night because he had a scheduled bout at the Showboat a week later.

Pep had by some accounts been the more promising amateur, but by the time he turned pro he seemed to have lost interest. He retired after less than two years as a professional with a 7-2-1 record.

Joey, though, shared the same card with Freddie on several other occasions. The handwriting may have been on the wall in late 1985 when, at the Hollywood Palladium, he faced '84 gold medalist Paul Gonzales. Joey had lost just one of ten fights, while Gonzales was fighting for just the second time as a pro, but the Olympian won eight of eight rounds on all three cards.

The next year Joey got knocked out by a guy (Mauro Diaz) who was 1-7-1. He never boxed again, finishing up 8-3-3.

An ESPN fixture from the network's inception, Freddie was a popular draw, but as has been well documented since, he spurned Futch's advice and overstayed his welcome, continuing to fight until 1986. He finished with a record of 39-15, but the fights he engaged in over those last couple of years may well have sown the seeds of the Parkinson's disease he would encounter later in life.

The brothers remained close even after going their separate ways. As has been recounted in painful detail elsewhere, they had shared not only their boxing experiences but an abusive childhood at the hands of their father as well. Paul Roach might have been the driving force in turning his kids into successful boxers, but by most accounts he wasn't averse to using each of them as punching bags along the way.

One can only assume that there were some lively scraps around the Roach household while the three were sharing their boyhood home in Dedham, but they loved one another as only brothers can.

While Freddie and I saw each other regularly over the years, I occasionally ran into Joey and Pepper too. The first time I saw Joey after he'd stopped boxing he grinned and told me he was working as a telemarketer.

"Who'd buy anything from *you*? Over the *phone*?" I kidded him.

That's how much I knew.

Once he stopped boxing, Freddie worked as an assistant trainer under Futch, and then, after Eddie's automobile accident, took over as head trainer for a few of his boxers. Next thing you knew he was the head trainer for a couple of world champions and was regarded as one of the bright young minds in the business.

It was along about that time that Freddie told me Joey had so taken to the telemarketing business that he'd quit his job and started his own telemarketing company.

"I can't believe it," said Freddie. "He's making more money than I am."

Barbara Roach eventually moved to Las Vegas and into the house Freddie had built there. Once Freddie's base of operations became the Wild Card Gym in Hollywood (where he was eventually joined by Pepper), she remained in Vegas where Joey could look after her the way she'd always looked after him and his brothers.

Just as Freddie went on to become a superstar in his field, so did Joey in his. Freddie won three Trainer of the Year Awards (and already has a leg up on a fourth), but Joey was pulling down million-dollar purses even before Freddie was. He employed over a hundred workers at his telemarketing firm, and owned so many cars he could pick his ride of the day by color-coordinating it with his clothes. He had two college-age kids by his first marriage, and there was no way in hell either of them was ever going near a boxing ring.

A few weeks ago he told Freddie it was time to relax and enjoy life. He planned to sell his business and retire by the end of 2009.

Last week Joey and his wife, Jacqueline, returned from a family vacation in Michigan. On Saturday morning Jackie woke up, and when she looked at her husband in the bed beside her, the first thing she noticed was that he had turned a ghastly shade of blue. Joey Roach had, at the age of forty-seven, died in his sleep. Although the cause of death has yet to be determined pending an autopsy, a heart attack is suspected.

It was left to Barbara Roach to break the news to Freddie and Pepper. Freddie, who had been training Manny Pacquiao for his November 14 date with Miguel Cotto, immediately suspended camp.

"She's trying to be a trouper, and Freddie is trying to be strong," said a close family friend. "But you know how close they all were. You can imagine how hard this has hit them."

Arrangements have yet to be finalized pending the autopsy, and while there's no indication Joey had the slightest reason to suspect that his days might be numbered, he had recently addressed the subject in terms that some might find surprising.

"When my time comes," Joey had said, "I think I'd like to be buried back in Boston—next to my father."

TheSweetScience.com
2009

More Than a Contender

Budd Wilson Schulberg, 1914–2009

New York

It began with Archie McBride, the heavyweight contender Budd Schulberg managed almost 60 years ago, tolling the final 10-count, and ended with a solo from the great jazz trumpeter Jon Faddis while behind him on the stage, a slide show provided vignettes depicting Budd Schulberg's remarkable ninety-five-year life. Several hundred relatives, friends, and admirers gathered at the Society for Ethical Culture in New York on Saturday to say their final good-bye to the Boxing Hall of Famer, Academy Award–winning screenwriter, and acclaimed novelist, who had passed away on August 5.

Budd's son Benn served as the promoter and ring announcer for his father's final main event, while a succession of heavyweights from the worlds of boxing, literature, film, and drama—whose tributes were interspersed with television clips depicting seminal moments in Schulberg's career(s)—provided the undercard for the three-hour event.

Just as his first novel, *What Makes Sammy Run,* had rendered Budd *persona non grata* in Hollywood circles in 1941, the 1947 publication of *The Harder They Fall* guaranteed a frosty reception in certain ringside circles. It was along about this time that Schulberg, having already made the transition from lifelong fight fan to boxing writer, took on his first and only hands-on involvement in the sport he had recently scourged by agreeing to manage McBride, at the time an up-and-coming heavyweight from Trenton, whom at one point Budd got to 19-2 and a position in the heavyweight rankings.

Schulberg had had a ring erected in the barn of his country home in Pennsylvania which he converted into a training camp. What he had not foreseen was that the remote location would occasionally discourage the usual suspects from traveling from the busy gyms in Philadelphia and New York to box with McBride. One such occurrence came at a critical stage in

McBride's career—on the eve of Archie's 1955 fight against Floyd Patterson, and in the absence of other sparring partners, Budd had to put on the gloves himself. The sparring session ended predictably, with the fighter bloodying his manager's nose. A few nights later Patterson would bloody Archie's, knocking him down three times on the way to a seventh-round stoppage.

The TKO to McBride was a rare loss for Budd, who was 2-0 in bouts with Ernest Hemingway and Norman Mailer, but Benn Schulberg provided an account of another. From the time he was old enough to stand, the Schulbergs *père et fils* had engaged in family sparring sessions at their Long Island home, with Benn flailing away at his father, who was obliged not only to fight while on his knees but to simultaneously provide a blow-by-blow narration of the bout in progress. The tradition continued for several years, by which time Benn had not only somewhat improved his boxing technique but also advanced through several weight classes. One morning, Benn related, he cut loose with a left to the body followed by a right that knocked his surprised father, by then well into his seventies, ass over teakettle, producing divergent responses from his parents.

"Gee, Benn, I think you just broke my jaw," said his father.

"That's it. No more fighting!" ordered Betsy Schulberg, whose word was law.

On the Waterfront, for which Budd received the Academy Award, might not have been in the strictest sense a "boxing movie," but Marlon Brando's character, Terry Malloy, is the ex-pug who "coulda been a contender," and at Budd's insistence, a trio of charter members of the Bum-of-the-Month-Club—Two-Ton Tony Galento, Tami Mauriello, and Abe Simon—were cast as burly longshoremen in the film. One highlight of the program was the telecast of the 1954 Oscar ceremony, when, after director Elia Kazan and Brando had already won their statuettes, Bob Hope and Brando opened the Best Screenplay envelope and summoned Budd from the audience to receive his. (And let history record that he didn't even try to look surprised. He knew what he'd done.)

Pete Hamill recalled having first met Budd at the 1962 Sonny Liston-Floyd Patterson fight in Chicago, an occasion far more memorable for the press room cast publicist Harold Conrad had assembled than for the barely two minutes of action in the ring. "You'd look in one direction and there would be Norman Mailer and A.J. Liebling," recalled Hamill, then just in his second year as a newspaperman, "and you'd look the other way and there would be Nelson Algren and James Baldwin and Budd Schulberg."

(Liebling, recounting the same scene in the *New Yorker,* wrote that "the press gatherings before this fight sometimes resembled those highly intellectual *pourparlers* on some Mediterranean island; placed before typewriters, the accumulated novelists could have produced a copy of the *Paris Review* in forty-two minutes.")

Hamill also recalled that on the evening of June 6, 1968, he and his brother Brian had driven across Los Angeles to pick up Budd in their rental car, and driven from there to the Ambassador Hotel, where Robert F. Kennedy would be speaking once the returns were in from that day's California primary. Budd, said Hamill, remembered the hotel from his youth as the scene of some memorable Hollywood debauchery. Both Hamill and Schulberg were waiting in the kitchen that night when Sirhan Sirhan shot Kennedy. Hours later, once the East Coast deadlines had passed, everyone reconnoitered, still battered by the shocking assassination. Everyone was grieving, but Schulberg made it his particular point that night to console Hamill, whom he knew had lost a close personal friend.

The poet (and Miles Davis biographer) Quincy Troupe, as it turned out, had another memory of Budd's and RFK's final days. Two days before the candidate was killed, Budd had brought the candidate by 9807 B Street to visit Watts 13, a byproduct of the Watts Writers Workshop Budd had founded in response to the 1965 Watts riots. The premises consisted of a modest inner-city house, fronted by what Troupe, perhaps the most prominent product of Schulberg's Watts initiative, described as "a really tiny lawn." The poet Jimmie Sherman, another workshop member, had made the cultivation of the lawn his personal project.

"It was his pride and joy," said Troupe. On the day of the visit Schulberg and Senator Kennedy stepped out of a large black sedan. Budd, aware of Jimmie Sherman's vested interest was careful to go around by the walkway. RFK decided to short-cut across the lawn.

"What the hell do you think you're doing?" thundered Jimmie Sherman. *"Get off the goddamn grass!"*

The presidential candidate, remembers Troupe, "jumped. But when he came inside he talked with all of us, and more important, he seemed to listen."

Budd's own memory of RFK's visit to Watts was that later that day, in his suite at the Ambassador, the doomed candidate had talked of initiating a federally sponsored program based on Schulberg's concept.

Gene Kilroy, Muhammad Ali's old camp facilitator, noted that although Howard Cosell and others climbed on the bandwagon later, Budd Schulberg had been Ali's first and most prominent defender, railing against the injustice when the champion was stripped of his title and his boxing license for his stance against the Vietnam War. And Bert Sugar recalled attending a fight at Foxwoods a few years ago, when Budd arrived to discover that there were no remaining seats in the press section. There were, however, a dozen empty seats in an immediately adjacent ringside area. Upon inquiry, a spokesman for the Mashantucket Pequod tribal nation explained that the seats had been reserved for "The Elders."

"Elder? Show me somebody who's more elder than Budd," replied Sugar, and the ninety-two-year-old Elder got his seat.

There was also a film clip of Budd's appearance on *Person to Person* with Edward R. Murrow. Watching Murrow conduct the entire interview while puffing on his trademark smoke, I found myself thinking that modern-day New York laws probably would have ordered Murrow's cigarette to be airbrushed out of the picture.

My turn to speak immediately followed the Murrow interview. "Does Bloomberg know about this?" I asked.

Budd, who had stayed busy right up to the end, was involved in recent years in a couple of intriguing projects that never quite got off the ground: Spiko Lee's documentary on Joe Louis and Max Schmeling, based on a screenplay Budd had written, and a film version of *What Makes Sammy Run,* which Ben Stiller had optioned more than a dozen years ago. Both Lee and Stiller recalled that, although no one was more aware of the purgatory in which Hollywood scripts can reside for years than Budd, he still made regular phone calls asking about the status of the films. And both seemed equally contrite that the projects didn't come to fruition in Budd's lifetime.

When they showed up for their first story conference in Hollywood, Stiller recalled, the retyped script circulating around the table had somehow omitted the title page notation "based on the novel by Budd Schulberg," which didn't exactly get the relationship off to a flying start.

"Ben Stiller, fresh off *The Cable Guy.* Jerry Stahl, fresh off a park bench in MacArthur Park," Stahl, Stiller's writing partner on the *Sammy* project, recreated the scene at Budd's memorial. "In retrospect, I can imagine how thrilled Budd Schulberg, the man who wrote *On the Waterfront,* must have been to have a couple of giants adapting the greatest work of his lifetime."

"But still, we stayed in touch, years after there was any real talk of mounting the movie," said Stiller. "Whenever I'd re-connect with Budd, he'd look at me with those alarmingly blue eyes. 'Well . . . ?'

"And I'd just sigh and say 'Not yet, Budd, not yet.' I had to get over the feeling that every time we saw each other we were both reminding ourselves of the unfinished business between us, and the frustration we both felt. I don't know if I ever did.

"I gave him an award a couple of years back at a film festival in Culver City," added Stiller. "I dropped it off the podium, of course, and Budd just laughed. At some point he really could have just said, *'Enough of you, Stiller, and your pseudo Sammy crusade. You had my baby, and you didn't get it done!!'* It would have been easy, even expected. But he didn't. Never. He always asked how my dad was, or how the project I was working on was going."

Spike Lee, who expressed remorse over having to repeatedly offer similar responses when Budd asked about their project, recalled that it was only after committing himself to the Louis-Schmeling film that he fully realized that he'd be working with a living piece of both boxing and Hollywood history.

"Budd *knew* Joe Louis. He *knew* Max Schmeling," said the filmmaker. "That was impressive, but then when I found out he'd personally arrested Leni Riefenstahl, *wow!*"

(The apprehension of Hitler's favorite filmmaker came in connection with Schulberg's naval service in World War II and its aftermath, when he was charged with compiling the photographic evidence presented at the Nuremberg Trials.)

Steven Berkoff, the British director of the stage version of *On the Waterfront* that played to rave reviews in London's West End earlier this year, announced his pride at having "directed the first production of *On the Waterfront* performed in English." When that one sailed right over the heads of pretty much the entire audience, Berkoff (who also played Johnny Friendly in the London production) had to lapse into Hobokenese to explain the joke.

There were messages from Hugh McIlvanney, the Boxing Bard of Scotland, from Andy Griffith (whose first starring role had come when he played Lonesome Rhodes in Budd's *A Face in the Crowd*), and from Christopher Plummer, whose film debut had come when he was cast in Budd's *Wind across the Everglades*. (Plummer recalled his astonishment at Budd's capacity for alcohol, and his own performance by saying, "Burl Ives was great; I was terrible.")

Nephew K.C. Schulberg recalled last February's trip with Budd and Betsy from London to Paris—the morning after opening night for the London *Waterfront* play, which had been followed by an all-night piss-up with Berkoff and the cast. And Budd's niece, Chris O'Sullivan, read a heartfelt message from Budd's younger sister Sonya at the New York memorial.

Dr. Nicholas Beck, who authored a 2001 biography of Schulberg, recalled that in its first incarnation when it was written as a short story for *Liberty* magazine, *What Makes Sammy Run* had been entitled *What Makes Manny Run*. It was changed at the suggestion of Budd's father B.P. Schulberg, who feared that Emanuel "Manny" Cohen, the man who had replaced him when he was dumped as head of Paramount Studios, might interpret it as "an act of petty revenge."

So Manny became Sammy, but the name change backfired in the end anyway. By the time *Sammy* came out as a book, Budd was working as an in-house screenwriter for Samuel Goldwyn. An underling, pointing out that Sammy Glick's initials were also SG, convinced Goldwyn that Sammy had been based on him, and Budd was fired and ordered off the MGM lot before he even knew of the accusation.

Ivan R. Dee, the Chicago publisher who in recent years reissued *The Harder They Fall* and published two collections of Schulberg's boxing pieces, said that to appreciate how good a writer he was one had only to compare his work with that of the other, "supposedly respected" boxing writers, whose work he described, I believe, as uniformly vapid. Dee presumably thought he was doing a service to Budd's memory, but it wasn't a very smart thing to say in a room full of boxing writers.

In the late 1960s the Broadway composer Frank Loesser had written the score for a Broadway adaptation *(Señor Discretion Himself)* of a short story by Budd, but Loesser *(Guys and Dolls; How to Succeed in Business Without Really Trying; The Most Happy Fella)* died in 1969 before it could be finished. Jo Sullivan and Emily Loesser, the composer's widow and his daughter, performed a moving duet of the play's show-stopper, "You Understand Me."

Señor Discretion Himself was revived five years ago at the Arena Stage in Washington, under the direction of Charles Randolph Wright, who suggested engaging the Los Angeles–based Chicano ensemble Culture Clash to complete Loesser's unfinished book and libretto. Culture Clash co-founder Richard Montoya came East to confer on the project and met with Wright and Schulberg at one of those swank restaurants in the Hamptons. The trio was standing near the front door when one of those celebrity wannabes who flock to the Hamptons each summer pulled up to the front door in his Mercedes. Assuming that the Mexican American standing beside the African

American must be a valet parking attendant, he wordlessly tossed his car keys to Montoya and rushed inside.

Wright said that Budd, having watched this exercise in profiling unfold before his eyes, turned to Montoya with what sounded more like an order than a suggestion.

"He looked at Richie and said, 'Keep them!'"

TheSweetScience.com

2009

The Man in the Middle
Kept a Low Profile

Arthur Mercante, 1920–2010

New York

Arthur Mercante had been a professional referee for only half-a-dozen years when he was appointed to work his first world title fight—the 1960 rematch between Ingemar Johansson and Floyd Patterson, whom the Swede had dethroned a year earlier to become heavyweight champion of the world.

The return bout, contested before 32,000 at the old Polo Grounds in upper Manhattan, had been largely unremarkable before the fifth round, when Patterson unloaded a massive left hook that had separated Johansson from his senses even before he crashed to the canvas. The Swede's left leg briefly twitched, and then he became quite still.

Patterson had become the first heavyweight champion to regain his title, but at that moment the concern was for Johansson. As Mercante recalled in his 2006 memoir *Inside the Ropes:*

> I looked on helplessly, dreadfully worried about Johansson's condition and thinking how ironic it would be if I finally got my turn in the national spotlight only to have a guy get killed on my watch. Suddenly, as only he could do, broadcaster Howard Cosell insinuated himself in the middle of the maelstrom.

"Is he dead? Is he dead, Whitey?" Cosell hollered at Whitey Bimstein.

Bimstein, the Runyonesque New York cornerman A.J. Liebling lauded as one of his "explainers," had been brought in to supplant Johansson's Swedish trainer, Nils Blomberg. From the ring he turned and bellowed back to Cosell: "No, but he oughta be. I *told* him to watch out for the left hook."

That Mercante, who died at ninety last Saturday, was fond of recounting that story, in which he was neither the author nor the target of the punch-line, typified as well his presence in the ring, in which he understood that the work of the best referee is seldom seen, heard, or remembered.

"Know when to stop the fight, stay out of the picture, but be there when you have to be there," he explained.

His obituary in Sunday's *New York Times* described him as "boxing's most prominent referee of the past half-century." His most high-profile assignment came in 1971, when he was the third man in the ring for the Fight of the Century—the epic first bout inaugurating the Muhammad Ali-Joe Frazier trilogy. Frazier won that one, but two years later in Kingston, Jamaica, George Foreman pounded him to the canvas six times in less than six minutes. Cosell's animated refrain from that night—*"Down goes Frazier! Down goes Frazier!"*—is embedded in the memory of even the most casual fan. Hardly anyone remembers that Mercante was the referee.

He had been a successful amateur boxer in his youth, and during his World War II Navy hitch served as a boxing instructor and referee as part of a physical fitness program established and supervised by former heavyweight champion Gene Tunney. He was active in amateur boxing until 1954, when he received his first professional license.

In all, he worked 147 world title bouts, including Marvelous Marvin Hagler's second fight with Mustafa Hamsho in 1984 (which shared the Madison Square Garden bill with Mike McCallum-Seán Mannion), and Steve Collins' 1992 majority decision loss to Reggie Johnson at the Meadowlands in New Jersey.

The result of that bout hinged on a single point deducted by Mercante after the Irishman attempted to retaliate against Johnson's repeated use of elbows and forearms by clumsily throwing one of his own.

Collins, to his credit, didn't blame Mercante for taking the critical point for the foul.

"[Johnson] has obviously had a lot more practice at it than I have," he wryly noted.

Although he is remembered as a lifelong New Yorker, Mercante was actually born in Brockton, Mass.—the same city fellow Hall of Fame members Hagler and Rocky Marciano called home. I hadn't been aware of this connection until Mercante apprised me over breakfast a few days before the Hagler-Hamsho fight. (Suffice it to say, Hamsho's handler, Al Braverman, didn't know about it either; he'd have raised holy hell if he had.)

Although Mercante's courtly, dignified manner and elegant speech suggested a privileged upbringing, his father, like Marciano's, had been a Brockton shoe-factory worker. Arthur, who held bachelor's and master's degrees from New York University, had been the first college graduate in his family.

In conversation he sounded more like a tenured professor than an authority in the school of broken noses.

He was also a physical fitness buff. At Tuesday night's wake on Long Island, Benn Schulberg recalled that when his father, Budd, introduced him to Mercante, the referee offered up his abdomen and invited him to throw his best punch.

"I was ten years old then, and every time I saw him after that he did the same thing," recalled Schulberg *fils*. "The last time he challenged me to hit him in the stomach, I was twenty-five—and he was eighty-five!"

Mercante, who had been in ill health for the past few years, expired peacefully on Saturday.

That night, just before the Andre Berto-Carlos Quintana welterweight title fight at the Bank Atlantic Center outside Fort Lauderdale, ring announcer Michael Buffer revealed his death on HBO's national telecast, and called for a moment of silence while the ring bell tolled a final 10-count.

He was buried yesterday following mass at St. Joseph's Church in Garden City.

Perhaps as a result of his devotion to fitness, Mercante remained active as a referee into the present millennium; he oversaw several world title fights after his eightieth birthday, and was still working as a ringside judge at eighty-five.

By that time he had been followed into the family business by his son Arthur Jr., who took charge of the 1999 Lennox Lewis-Evander Holyfield fight at the Garden.

A few years ago, the younger Mercante recalled, he was appointed to referee a fight at one of the Connecticut tribal casinos, and his father tagged along for company. They shared a room that night, and around dawn Arthur Jr. was awakened by what sounded like an ominous thump from across the room.

"I was afraid my dad had fallen out of bed, so, expecting the worst, I switched on the light to check on him," he said.

What he discovered instead was eighty-seven-year-old Arthur Mercante doing his morning push-ups on the floor of the hotel room.

TheSweetScience.com
2010

Chapter VI—The Last Great Heavyweight Rivalry

Ali, Frazier, Foreman, and Norton

In February of 2010 I was invited to participate, along with George Foreman and Dr. Robert Rodriguez, in a Boxing Symposium at the University of Kansas. Entitled The Last Great Heavyweight Rivalry, my presentation at the KU event anecdotally compared the 1970s heavyweight nexus of Muhammad Ali, Joe Frazier, George Foreman, and Ken Norton with that of the middleweight rivalry celebrated in my earlier book **Four Kings: Leonard, Hagler, Hearns, Duran and the Last Great Era of Boxing**. *That lecture, in turn, was expanded and serialized on TheSweetScience.com, forming the basis for this chapter.*

Four Kings recounted the historic rivalry between Sugar Ray Leonard, Marvelous Marvin Hagler, Thomas Hearns, and Roberto Duran. Between 1080 and 1989, those four men engaged in nine fights between them. Each of them beat at least one of the others, and each of them lost to at least one of the others.

While the era of the Four Kings was a watershed moment in boxing history, it was not entirely unique. A remarkable parallel existed between four great heavyweights just ten years earlier. Like my middleweight Four Kings, each member of this quartet—Muhammad Ali, Joe Frazier, George Foreman, and Ken Norton—beat at least one of the others and lost to at least one of the others. These heavyweights engaged in ten fights against one another, and during an even briefer—six years in all—time frame than my middleweights of a decade later.

Yes, I described that of the Four Kings as "the last great era of boxing." But I never claimed it was the *only* one.

The principal difference between them was that while Leonard-Hagler-Hearns-Duran was a proper round-robin, Joe Frazier and Ken Norton never fought each other. The principal reason for this was that both men were trained by the late Eddie Futch, a highly principled man who would have been extremely reluctant to match them against each other. (When Larry Holmes and Michael Spinks fought for the first time in 1985, Futch elected to watch from the sidelines rather than take sides. Spinks understood this decision, but Holmes was critical. When the two met in a rematch the next year, Eddie was in Spinks' winning corner.)

Futch, in fact, played an important role in these proceedings—that of the demystifier of Muhammad Ali. As my old friend pointed out to me on a number of occasions, "In his whole career Ali only lost to five guys—and I had three of 'em."

The basis for this great heavyweight rivalry would have been apparent to no one in 1964 when Cassius Clay, as he had predicted that he would, "shook up the world" by upsetting the fearsome Charles (Sonny) Liston. When Liston failed to answer the bell for the seventh round in Miami Beach, Clay, who had gone into the fight a 7-1 underdog, assumed a place in boxing history as the legitimate heir to Jack Johnson, Jack Dempsey, Joe Louis, and Rocky Marciano.

On the night of February 25, 1964, Joseph William Frazier was an amateur heavyweight who still answered to the name "Billy." Billy Frazier had just celebrated his twentieth birthday and was still hoping to land a berth on the Olympic team the United States would send to Tokyo. Down in Houston, a juvenile delinquent named George Foreman had just turned fifteen and appeared destined for a life of crime. Ken Norton was a twenty-year-old Marine Corps Lance Corporal, stationed at Camp Pendleton, California.

In the first list of worldwide rankings to emerge after Clay's defeat of Liston, the world's Top Ten heavyweight contenders were, in order, (1) Liston, (2) Floyd Patterson, (3) Ernie Terrell, (4) Cleveland Williams, (5) George Chuvalo, (6) Zora Folley, (7) Karl Mildenberger, (8) Roger Rischer, (9) Eddie Machen, and (10) Doug Jones.

At the time he won the title, Clay had faced only one of these. A year earlier, in 1963, he had won a disputed decision over Jones at Madison Square Garden. But beginning with his 1965 rematch against Liston, over the next three years the new champion took on numbers one through seven on the aforementioned list of contenders and defeated them all, five inside the distance. Only Chuvalo and Terrell survived to hear the final bell.

(The two he *didn't* fight? Rischer, ranked eighth in 1964, quickly took himself off the list when he suffered back-to-back losses to Thad Spencer and Brian London the next year. The thirty-year-old Machen's fall was even more dramatic. Of the five fights in which he engaged beginning in July of

1964, he lost four, drew the other, and had ceased to be a contender in anyone's mind.)

Cassius Marcellus Clay Jr. had seemed a breath of fresh air. Handsome, engaging, and youthfully exuberant, the youngster from Louisville, Ky., had returned from the 1960 Rome Olympics with the light-heavyweight gold medal, and was soon making the rounds of the popular television talk shows of the day.

A consortium of well-heeled Louisville businessmen had banded together to underwrite Clay's professional career. They in turn made the decision to pack him off to Miami Beach, where the respected trainer Angelo Dundee had set up shop in a gym owned in conjunction with his older brother, pro-moter Chris Dundee.

Although his status today is that of an iconic and almost mythical American hero, it should be noted that Clay was not universally beloved—and that in short order he would come to be roundly despised by many of his country-men. Although his professional trajectory was impressive from the outset, Clay had already begun to dissipate some of the residual goodwill from the Olympics with his penchant for self-promotion. Not long after turning professional, Clay found himself intrigued by the public image the wrestler Gorgeous George had constructed for himself, and made a conscious de-cision to adopt a similar public personality.

Increasingly wont to describing himself as "the greatest," Clay took to taunting prospective opponents, jibes which were often expressed in rudi-mentary poetry. He sported brightly colored satin robes and trunks, wore tasseled shoes, and in the ring often seemed more flash than dash.

Although the term "trash-talking" had yet to gain currency, Clay was an early proponent and, eventually, master of that medium, and in an age in which boxers were expected to respect their opponents, his boastful style did not sit well with many American sporting fans—particularly those of the Caucasian persuasion, many of whom had come to regard his posture as that of the prototypical "uppity nigger."

By the time Clay was scheduled to meet Liston in Miami Beach, for ev-ery white American who found his antics refreshing there were three more openly rooting for Liston to put him in his place. And in the days immediately preceding the fight, another factor emerged that would profoundly influence the way he was perceived. Reports that he had increasingly become involved with the Nation of Islam and its mysterious leader, Elijah Muhammad, seemed to have been confirmed when he was spotted in the company of the man then considered to be Elijah's consigliere, Malcolm X.

Although Dundee and publicist Harold Conrad worked out a behind-the-scenes deal and persuaded Malcolm to get out of town until the night of the fight, the rumors continued to swirl. The morning after he defeated Liston, Clay confirmed his Muslim affiliation and announced that he was renouncing what he described as his "slave name."

Henceforth he would be known as . . .

Cassius X.

(The name Muhammad Ali would come later and was personally conferred on him by Elijah Muhammad.)

Usually described by the mainstream media as "the Black Muslims," the Nation and its separatist policies were considered a major threat to the integrationist goals of the fledgling Civil Rights movement. Both white liberals and black progressives distanced themselves from Clay/Ali as a result.

An ironic development was the Elijah-Malcolm schism that developed shortly after the first Liston fight. Malcolm X came to embrace a more traditionally orthodox interpretation of Islam, rejecting some of the more bizarre accoutrements of Elijah's personally contrived theology. Although Malcolm's universalist view was very much in keeping with the Sunni/Sufi teachings Ali would himself eventually practice, at the time his allegiance remained with Elijah Muhammad, and following Malcolm's assassination there were genuine fears that Ali would be a target of retribution by Malcolm's followers.

Ali had already earned the enmity of tradition-minded fans and disaffected liberals alike, but in short order he would become the most despised sporting figure in America when he came down on what was at the time considered the "wrong" side of the most polarizing issue of the day—the Vietnam War.

When he was reclassified 1-A in early 1966, making him eligible for the draft, Ali almost immediately signaled his unwillingness to participate as a matter of conscience. "I ain't got nothing against them Viet Congs," he famously said, and on another occasion he pointed out that "no Viet Cong ever called me 'nigger.'"

On April 28, 1967, Ali reported to the induction center in Houston, but declined three commands to take the ceremonial step forward that would have confirmed his willingness to be drafted. Within a matter of hours his boxing license had been revoked by the New York State Athletic Commission, and other governing bodies rapidly followed suit. Even though he would not stand trial on the draft evasion charge until June, by nightfall most jurisdictions had already withdrawn recognition of his heavyweight championship.

Even while preparing himself for a prison stretch he considered a virtual certainty (his five-year sentence was stayed pending the resolution of his appeal), Ali had staged a scorched-earth campaign through the heavyweight division in which he had eliminated virtually every credible challenger, and by any reasonable definition would have been approaching the prime of his career.

Even though his great rivalries were yet to come, Muhammad Ali's career never *had* a "prime." He had just turned twenty-five when he was prevented from earning a living for more than three and a half years.

As much as this injustice might be deplored today, Ali's banishment was widely applauded at the time. Most of mainstream America, in fact, wondered how he could be speaking on college campuses and walking alongside Martin Luther King in antiwar marches instead of being where he belonged—behind bars.

Many sportswriters shared that view, although a number of writers and intellectuals did support Ali's position—on the due process issue, if not on the war itself. More typical was the reaction of Ali's predecessor Floyd Patterson, who in an *Esquire* story ghostwritten by Gay Talese and amusingly entitled "In Defense of Cassius Clay," claimed that "right now the only people in America who are not booing him are the Black Muslims," and offered as his solution: "I do not see how Clay can get himself out of the mess he got himself into unless he quits the Muslims."

In expressing the latter viewpoint Patterson and Talese were guilty of trivializing Ali's religious commitment. In the other, they had essentially dismissed the swelling tide that would shortly sweep its way across America—the antiwar movement, to which the bravery of Muhammad Ali's stance had made him nothing less than a hero.

It would be October of 1970 before Ali boxed again. Georgia was not regulated by an officially recognized boxing commission, and supporters were able to cut through the red tape and clear the way for him to fight Jerry Quarry in Atlanta. (The fight lasted less than three rounds and ended with Quarry, not for the first time, cut to ribbons.)

Later that same month, the New York State Supreme Court ruled that Ali had been unfairly deprived of his boxing license, clearing the way for a return to Madison Square Garden, where, in December, he knocked down Oscar Bonavena (who had given Joe Frazier his two toughest fights) three times in the 15th round for a TKO win. This in turn set the stage for what was widely described as the Fight of the Century between Ali and Frazier at the Mecca of Boxing the following March. (The forestalled threat of a prison sentence would linger until June 28, 1971, when the United States Supreme Court, by an 8-0 unanimous decision, overturned his conviction on the draft evasion charge.)

Frazier was the son of a South Carolina sharecropper who had moved north to Philadelphia. There, he had worked in a slaughterhouse, where he originated a technique—pounding away at frozen slabs of beef—that would later be given widespread currency by another Philadelphia heavyweight named Rocky Balboa.

Frazier had retained his amateur status through the 1964 Tokyo Games, in which he hoped to represent the United States. His dream appeared to have been dashed when he lost in the Olympic Trials to Buster Mathis. When Mathis broke a hand in training, he was replaced by the first alternate, Frazier, who then proceeded to win all of his bouts and return with the gold medal.

Frazier had not yet made his pro debut when he visited Ali at his New England training camp, where he was preparing for his rematch against Liston. There, the youngster asked the champion if he had any advice for him.

"Yeah," joked Ali. "Lose some weight and become a light-heavyweight."

Ali-Frazier matched two undefeated champions, each of whom could legitimately claim that designation. Ali referred to himself as "the people's champion," and pointed out, correctly, that he had never lost his title in the ring. On the other hand, he had officially "resigned" his title to confer legitimacy on the winner of the 8-man tournament the WBA conducted to determine his successor—who turned out to be his boyhood friend and sometime sparring partner, Jimmy Ellis.

Frazier, on the recommendation of Eddie Futch, had declined to participate in the WBA exercise. Instead, in March of 1968 he was matched against his old amateur foe Mathis at Madison Square Garden for what was recognized as the "world" heavyweight championship by the New York commission, along with the governing bodies of four other states—Massachusetts, Pennsylvania, Maine, and Illinois. He defended this limited version of the title on four occasions before being matched against Ellis for what was billed as the "undisputed" championship—although it was surely disputed by those who maintained that Ali had never lost his championship in the ring. In New York in March of 1970, Frazier won the WBA belt from Ellis on a fifth-round TKO, and then in November, a month before Ali fought Bonavena, knocked out light-heavyweight champion Bob Foster in Detroit.

The win brought Frazier's record to 26-0 on the night of their epic encounter. Ali was 31-0, but he was fighting for just the third time in four years.

As much event as boxing match, Frazier-Ali I was unlike any heavyweight championship fight before or since. A Hollywood producer named Jerry Perenchio, having ponied up $5 million in guarantees to bypass boxing's traditional power structure, was the promoter of record, and it shortly became apparent that Frazier-Ali would be catered to by Perenchio's constituency, an audience in which A-list celebrities outnumbered hard-core boxing fans. It was a night, said Bobby Goodman, for "plumage, pimps, and hustlers."

The nation's two top blow-by-blow announcers, Don Dunphy and Howard Cosell, had so desperately coveted the assignment behind the microphone that night that either would have gladly done it for free. Each monitored the other in the run-up to the fight, fearful that his rival might outmaneuver him to gain Perenchio's ear. One day Dunphy's son, an ABC assistant director, phoned his father to report a stunning piece of news.

"I'm not going to do the Ali-Frazier fight, and neither is your father," Cosell had told Don Jr. "They're going to use Andy Williams, Kirk Douglas, and Burt Lancaster."

That had in fact been Perenchio's plan, but, happily, cooler heads eventually prevailed, and by fight night only the Birdman of Alcatraz remained on the broadcast team. Dunphy was the lead announcer, with Archie Moore joining him and Lancaster at ringside.

As he looked down from Frazier's corner that night, Eddie Futch recalled "a sea of glitter." As he climbed the steps to Ali's corner across the ring, Angelo Dundee heard someone call his name. He turned in response, just in time to have his picture snapped by *Life* magazine's photographer at ringside—a fellow named Sinatra.

Bill Nack recalled the occasion in *Sports Illustrated* a quarter-century later:

> There had never been a night like this one in New York City. By 10:30 p.m. on the evening of March 8, 1971, when the two fighters climbed into the ring at Madison Square Garden, Ali in red trunks and Frazier in green-and-gold brocade, there was a feral scent and crackle to the place. The Garden was a giant bell jar into which more than 20,000 people had drifted, having passed through police barricades that rimmed the surrounding streets. They came in orange and mint-green and purple velvet hot pants, in black

leather knickers and mink and leopard capes, in cartridge belts and feathered chapeaux and pearl-gray fedoras. Some sported hats with nine-inch brims and leaned jauntily on diamond-studded walking sticks. Manhattan listed toward Babylon.

Although Ali was able to battle on fairly even terms over the first ten rounds, it was clear for most of the night that three rounds with Quarry and fifteen with Bonavena had not been enough to clear the accumulated ring rust from his protracted, though involuntary, layoff. When Frazier began to pour it on over the final few stanzas, Ali needed one of his old miracles to turn the tide, but his reflexes, the timing, and ultimately the stamina that had characterized his first career were absent on this night.

Only the ring ropes had kept Ali on his feet when he was crushed by a Frazier left late in the eleventh, and Ali's jaw had swollen to grotesque proportions even before Frazier decked him with the left hook that put the fight out of reach.

When the scorecards were tallied, one judge, Bill Recht, had scored just four of the fifteen rounds for Ali. The other, Artie Aidala, had it 9-6 for Frazier, while referee Arthur Mercante had Frazier the winner, 8-6-1.

In handing Muhammad Ali his first professional defeat, Joe Frazier had drawn first blood in what would become a four-way rivalry for the ages. Ali, Frazier, George Foreman, and Ken Norton would engage in nine more of these encounters over the next five years, and Joe Frazier would be a participant in four more of them. He could not have known it at the time, but within the confines of this select company, Frazier would never win another.

As would become a regular occurrence over the course of their rivalry, both Ali and Frazier wound up in the hospital after the Fight of the Century. X-rays on Ali's jaw were negative, and by the next day he was entertaining reporters who visited his suite at the New Yorker hotel. Frazier's stay was even longer. The newly confirmed undisputed champion was passing blood for several days.

After taking four months off, Ali fought three more times in 1971, and six the following year. Frazier took longer to recuperate. He didn't lace on the gloves again in '71, and in '72 fought just twice. The opponents in both cases were plodding white journeymen, neither of whom lasted five rounds.

Frazier's first post-Ali defense, against Terry Daniels, took place at New Orleans' Rivergate Auditorium on January 15, 1972. Super Bowl VI (Dallas

24, Miami 3) would be played at Tulane Stadium less than 24 hours later, guaranteeing that a substantial ringside presence of national media in town for the game would witness New Orleans' first heavyweight championship fight since Corbett-Sullivan in 1892.

What they witnessed instead was a terrible mismatch. Before the first round was over a Frazier left hook had sent Daniels plowing, face-first into the canvas, and there would be three more knockdowns before the Louisiana referee, Herman Dutrieux, stopped it at 1:47 of the fourth. In the eyes of most, including, apparently, Joe Frazier, that was at least two knockdowns more than should have been necessary.

As the groggy Daniels tried to haul himself up from one of them, in fact, it appeared to me that Frazier had, if only for an instant, looked imploringly toward Dutrieux as if begging him to stop the fight, but when the referee ignored his apparent plea for mercy, Smokin' Joe recognized that the burden of ending the torture would fall solely on him and reluctantly returned to that task.

By the time Dutrieux finally did stop it, Daniels had been effectively destroyed as a fighter: His record was 28-4-1 when he met Frazier, 7-26 thereafter.

On my way out of the arena that night I found myself walking in near-lockstep with George Foreman, and mentioned what I thought I'd seen in Joe Frazier's eyes for that instant in the third round. Foreman stopped walking and arched his eyebrows as he looked at me in surprise.

"You saw that too?" he asked.

I was young and comparatively new to the boxing game at this level, so I didn't realize that I had just been a participant in what, in 1972, represented one of George Foreman's longer conversations.

A coda to the Frazier-Daniels fight, incidentally, is that its aftermath produced the first appearance of a characterization that would lead to a lifetime of bitterness in Joe's relationship with Muhammad Ali. And on this occasion it was Frazier himself who introduced the "G" word.

At the post-fight press conference Daniels, who had gone the distance with Floyd Patterson and beaten the highly regarded Manuel Ramos the previous year, recalled having thrown punches at Frazier that "would have kept a normal guy off me."

"What am I?" bristled Frazier. "A gorilla?"

"I would rather," replied Daniels, "have *fought* a gorilla."

• • •

The term "poster boy" has become hopelessly hackneyed today, but when he returned from the 1968 Mexico City Olympics, George Foreman literally became a poster boy—for the Job Corps. A Great Society program headed up by Kennedy in-law Sargent Shriver, the Job Corps' mission was to turn the nation's wayward youth into productive citizens.

Few youths in America had been more wayward than Foreman, a one-time street mugger from Houston's Fifth Ward, who now appeared to have been thoroughly rehabilitated by the experience. At the Mexico City Games, he had celebrated his Olympic title by prancing around the ring waving a miniature American flag—in stark contrast to the gloved-fisted Black Power salutes of Tommie Smith and John Carlos that endure as a symbol of that Olympiad.

In addition to re-channeling his baser instincts, Foreman had learned to box in the Job Corps, and his face stared back from Job Corps recruiting posters adorning every street corner in urban America. The message seemed to be that if George Foreman could be deterred from a life of crime, anybody could be.

The truth probably lay somewhere in between. Foreman might have been rootless, but his future in the field of petty crime wasn't particularly promising, either, simply because he wasn't very good at it. He and his friends stole things, but rarely at a profit, because they had no idea where to sell them; as a purse-snatcher he proved an even more abysmal failure. At no point had he been a candidate for the Juvenile Delinquents' Hall of Fame.

But at 6'4" and 220 pounds (then) he was bigger than any heavyweight champion since Primo Carnera, and he could punch like a mule. He had turned professional in 1969, and at the dawn of 1973 had knocked out all but three of his 37 victims to date.

Despite these prodigious accomplishments, the widespread feeling was that Foreman was still a year or two away from being ready for the likes of Joe Frazier. When the two were matched at the National Stadium in Kingston, Jamaica, on January 22, 1973, Foreman was a significant betting underdog.

Ironically, Frazier and Foreman shared another thing in common: the most difficult opponent for each had been an Argentine. Bonavena had floored Frazier twice in losing a controversial split decision in 1966, and extended him the 15-round distance in their 1968 rematch, while Gregorio Peralta, a middle-aged, undersized light-heavyweight, had twice gone ten rounds with Foreman.

The local on-site promoter was Lucian Chin, a Jamaican of Chinese extraction who owned a racecourse and was the island nation's most prominent legal bookmaker. A dapper *bon vivant,* Chin represented Jamaica in international bridge competitions, and later would stake out another field of expertise on the professional poker circuit.

The allure of two undefeated contestants, the appeal of a warm-weather escape in January, and the exotic mystique of Kingston at the dawn of the Bob Marley era combined to make Jamaica a site unlike any that had ever previously hosted a heavyweight title fight.

Although this was the second time the heavyweight championship had been contested in the Caribbean, it seems doubtful that members of the fight mob stepping off the boat for the 1915 Willard-Johnson bout in Havana were welcomed with the ceremonial, hand-rolled ganja cigars that were handed out in Kingston.

One visiting boxing dignitary answered a knock on his hotel room door and was presented with a medium-sized paper sack literally brimming with local loco weed. Upon sampling it, he was reduced to such a state of near catatonia that he swore off it for the rest of the week. On the night of the fight, he brought it along to the arena and gave it to a journalist friend, saying, "I can't handle this stuff. You can have it."

Now flash forward a few hours. In what was not only an upset but one of the most action-packed performances by a heavyweight challenger in at least half a century, Frazier was making like a yo-yo as Foreman knocked him down six times in less than six minutes, while Howard Cosell shouted *"Down goes Frazier! Down goes Frazier!"*

In the midst of this chaos the boxing dignitary stole a glance at the working press section across the ring, where several snoring sportswriters were using their typewriters as pillows. Three or four more were marginally conscious; wide-eyed and wearing silly grins, the words *"oh, wow, man"* and *"far out"* periodically escaped their lips.

So if you're wondering why so few great fight stories were filed from Kingston, there's your answer. Half the guys who covered the first Foreman-Frazier fight *still* don't remember it.

Foreman's emotions ran the gamut that night. After the first knockdown—and indeed, throughout the first round—he kept reminding himself that this was Joe Frazier, whose previous experiences with having been knocked down suggested that it only made him meaner.

By the third knockdown, which came just before the bell ended the first, Foreman's confidence had returned. Not only had putting Frazier on the floor not been a fluke, he could do it pretty much any time he wanted to. As a result, he spent most of the next 2 minutes and 28 seconds knocking Frazier down three more times and quizzically glaring at Arthur Mercante with the same expression he and I had seen on Frazier's face a year earlier in New Orleans.

"It was a pity they let it go on for so long," he would say later.

A viewing of the tape from that night reveals two shifts in allegiance in the brief time it took the fight to play out. Cosell spent the first minute of the telecast describing Frazier's vaunted left hook and what the champion was likely to do to Foreman as the evening wore on, but not only had he deftly switched to the Foreman bandwagon by the time of the first knockdown, in his post-fight interview with Foreman he did his best to make himself sound like the architect of the challenger's victory.

The other turncoat was even more brazen. An aspiring promoter and recently released ex-con named Don King had accompanied Frazier on his flight to Jamaica, attached himself to the champion in the days before the fight, and even walked him into the ring. Six minutes later King was a conspicuous figure as he jumped up and down, celebrating with Foreman in the new champion's corner, and departed the ring as a member of the Foreman entourage.

In a recent conversation with former Kronk assistant trainer Prentiss Byrd, I noted that for all their talents, it seemed unlikely that Sugar Ray Leonard, Marvelous Marvin Hagler, or Roberto Duran could have achieved the same heights in another sport as they did in boxing; in the case of Thomas Hearns it didn't seem a stretch at all. Hearns was such a gifted athlete that had he applied the same diligence to another sport as he did to boxing, it wasn't hard at all to imagine him playing professional baseball or basketball or even football.

With all due respect to Ali, Frazier, and Foreman, it's hard to envision any of them dunking on Kareem or hitting the curve ball with anything approaching the efficiency with which they hit opponents, but there was one such specimen within this heavyweight group.

As a schoolboy in Jacksonville, Ill., Ken Norton once entered eight events at a track meet. He won five of them and finished second in the other three—a feat which will most assuredly never be duplicated, at least in Illinois, because the state interscholastic governing body responded with what is still called "the Norton Rule," limiting competitors to four events in any one meet.

He was an all-star in basketball and a football player of such accomplishment that as a high school senior he was recruited by 85 colleges—including the University of Kansas. When it comes to football, today's fans might be more familiar with Ken Norton Jr., an All-Pro linebacker who won Super Bowl rings with the Cowboys and 49ers, but there are old-timers who saw them both who claim that his father was even better.

Norton wound up accepting a scholarship to Division II Northeast Missouri State, but by his sophomore year, finding life on the Kirksville campus tedious, he left school and joined the Marines. Although he had never so much as laced on a pair of gloves, he signed up for the boxing program at Camp Lejeune and soon proved to be as naturally equipped for his new sport as he had been for his former ones.

Between 1963 and 1967 he won three U.S. Marine Corps championships, amassed an amateur record of 24-2, and had qualified to represent the U.S. in the '67 Pan-Am Games before American amateur officials intervened to leave him off the team on the grounds that his style was unsuited to international amateur competition—which it probably was.

Discharged at Camp Pendleton, he elected to remain in San Diego, where his sponsors hooked him up with one of the game's acclaimed trainers, Eddie Futch. When Futch later joined Yank Durham in Joe Frazier's corner this, in turn, led to several stints as a Frazier sparring partner, where Norton picked up invaluable experience that helped offset his belated entry into the sport. Although Frazier and Norton never fought in anger, they probably boxed more rounds against each other than any other pairing in this quartet.

Norton employed a cage-like, cross-armed defensive posture for blocking punches that seemed unique in its time, but its efficacy was underscored years later when Foreman adopted a variation of the style during his remarkable second career.

After reeling off 16 consecutive wins at the outset of his pro career, Norton suffered a stunning defeat when Jose Luis Garcia, outweighed by nearly 20 pounds, dropped him in the first round and knocked him out in the eighth of a scheduled ten-rounder at the Olympic Auditorium in L.A. A light-heavyweight from Venezuela, Garcia would later be regarded as a credible heavyweight trial horse, but at the time he was 12-2-1 and had himself been knocked out in his only previous U.S. fight.

Stunned by the loss and filled with self-doubt, Norton credited his reading of a motivational book called *Think and Grow Rich,* by Napoleon Hill, with restoring his shaken confidence.

Fighting almost exclusively in California, Norton had accumulated a 29-1

George Kimball

record by March of 1973, when he was matched against Muhammad Ali at the San Diego Sports Arena in a Saturday afternoon fight carried on ABC's *Wide World of Sports.* Although the NABF title was at stake, Howard Cosell described the bout as "the worst mismatch in boxing history."

There seems little question that Ali underestimated Norton and was lackadaisical in his preparation for the bout, but it didn't take Norton long to remind him he was in a fight. The ex-Marine had broken Ali's jaw before the second round was over, and at the end of 12 Norton had prevailed on a split decision. Referee Frank Rustich scored it 7-4 for Norton, while the two judges—Hal Rickard (5-4 Norton) and Fred Hayes (6-5, Ali)—split their verdicts.

The doctor who operated on Ali's jaw after the Norton fight found it unfathomable that he could have fought for ten rounds with the injury. Ferdie Pacheco later told Ali's biographer Thomas Hauser that the break was so complete that he could feel the separation with his fingertips. Pacheco, in fact, would later express regret for not having intervened at the time of the injury.

"When the bell rang, I was no longer a doctor, I was a second," said Pacheco. "As a doctor, I should have said 'Stop the fight!'"

For future Nat Fleischer Award–winner Tom Cushman (who would later become sports editor of the *San Diego Tribune*), in San Diego to cover the bout for the *Philadelphia Daily News,* the best moment came afterward, when Cosell had to interview the winner on-camera. (The loser, in this instance, could not speak.) Cosell began by apologizing for having labeled the matchup "a disgrace."

"Kenny," said the broadcaster, "you made me look silly."

"That's all right, Howard," Norton replied. "You *always* look silly."

Ali had won ten fights in a row since the Frazier fight, and the loss to the unknown Norton led most evening newscasts. Frazier's manager/trainer Yancey Durham, who had traveled to San Diego hoping to conclude negotiations for a lucrative Ali rematch, had fretted that Ali might be underestimating Norton.

"He could cost us all a lot of money," he told Cushman.

In fact, Durham would die that August and never see Ali-Frazier II and III.

For a man trying to battle his way back into contention after the Frazier loss, the defeat by Norton was a giant step backward, but for Norton's career it represented a quantum leap.

"I took a nobody and created a monster," said Ali. "I put [Norton] on *The Dating Game.*"

The economic imperative for both Ali and Norton was a rematch, as soon as one could be safely arranged. Because Ali needed time to recuperate from his injury, it was September of '73 when the pair resumed hostilities, this time at the Forum in L.A.

Ali obviously didn't sell Norton short going into this one, and while there were no broken jaws, the second fight was every bit as close as the first had been, and Ali needed to win the last round to get the decision. Once again, two judges disagreed on the winner—Hal Rickard had it 5-4, Ali; George Laika 6-5, Norton—but this time the referee (Dick Young) had Ali the winner, by a 7-5 margin.

"Ken Norton is the best man I've ever fought," Ali told Cushman afterward. "He's better than Joe Frazier, Jerry Quarry, Sonny Liston—all of them."

There can be little question but that he was Ali's most difficult opponent, in any case. Ali's trilogy with Frazier might be better remembered, but his fights against Norton resulted in two split decisions followed by a unanimous one that may have been the closest of the three. In their back-to-back 1973 fights they had boxed 24 rounds against each other, and on the aggregate scorecards of those two fights, six scoring officials gave Ali and Norton 33 rounds apiece, while deeming 6 more even.

Although it is considered but a historical footnote in the spectrum of this rivalry, the second Ali-Frazier fight, on January 28, 1974, was witnessed by more spectators than had seen the first. The announced attendance of 20,748 remains to this day the largest for a boxing event in Madison Square Garden history.

Only the NABF title was at stake in the 12-rounder, but both men had a lot on the line. Still licking his residual wounds from the Foreman humiliation a year earlier, Frazier was trying to climb back into the heavyweight picture. Ali not only sought to avenge his loss to Frazier three years earlier but to establish the credibility that might force a challenge to Foreman—a fight few thought he could win, but one that might be worth millions.

The two met at an ABC studio for a *Wide World of Sports* segment designed to hype the rematch with a review of their first fight. That day it became clear that the bad blood between the two transcended anything that had happened in the boxing ring. This was personal, and it was a feud that has endured for the rest of their lives.

They knew how to push each other's buttons. Frazier tried to needle Ali, noting that he'd sent him to the hospital after their first fight.

"I was in the hospital for ten minutes. You were in the hospital for three weeks," shot back Ali, who then described Smokin' Joe as "ignorant." When this brought Frazier out of his chair, Ali seized him by the neck and forced him to sit down again. The next thing anybody knew the two were rolling around on the floor.

Although both men were fined by the New York commission, it had made for pretty good theater. And while it had erupted spontaneously, many assumed the brawl to have been staged. In this respect it became the antecedent of every silly press conference melee that has occurred since. The impromptu scrap aired on January 26, 1974, and viewers probably saw a better fight than the one in the ring two nights later.

Even at thirty-two, Ali, who had fought 13 times (to Frazier's four) since their 1971 meeting, was in better fighting trim than he had been three years earlier when he was still shaking off the effects of the years away from the sport. In the second round he nailed Frazier with a right that buckled his knees. Frazier looked like a man trying to learn the boogaloo as he tried to remain upright while his legs jerked spasmodically beneath him. He never did hit the canvas, but Ali moved in and drove him to the ropes, ready to administer the coup de grâce.

At that instant, referee Tony Perez mistakenly thought he had heard a bell and separated the fighters. By the time the mistake was rectified only seconds remained in the round, and Frazier survived it.

The bout turned into a boxing match over the final ten rounds. Having established a big early lead, Ali was content to jab from a distance, smothering Frazier with clinches whenever Joe tried to burrow his way in to hooking range. Neither was even close to going down again, and while by the end Frazier had become the more effective of the two, he could only make it closer on the scorecards. Perez scored it 6-5-1, Tony Castellano 7-4-1, and Jack Gordon 8-4 as Ali coasted to a unanimous decision.

After winning the title from Frazier, Foreman had defended it in Tokyo against Jose (King) Roman, whom he knocked out in two minutes. By now considered as fearsome a puncher as had ever worn the heavyweight belt, Foreman had knocked out 36 of 39 opponents, a stunning 94.9 percentage, but he was still perceived as "difficult" by the media.

By his own description Foreman had become "the stereotypical heavyweight champ—surly and angry."

Unsure of exactly how a heavyweight champion was supposed to act, Foreman was no more suited to Ali's Gorgeous George act than to Frazier's earnest, blue-collar meatpacker approach. So he had modeled himself on the only other of his predecessors with whom he had a firsthand relation-ship: Sonny Liston.

And "to say that Sonny Liston was a man of few words is to say that the sun is warm," Foreman would later recall. "Mostly, he just glared."

The intelligence and sensitivity that would not be revealed to the world until his 1987 comeback rarely intruded on accounts of Foreman's first box-ing incarnation. It might be a surprising revelation to sportswriters who recall the glowering, menacing figure that was George Foreman in 1974, but even then the novelist Leonard Gardner, in Caracas that spring to cover Foreman's fight against Ken Norton, was able to cut through the veneer to separate the public image from the man.

Gardner's 1974 *Esquire* piece opened with a description of one of the many press conferences Foreman and Norton were obliged to endure in the run-up to the first heavyweight championship fight ever contested in South America, and while the novelist could empathize with the plight of the news-men obliged to create daily dispatches even when nothing much actually seemed to be happening, Gardner was even more sympathetic to the boxer besieged by all these silly questions.

Gardner, in his *Esquire* story, described an interlude during one of these media cluster-plucks when a particularly dumb interrogatory was met by a stony silence.

> Foreman did not answer. The man kept holding out his micro-phone. Close to twenty reporters were crowded into the cubicle and all looked expectantly at Foreman, whose mouth and eyes remained closed. The silence became unsettling, then bewilder-ing and a little demeaning. It went on for what seemed a minute. Had he fallen asleep? At last someone spoke.
>
> "Why wouldn't you answer that question?"
>
> "Oh, that was a question? I thought it was a statement."
>
> There was some uneasy laughter at this, and the questions that followed became progressively more halting and desultory.

Although Gardner was in the midst of the posse of newsmen, he seemed in his account to be taking great pains to make it clear that he was not one of them. The press was headquartered at the Caracas Hilton, as, ostensi-bly, was Foreman, although the champion had several days earlier slipped off and quietly relocated to a small, less bustling hostelry called the Avila. Gardner, accompanied by press agent Bill Caplan, went to visit him there.

While initially resistant, Foreman's defenses eventually came down as the two conversed beside the swimming pool:

> He spoke slowly and carefully, without gestures and with little change in pitch, his voice low and restrained and softened by a black Texas accent. He had grown up in Houston, one of seven children supported by his mother, who had been a cook and a barber and a strong influence on him, and as he talked about her now it was evident there were still close ties between them. When he was fourteen she had suffered an emotional collapse and been hospitalized, and in the time she was away Foreman had dabbled in drunkenness, truancy, vandalism, strong-arm robbery and purse-snatching. But depressions had come with the hangovers, he quit the robberies for fear his violent partner was going to hurt someone, and as a purse-snatcher he was a total failure; undone by his victims' cries for God's assistance, he was compelled to run back and return all the purses.

Much has been made of Foreman's ability to re-cast his image in concordance with his religious conversion and subsequent comeback, but in looking back at Gardner's rendition of that soul-baring conversation 36 years later, one can't help but wonder how much of it was a matter of Big George reinventing himself in his second incarnation, and how much the result of people just not asking the right questions during his first.

Norton's two strong performances against Ali had earned him the challenger's role against Foreman. I was in spring training with the Red Sox, and Orlando Cepeda and I had made plans to drive to a dog track in Sanford that night to watch the closed-circuit telecast. Cepeda was a big boxing fan; as a boy he had grown up in Ponce with José Torres, and as a man he had named one of his children after Ali.

On the morning of March 26, 1974, Red Sox manager Darrell Johnson announced the outright releases of Cepeda and another future Hall of Famer, shortstop Luis Aparicio, resulting in a virtual day of mourning in Winter Haven, particularly among the club's younger Latino players, who had come to regard Cepeda as a father figure.

In the midst of that day's doom and gloom, I finally dragged my way over to Cha-Cha's room to see if he still wanted to go watch the fight. It would have been completely understandable, under the circumstances, if he hadn't.

"Of *course* we're going to the fight," he said.

So that night Cepeda and yet another future Hall of Famer, his old Giants' teammate Juan Marichal, and I piled into my rental car and drove over to watch the Foreman-Norton telecast from Caracas. The venue was set up in the manner of a drive-in theatre. There was a large screen in the infield, with loudspeakers to hang from the inside of your car window. We'd prepared ourselves to settle in for a long evening, and I had a case of beer iced down when the bell rang. There were something like 21 bottles left when it was over. Norton might have gone the distance twice with Ali, but against Foreman he didn't last much longer than Frazier had. Foreman walked right through Norton's crab-like defense and knocked him down three times in five minutes.

If Foreman fought like a man consumed by anger, he was. Having become heavyweight champion had not brought the respect he felt was his due, and in his own mind he was so determined to annihilate his opponent that he literally wanted to kill Norton. That rage had diminished with the intervention of referee Jimmy Rondeau two minutes into the second. In Jamaica Foreman had pleaded with Mercante to rescue Frazier, but in Venezuela he was furious because the referee had rescued Norton.

No longer able to vent his rage on Norton, Big George looked around for the next available target. He walked across the ring, leaned across the ropes above the press section, and pointed to Muhammad Ali at the television table.

"I'm going to kill you," he promised, sounding as if he meant it.

In Caracas, the local promoters had been somewhat displeased when Don King and his business partner, Hank Schwartz, rolled into town two days before the fight to upstage the Norton fight with their announcement of Foreman's *next* defense. Although King would become the face of the fight that would come to be known as The Rumble in the Jungle, his initial involvement had been that of a middleman. In early 1974 he had separately approached both Muhammad Ali and George Foreman, even though the heavyweight champion had yet to defend his title against Norton in Venezuela.

By assuring both Ali and Foreman that the other had already agreed to its terms, King was able to persuade both Foreman and Ali to sign contracts guaranteeing them $5 million apiece to fight later that year. The fact that he didn't have $10 million was a matter of slight consequence to King, who was able to use the contracts as leverage to round up the necessary capital.

Schwartz' Video Techniques, in which King already had an interest, was one investor, and a British financier named John Daly, who owned Leisure Technologies, became a major one.

The final piece to the puzzle came when Mobutu Sese Seko, the dictator who had reorganized the former Belgian Congo and renamed it Zaire, agreed to cover the rest of the financing in the hope of boosting the image of his country (to say nothing of his own image) among the nations of the world. The bout would be held that September at the Stade du 20 Mai in the capital city of Kinshasa, formerly known as Leopoldville.

Before he had even left the United States, Ali warned Foreman that "my African brothers are going to cook you in a pot and eat you," and once he reached Kinshasa he continued a relentless campaign calculated to isolate the champion and turn a fight he described as The Rumble in the Jungle into a home game for himself. Foreman, newly divorced, had brought along his dog to keep him company, blissfully unaware that the Alsatian—what we in this country would describe as a German Police Dog—was the breed the Belgian police had used in crowd-control operations during the colonial era. At every opportunity, Ali referred to Foreman's pet as a "Belgian Shepherd."

Ali and his entourage were quartered in the luxurious presidential villas at N'sele. Foreman, though the champion, was assigned housing at a military complex surrounded by barbed wire and manned guard towers that had every appearance of being a prison. Not that Foreman seemed anxious to leave and mingle with the natives, but he did find the atmosphere so stifling that he eventually moved into a Kinshasa hotel. (There, having spurned the military guard provided by the government, he was obliged to reach into his own pocket to pay for round-the-clock security.)

Ali, on the other hand, made it a point to court the favor of the locals. He made frequent forays into the cities and towns, and even to small villages. Even in places that had never known electricity he was instantly recognized and embraced by the natives. The chant *"Ali bomaye!"*—a phrase in the Ngala tongue meaning, literally, "Ali, kill him!"—became his clarion call. The sum effect was to create the widespread impression that the Congolese people considered Ali one of their own and Foreman a hostile invader.

That Ali seemed to spend much of his daily training lying against the ropes while his sparring partners flailed away was considered unremarkable; he often conserved his energy the same way back at Deer Lake. Foreman, on the other hand, seemed to regard his training sessions as an opportunity to vent his rage, which he took out on his sparring partners. Eight days before the bout, he was sparring with Bill McMurry, who, trapped against the ropes, saw Foreman coming at him and threw up his arms to protect himself. One of his elbows caught the champion above the right eye, just below the head-gear, and blood immediately spurted forth from the cut.

Word of the injury to the champion spread like wildfire. It was shortly confirmed that the fight would be postponed for a month. Trainer Dick Sadler had immediately patched the wound with a butterfly, but Foreman voiced hope of flying to Europe to have the injury treated by a specialist in France or Belgium. Mobutu, fearing that if Foreman were allowed to leave Zaire he might never return ("and he was right about that," Foreman says today), refused permission for either fighter to leave the country during the delay.

Foreman viewed this restraint as one more indication that the field had been tilted in Ali's favor, but the truth of the matter is that Ali was almost as anxious to get away from monkey meat as Foreman was. Once it became clear that he wasn't going anywhere, Ali continued to train, and the extra month gave him time to achieve a level of fitness he hadn't approached since before his exile.

Foreman told himself he was doing it to guard against re-opening the cut, but between the date of the injury and the night of the fight, he didn't spar a single round.

Most of the traveling media contingent had already arrived on-site when the injury occurred. Foreman and Ali were under orders to remain in Zaire; the press corps became a hostage to simple economics. The sweetheart arrangement under which most of them had flown to Africa on Air Zaire did not cover the postponement, and most newspapers discovered it was a lot cheaper simply to keep their representative in Kinshasa for a month than to fly him home and back again.

Bob Waters, *Newsday*'s boxing writer, wound up authoring what proved to be an award-winning series on famine in Africa during this interlude. Budd Schulberg, who filed dispatches from Zaire for the same newspaper, flew back to the United States at his own expense. The night before his departure from Kinshasa, Ali invited Schulberg to dine with him at N'sele. Although he didn't consider it particularly noteworthy at the time, Schulberg later recalled that after dinner he and Ali watched some videotape of Foreman's fights, including those against Gregorio Peralta. Ali sat fixated upon the screen, where the Argentine seemed to have contracted into a little ball, his back to the ropes, while Foreman flailed away with both fists.

Foreman, Ali pointed out to Schulberg that night, "thinks he's killin' him—but all he's doin' is getting arm-weary."

As the anecdote related by Schulberg makes clear, Ali was obviously aware of the possibility that should all else fail Foreman might be lured into expending his energy in a similar manner, but the notion that either he or trainer Angelo Dundee had plotted the strategy that became known as the "Rope-a-Dope" beforehand is misplaced. This myth has survived in part because Norman Mailer, one of many literary luminaries in Africa to cover the Ali-Foreman bout, included in his narrative an account in which he claimed to have witnessed Dundee marching from corner to corner and using a wrench to deliberately loosen the ring ropes just before the fight, and with Ali already in the ring. In point of fact, Mailer could not have seen this, because it never happened.

Mailer's account in *The Fight* also included an evocative scene in the challenger's dressing room just before the fight, in which he inserted his own name, along with that of fellow author George Plimpton's, into a list of those present: "Dundee, Pacheco, Plimpton, Mailer, Walter Youngblood, Pat Patterson . . ." But it seems extremely doubtful that Mailer could have been there at all, particularly at the critical juncture he described in his book.

"Mailer was in the dressing room? He was never in the dressing room," said Dr. Ferdie Pacheco. "I was the one who kept him out."

In Bobby Goodman's recollection, "I was assigned to stay with Ali, while my Dad (publicist Murray Goodman) was going to bring out Foreman. I recall seeing Norman stick his head in for a second, but he didn't remain with us."

The bout was scheduled for 4 a.m., Zaire time, on October 31, which would coincide with a 10 p.m. closed-circuit showing back in the states. The previous afternoon, in daylight, Dundee and Goodman drove out to the stadium to inspect the venue. Both men had repeatedly implored the locals who would be setting up the ring to wait until the last possible moment, but when they got there the ring was already in place, and the ropes were already sagging nearly to the floor after exposure to the heat and humidity. Worse, the turnbuckles had been fully tightened and couldn't be readjusted. The two men spent the better part of the afternoon cutting the ropes with razor blades, re-clamping them, and then hand-tightening the turnbuckles to allow for further adjustment in the wee hours of the following morning.

All of this, it should be noted, was done to *tighten,* not loosen, the ring ropes.

Ali and Foreman entered the ring at the conclusion of the undercard, and, recalls Goodman, "after the prelims, the ropes had stretched out. All along the strategy had been for Ali to dance. He was supposed to stay off the ropes, but once he got in the ring he realized that the Ensaflor padding had become soft and spongy in the heat and that he wouldn't be *able* to dance—but when he went to test the ropes they went back so far that he could lean with his head more than a foot outside the ring.

"Just before the fight Angelo and Youngblood and Bundini and I were going to tighten the ropes with a screwdriver or a wrench or just our hands, but Ali told us to leave them alone," said Goodman.

When the two men removed their robes in their respective corners just before they were summoned to the center of the ring, a wide-eyed Ali poked Dundee and pointed to Foreman's biceps as he mouthed the word "Big!" He was doing his best to appear overawed, and he made sure Foreman took notice.

Once the bell rang, Foreman approached his task with the same disdain he had had for Frazier and Norton, and there is every indication that he expected to finish off Ali as easily as he had those two. In a startling display of impudence, Ali ducked inside a Foreman charge and landed a right-hand lead. Though not hurt, Foreman had been served notice that he was in a fight against an opponent who would not go quietly.

In the second round Ali unveiled his backup strategy when he retreated to the ropes and, seemingly offering but token resistance, allowed Foreman to flail away. Taking advantage of the loose ropes, he was able to keep his head out of the optimal range of Foreman's most dangerous blows, and while some of Foreman's punches missed and others were blocked, the champion was able to subject Ali's body and arms to some of his heaviest artillery.

From the corner Dundee was shouting "Get off the ropes!", and when Ali returned to his stool at the end of the round the trainer admonished him, "What are you doing?"

But even as he plunged ahead with what seemed a suicidal strategy, Ali was able to periodically emerge from his cocoon against the ropes to land sneaky punches of his own. Even though he spent most of each round pounding away without meeting much resistance, this happened often enough that the champion's face grew increasingly puffy as the night wore on.

On several occasions Foreman was able to land punches that seemed as solid as the ones that had put Frazier and Norton on the floor. Ali not only took them but sneered back, "Is that all you got, George?" and "They told me you could punch."

Even as it unfolded, nobody described the tactic as the Rope-a-Dope that night. In fact, when he saw Ali do it for the first time, Plimpton turned to Mailer and said, "Christ, it's a fix!"

The descriptive phrase would shortly become so identified with the fight that spawned it that even Foreman employs it today in recalling the events of that evening.

"Yeah," he says. "And I was the dope."

Another myth that has grown up around this fight over the intervening 36 years is that Foreman was on his way to a rout until he tired. In fact, on the scorecards of the three officials after seven completed rounds, Foreman had taken two rounds on referee Zach Clayton's tally. One of the judges, James Taylor, had Foreman winning one round, the other, Nourridine Adalla, none. (Clayton, Taylor, and Adalla had between them scored seven rounds even.)

Ali's inspired tactic was soundly rooted for yet another reason: Foreman was so accustomed to putting opponents away early that he rarely had a Plan B. Only the two Peralta fights had lasted as long as ten rounds. Since the second of those, three and a half years earlier, the champion had fought a dozen times, and only one of those—a fifth-round TKO of the Brazilian Luis Faustino Pires—had gotten past the *second* round.

In the champion's corner Dick Sadler was telling him to keep pressing the attack on Ali. Archie Moore was also in the corner and could sense that a failure to adjust might further sap Foreman's waning stamina, but since he was not the chief second felt it imprudent to countermand the instructions.

By the fifth it was apparent that Foreman's punches were losing their steam. He continued to pound away, but Ali seemed unaffected, and before the seventh ended the fight had taken yet a new turn. Ali had become the aggressor.

Even so, Foreman continued to regard the man across the ring with disdain and vowed to knock him out the next round. When Foreman missed with a sweeping punch, Ali countered with a jarring left hook that snapped Foreman's head into position to receive the right hand that came whistling after it. Foreman went lurching across the ring, seeming to spin in a futile effort to keep himself erect, and eventually crashed down.

Foreman initially seemed alert as he took Clayton's count, even looking toward his corner for instructions on when to get up. The signal was a bit late in coming, considering how much trouble the weary champion had making it to his feet, but he still seemed to have beaten the count and was surprised to see Clayton waving his arms to signal the most improbable upset in boxing history.

What closed-circuit viewers around the world heard was the breathless announcement of David Frost, who was shouting *"Ali wins by a knockdown! Ali wins by a knockdown!"*

Eight-and-a-half years after his title had been taken away from him, Muhammad Ali had become just the second heavyweight champion in history to regain it.

It was the rainy season in Central Africa, and the predicted rainstorm had held off just long enough for the miracle to take place. (The anticipated downpour would not have postponed the bout, since the ring was covered, but it might have seriously tested the resolve of the nearly 60,000 who packed the Stade to watch it.)

Dawn was already breaking when Ali finally emerged from his dressing room and commenced the drive back to N'sele. Every step of the way the roads were lined with happy Congolese. Ngala is but one of six or seven Congolese languages, and no more prevalent than the others, but on this morning regardless of tribal affiliation every man, woman, and child seemed to be chanting *"Ali bomaye!"*

Sleight of Hand

Can't tell you how many times
I'd be walking through
a crowded corridor at Caesars
ice clinking in glasses
rattling dice and the bells
of slot machines
or maybe just standing
in the buffet line at
the Elvis Hilton when
I'd hear a bug buzz past my ear
just before it
landed in my hair

He got me every time

I'd instinctively stop
to slap it away
smack myself in the head
then turn around and there he'd be
laughing his ass off

By an 8-0 vote the Supreme Court
agreed he was a
Minister of Islam but
how many Holy Men you know
walk around with a deck
of cards in their pockets?

Back then when his hands
still listened he could make the
Jack of Diamonds
jump out of the pack
and spit in your eye

He specialized in making
silver dollars disappear
but those who know
could tell you that his
greatest magic trick of all
came in Zaire

No not the Rope-a-Dope:
Before the fight when he
turned George Foreman
into a white man

Somehow "It will be a killa and a chilla and a thrilla when I get the gorilla in Honolulu" just wouldn't have had the same ring to it.

In April of 1975, just a few weeks before Ali's scheduled defense against Ron Lyle, Don King summoned the press for a breathtaking announcement: the long-awaited rubber match between Ali and Frazier would take place that September, opening a new, 50,000-seat stadium in Honolulu—and he himself would be the promoter of the extravaganza.

Although most reporters still regarded King as a self-promoting blowhard, he had retained some bona fides for his part in arranging the extravaganza in Zaire. King went on to reveal his plans for Ali to make an interim defense, against England's Joe Bugner, in Malaysia that June, and if he'd stopped right there he'd probably have had his captive audience eating out of his hands. Instead, King went on to tell the press that day that, having assembled a consortium of Middle Eastern businessmen as backers, he was deeply involved in negotiations to purchase Madison Square Garden.

The notion that the Mecca of Boxing would be controlled from, well, Mecca, and that a huckstering ex-con would be its front man was difficult to swallow. Michael Burke, then the president of MSG, found it extremely amusing, but like everyone else associated with the Garden, knew of no negotiations to buy a building that was not for sale in any case. (Burke did, on the other hand—with tongue firmly in cheek—wish King all the luck in the world with his venture in Hawaii.)

One phone call to Honolulu similarly established that there was no deal to stage a fight there, either. Mackay Yanagisawa, the manager of the as-yet-unnamed Aloha Stadium, said that it was by no means certain that the new facility would even be completed by September. (Although the Hawaii option faded from view, the cover of the August 1975 issue of *The Ring* was a facsimile poster for Ali-Frazier III—at Nasser Stadium in Cairo, Egypt.)

One of King's seemingly fanciful boasts did come to pass when on June 30 of that year Ali defended against Bugner in Kuala Lumpur and won a unanimous decision, and another proved partially true. It didn't take place in Hawaii and it didn't take place in Egypt, but before the summer was out King had entered into an alliance with yet another Third World dictator. With Ferdinand Marcos assuming the role Mobutu had played in Zaire, and for pretty much the same reasons, a deal was struck for Ali and Frazier to consummate their trilogy in the capital city of the Republic of the Philippines.

The buildup to the October 1975 fight was dominated by two subtexts, both of which would have enduring consequences. One was Frazier's reaction to Ali's constant needling. If Smokin' Joe had been ready to come to blows over being called "ignorant" before Ali-Frazier II, we can only imagine how he felt about being characterized as a gorilla at every turn in the buildup to this one. It was classic Ali gamesmanship, and he flung the term around so incessantly that it found its way into local English-language stories whose authors assumed it to be Joe's adopted *nom de ring*. Thirty-five years later we can only speculate how the entire future of the Ali-Frazier relationship might have been affected had their third meeting taken place in a city that didn't lend itself to such an easy rhyme.

The other pre-fight contretemps came because Ali's traveling party included the lovely Veronica Porche. As a pre-med student at USC, the aspiring actress had met Ali in Zaire after winning a contest to become one of four "poster girls" for the Rumble in the Jungle and had regularly been seen in the champion's company over the intervening year. Since the American sporting press generally turned a blind eye to Ali's womanizing, the relationship had not been widely publicized, but it had been so brazenly conducted that Belinda Ali could hardly have been unaware of it, but she had apparently determined to keep her counsel for the sake of her family rather than be publicly embarrassed.

All of that changed when Veronica accompanied Ali to an official function at the presidential palace. Ms. Porche's presence might have been innocent enough (she probably just wanted to compare shoe collections with Imelda Marcos), but in the course of the state visit, Ferdinand Marcos introduced Veronica as "Mrs. Ali." Ali himself certainly had the opportunity to correct him, but when he did not, stories describing her as his "wife" were circulated all around the world. A steaming Belinda Ali was shortly on a flight to Manila, and after a noisy and unpleasant confrontation at the champion's hotel, departed again.

It was the end of Ali's second marriage. He would marry Veronica Porche in 1977, a union which produced two daughters—Hana Ali, who would write *The Soul of a Butterfly*, and Laila Ali, who would accumulate a 24-0 record as a professional boxer.

The turmoil surrounding Ali's personal life so dominated the run-up to the Manila fight that many assumed it would prove a distraction; even Frazier joked about it. When he encountered Tom Cushman he indicated the lady next to him and said, "I'd like you to meet *my* girlfriend. Florence is also my wife."

The bout was held outside Manila, at the Araneta Stadium in Quezon City. Television was once again calling the tune, and it commenced at 10:45 in the morning, Philippines time. Officially, Ali (224 1/2) and Frazier (215) were significantly heavier than they had been for the earlier two meetings; there's no telling how much they weighed at fight time since the weigh-in was conducted five days beforehand. There were 28,000 eyewitnesses, including the Marcoses. The referee, a little-known Filipino named Carlos Padilla, would capitalize on the exposure he received in the Thrilla by moving to Las Vegas soon afterward, and by 1975 was working high-profile bouts in his adopted hometown.

There were three distinct phases to the Thrilla in Manila. Ali dominated the first act, outboxing Frazier while he peppered him with long-range jabs and combinations to the head, simultaneously negating Joe's favored weapon as he grabbed him behind the neck before he could unload with the hook.

Act II, comprising the middle rounds, went to Frazier almost by default once Ali wearied and stopped punching. Joe had opened the sixth by landing three solid hooks to the jaw, any one of which, in his own estimate, "could have knocked down a building."

As he took one of them, Ali supposedly said to Joe, "And they told me you was all washed up," to which Frazier replied, "They lied to you, didn't they?"

At this point Ali once again retreated to his refuge on the ropes, but if the Rope-a-Dope had been an inspired tactic in the Foreman fight, it was all wrong for fighting Joe Frazier, who was not only much better conditioned, but seemed to delight in the opportunity to punish his despised rival without meeting serious resistance. Ali appeared ready to quit after both the tenth and eleventh, but Dundee was able to haul him off his stool and force him back into the ring.

After 11 rounds in the hot, late-morning sun, both men seemed exhausted, but Ali summoned a second wind that saw him take the fight to Frazier. By now Frazier's eyes were rapidly closing, and he occasionally looked like Mr. Magoo in the ring, turning the wrong way in his confusion. "He can't see you!" Dundee shouted to Ali from the corner.

Ali appeared to stagger his foe several times in the 12th, and in the 13th he unloaded a punch with such ferocity that Joe's mouthpiece threatened to go into orbit. The mouthpiece, which had landed in the audience, was not replaced until the end of the round, and after 13 Frazier's mouth had accumulated several new lacerations. By the 14th Ali's punches had completely closed Frazier's left eye; the right one wasn't much better. The scorecards would later confirm that Ali's lead at this point was virtually insurmountable—he was up 66-60 on Padilla's, 67-62 and 66-62 on those of the two judges. In other words, Frazier's only hope lay in a knockout of a target he couldn't even *see,* much less hit.

When the bell sounded for the final round, Frazier could be heard pleading with Eddie Futch, saying, "I want him, Boss!", but the trainer held Frazier down, saying, "It's all over. No one will forget what you did here today," as he motioned to Padilla that his man had had enough.

Ali could have been speaking for both of them when he pronounced the experience "the closest thing to dying I know of."

For all the rancor that had passed between the two, Ali said afterward, "If God ever calls me to a Holy War, I want Joe Frazier fighting beside me."

• • •

Ali had followed the Thrilla in Manila by making three title defenses (against Jean-Pierre Coopman, Jimmy Young, and Richard Dunn) in the first five months of 1976. Frazier didn't fight again until the next June, when he was matched against Foreman before just over 10,000 at the Nassau Coliseum in what may well have been the least-memorable of any of the ten bouts between the members of the quartet. The meeting of the two former champions was even overshadowed by Ali's "fight" against the Japanese wrestler Antonio Inoki in Tokyo three nights later.

(Trivia Question here: *Who was the last opponent to have Ali on the floor?* A: *Inoki.*)

The Long Island fight was promoted by an odd coupling of Jerry Perenchio, the Hollywood guy who had staged Frazier-Ali I, and Caesars Palace. Foreman had sent Sadler, Saddler, and Moore packing after the debacle in Zaire, and while he would team up with Hall of Fame trainer Gil Clancy later that year, Charlie Shipes and Howie Albert were in charge of the Foreman corner.

Frazier was actually the bigger of the two for this one, at 224 ½, outweighing Foreman by half a pound. A boxing apothegm holds that people born round don't die square, but Joe attempted a complete makeover for this bout: he had shaved his head, could be seen woofing and jabbering away during the referee's instructions, and had even jettisoned the boxing style with which he had been identified throughout his career in favor of a bobbing, weaving, and sometimes even dancing approach.

Foreman ("I was under the impression Frazier could only fight one way") admitted that he was surprised to find himself facing this strange new opponent, but while what Eddie Futch termed "a change in tactics" made Frazier marginally more elusive and difficult to hit, his most feared weapons were also left without a launching pad.

Foreman had dominated each of the four completed rounds, and the more punishment Frazier took, the more he lapsed back into the Frazier of old. In the final minute of the fifth Foreman crushed Frazier with a short right. Joe stopped moving and provided a stationary target as Foreman followed that by using Frazier's head for a speed bag, and when Foreman landed a sweeping left hook it knocked Frazier off his feet; all four limbs flailed simultaneously as he sailed sideways across the ring.

Frazier bounced up, but then delivered himself straight back into the fire.

When Foreman put him down with a left uppercut, it was looking like Round One in Jamaica revisited. Frazier made it up at seven, but Harold Valen's decision was made for him when Futch came up the steps and raced along the apron, imploring the referee to stop it.

Foreman was encouraged enough by his own performance that he spoke of being ready to challenge for the title again, but he was solidly outpointed by Young in Puerto Rico and would hang up his gloves for the next ten years. Frazier formally retired immediately after the Nassau fight, but five years later came back to meet Jumbo Cummings in Chicago, and was probably lucky to escape with a draw. Smokin' Joe had been 29-0 when he stepped into the ring against Foreman the first time; in his last eight bouts he was 3-4-1.

The third match in the trilogy between Ali and Ken Norton at Yankee Stadium on September 28, 1976, rang down the curtain on the ten-fight series. As had been the case with its two predecessors, there wasn't much to separate Ali and Norton in this one, either. No one could have known it at the time, but while the House That Ruth Built would endure for another three-and-a-half decades, Ali-Norton III would be the last boxing event ever to take place there.

As fate would have it, the bout was scheduled in the midst of a job action by the NYPD, and the only visible police presence inside or outside the stadium were those walking picket lines, and chaos reigned. Pickpockets and small-time hoods operated with virtual impunity; the *Times'* Pulitzer Prize–winning columnist Red Smith wondered the next morning what the fellow who stole his wallet would buy with his Brooks Brothers charge card—and several scribes on their way through the press gate had their tickets ripped right out of their hands by brazen thieves despite the presence of picketing cops just a few feet away.

And on this night the robbery was by no means the exclusive province of the purse-snatchers. In several otherwise close rounds Ali staged showy flurries just before the bell in the hope that that was what the judges would remember, and he appears to have gauged their response accurately. Although their third fight produced the only unanimous decision of the Ali-Norton trilogy, the bout was in many respects even closer than the two split decisions had been: Mercante, the referee, had Ali up 8-6 with a round even, while Harold Lederman and Barney Smith both scored it 8-7.

Switching just one round (and there were many extremely close ones) on the judges' cards would have tilted the decision to Norton.

At most of Ali's bouts for the previous decade he had enjoyed the support of the crowd, but the audience seemed almost divided in its loyalties. Given the pervasive atmosphere of danger hanging over the ballpark that night, it occurred to me that ringside probably wasn't going to be a great place to be sitting when the verdict was read; I'd already begun to ease my way toward safety as the 15th round played out.

As I quickly made my way to the home team dugout along the first base line, where a tunnel offered the best means of escape, the angry mob was already laying siege to the ring. Behind me I could hear the recitation of the scorecards periodically interrupted by the splintering of wood as they surged forward, climbing across the makeshift plywood tabletops that had been installed in the ringside press section.

In lieu of credentials, the working press had been issued red, white, and blue baseball caps bearing the fight logo, presumably to make us more readily identifiable to the skeleton crew working security that night, and when I reached the tunnel the preoccupied guard waved me on through, simultaneously denying access to a squeaky-voiced fellow wearing a suit, but lacking the requisite baseball cap.

"But you've *got* to let me through," I heard him pleading as he peered nervously over his shoulder. "I'm one of the *judges.*"

I turned to the guard, and pointed back toward the ring, where utter chaos now reigned.

"I think you'd better let him get out of here. Now," I said. The security man relented, and the judge followed me through the tunnel to safety.

And that was how I met Harold Lederman.

Although their shared rivalry in the ring would end with the debacle at Yankee Stadium, the boxing world hadn't seen the last of the four.

Ali lost and regained the heavyweight championship in fights against Leon Spinks in 1978. That his once remarkable skills were deteriorating was evident when he fought twice in the 1980s, and lost both times. A year after he was battered into submission by Larry Holmes in their 1980 fight at Caesars Palace, he traveled to the Bahamas and in a ring erected atop a dusty softball diamond outside Nassau, lost a ten-round decision to Trevor Berbick. Because the fight's amateurish promoters had failed to provide a regulation bell, the end of Ali's career was signaled by the clapping of a Bahamian cowbell.

More universally beloved today than at any point in his fistic career, Ali, his hands trembling as the result of the Parkinson's that had claimed his body, poignantly climbed the stairs to ignite the Olympic torch to begin the 1996 Atlanta Games.

Late in 1977, Ken Norton edged Jimmy Young in what the World Boxing Council had designated as a heavyweight title eliminator. When Leon Spinks, who upset Ali in just his eighth pro fight, agreed to a 1978 rematch in contravention of WBC rules, the organization stripped him of its title and retroactively declared Norton its champion. In his very first defense, he was edged by Holmes in a split decision that came down to a single point on all three scorecards. Norton's place in boxing history was thus defined not as the man who endured three hard fights with Ali, but as the only heavyweight champion in the annals of the sport to have lost all three title bouts (Foreman, Ali III, and Holmes) in which he participated.

Norton fought until he was nearly thirty-eight, and the trajectory of his late career suggested a boxer in decline. He managed just one win—that a split decision over Randall (Tex) Cobb—in his last four fights. Sandwiched around a draw with Scott LeDoux were first-round knockout losses to Ernie Shavers and, in his final fight, on May 11, 1981, to Gerry Cooney. His final record was 42-7-1.

Although Norton emerged from boxing with his physical and mental faculties unimpaired, the fates were less kind once he hung up the gloves. One night in 1986, Norton was driving home from a dinner at which he had been honored by Los Angeles Mayor Tom Bradley when he lost control of his car and jumped the curb on the Santa Monica freeway. His Escalade wound up in a crumpled heap in a ditch below, trapping Norton inside. He was rescued and eventually transported to Cedars-Mount Sinai Hospital, suffering from a fractured skull, a broken jaw, and a fractured left leg. In and out of a coma for months, Norton today has no memory of this interlude in his life—including Ali's vigil at his bedside. ("I couldn't have talked to him anyway," said Norton when told later of the visit from his old rival. "My jaw was wired shut.")

Although Norton eventually recovered, his vocal chords were permanently damaged, putting an end to his movie career. When we last encountered him, Norton had traveled with his wife to the induction weekend at the International Boxing Hall of Fame in Canastota, N.Y., in the summer of

2010. His voice had been rendered a barely decipherable whisper, and the man whose body had been likened to that of a Greek god now required a walker. Norton's infirmities are the residue of the auto accident, not of his boxing career.

Neither did Joe Frazier ease gracefully into old age. More than five years after losing what seemed to have been his final fight against Foreman, he re-emerged to participate in an embarrassing sham of a fight in which he was awarded a draw against Floyd (Jumbo) Cummings. Frazier's obsession with Ali has hardened into a bitter animus that does not serve him well. Frazier sometimes sounds as if he's claiming credit for Ali's Parkinson's, which he sneeringly describes as "Joe Frazieritis" and "left hook-itis."

After watching his old rival light the Olympic cauldron that night in Atlanta, Smokin' Joe told Bill Nack, "It would have been a good thing if he'd lit the torch and fallen in. If I had the chance I would have pushed him in myself."

If Ali, Frazier, and Norton had each overstayed his welcome in the fight game, that Foreman had not did not become apparent until 1987, when, following a hiatus of ten years, he returned to the heavyweight stage for a second career that was in many respects more remarkable than its predecessor.

The menacing figure who had intimidated reporters and opponents alike had disappeared, replaced by the roly-poly "Punching Preacher" who claimed that he trained on cheeseburgers. Foreman had initially returned because his Houston Youth Center was low on funds, but as the exercise continued well into his forties, money was the least of his worries, as the comeback led to roles as a television pitchman for everything from fast-food and auto-repair chains to the George Foreman Grill, which earned him several hundred million dollars.

When he was accused of hand-picking opponents, he would smile and reply, "They're only saying that because it's true," but for the most part Foreman was not seeking out soft touches but opponents who were stylistically suited to his particular talents.

In his forties Foreman could punch as effectively as he had in his twenties. The one thing he could not do was chase an opponent all over the ring, so his preference was to take on opponents who, it could reasonably be inferred, would actually try to fight him. But guys who had never taken a backward step in their lives abruptly turned into acrobats and ballet dancers when placed in the ring with Foreman.

Despite losses to Evander Holyfield and Tommy Morrison, on November 5, 1994, Foreman found himself the challenger to twenty-six-year-old Michael Moorer, an undefeated southpaw from Pennsylvania who that April had defeated Holyfield to win the WBA and IBF heavyweight titles.

I'd just checked into the hotel and hadn't even visited my room yet when I ran into Foreman. We chatted for a few minutes, and then I told him I had gone on record in my newspaper picking him to win. Big George seemed to think that was the funniest thing he'd ever heard, and next thing I knew he was laughing so hard he wound up flat on his back, rolling around on the carpet. It wasn't that he didn't think he could win himself; he was merely suspicious of whatever thought process I might have employed to arrive at that conclusion.

"You're not the first one," he explained. He'd finally stopped laughing, but the tears were still coming down his cheeks. "A *bunch* of you old guys are picking me. Everybody wants to roll back the clock."

For ten rounds against Moorer it looked as if the clock had caught up with George. The seat next to me was vacant, and seemingly every round either Mort Sharnik or Bill Caplan would slide into it, watch for a few minutes, and ask how I had it scored. My recollection is that up until then I hadn't given Foreman a round.

Foreman's face, as it had in the Holyfield fight, had accumulated a ghastly collection of lumps, and both eyes had been reduced to narrow slits, as if he were wearing some particularly gruesome relic left over from Halloween. The younger man had simply been too quick for him. In Teddy Atlas' game plan Moorer was able to get in, land a couple of quick punches, and get out before Foreman could even set up behind his jab. And the boxer George Foreman had become at forty-five could still pulverize you with his right, but he needed to be able to land the jab to do it.

Then in the ninth round the voice next to me was the first to take note of the almost imperceptible shift in the action. Because Moorer was not being hit by any clean shots, most people, including the television announcers, didn't even notice, but while he was still unable to get to Moorer with the full force of his punches, the champion had slowed just enough that Foreman was for the first time all night able to jab—and each jab was the first half of a one-two combo.

"That's it, George. That's it," the barely audible voice to my left said. "You've got him now."

And if you'll watch the tape carefully now the shift in momentum is retrospectively clear. Even though Moorer was blocking everything Foreman threw with his gloves, he was still feeling the impact, because each time Foreman hit Moorer's gloves with that thumping left-right combination, Moorer's gloves hit Moorer—sometimes hard enough to snap his head back.

By the time Caplan arrived in the tenth he was also beaming at what to him loomed a foregone conclusion. To the crowd, and to much of the ringside press section, it might not have been clear that Foreman had just taken over the fight, but he had.

There was more of the same in the tenth. Moorer, winded, could no longer get in quickly enough and still keep himself out of harm's way, so he was no longer an offensive threat. He had all he could do to keep his hands up to ward off the bombs Foreman was throwing his way, but he was paying a price for that as he continued to absorb the punches secondhand.

The ending came swiftly. Foreman threw another left-right, and this time managed to split Moorer's gloves to land the jab, and came around them with the right that immediately followed. A look of surprise came over Moorer's face, and his gloves dropped just enough for Big George to find the opening. He cracked Moorer with another jab and came right up the middle with a right hand, and the next thing anybody saw was Michael Moorer, stretched out on the canvas while Joe Cortez counted over him.

More than 20 years after losing his title, in one of the more improbable upsets in heavyweight annals, George Foreman had, at forty-five, done what many considered impossible. But for all the drama that accompanied that emotional moment, when I look back on it 16 years later, as I often do, the knockout punch isn't what springs to mind.

Hours later, I'd filed my story for the paper, but as exhausting as the evening had been, sleep wasn't going to come easily on a night like that. Having decided to go down to the casino to unwind, I had to walk the length of a football field before I located a $25 table. (On fight nights in Vegas, a game with a $25 minimum is considered a small-stakes game.)

I'd been there for 15 or 20 minutes when, far down at the other end of the hangar-like casino, I heard the noise commence. At first it sounded as if a freight train were coming through the building, and the din steadily picked up momentum until it became a rolling roar. It was happening so far away that at first it was difficult to see what all the commotion was about, but it gradually came into focus: George Foreman, accompanied by a couple of his sons, was headed for the MGM exit out on the Strip, and to get there he had to walk a couple hundred yards along a carpeted walkway that bisected the floor-level casino.

And as he and his party passed by, every game in the joint was briefly suspended. Gamblers stopped gambling and leapt to their feet to join in the deafening applause. Dealers stopped dealing, croupiers stopped raking, and they and the pit bosses and the cocktail waitresses and everyone else committed themselves to the joyous task of saluting Foreman.

When George and his party drew abreast of my table, I wasn't even sure he saw me, but I gave him a quick thumbs up anyway. Only then did I pause to even think about it. Back east it was almost three in the morning. In Vegas it was drawing close to midnight. Where was Foreman going at this hour?

Almost as soon as I asked myself the question, the answer became apparent: he was headed for the airport.

Two hours earlier he had become the oldest man in history ever to win the heavyweight title, but right now George Foreman was on his way to catch the red-eye back to Houston. He still had to preach in the morning.

2010

Notes on Chapter VI

The concept of *Manly Art* already existed on the drawing board early in 2010 when I was invited, along with George Foreman and Dr. Robert Rodriguez, to participate in a Boxing Symposium presented at the University of Kansas. Upon learning that my presentation that night would be a lecture recounting the history and backstories of the ten fights involving Ali, Frazier, Foreman, and Norton, it was the suggestion of my editor at McBooks, Jackie Swift, and the publisher, Alex Skutt, that the material be expanded and adapted as a separate chapter for this book. That chapter also formed the basis for a four-part series serialized on TheSweetScience.com.

As was the case with *Four Kings,* much of the material included in this presentation turned out to be my own stories, notes, and recollections of the era, many of which were enhanced and refreshed (and sometimes corrected) through conversations, interviews, and anecdotal dialogue over the intervening four decades with a number of friends and colleagues (many of whom are sadly no longer with us), including, but not limited to: Bob Arum, Howard Bingham, Bill Caplan, Bill Cardoso, Lucian Chin, Harold Conrad, Angelo Dundee, Eddie Futch, Leonard Gardner, Bobby Goodman, Pete Hamill, Jerry Izenberg, Michael Katz, Hugh McIlvanney, Larry Merchant, Leigh Montville, Ferdie Pacheco, Budd Schulberg, Hunter Thompson, Bob Waters, and Vic Ziegel, as well as the personal recollections of Muhammad Ali and George Foreman.

I also relied upon (and sometimes quoted from) a number of published resources including:

Cushman, Tom. *Muhammad Ali and the Greatest Heavyweight Generation.* Southeast Missouri State University Press, 2009.

Dunphy, Don. *At Ringside*. Henry Holt & Co., 1988.

Foreman, George (with Joel Engel). *By George*. Villard Books, 1995.

Gardner, Leonard. "Stopover in Caracas." *Esquire,* October 1974.

Hauser, Thomas. *Muhammad Ali: His Life and Times*. Simon & Schuster, 1992.

Kram, Mark. "Lawdy, Lawdy, He's Great." *Sports Illustrated,* October 13, 1975.

Nack, William. "The Fight's Over, Joe." *Sports Illustrated,* September 30, 1996.

Patterson, Floyd (with Gay Talese). "In Defense of Cassius Clay." *Esquire,* August 1966.

Remnick, David. *King of the World*. Random House, 1998.

Schulberg, Budd. Newsday dispatches from Zaire included in *Sparring with Hemingway*. Ivan R. Dee, 1995.

Thank Yous

Thanks to the platoon of editors—Nate Dow and Hank Hryniewicz, the late Joey Hamill, Greg Leon, Darius Ortiz, Sean Sullivan and Robert Ecksel, Malachy Logan, and Michael J. Woods—under whose aegis the stories in this book initially appeared, as well as to Jackie Swift and Alex Skutt at McBooks for their enduring faith. Gratitude, as always, is due my friends and colleagues at ringside: Tom Hauser, Michael Katz, Robert Rodriguez, John Schulian, and the late Budd Schulberg; along with my agent, Farley Chase; and a trifecta's worth of George Foremans (Big, Monk, and Bigwheel). Thanks as well to my own explainers: Freddie Roach, Emanuel Steward, Lou DiBella, Randy Neumann, Jim Borzell, and Thomas (Mutley) Rohan; to my wife, Marge, for her patience; to Darcy and Teddy for being a source of great joy; to Tom Russell, Anne Tangeman, and Carlo Rotella, Ph.D., for their contributions to this book; and to Manish Shah, M.D., for arranging the extra innings.

Acknowledgements

Gratitude is hereby expressed for permission to reprint the stories, articles, columns, and reviews in this book by the following periodicals, newspapers, and online publications in which they originally (sometimes in slightly different form and under a different title) appeared:

The Boston Herald: Irish Thunder

Boxing Digest: Deconstructing the Champ; Abraham–Miranda II: Stomping through the Swamp; Bute: Saved by the Bell at the Bell; Calzaghe Tames a Legend; The Wrath of Khan's Army; A Bronx Tale; Vaya con Dios

BoxingRanks.com: Tyson Makes Golota Quit

BoxingTalk.com: A Man You Don't Meet Every Day; MSG's Loss Is Canastota's Gain; The Reinvention of the Ambling Alp; Luis Resto Billy Collins Redux; Mayweather Outboxes Oscar for Fifth Green Belt; The Pac-Man Politician; Paulie's Hair; Semper Fi or Swift Boat Redux?; Bring Back the Titans; Hopkins-Wright: "Title Fight" or Flim-Flam?

ESPN.com: Sometimes the Scale *Do* Lie . . .

The Irish Times: Mississippi Riverbank Hustle; Arm and the Man; The Babylonian Heavyweights; What Would Liebling Do?; A Look Inside Tyson's Head; Savage Beating by Lewis Ends Tyson's Claims as a Pretender; Pretty Boy: Money Boy; Chico Goes Down for the Last Time; The Kronk's White Shadow. Copyright (c) 2002, 2006, 2007, 2008, 2009 by the Irish Times Newspaper Company, Ltd.

TheSweetScience.com: The Great St. Patrick's Day Hooley; Separate But Unequalled; Arm and the Man; A Catalyst for Consensus?; Fat City and *Fat City*; The Cut Man's Baby; Trying on the Glass Slipper; Terry Malloy Meets Paulie Walnuts; Ali, Holmes, and Maysles; Stallone Takes a Final Crack at Rocky; Duddy-Puddy Smackdown at MSG; Dawson Overwhelms Adamek, Wins WBC Crown; Bad Mojo at the Joe; From the Tail of a Pony; The Prisoner of Hell's Kitchen; Baghdad's Friday Night Fights; Golden Boy's Gold Rush; High Blood Sugar and Sour Excuses; Termite: A Pest by Any Other Name; Forbes: The New Bible of Boxing?; Hailed as "Brilliant," Bradley's Move Wasn't; What's This? A Boxing Promoter with a Conscience?; Debbies Do New York; The Accidental Trainer; Johnny, They Hardly Knew You; The Ref Strikes Out; Arthur Curry, Come on Down!; Counting the House in Wise-Guy Heaven; The Human Highlight Film; Pal Joey; More Than a Contender; The Man in the Middle Kept a Low Profile

A version of "Freddie vs. Ugly Boy" appeared in the annual journal of the Boxing Writers Association of America, June 2009.

The review of *Jacobs Beach*, "Bad Day at the Beach," and the article "Survival of the Greatest" originally appeared in *The Irish Times Weekend Magazine.* Copyright (c) 2009 by the Irish Times Newspaper Company, Ltd.

The poem "Sleight of Hand" (Copyright (c) 2010 by George Kimball, from the collection entitled *The Fighter Still Remains: A Celebration of Boxing in Poetry and Song* [Fore Angels Press, 2010]) was publicly presented for the first time as part of the University of Kansas Heavyweight Boxing Symposium on February 4, 2010, and subsequently included in the online version of Chapter VI serialized on TheSweetScience.com.

"Mississippi Riverbank Hustle," "Savage Beating By Lewis Ends Tyson's Claims as a Pretender," and "Pretty Boy: Money Boy" were previously included in the collection *American at Large* (Red Rock Press). Copyright (c) 2008 by George Kimball.